1973

HD
905
S85

93408

DATE DUE

LENDING POLICY

IF YOU ~~DAMAGE OR LOSE THIS BOOK~~ YOU
WILL B~~E CHARGED FOR REPLACEMENT~~MENT.
FAILURE TO PAY AFFECTS REGISTRATION,
TRANSCRIPTS, AND LIBRARY PRIVILEGES.

PERALTA COMMUNITY COLLEGE DISTRICT

Laney College Library
900 Fallon Street
Oakland, Ca. 94607

DEMCO—FRESNO

POPULAR UPRISINGS
IN THE PHILIPPINES
1840–1940

POPULAR UPRISINGS
IN THE PHILIPPINES
1840-1940

David R. Sturtevant

Cornell University Press ITHACA AND LONDON

Copyright © 1976 by Cornell University

All rights reserved. Except for brief quotations in a review, this book, or parts thereof, must not be reproduced in any form without permission in writing from the publisher. For information address Cornell University Press, 124 Roberts Place, Ithaca, New York 14850.

First published 1976 by Cornell University Press.
Published in the United Kingdom by Cornell University Press Ltd., 2-4 Brook Street, London W1Y 1AA.

International Standard Book Number 0-8014-0877-6
Library of Congress Catalog Card Number 75-36521
Printed in the United States of America by York Composition Co., Inc.

To Joy

93408

35108

Acknowledgments

Those who engage in historical research accumulate obligations. Like other American students of the Philippines, I have collected more than my share on both sides of the Pacific. Scores of kind people have assisted me—too many by far to thank individually. The help of foundations and the important contributions of several colleagues and friends, however, must be acknowledged.

The book would have been impossible without grants for extended study in Washington, D.C., and Manila. Through its Mack Foundation Program, Muskingum College supported research and writing over two summers. The Committee on International Exchange of Persons subsidized a year in the Philippines as a Fulbright-Hays Researcher. And a grant from the Joint Committee of the American Council of Learned Societies and the Social Science Research Council enabled me to complete my investigations and finish the manuscript. Theodore Friend and John Larkin read the draft and offered pertinent criticisms to strengthen the final product. While the aid of these organizations and individuals was indispensable, none of them should be held responsible for any errors of fact or interpretation contained in the text.

Among the Americans who moved me or my work forward at critical junctures six deserve special thanks. I would like to express indebtedness to Claude Buss, Felix Keesing, Russell Fifield, Arthur Wright, Frank Golay, and—for advice and help beyond measure—the late Harry Benda. Numerous Filipinos also facilitated my inquiries in Manila and the provinces. For gracious counsel and constant encouragement, I owe particular debts of gratitude to Josefa Saniel, F. Sionil José, Teodoro Agoncillo, Jeremias Adia, and the Reverend Conrado Generalla.

Friends and neighbors in New Concord contributed much of their energy and time to the completion of this book. For converting my cramped scrawl into type and for attempting to shape my unrestrained prose into a rough approximation of the English language, I am especially grateful to Josephine Maddox. Similar appreciation is due Marge Hawkenberry and Eleanore Smith for preparing the final manuscript. John Armstrong read proof and thoughtfully restricted himself to Scot-like observations on diction or punctuation. Administrators and fellow teachers at Muskingum, moreover, always tried to help my work toward completion.

Several publications and publishers granted permission to use sections of my articles. For their courtesy I would like to thank the *Journal of Asian Studies, Solidarity, Asia Studies,* and the Publications Office of the Ohio University Center for International Studies. Document depositories were equally cooperative. The Manuscript Division, Library of Congress, consented to the reproduction of a letter from the Leonard Wood Papers; and the Ayer Collection of Newberry Library approved the incorporation of several brief quotations from a nineteenth-century manuscript by Manuel Sancho. Robert Warner of the Michigan Historical Collections and Betty Hayden of Ann Arbor extended every kindness to me—including unrestricted use of important materials from the Joseph R. Hayden Papers.

Last but not least, I must acknowledge the four people who assisted most of all. For constant and good-humored toleration, I thank Lynne, Mark, and Jim Sturtevant. And for putting up with me and this book far longer than I had any right to expect, I express profound admiration and love for my wife, Joy.

DAVID R. STURTEVANT

New Concord, Ohio

Contents

Maps

POPULAR UPRISINGS
IN THE PHILIPPINES
1840–1940

Prologue

Serious history is not a form of suspense literature. Readers should not be required to search for clues concerning the thesis, nor be compelled to await an exposition of camouflaged themes in the final chapter. Before beginning a book they deserve an indication of the orientation that has shaped it. This study applies the perspectives and methods of social history to a series of peasant movements in the Philippines. It is hoped the approach will challenge stereotyped political and economic interpretations of agrarian unrest, while suggesting an alternate focus for analyzing the problem.

When compared with the lengthy traditions of European and American studies, systematic scholarship on Southeast Asia is still in its infancy. Until recently most investigations have been of an essentially political nature. A handful of specialists—many of them full- or part-time colonial civil servants, the others native advocates of self-determination—concerned themselves with two seemingly antagonistic themes: imperialism and nationalism. The concentration inevitably produced polarized results. On the one hand, it led to a discussion or justification of governmental policies and their implementation. On the other, it contributed to an examination or glorification of indigenous elites struggling to achieve national identity and freedom.

A few individuals realized there was no fundamental contradiction in the tension between metropolis and dependency. To them, the contending forces represented different sides of the same political coin. "Nationalism," as Teodoro Locsin laconically observed, was simply "colonialism in reverse."[1] The cooperation that characterized the relationships between American administrators and Filipino politicians from 1901 to 1941 demonstrated the validity of his generalization. Occasionally friction developed over the readiness of prominent

1. *Philippines Free Press,* May 13, 1967, 1.

Nacionalistas to guide their constituents along an independent course, but there was never a serious question on either side of the Pacific as to the desirability of granting sovereignty to the Islands. It was not coincidental that the foremost prewar work on the Philippines bore the subtitle *A Study in National Development.*[2]

Emphasis on political phenomena—understandable as it might have been in the colonial context—exercised a lamentable influence over inquiries into the past. Philippine historical studies tended to focus upon formal relations with Spain and the United States, so that practitioners of statecraft in Manila, Madrid, and Washington enjoyed the spotlight. Governors general such as Primo de Rivera and Leonard Wood, and nationalist leaders such as Emilio Aguinaldo and Manuel Quezon, often emerged from those chronicles as herculean antagonists engaged in a struggle between good and evil. But Filipinos in the broadest sense seldom infringed on the morality play. Nationalism, together with what helped and hindered it, came to be the only real subject of the discourse.

Primary concern with transoceanic relations and Manila politics led students of Philippine affairs to ignore or to miss the significance of intermittent peasant uprisings. Village rebellions under the Spanish regime, for example, received two conventional treatments: either they were dismissed as comparatively unimportant local protests against Iberian cupidity and misrule, or they were accorded the scant coverage reserved for provincial matters.[3] An unstated premise guided most discussions of rural challenges to Spanish authority, in that many scholars regarded the upheavals as spasmodic, reflex actions against autocratic rule by inept aliens. The viewpoint produced a comforting conclusion: if Filipinos had directed their own destinies, the violent protests might not have occurred.

American governmental methods undermined the political interpretation. Almost from the outset of United States rule a large measure of responsibility for the conduct of provincial affairs was placed in the hands of local leaders. The innovation proved so successful that it was quickly applied to the expanding institutions of central government in Manila. "Filipinization," as the policy was called, led to a

2. J. R. Hayden, *The Philippines: A Study in National Development* (New York, 1942).
3. For the view of prominent Filipino historians on the subject see T. A. Agoncillo and O. M. Alfonso, *A Short History of the Filipino People* (Quezon City, 1960), iii; and G. F. Zaide, *The Philippines since Pre-Spanish Times* (Manila, 1949), 439–440.

comparatively brief transition from a regime administered by Americans assisted by Filipinos to one run by Filipinos advised by Americans. Reinforced by an early institution of general elections, the technique produced a more responsive and popular government. Within a generation Filipinos achieved complete autonomy. But peasant protest movements did not disappear. Abortive uprisings continued to occur with approximately the same frequency that had prevailed prior to 1898. Something other than political tension, quite obviously, was generating discord in the countryside.

Another explanation for the intermittent upheavals emerged from an examination of rural living conditions. Studies made during the latter stages of American jurisdiction (the 1930's and 1940's) revealed economic inequities and social dislocations of sufficient magnitude to produce chronic hostility among villagers.[4] Liberal American analysts and their Filipino counterparts compiled a catalogue of mass misery to demonstrate the necessity of sweeping reforms. In broad terms their circular indictment ran as follows: inequitable income distribution, reinforced by debt bondage and usurious interest charges, produced soaring tenancy rates; ever-increasing tenancy, linked to population pressures, led to further concentration of wealth in the hands of a socially irresponsible minority; the minority, in turn, monopolized political power and used its influential position to perpetuate and expand control over the key resource in an agrarian economy, namely, land. Unless reversed, the chain logic of that downward spiraling cycle suggested only one dismal conclusion: eventual revolution.

During the years immediately preceding and following World War II, economic interpretations replaced political explanations of rural discord. Erich Jacoby, one of the leading exponents of the emerging outlook, summed it up succinctly. Contact with the United States, he maintained, did not change "the fundamental features of the country: a precapitalist agrarian economy and a semi-feudalist structure of society; . . . unrest will smolder, and perhaps ignite, as long as the land problem is not solved."[5]

Unquestionably, the economic approach to the sources of discon-

4. Articles on tenancy systems and rural living levels began to appear systematically in the mid-1920's. Some of the best surveys were conducted by the College of Agriculture of the University of the Philippines. For the years 1924 to 1940, see *Philippine Agriculturist*.

5. E. H. Jacoby, *Agrarian Unrest in Southeast Asia* (New York, 1949), 221–222.

tent provided a far more valid basis for understanding the problem than its political precursor. But it too led to narrow and in some instances oversimplified inquiries. The political rule implied: aliens cause unrest. The economic maxim suggested: high tenancy rates create unrest. Proceeding from that premise, students concentrated on the tenant-ridden provinces of central Luzon—a region which appeared to produce rice and rebellions in comparable quantities.[6] They also conducted a few surveys of labor conditions on the sugar estates of Negros[7] and briefly canvassed living levels along the crowded coasts of the Ilocos.[8] From those limited investigations they developed a comprehensive diagnosis of Philippine social ills and prescribed a specific remedy: land reform.

While the research techniques of the years before and after World War II contributed depth to the study of provincial tension, some diquieting data were either overlooked or conveniently ignored. Historically, violent protest has not been restricted to central Luzon. It has flared recurrently throughout the archipelago, both in areas with high- and low-tenancy rates and in provinces with dense and sparse populations. Advocates of the economic interpretation made little effort to examine the historic and geographic distribution of rural rebellions. They also failed to scrutinize the diverse forms assumed by peasant protest movements. In simple terms, they replaced a one-dimensional analytical design (politics) with an inadequate two-dimensional model (politics and economics).

Agrarian unrest, unfortunately, was not a problem in plane geometry. Discord in the Philippines, as elsewhere, evolved as a multifaceted phenomenon. To be understood it had to be examined from many sides. Most recommendations for resolving the knotty equation have been based upon inquiries into the rise and fall of the Hukbalahap. The Communist-led rebellion of the 1940's and early 1950's, however, represented neither the end nor the beginning of the rural Filipino's dissident heritage. All too many of those studies, moreover,

6. See, for example, J. S. Allen, "Agrarian Tendencies in the Philippines," *Pacific Affairs,* XI (1938), 52–65; and H. R. Crippen, "Philippine Agrarian Unrest: Historical Backgrounds," *Science and Society,* X (1946), 337–360.
7. I. T. Runes, *General Standards of Living and Wages of Workers in The Philippine Sugar Industry,* Institute of Pacific Relations, Philippine Council (Manila, 1938).
8. H. C. Lava, *Levels of Living in the Ilocos Region,* Institute of Pacific Relations, Philippine Council (Manila, 1938).

projected essentially Western and urban motives or aspirations on dissenting villagers. Others emphasized contemporary developments while ignoring the peasantry's stormy record. Discussions of the subject, in short, have tended to be both acultural and ahistorical. This examination will attempt to rectify some of those oversights by emphasizing the social settings and historical patterns of agrarian unrest. The period under investigation, 1840 to 1940, was selected for two reasons. First, available source materials supplied basic information on a series of little known but important uprisings and protest movements. Second, the century in question provided sufficient perspective to reveal the broad configurations of the hamlet dweller's turbulent tradition.

That heritage was not based upon fundamental quests for material improvements. Few if any movements between 1840 and 1930 were organized around purely economic symbols. Few if any, furthermore, made the redistribution of land a basic objective. If a connecting link or common theme existed in the outbreaks, it was a religious or supernatural element. From 1840, when the villagers of Tayabas and Laguna rallied to Apolinario de la Cruz, to 1930, when the tenants of eastern Pangasinan gathered behind Pedro Calosa, Filipino farmers followed scores of charismatic local leaders down the dusty road toward temporal and spiritual salvation. Some of them found only death. Many received prison sentences. Most experienced disillusionment. But while individual uprisings failed, the discordant tradition could not be suppressed. The repetition of otherworldly patterns in widely separated regions of the archipelago indicated the existence of highly developed millennial themes in peasant society.

The importance of those popular "revitalization" efforts cannot be overemphasized. Their recurrence pointed to the existence of serious cultural tensions in the Philippines and suggested that the basic conflict in the countryside came primarily from neither economic nor political factors. Instead, it grew from a complex clash between customary and modern tendencies. The uprisings, in short, should be regarded as by-products of the stress between what Robert Redfield called the little and great traditions.

Between 1930 and 1940, the supernaturalism that had characterized earlier agrarian flare-ups appeared to give way to secularism. Educated members of the middle and upper classes assumed leadership of peasant movements in central and southern Luzon. They directed villagers toward radical but, on the whole, realistic objectives. For the first time in Philippine history, provincial dissenters sought change via legitimate means and repeatedly issued manifestos calling for a more equitable society. Commonwealth President Quezon's Social Justice program clearly indicated that the highest echelons of the *Nacionalista* establishment felt and were influenced by mounting pressures from below.

The transition from mysticism to relative sophistication constitutes the central theme of this four-part study. Part I surveys the evolution of colonial society under two metropolitan powers and describes the complicated sources of stress that converged on Filipino villagers. Part II deals with violent popular responses in the nineteenth and early twentieth centuries and treats a variety of reactions ranging from nativism and millennialism through social banditry. Part III evaluates the activities of conventional religious dissenters and unconventional political zealots during the 1920's and points up the appearance of patriotic secret societies in the countryside. Part IV assesses several efforts to combine rural and urban elements behind radical objectives and traces the rise and fall of Sakdalism—the first movement to forge a successful, if ephemeral, coalition between Manila and the hinterland.

What follows was written in total awareness of the fact that it represents neither the first nor the last word on a complex subject. It is hoped, nevertheless, that the study will contribute perspective and a measure of insight into agrarian unrest in the Philippines. It should strip away some of the obscurity surrounding a series of intriguing lost causes. It should also restore a degree of humanity to generations of defiant rebels who have been consigned through neglect to historical anonymity.

PART I

THE SOURCES OF STRESS

Forasmuch therefore as ye trample upon the poor, and take
exactions from him of grain: ye have built houses of hewn stone,
but ye shall not dwell in them; ye have planted pleasant vine-
yards, but ye shall not drink the wine thereof. For I know how
manifold are your transgressions, and how mighty are your sins
—ye that afflict the just, that take a bribe and that turn aside
the needy in the gate *from their right* . . . saith Jehovah the
God of hosts: I abhor the excellency of Jacob, and hate his
palaces; therefore will I deliver up the city with all that is
therein.

Amos 5 : 11–12; 6 : 8

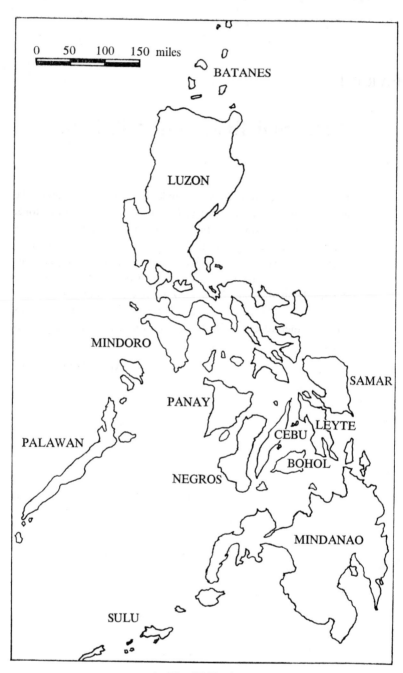

1. The Philippines

CHAPTER 1

The Origins of Rural Society

The genesis of the peasantry antedated by centuries the appearance of a coherent Philippine culture. Long before Magellan made his fatal landing on Mactan, Malayan chieftains and their tribal retainers migrated to the sprawling archipelago from the southeast Asian mainland and Indonesia. They came with warriors, women, children, and economic dependents in gale-defying craft called *barangays*. Upon completing the demanding voyage they established tightly knit settlements named after their rugged outriggers.[1] The small, self-sufficient, kin-integrated, sacred communities which grew out of that maritime trek encompassed the essential ingredients of a persistent folk tradition. Primitive economic, social, and political arrangements, together with the primordial religious outlooks that developed in the new setting, exerted profound influence over the course of village affairs well into the twentieth century.

For the settlers and their descendants life revolved around the hamlet. Houses were constructed to meet the requirements of a torrid climate. Dwellings, built of bamboo and woven fiber, stood close together to serve the defensive needs and gregarious tastes of their occupants. Topped by steep thatched roofs, the residences consisted of little more than an enclosed sleeping quarter elevated on hardwood corner posts. The open space beneath the dormitory served a variety of functions. At night livestock was tethered there. During the daylight hours women used the area to perform a multitude of domestic tasks. Noontime heat drove men back to the sheltered rectangles, where they joined their families for lengthy siestas before returning to late-afternoon routines. Squat banana trees and stately coconut palms grew in haphazard profusion among and around the cluster of

1. In Filipino, *barangay* refers to the kinship group. See H. de la Costa, *The Background of Nationalism and Other Essays* (Manila, 1965), 16.

buildings. Their filigreed shade marked the dividing line between the islandlike *barangay* and its surrounding rain- or sun-drenched paddies. Existence fell into a rhythm foreordained by the seasonal ebb and flow of monsoon Asia. An apt Spanish proverb described the annual sequence: *"Seis meses de polvo, seis meses de lodo, seis meses de todo* ("Six months of dust, six months of mud, six months of everything").[2] Throughout the year villagers regulated their activities to coincide with the climate's commands. While fields slowly alternated between succulent green and bitter brown, the people of the *barangay* labored on the land, fished in adjacent waters, hunted in nearby forests and mountains, and occupied themselves with all the diversified chores of a self-sustaining small community. Wealth consisted largely of the soil and its products. But hamlet dwellers supplemented the yield of the rich volcanic loam with hand-crafted ornaments, fabrics, and weapons of appropriately delicate or deadly design. Coastal residents used a portion of that secondary output to conduct limited trade with other *barangays* and with seafaring Chinese.[3]

The class system broke down into four reasonably distinct segments: chiefs, warriors, and two gradations of economic dependents. Early Spanish accounts, however, projected Iberian social categories onto the islanders by inaccurately labeling them "nobles, freemen, serfs, and slaves."[4] The *datu,* or headman, usually achieved his position by hereditary right. His responsibilities were those of a near-absolute priest-chieftain. He led religious ceremonies, oversaw divination, commanded military expeditions, held the largest and best land parcels, interpreted customary law, and defined punishments for those who violated established practices. He was, in short, the final arbiter on all community affairs. The only checks on his authority emanated from a council of elders, generally made up of old or infirm *datus,* and his own sense of what was feasible. That pragmatic constraint was far more effective than autocratic Spanish observers were willing or able to recognize. The *barangay*'s sentimental interrelationships—like those of any face-to-face society—tipped the scales toward mea-

2. Paulino Lim, "The Victorian Visitor's View," *Philippines Free Press*, Jan. 15, 1966, 14.
3. Aurora Roxas-Lim, "Chinese Pottery as a Basis for the Study of Philippine Proto-History," in Alfonso Felix, Jr., ed., *The Chinese in the Philippines, 1570–1770* (Manila, 1966), 233–244.
4. J. L. Phelan, *The Hispanization of the Philippines* (Madison, Wis., 1959), 20.

ured applications of power and made for compassionate leadership.[5] *Maharlikas* constituted the second stratum. As independent warriors they provided services for the *datu* in keeping with their station. In addition, they acted as his escort on important occasions and furnished laborers or supplies when the headman constructed a new residence. In return they received traditional rewards: feasts for ceremonial or material assistance, and a share of the spoils for participating in successful forays. Their primary role as fighting men assured a position of prominence in the tribal scheme of things. Like the *datu,* furthermore, they held land and were served by social inferiors.

The third and fourth classes, *namamahays* and *sagigilids,* existed under increasing degrees of restraint. In the manner of modern Filipino tenants, *namamahays* labored for landholders and turned over a portion of the harvest to their patrons. Periodically, they also carried out additional assigned duties. Members of the class, however, enjoyed well-defined rights and owned property in the form of dwellings and personal belongings. *Sagigilids* possessed nothing other than limited physical energy and a conditioned capacity for servile conduct. They toiled in the fields and houses of their superiors, performing the most menial tasks. Their social degradation resulted from a variety of circumstances. Some were war captives. Others had been sentenced to servitude for legal violations. But the vast majority had been cast down by accumulating unpaid debts to the chieftain or his martial retainers.

For several reasons, *barangay* social stratification escaped rigidity. The delicate web of kinship which bound the community together blurred any tendencies toward caste. Landholding arrangements differed sufficiently to assure a gradual rise and fall of individual fortunes.[6] Complex marital patterns, together with intricate social gradations growing out of them, alleviated the long-term impact of status. Women also occupied elevated positions and constantly influenced their offspring's destinies through gentle or shrewish treatment of husbands and male relatives. The system, in brief, functioned in

5. For a discussion of the "compassionate function" of leadership in folk societies see Mehmet Beqiraj, *Peasantry in Revolution* (Ithaca, N.Y., 1966), 10–14.
6. Juan de Plasencia, "Customs of the Tagalogs," in E. H. Blair and J. A. Robertson, eds., *The Philippine Islands, 1493–1898* (Cleveland, O., 1903–1909), VII, 174–175. (Hereafter references to Blair and Robertson will be cited as *BR.*)

accord with tribal dynamics. Its relatively simple forms bore little or
no resemblance to European corporate and contractual configurations.
Despite that fact, Spanish chroniclers attempted to force *barangay*
society into feudalism's familiar mold.[7]

An individual's martial role and relationship toward land were not
the only determinants of position. The mystery-permeated world of
the *barangay* granted automatic prominence to any person with
reputed influence over natural or supernatural phenomena. In every
hamlet, priests, priestesses, mediums, sorcerers, soothsayers, witches,
warlocks, and covert disciples of benevolent or malevolent spirits
plied their black or white arts in awe-inspiring rivalry.[8] Divination
preceded all important community undertakings. A pantheon of omnipotent deities personifying nature received regular worship. Villagers also took heed of dead relatives' ghostly requirements through
periodic offerings and memorial ceremonies.

To that array of beliefs and practices were added the ramifications
of animism. The archipelago's ever-changing terrain and lush vegetation induced predictable fear or adoration. Volcanoes, precipices,
chasms, waterfalls, caverns, pools, forest glens, gnarled trees, eroded
rocks, and surf-swept reefs were all regarded as the habitation of gods
and ancestral phantoms. A multitude of rites evolved to placate their
influence. Bluebirds, crows, and alligators were looked upon as divine
beings. Islanders attributed good or bad fortune to those and other
forest creatures and treated them accordingly. Daily activities were
also affected by an accumulation of quasi-spiritual beings. Villagers
traced lucky and unlucky days to the whims of sprites and goblins
who helped or hindered them at work and play. Great and minor
denizens of the otherworld were all recognized in religious obser-
vances. *Barangay* people fashioned wood and metal images in their
honor, placed the idols in houses and fields, and regularly paid
homage to them. No effort was made to distinguish between the spirits
and their material symbols. Both were called *anitos*.

Popular acknowledgments of benign and malignant powers were
not limited to rituals. Pre-Spanish practitioners of magic evolved a

7. Feudalism in the historical sense (a decentralized political system in
which power is exercised by a military aristocracy owing fealty to an overlord)
never existed in the Philippines. For a careful definition of the abstraction see
Rushton Coulborn, ed., *Feudalism in History* (Princeton, N.J., 1956).
8. Tomas Ortiz, "Superstitions and Beliefs of the Filipinos," *BR*, XLII,
103–110.

repertoire of techniques and devices to assist fellow villagers through the maze of a supernatural milieu. Hexes, incantations, and miraculous formulas protected hamlet dwellers from unearthly influences. Equally impressive methods were developed to ward off the intentions of human foes. *Anting-anting,* in the form of talismans, guaranteed invulnerability to their possessors. Enchanted clothing held forth a similar promise. Sorcerers gained renown for their ostensible ability to conjure love potions, devise concoctions to incapacitate and subjugate enemies, create amulets granting invisibility to their fortunate owners, and formulate charms which permitted men to swim rivers and lagoons without getting wet.[9]

Like other participants in the primitive tradition, prehistoric Filipinos devoted much of their intellect and energy to the propitiation of good and evil forces. Concern with those issues, and involvement with the implications of kinship and status, undermined any latent tendencies toward the development of elaborate political or economic institutions. The *barangay* did not give birth to embryonic states. Although a few imaginative *datus* acquired shaky hegemony over neighboring settlements, most chieftains remained too parochial to overcome tribal loyalties and village orientations. When the Spaniards arrived, lowland people were still living in isolated small communities. Such fragmented units could not organize a coherent response to the alien challenge. After sporadic, token resistance, their inhabitants subordinated themselves to the representatives of a new sacred order.

Subjugation of the northern and central islands was also attributable in part to the character of late sixteenth-century Spanish imperialism. A generation earlier, insubordinate swashbucklers had broken the New World's high cultures and seriously challenged Madrid's authority. Veteran campaigners led by the disciplined servants of a devout monarch came to the Philippines. Their orders involved challenging objectives. Legaspi's first responsibility was to make good Spain's claim to the archipelago. His second was to discover a return route to Mexico. Those purposes, however, paled into insignificance beside the expedition's religious goals. Churchmen were to introduce islanders to the word of God. More importantly, they hoped to develop a Christian colony on Asia's periphery which could serve as a base for the conversion of China.[10] In those early years the heady desire to

9. T. A. Agoncillo and O. M. Alfonso, *A Short History,* 44–45.
10. "Bishop Salazar's Report to the King," in Felix, 133.

spread the gospel, far more than greed or glory, drew Spaniards into the western Pacific. For the next two centuries, furthermore, ecclesiastical priorities continued to determine the destiny of Spain's most remote outpost.

The fact that spiritual matters took precedence over temporal affairs facilitated the penetration of the Philippines. True to their proselytizing intentions, the invaders seldom found it necessary to resort to naval or military displays. They relied instead on Catholicism's devastating impact. Clerical garments, a divine book, crucifixes, images, chants, prayers, and the stately intricacies of the mass proved more effective than muskets or cannons. Credulous *barangay* folk were captivated by sacerdotal pomp and circumstance. The institutionalized mystery from the West thwarted indigenous supernaturalism. Dedicated priests and friars rather than dashing *conquistadores* won the islands for Phillip II and retained them for his successors. With relative ease churchmen superimposed the elements of their faith on the lowlanders of Luzon and the Visayas. They also set in motion the long-term processes which led to the formation of peasant society.

To most villagers the subtle transformation of conventional ways must have been almost imperceptible. Until the latter half of the nineteenth century, the Spanish lay community in the colony remained small.[11] Its members tended to limit their activities to the fortified sanctuary of Manila and to strategically located lesser bastions to the north and south. Aside from a handful of estate holders, a few administrators, and occasional commanders of punitive expeditions, village exposure to the conquerors was restricted almost exclusively to churchmen. But even the mission enterprise suffered from chronic personnel shortages and inadequate support. Overburdened friars, consequently, learned to make do under trying circumstances by developing techniques compatible with the cultural conditions confronting them. The existence of numerous, small, stable communities frustrated the creation of baronial establishments comparable to the vast *reducciones* which emerged among nomadic folk on Latin American frontiers. Missionaries in the Philippines were forced to work

11. Spaniards, including regular military personnel, were so few that the colonial government relied on native levies to maintain order. From 1570 to 1828 there was no European garrison in the Philippines. From 1828 to 1883, only 1,500 artillerymen were stationed in the Islands. F. H. Sawyer, *The Inhabitants of the Philippines* (London, 1900), viii.

within a network of sedentary social units. Under the new dispensation, most *barangay* people lived in the same locales and remained loyal to ancestral norms. They conceived of Hispanic authority in terms of the resident curate. For all practical purposes one style of religious leadership had simply been supplanted by another.

Pioneer churchmen organized their endeavors systematically.[12] After baptizing a region's population, they devoted themselves to language study. Dialect mastery enabled clerics to work toward permanent institutions. As soon as possible they erected a massive church and *convento* (parish house) in or near a well-situated community. *Visitas* (satellite chapels), also of hewn stone, were constructed in encircling settlements. From that fortresslike base and its dispersed outerworks pastors shepherded their flocks. The religious edifices— more lasting than any structures built in the Philippines before or since—supplied a centripetal element which had been absent from pre-Spanish life. Confessionals, christenings, marriages, funerals, and repetitive masses interrupted everyday routines. The holy aura surrounding such services regularly lured converts away from hamlet tedium into relatively animated church and chapel communities.

As elsewhere, the attraction exercised by sacred ceremonies stimulated more earthy activities. Sunday markets and cockpits sprang up alongside church walls. Planting and harvest festivals erupted periodically in adjoining plazas. Villagers found both restraint and release "under the bells." Ecclesiastical domination not only contributed discipline and order to remote districts, it also provided spiritual comfort and exaltation. In addition, churches furnished sites for the exchange of goods or gossip, convenient locations for wagering on fighting cocks, and authorized arenas for the semiannual catharsis of accumulated frustrations. Given those broad inducements, *barangay* folk voluntarily joined the Sabbath pilgrimage. Without realizing it, they moved toward the Hispanic tradition along paths worn smooth by the sandals of adaptable clerics.

Political modifications of indigenous society lagged far behind religious alterations. Manila, to be sure, emerged relatively quickly as a legal and cultural extension of New Spain. Beyond the city's somber wall, however, Spanish administrative influence diminished with each additional league. In the foothills and mountains it vanished alto-

12. For a discussion of the techniques of one influential order, see H. de la Costa, *The Jesuits in the Philippines, 1531–1793* (Cambridge, Mass., 1961),

gether. Secular authority in secured regions developed slowly from diffusion of governmental institutions. The gradualness of the process lessened its traumatic impact. Executive and bureaucratic shortages, furthermore, forced colonial officials to incorporate traditional leaders into the evolving system. Agencies for the conduct of local affairs, accordingly, took on a strong native character. Nomenclature changed. *Datus* became village headmen. *Barangays* gave way to "barrios." Hamlet life patterns and social relations, however, remained constant. Madrid dominated Manila. But hereditary chieftains continued to hold sway in the villages.

Between the city and Christian settlements, Spain interjected rudimentary political machinery. Military zones and pioneer parishes were incorporated slowly into manageable districts. Each province was divided into towns or *poblaciones,* and each town was subdivided into barrios and *sitios* (three or four isolated dwellings). A Spanish governor, stationed in an accessible municipality, oversaw administrative operations. His responsibilities consisted of little more than peace keeping and tax collection. Prominent *"indios,"* as Spaniards referred to the islanders, assisted him in those duties. In the *poblaciones,* appointed *gobernadorcillos* (petty governors) assumed obligation for maintaining order and accumulating revenue. In the barrios, *cabezas de barangays* (village headmen) carried out similar functions. Under the system, former *datus* emerged as local legates of Spain. To villagers the changes were perhaps not as real as they seemed: although the machinery of government bore an alien stamp, familiar hands operated the strange contrivance in a reassuringly conventional manner.

The pattern of Spanish rule produced predictable results. Insulated village populations learned little of Hispanic political processes. But exposed municipal and barrio leaders acquired increasing knowledge of Spanish managerial techniques. By necessity, *gobernadorcillos* and *cabezas* turned away from local orientations. At first they looked only to the governor and the provincial capital. Soon, however, they gained a glimpse of broader vistas. In time Manila, Mexico, and Madrid became components of an expanding political horizon. Survival in that imposing context involved comparative sophistication. Slowly but surely they took on the language, dress, manners, and style of their Iberian mentors, and by 1800 an embryonic gentry had emerged in rude provincial towns. Spanish domination, accordingly, not only created a cultural climate favorable to the formation of the peasantry, it also produced conditions that led to the growth of the Hispanicized *principalia* (first citizens or notables).[13]

For two centuries, concentration on religious and political matters hindered the growth of a colonial economy. Manila constituted the only important commercial center in the Philippines. While the city stimulated farming and fishing in contiguous areas, its role as a catalyst for widespread provincial activity was negligible. For the most part, the seaport's Spanish population ignored the countryside's rich potential and gambled available resources on the unpredictable outcome of the Acapulco trade.[14] Until the New World was lost to Spain, Manila remained little more than a somnolent way station between China and Mexico. Once a year, wares from the Middle Kingdom and silver from New Spain arrived in the choppy anchorage at the mouth of the Pasig River. When the ensuing commodity exchange ended, nondescript junks and stately galleon plunged into the gentle swells of the China Sea. Their departure signaled a return to less demanding routines.

The superficial commerce did little to develop the productive capacity of the countryside. But it stimulated an unforeseen migration that directly affected village economies. Mexican silver tempted Chinese to Manila in ever-increasing numbers. Many took up permanent residence. Merchants were reinforced by artisans, coolies, and farmers. The energetic newcomers from Fukien and Kwangtung soon outnumbered the Spanish community and played a strategic role in the colony's life.[15] More frugal than comfort-loving Spaniards, and more ingenious than subsistence-oriented islanders, they won and retained a strategic position between overlords and subjects. As early as 1600, three interdependent systems had emerged: an embryonic Western economy, concentrated in Manila; a traditional economy, centered in the villages; and a Chinese economy, uniting and dividing the two extremes.[16]

13. The gentry developed from municipal councils of elders. Made up of former *gobernadorcillos* and *cabezas de barangays,* the groups supervised preparation of tax rolls, collected census information, and planned town fiestas. J. H. Romani and M. L. Thomas, *A Survey of Local Government in the Philippines* (Manila, 1954), 16.
14. W. L. Schurz, *The Manila Galleon* (New York, 1939).
15. Rafael Bernal, "The Chinese Colony in Manila," in Felix, 40–60.
16. For a stimulating discussion of the Chinese role in the pre-nineteenth-century economy, see Edgar Wickberg, *The Chinese in Philippine Life, 1850–1898* (New Haven, Conn., 1965), 3–41.

Since Spaniards tended to restrict their activities to Manila, commercial intrusions on the countryside fell to the Chinese. Although legal barriers were erected to frustrate such a development, peddlers and purveyors circumvented the obstructions. Moving first through the region surrounding Manila, they cautiously ventured outward into remote municipalities and barrios. Impoverished itinerants opened the hinterland, but more affluent storekeepers, rice merchants, and usurers exploited the promising breach. Eventually, profit-seeking Chinese became as common as church steeples in the provincial landscape. Unfortunately, they never blended into the bucolic backdrop. Neither Spaniards nor indigenous converts could bring themselves to accept the enterprising outlanders. Economic and cultural animosities led them to regard the Chinese as alien money grubbers and amoral heathen. The label "Sangley" (merchant), which gradually took on pejorative connotations, captured the essence of Christian attitudes toward the interlopers. In the face of fluctuating official antipathy and chronic popular hostility, the Chinese persevered. Their patient pursuit of wealth brought another glimpse of the outside world into the narrow purview of the village.

Except for the conquest and the mass conversions growing out of it, none of the changes initiated during the first two centuries of Spanish rule occurred suddenly. The deliberate pace and lengthy duration of the transition minimized cultural dislocations. Adaptation rather than mutation characterized the initial stage of the acculturation process: foreign outlooks, institutions, and techniques penetrated the interior; village political and economic life took on new shapes; and pre-Spanish religious beliefs came under intense pressures. But the Malayan infrastructure of the barrio held firm. Hamlet dwellers cultivated paddies in the age-old manner; they communicated with one another in ancient dialects, lived in the same houses, and—as in the past—followed familial leaders. Customary supernaturalism, furthermore, with all its emotional depth and intensity, persisted under a lacquer-thin Catholic veneer.[17] Broadly speaking, the established ways of a face-to-face world continued in near uninterrupted form.

17. See, for example, Jose Nuñoz, "Present Beliefs and Superstitions in Luzon," *BR,* XLIII, 310–319; Richard Arens, "Witches and Witchcraft in Leyte and Samar Islands, Philippines," *Philippine Journal of Science,* LXXXV (1956), 451–465; R. W. Leiban, "Sorcery, Illness, and Social Control in a Philippine Municipality," *Southwestern Journal of Anthropology,* XVI (1960), 127–143; and D. V. Hart, "The Filipino Villager and His Spirits," *Solidarity,* I (1966), 65–71.

The patterns of cultural modification followed Robert Redfield's classic model. Under Spanish rule three distinct configurations came into being. Manila, together with its bayside suburbs and rural environs, constituted a partially Westernized enclave: the Walled City's narrow streets sheltered and fostered an expanding urban or great tradition. Away from the colonial capital pristine folk societies lingered: Northern Luzon, Mindoro, Palawan, and most of Mindanao remained strongholds for primitive peoples. While on connecting plains and intervening islands, converted lowlanders combined ingredients of the contrary heritages into an uneasy equilibrium. Conscious of both extremes, repelled and attracted by each, villagers fashioned a relatively stable world of their own. The barrio involved a working synthesis of elements from Manila and the defunct *barangay*. From that "half-way house" the peasantry emerged.[18] Their appearance marked the birth of the Philippine little tradition.

After 1800, leisurely cultural interactions came to an end. A more dynamic atmosphere did not materialize abruptly. The rate of transition merely quickened at a pace that became discernible and vaguely disconcerting to village populations. In its early stages, the subtle acceleration must have been roughly comparable to the passage from winter to summer in Manila. Unlike soaring temperatures, however, the mounting pressures of the acculturation process did not moderate. Throughout the nineteenth century Spanish efforts to rationalize the insular economy introduced additional catalytic agents into Philippine society. Under their influence a climate of comparative stability gave way to one of equilibrium-eroding change.

The inconstant quality of the new environment emanated from a reorientation of imperial objectives.[19] Staggered by the loss of vast New World possessions, Madrid was forced into a reconsideration of assumptions and purposes. In the Western Hemisphere paternalism, absolutism, state Catholicism, and mercantilism had ceased to function as stabilizing factors. The implementation of those policies, in fact, contributed to the formation of nationalistic undercurrents which developed into a revolutionary flood tide. By 1823, Mexico and

18. Robert Redfield, "The Natural History of the Folk Society," *Social Forces*, XXI (1953), 225. For the development of Redfield's thinking on the little and great traditions see his *The Primitive World and Its Transformations* (Ithaca, N.Y., 1953); *The Little Community* (Chicago, 1964); and *Peasant Society and Culture* (Chicago, 1965).
19. The best short study of the entire Spanish era is that of N. P. Cushner, *Spain in the Philippines* (Manila, 1971).

South America had been swept away. From the perspective of the Spanish capital little of value was left. Only one path to survival remained open. Colonial liabilities obviously had to be converted into assets. But the delicate alchemy required extreme caution. Otherwise, the off-shore islands would follow the divergent course pursued by lost continents.

The Philippines constituted a particularly demanding challenge. Perpetuation of Spanish sovereignty required the transformation of a subsidized mission establishment into a profitable dependency. Although conservative Spaniards feared the long-range political implications of the process, they had no realistic alternative other than to begin. The focus of Madrid's attention shifted from religion to commerce and agriculture. Prudent experimentation produced an impressive increase in the output of tobacco, hemp, sugar, copra, and coffee throughout the nineteenth century.[20] The higher yield of export crops brought the Islands a favorable balance of trade. Custom returns, in fact, grew to such respectable dimensions that surplus revenue became available for use elsewhere in the impoverished empire.[21] Material improvements, however, were not an unmixed blessing, for policies that stimulated production also spurred the development of insular elites dedicated to nationalistic goals. The same policies also injected new sources of tension into the rural milieu.

The reforms began with modifications of mercantilism. After 1820, stultifying restrictions were gradually abandoned in favor of limited laissez-faire incentives. Manila became an open port. Inducements for Hispanic investors were established to augment the efforts of royal monopolies. Prohibitions on non-Spanish participation in the insular economy fell by the wayside. Colonial administrators cast aside stringent, eighteenth-century bans on Chinese immigration. In a farewell gesture toward the confining policies of the past, the *Cortes* also lowered preferential tariff rates to competitive levels.[22] When the locks of the Suez Canal went into operation in 1869, Spain's Pacific de-

---

20. Trade figures revealed an impressive growth rate. Between 1841 and 1894, imports climbed from 3,092,432 to 24,558,552 pesos; and exports from 4,370,000 to 33,149,984 pesos. See G. F. Zaide, *Philippine History* (Manila, 1961), 190.
21. Agoncillo and Alfonso, 117.
22. For a detailed discussion of policy changes see Benito Legarda, Jr., "Foreign Trade, Economic Change, and Entrepreneurship in the Nineteenth-Century Philippines" (Doctoral dissertation, Harvard University, 1955).

pendency was ready to contend for a share of the burgeoning commerce that soon developed between Europe and maritime Asia. All the economic catalyzers worked directly on Manila. Under their influence the city's conventional austerity, sanctity, and stability began to evaporate. Within two generations a parochial religious and administrative center took on many of the cosmopolitan qualities normally associated with modern commercial life. Beyond the ramparts of old Intramuros, a new Manila grew without regard for order or amenities. Warehouses, business establishments, export-import concerns, and financial institutions went up along the Pasig and its serpentine *esteros* (drainage canals). Ramshackle *indio* quarters, in the form of rambling, interconnecting barrios, proliferated beside the bay. Chinese in unprecedented numbers flowed once again into the city and quickly recaptured their strategic positions in its economic life. No longer able to hope for success in the New World colonies, Spaniards increasingly sought their fortune in Manila. They were joined by a small but influential group of British and American entrepreneurs and European investors. Rapid growth and intensifying secularization changed Manila's raison d'être.[23] By 1870, it had emerged as the hub of a developing hinterland.

While provincial transmutations lagged behind those occurring within the colonial capital, more and more rural areas became directly involved in the city's destiny. Manila's influence spread along the lines of an evolving transportation network. Roads and bridges eased the transfer of goods to and from the hinterland. Steam navigation contributed to a steady expansion of interisland shipping. Ports in the Visayas, Mindanao, and Luzon tied formerly remote areas to the city. Late in the century inauguration of railway service to Lingayan Gulf gave Manila's commercial interests direct access to the fertile fields of central Luzon and the Ilocos. Harbor and terminal towns inevitably emerged as collection and processing centers. The developments so forged served to link production and distribution systems throughout the colony. They also broke down regional barriers to the flow of merchandise and the movement of people. The comprehensive effort, in short, inaugurated profound changes and, above all, created the primary elements of an integrated Philippine economy.[24]

23. Manila's population grew from 93,595 in 1876, to 176,777 in 1887, to 219,928 in 1903. See *Census of the Philippine Islands 1903*, II (Washington, D.C., 1905), 20.
24. Wickberg, 45.

Commercial impulses were not the only transforming tendencies radiating from Manila. Mounting production and a reasonably reliable transportation system required a modicum of internal order. Law enforcement, consequently, became a primary concern of colonial administrators. Officials responsible for imposing restraint on insular residents faced a variety of challenges: in the mountains, tribesmen settled old scores with poisoned darts and head axes; from Sulu and Mindanao "Moro" freebooters regularly attacked merchantmen on the high seas; when not engaged in piracy, they conducted raids on coastal settlements in the Visayas, carrying off survivors to slave marts in Jolo and Borneo; hostilities between lowlanders and mountain people, and antipathies between Christians and Moslems, kept frontier zones in a state of chronic tension which flared periodically into irregular warfare. Even in ostensibly stable areas, conditions left much to be desired.[25] Blood feuds, personal vendettas, bandits, rustlers, highwaymen, and individual hellions kept many provinces on the ragged edge. The general condition meant that Spanish authorities could begin pacification efforts almost anywhere.

From 1850 onward, the endeavor was made. Steam gunboats halted slave hunts in the central islands and reduced piracy to tolerable levels. When the Sultan of Sulu accepted Spanish suzerainty in 1878, southern sea lanes became relatively safe for interisland and world shipping.[26] Stabilization proved more difficult in insular interiors. Small military garrisons contributed a measure of order to troubled areas in the foothills. Protection of lowland lives and property, however, involved a far more extensive and persistent operation. In 1868, accordingly, the Spanish organized the *Guardia Civil*. Police companies, headquartered in provincial capitals with detachments in major towns, brought an unprecedented degree of external surveillance and control to the countryside. Native Civil Guards, commanded by Spaniards, gained neither the fame of Canadian Mounties nor the notoriety of Mexican *Rurales*, but they produced detectable results. Lawlessness did not vanish. Regular patrols and

25. During the early nineteenth century *ladrones* (bandits) flourished in the provinces around Manila. Several large municipalities in Laguna, in fact, were known as *"ladron* towns." See V. S. Clark, "Labor Conditions in the Philippines," *Bulletin of the Department of Labor*, X (1905), 729.
26. C. A. Majul, "Chinese Relationships with the Sultanate of Sulu," in Felix, 156.

heavy-handed punishments, however, reduced it to endurable proportions.[27]

The expansion and consolidation of central authority required additional revenues. When old-style levies proved inadequate, they were gradually abandoned in favor of more comprehensive systems. Of these, the head tax, or *cedula,* carried the greatest potential for increased returns.[28] Those who could not pay the annual three-peso fee were required to perform equivalent labor service for the state. But the new exaction could not be levied until valid census data and reliable municipal tax rolls had been accumulated. Spanish authorities encountered unforeseen difficulties when they began the tabulations. Most village dwellers existed in a world without surnames. The face-to-face quality of barrio life made family designations superfluous. In rural hamlets everyone knew everyone else.[29] Everyone, furthermore, knew to whom everyone else was related. The custom frustrated Spanish record keepers and hindered efficient revenue collection. A decisive governor general finally resolved both problems by decreeing that all *indios* must adopt Hispanic surnames.[30] Within one year mass anonymity began to disappear. Family names made individual taxation feasible. Civil Guards, moreover, made it almost inevitable.

Cedulas and the *Guardia Civil* symbolized the arrival of impersonal law. Prior to the nineteenth century, *provincianos* seldom experienced direct contact with alien authority.[31] Villages had been controlled by traditional leaders, and most disputes between individuals or families had been settled according to time-honored practices. A kind of rustic *lex talionis* based on personalistic folk conventions prevailed. With tax certificates and policemen came the complex legal paraphernalia of the modern state.[32] Courts, magistrates, lawyers, and notaries;

27. Wickberg, 59.
28. The head tax shifted the incidence from families to individuals. For a concise discussion of Spanish revenue policies, see C. C. Plehn, "Taxation in the Philippines," *Political Science Quarterly,* XVIII (1902), 684–689.
29. Barrio women still retain their maiden names and are referred to simply by diminutives. See B. H. Stoodley, "Some Aspects of Tagalog Family Structure," *American Anthropologist,* LIX (1957), 240.
30. Agoncillo and Alfonso, 126.
31. For a brief discussion of the divide and rule technique of the *Guardia Civil* see Felix Keesing, *Taming Philippine Headhunters* (Stanford, Calif., 1934), 78.
32. *Principales* used the new machinery to improve their position. See J. A. Larkin, "The Evolution of Pampangan Society: A Case Study of Social and

writs, titles, torts, and claims; all the hair-splitting niceties of ab-
stract depersonalized jurisprudence, with its neat division into civil
and criminal law, became part of normal existence in the *municipios.*
Behind the elaborate juridical machinery lurked an expanding
penal system. Increasingly, those who consciously or unconsciously
challenged authority found themselves behind bars: misdemeanors led
to sojourns in crude provincial *carcels* (jails); felonies led to extended
sentences in the dungeons of Bilibid Prison; capital crimes led to Fort
Santiago and to public executions in Bagumbayang Field. Most prisoners probably found it difficult to understand the legal assumptions
and procedures that reduced them to captivity. Activities that had
been either overlooked or considered socially acceptable in 1800
were classified as crimes against the state by 1887.[33] Many villagers
must have concluded that simple forthright justice had vanished. In
their minds it had been replaced by intricate inequitable law. By every
measurement a formerly light regime had given way to an ever-more-
intrusive and burdensome government.

The sources of stress, however, were not restricted to external factors. Within the most developed *municipios* internal social pressures
also heightened. Until 1800 the gap between villagers and their local
betters remained small. Differences in rank were matters of degree
rather than kind. Class relations had been characterized by symbiosis.
Peasants supplied sustenance and labor for the *principalia.* The *principales,* in turn, provided reciprocal assistance and acted as effective
buffers between hamlet dwellers and colonial overlords. During the
nineteenth century, mutuality started to break down. Instead of de-
flecting Spanish intentions, provincial elites increasingly reflected them.
Instead of resisting foreign innovations, more and more local leaders
adopted alien methods and applied them to rural settings. Predictably,
they reaped the primary benefits of change. The *principalia* began to
extract far more from barrio people than they granted in the form of
reciprocal services. As a consequence, the first symptoms of class
antagonism appeared among village populations.

Social animosity emerged from the transformation of the countryside. Emphasis on export crops led to radical changes in agricultural

---

Economic Change in the Rural Philippines" (Doctoral dissertation, New York
University, 1966), 80.
    33. In that year the Spanish Penal Code was applied to the Philippines. See
Zaide, *History,* 202.

patterns, for, as subsistence farming gave way to production for foreign markets, land became the primary source of wealth. Under the new dispensation, rural elites found themselves in an enviable position: proximity to Spanish authorities assured foreknowledge of transportation improvements; familiarity with Iberian legal procedures facilitated the acquisition of land titles; and political influence in provincial capitals and municipalities guaranteed near immunity from external interference. Throughout the nineteenth century, consequently, prominent families devoted a large portion of their energies to the accumulation of agricultural properties.[34] The thrust of their activities started the wholesale dispossession of village populations.

The character of rural society changed even more rapidly than landholding patterns. Until the middle of the eighteenth century, most provincial leaders had been *indios*. Many, in fact, had inherited their status directly from pre-Spanish *datus*. Between 1750 and 1850 an important alteration occurred. During that hundred-year interval, Spanish decrees forbade further Chinese immigration to the Philippines. Strict prohibitions were also issued against Chinese participation in rural economic life. The exclusion policy effectively removed alien middlemen from the *municipios*. It also provided an unprecedented opportunity for a frustrated minority. *Mestizos*, or mixed bloods—primarily of Chinese descent—filled the void. They flourished as provincial wholesalers, retailers, rice merchants, and moneylenders.[35] Soon, they began systematic investments in land. *Mestizo* success, furthermore, threatened the position of the predominantly *indio* elite, and many old families headed off disaster by arranging well-timed marital alliances with promising members of the "third class."[36] The process produced a dynamic new generation of rural leaders.

While most Spanish policies favored the reanimated *principalia*, one nineteenth-century reform threatened their new-found prosperity. In 1850, the colonial government repealed Chinese exclusion. "Sangleys" immediately returned to the countryside. They not only won back their old position as provincial middlemen, but also expanded

34. Wickberg, 142–143.
35. The development was predicted by Spanish churchmen. See Lourdes Diaz-Trechulo, "The Role of the Chinese in the Philippine Domestic Economy," in Felix, 175.
36. For a discussion of the group's origins and development see Edgar Wickberg, "The Chinese Mestizo in Philippine History," *Journal of Southeast Asian History*, V (1964), 62–100.

into new regions and subsidiary endeavors. Nascent *mestizo* entrepreneurs found it impossible to meet the new Chinese competition. Most of them abandoned the demanding world of commerce and turned to the less rigorous and still protected field of agriculture. There, skills and capital acquired by the *mestizos* during the era of Chinese exclusion stood them in good stead. Throughout the last half-century of Spanish rule, displaced *mestizos* engaged in a race with established *principales* and newly arrived Spaniards to amass farm holdings. After 1880, the rivalry deteriorated to the level of rampant land grabbing.[37]

All energies were not devoted to estate formation. Large landowners applied a portion of their gains to conspicuous consumption in the form of fine houses, fashionable clothing, and gem collections. More importantly, they used rising incomes to acquire higher education for their offspring.[38] As the level of sophistication rose, families doubled their efforts to forge strategic alliances. Mergers with rising kin groups continued, but they were complemented by an increasing number of intermarriages or *compadrazgo* (godparenthood) arrangements with affluent Chinese and influential Spaniards. Fusions of both types led to further elevations in wealth and status. By 1890, a clearly defined provincial gentry had come into being.

The new elite, however, bore little resemblance to its indigenous precursor. Predominantly *mestizo* in origin, and overwhelmingly Hispanic in orientation, it flourished with the characteristic vigor of genetic and cultural hybrids. The urbane ways of central Luzon's *principalia* proved impressive to foreign visitors. Frederick Sawyer, a nineteenth-century English observer, commented on their aristocratic life style:

> Their houses are . . . clean and the larger ones are well-suited for entertainment, as the *sala* [parlor] and *caida* [interior gallery] are very spacious, and have polished floors of *narra,* or some other hard close-grained wood very pleasant to dance on.
>
> A ball in a big Pampanga house is a sight that will be remembered. Capitán Joaquin Arnedo Cruz of Sulipan . . . a wealthy native sugar planter, used to assemble in his fine house the principal people of the neighbourhood to meet royal or distinguished guests. . . . Capitán Joa-

37. Philippine Islands, Bureau of Forestry, *Spanish Public Land Laws in the Philippine Island* (Washington, D.C., 1901), 51.
38. For a brief but provocative statistical evaluation of the role played by educated *provincianos* in the late nineteenth century, see Felix, 2–3.

quin possessed a magnificent porcelain table service of two hundred pieces, specially made and marked with his monogram, sent him by a prince who had enjoyed his hospitality.

He gave a ball for the Grand Duke Alexis of Russia, who afterwards declared that the room presented one of the most brilliant sights he had ever seen. This from the son of an Emperor might seem an exaggeration, but brilliant is the only word that can describe the effect produced on the spectator by the bright costumes and sparkling jewelry of the women.[39]

Few rural leaders lived in the grand manner of the *Capitán* (*gobernadorcillo*) of Sulipan. All of them, however, achieved levels of comfort and prosperity beyond the material cravings of their ancestors. The peasantry experienced nothing in the way of comparable satisfactions but continued to eke out a hand-to-mouth existence in traditional village settings. Steady population growth, in fact, probably made hamlet life more difficult than before.[40] Although large quantities of virgin land were opened to agriculture, the number of rural dwellers increased far more rapidly than the area under cultivation. A handful of great houses gracing municipal plazas, and jumbles of cane shacks along the squalid streets of proliferating barrios symbolized the Malthusian course of the social transition.[41]

As the century wore on, the developing contrast between classes took on a chiaroscuro quality. *Principales* were literate; peasants were not. *Principales* spoke Spanish; peasants used local dialects. More and more members of prominent families pursued the learned professions—particularly theology, law, and medicine; villagers continued to farm and fish. A simple mental-manual social dichotomy emerged. Sheltered faces, soft muscles, and long fingernails designated educated leaders or *ilustrados*.[42] Sun-ravaged flesh, wiry bodies, and work-worn hands distinguished commoners or *taos*. The fact that a Spanish superlative was reserved for the elite, while a Malay noun was retained for the peasantry underlined the cultural nature of the developing gap. As it widened, the basis for mutual trust and understanding diminished.

Popular awareness of the change manifested itself in less favorable

39. Sawyer, 245.
40. The insular population grew from 1,561,251 in 1800, to 6,490,684 in 1894. See *Census of 1903*, II, 19.
41. J. A. LeRoy, *Philippine Life in Town and Country* (New York, 1905), 173.
42. H. H. Miller, *Principles of Economics Applied to the Philippines* (Boston, 1932), 512.

attitudes toward the gentry. Envy began to supplant respect. Social variations had become so great they could no longer be attributed to the natural order of things. Marked contrasts in living levels, furthermore, were reinforced by pronounced dissimilarities in behavior and pigmentation. Obvious differences between the foreign conduct of fair superiors and the customary ways of swarthy inferiors generated a variety of wry comments. Most revealing, perhaps, was the growing tendency on the part of the peasantry to refer to themselves as "Filipinos of heart and face."[43]

One factor kept village views of the elite from deteriorating to the point of outright hostility. For the most part, class relations retained personalistic qualities. Social distance grew, but physical and psychological proximity survived. Since production for export required close supervision to assure maximum output, many landowners maintained houses in the barrios.[44] Regular visits enabled them to oversee tenant labor and keep in touch with village affairs. Peasant families who experienced misfortune took advantage of such occasions to request succor and sympathy, both of which were usually granted. In the final analysis, paternalism held the system together. Prominent men regarded their dependents as children and treated them accordingly, while tenants looked upon the landowner as a potential benefactor and usually addressed him as elder brother or father.[45] In a changing world, the intimate nature of the unequal relationship gave villagers an illusion of permanence and a false sense of security. Face-to-face interactions, however, did not persist everywhere. Absentee ownership—which prevailed on many church estates, and appeared on some private holdings—destroyed the last vestiges of sentiment and compassion. Its emergence signaled the death of social reciprocity and the simultaneous birth of class antipathy.[46]

Spain might have perpetuated its sovereignty over the Philippines by attempting to meet either the aspirations of the *principalia* or the needs of the peasantry. Instead, Iberian officials managed to alienate

43. *"Filipinos de corazon y cara."* Suppressed racial feelings asserted themselves in 1896 when rebelling villagers smashed the Caucasian noses of religious images. Theodore Friend, *Between Two Empires* (New Haven, Conn., 1965), 36.

44. Larkin, 115–16.

45. S. E. Macaraig, *Social Problems* (Manila, 1929), 98.

46. The development of symbiotic relationships in one province and the causes of their eventual breakdown have been traced and analyzed. See J. A. Larkin, *The Pampangans* (Berkeley, Calif., 1972).

both elements. If Madrid had manifested the same degree of cautious flexibility on religious and political issues it had demonstrated on economic matters, the Hispanized gentry would have had few grounds for discontent. Peninsular rigidity, however, frustrated the insular elite's desire for a larger role in determining ecclesiastical and governmental policies. Between 1872 and 1898, consequently, *ilustrados* led a disjointed drive for national independence. Like most nineteenth-century revolutionaries, they sought essentially political goals.[47] Other objectives—particularly the creation of a more equitable social order —held little allure for the men who challenged Spanish authority. By 1896, Filipino elitists were attuned to the great tradition. They challenged neither its basic assumptions nor its rational purposes. All they hoped to achieve was a transfer of power. *Ilustrados,* in short, aspired to direct the course of Philippine development.

Many peasants joined the *principales* in their effort to throw off the Spanish yoke, but popular desires differed radically from the aspirations of revolutionary leaders. The dissimilarities in purpose emanated from contrary sources of estrangement. Barrio people found themselves beset by incomprehensible forces. Familiar ways were disappearing even more rapidly than unqualified claims to land, while dispossession, *cedula* certificates, and policemen symbolized the dawn of a depersonalized era. Villagers, in brief, saw little of value in the new age. Like the gentry, they longed for freedom from Spanish interference. But, unlike their social betters, they yearned for the restoration of a less complicated world. As participants in the little tradition they sought the re-creation of the simple clarities inherent in a defunct moral order. If *ilustrados* looked toward the future, the peasantry looked toward the past. The difference in social perspectives led to mounting stress during and after Philippine hostilities with Spain and the United States.

47. For the goals and ideology that propelled the Revolutionary Era, see T. A. Agoncillo, *The Revolt of the Masses: The Story of Bonifacio and the Katipunan* (Quezon City, 1956), and *Malolos: The Crisis of the Republic* (Quezon City, 1960); and C. A. Majul, *The Political and Constitutional Ideas of the Philippine Revolution* (Quezon City, 1957), and *Mabini and the Philippine Revolution* (Quezon City, 1960).

CHAPTER 2

The American Impact

American intervention and occupation altered the course of Philippine development.[1] The unforeseen appearance of a second colonial regime compounded the difficulties facing Filipinos: novel Anglo-Saxon patterns replaced familiar Hispanic forms; an indigenous revolutionary sequence was interrupted, and in its stead an alien evolutionary order emerged. *Ilustrados,* preconditioned to the demands of cultural flexibility, quickly abandoned their initial hostility and adapted themselves to the expectations of a new metropolitan power. Peasants, far more subservient to traditional village requirements, found adjustment extremely difficult. While the United States brought the paraphernalia of popular government and guarantees of eventual independence to the Philippines, it did not transform the nature of insular society. Tensions between social groups persisted. American administration, in fact, contributed additional dimensions of discord to the rural scene.

The paradoxical character of American policy made such an outcome almost inevitable. Politically, the colonial program was extremely enlightened. Economically, it left much to be desired. The United States set out to create a working democracy in its Pacific dependency. Public health programs, educational reforms, transportation improvements, and administrative techniques reinforced the primary objective. Ill-conceived economic policies, however, worked in the opposite

1. For a standard account of the American era, see G. A. Grunder and W. E. Livezey, *The Philippine and the United States* (Norman, Okla., 1951). More detailed discussions by men who shaped policy can be found in J. A. LeRoy, *The Americans in the Philippines,* 2 vols. (New York, 1914); F. B. Harrison, *The Corner-Stone of Philippine Independence* (New York, 1922); W. C. Forbes, *The Philippine Islands,* 2 vols. (New York, 1928); D. C. Worcester and J. R. Hayden, *The Philippines Past and Present* (New York, 1930); and J. R. Hayden, *The Philippines: A Study in National Development.*

direction. Free trade with the United States completed agricultural and commercial processes initiated by Spain. A full-fledged colonial economy came into being. By 1940, Filipinos had achieved autonomy, but they governed an embryonic nation with the most dependent economic system in Southeast Asia. American inability or unwillingness to resolve pressing land problems, moreover, perpetuated conventional rural relationships and forms of cultivation. Tenancy increased rather than decreased, and poverty remained the lot of barrio people. By the eve of World War II, the gap between the prosperous minority and the deprived majority threatened to become a chasm.

Disproportionate social development grew out of the assumptions underlying American administration. The foundations for the brief colonial regime were hastily laid at the turn of the century and, predictably, they reflected attitudes then current in the United States. Like the Filipino revolutionaries they supplanted, American civil servants conceived of the world in essentially political terms. As early twentieth-century Progressives they believed that republican institutions produced free men. While they recognized the dangers of social and economic inequities, their limited conception of administrative responsibility militated against sweeping rectification. Ultimately, Washington acknowledged the necessity of assuming broad welfare obligations. The development, however, came too late to benefit Filipino villagers. In the final analysis, Theodore Roosevelt's nation rather than Franklin Roosevelt's America directed the course of Philippine social destinies.

The style of American colonialism, nevertheless, differed radically from that of Spain. Legal barriers went up immediately between the spheres of church and state. After consigning the spiritual fate of Filipinos to a disestablished clergy, the United States concentrated on secular problems. Public health received high priority.[2] While American forces still engaged Aguinaldo's revolutionary army, medical men and sanitation teams launched an assault on disease. Their efforts produced impressive results: cholera, smallpox, and plague came under control—in time, these age-old afflictions were virtually eliminated; systematic campaigns against anopheles mosquitoes and their breeding places cut the incidence of malaria to manageable propor-

2. For a vivid account by a participant, see Victor Heiser, *An American Doctor's Odyssey* (New York, 1936).

tions; new water supplies and sewerage systems reduced the ravages caused by intestinal parasites; leprosy was checked; and infant mortality rates—which had been among the highest in the world—declined precipitously.[3] Census figures bore witness to the effectiveness of the program. Within the span of one generation the archipelago's population more than doubled.

The commitment to public health programs was exceeded only by an abiding faith in the efficacy of mass education. In August 1901 the transport *Thomas*—which shuttled troops to and from San Francisco —brought a strikingly different cargo to the Philippines.[4] Six hundred American teachers disembarked. Within a month they were hard at work in Manila and the provinces. The contingent constituted the vanguard of an annual invasion which continued for more than a decade. "Thomasites," as the teachers were called, quickly gained the respect and affection of Filipinos. They pursued their profession with the same zeal manifested by early Spanish friars. In a cultural sense, they also achieved comparable results. Largely owing to their efforts, schools replaced churches as symbols of foreign domination.

The educational system which emerged reflected American beliefs and aspirations. Tax-supported and secular in orientation, its grade levels ranged from public elementary schools through a state university. Administrative patterns, textbooks, curricular and extracurricular programs—including parent-teacher associations and interscholastic athletics—were all imported from the United States. English became the vehicle for instruction. Primary instruction stressed reading, writing, arithmetic, citizenship, and community hygiene, while vocational subjects, other than industrial arts and home economics, received scant attention. High schools and the University of the Philippines emphasized academic or professional training. The system, in short, reflected all the strengths and weaknesses of its American model.

Educational innovations were not restricted to structure and content. An attempt was made to transfer seemingly contradictory values to youthful Filipinos. Classwork brought out the advantages of freedom and democracy while pointing up the necessity of "responsible

3. In Manila, infant deaths fell from 80 per 100 in 1900 to 6 per 100 in 1940. G. B. Cressey, *Asia's Lands and Peoples* (New York, 1944), 540.
4. For an appreciative description of the educational program see Agoncillo and Alfonso, *A Short History*, 435–437.

nationalism." Instructors who praised competitive endeavors also spoke glowingly of the advantage of teamwork and fair play. Many teachers and professors, furthermore, tried to revise established attitudes toward physical labor by elaborating on the dignity of manual pursuits. Students, for the most part, ignored the panegyrics to individualism and the work ethic. They concentrated instead on daily assignments and retained strong group orientations. Those fortunate enough to complete the lengthy process, moreover, tended to emulate the life styles and careers of their mentors.[5]

With all its imperfections, the experiment produced benefits. For one thing, literacy rates rose sharply. By 1939 at least 7,000,000 Filipinos were able to read and write—a figure equal to the total population at the turn of the century.[6] For another, increasing reliance on the English language helped break down regional linguistic barriers. In the same way that Catholicism created the initial base for unifying diverse Malay cultural components, a colonial lingua franca contributed an additional impulse to the forces working toward cohesion. More significant than either of these accomplishments, however, was the social role of public education. High schools and universities provided many Filipinos with an unprecedented opportunity to better themselves, and from the intermediate and advanced institutions emerged the lead elements of a potentially important middle class.

Improvements in transportation and communication approached the rates achieved in health and education.[7] Existing railroads were extended in central Luzon and the Ilocos—a new line passed between the slumbering volcanos south of Manila and traversed Bicol's languid valleys. Steel and concrete bridges, paved highways, graveled feeder roads, and a supplemental web of trails opened isolated regions to outside influences. Telegraph and telephone lines went up beside the expanding network. Interisland shipping improved both in quantity and quality, and regular passenger and cargo service linked new harbor facilities in the Visayas and Mindanao to Manila's deep-water port. The integrated system forged discrete segments of the archipelago into a new interdependence.

5. Macaraig, *Social Problems,* 49.
6. Hayden, 604.
7. When the Americans arrived only 990 miles of treacherous roads existed in the Philippines; by 1934, 13,000 miles of all-weather highways had been constructed. David Bernstein, *The Philippine Story* (New York, 1947), 122.

The greatest centripetal influences, however, emanated from American administrative patterns. Uncomfortable—if not unwilling—imperialists, pragmatic governors general from William Howard Taft through Frank Murphy directed their energies toward eliminating, and then avoiding, anything resembling the prelude to 1776. To a remarkable degree they succeeded. Their collective accomplishment rested on recognition and acceptance of the aspirations inherent in the truncated Philippine Revolution of 1896–1902.[8] By incorporating its primary goals—excluding, of course, immediate independence—into the machinery of the evolving colonial regime, they quickly won the support of *ilustrado* elements, and eventually attracted the loyalty of villagers. Through a strange historical quirk, therefore, the power originally responsible for inflicting grievous wounds on Philippine nationalism became, in time, its guardian.

The political fundamentalism of American policy affected every phase of life in the Philippines. Proceeding on the assumption that legitimacy sprang from the consent and participation of the governed, American administrators granted expanding spheres of action to prominent islanders. An orderly Filipinization process began shortly after Taft's arrival in Manila. From 1901 to 1907, the Philippine Commission controlled the dependency. Composed of five Americans and three Filipinos, it exercised both executive and legislative powers. In 1907, Commission authority was diluted by the creation of the Philippine Assembly. For the next nine years the Commission carried on the dual functions of an executive cabinet and upper legislative body, while the popularly elected Assembly operated as the lower house. The Jones Act of 1916 abolished the Commission, replaced it with an all-Filipino Senate, and converted the Assembly into a House of Representatives. From then until the inauguration of the Commonwealth in 1935, American governors general retained executive powers but delegated law-making authority to the bicameral Philippine Legislature. The process produced a systematic transfer of power and constituted a rare experiment in self-liquidating colonial management.

The emergence and growth of representative institutions entailed

8. For provocative discussions of the "co-optation" of Philippine nationalism, see O. D. Corpuz, *The Philippines* (Englewood Cliffs, N.J., 1965); and G. E. Taylor, *The Philippines and the United States: Problems of Partnership* (New York, 1964).

the formation of political parties.[9] But the factions and interest groups that materialized in the Philippines bore little resemblance to their ostensible models in the United States or Western Europe. If power was the immediate prize sought by ambitious politicos, their ultimate aim was national independence. Philippine parties, as Joseph Hayden observed, evolved as "instruments of freedom rather than government."[10] Sovereignty, after all, had been the primary goal of the abortive Revolution. Until 1935, it remained the one political desideratum denied by a generally benevolent metropolitan power. As such, it became the only electoral issue with universal appeal. Candidates for office, from rude provincial aspirants to suave senatorial incumbents, consistently stressed it desirability. "Independence," accordingly, became the rallying cry for statesmen and demagogues alike—the shibboleth of an era.

Paradoxically, the first party organized under American jurisdiction advocated annexation to the United States. Formed in 1900, while hostilities still raged in Luzon and the Visayas, the *Partido Federalista* advocated an early restoration of peace, complete cooperation with occupation authorities, and eventual statehood for the Philippines within the American union. *Federalista* aspirations proved irresistable to colonial administrators plagued by the savagery of protracted guerrilla warfare. From 1901 to 1907, consequently, appointments to government posts came almost exclusively from the party's ranks. Federalism, in fact, provided the initial base for the Filipinization process.

By 1906, the most dangerous military expressions of Philippine nationalism had been suppressed, and Americans broadened the role of Filipinos in the colonial regime. Calls were issued for the first general election in Philippine history. Restrictions on civil rights, together with bans against groups advocating independence, fell by the wayside. New parties representing all shades of opinion on the subject formed and received the freedom to advocate their causes before captivated voters. A *Partido Independista Inmediatista,* and a *Partido Urgentista,* along with other organizations bearing similarly exhilarating titles, appeared on all sides. Since the multiplication threatened to dissipate nationalism's potential strength, spokes-

9. Dapen Liang, *The Development of Philippine Political Parties* (Hong Kong, 1939).
10. Hayden, 316.

men for the contending groups advocated the formation of a working coalition. In March 1907, the various factions united under the banner of the *Nacionalista* Party. The campaign of 1907 for control of the Philippine Assembly revolved around the independence issue. *Nacionalista* candidates, many of whom were former officers in the revolutionary army, maintained that Filipinos were ready for complete sovereignty. *Progresistas,* as the *Federalistas* were then called, cautioned against such a course and denied the capacity of Filipinos to administer their own affairs. Pardo de Tavera, first Filipino member of the Philippine Commission and leader of the party, disputed his rivals' claims. "If this country were governed solely by Filipinos," he warned, "our government would not be democratic but autocratic and the people would be oppressed by those who would be in power."[11] Voters rejected Tavera's oligarchic argument. When the Assembly convened, fifty-eight of its eighty members were *Nacionalistas*.

The outcome set the mold for future campaigns. *Nacionalistas* won by monopolizing the independence issue. Thenceforth, parties contending for a place in the political arena were forced to adopt similar platforms. After the demise of the *Progresistas* in 1917, remnants of the organization merged with maverick *Nacionalistas* to form the *Democrata* Party. Their effort to establish an alternative for voters also failed. *Nacionalistas* retained overwhelming majorities and with them control of patronage throughout the archipelago. Other ephemeral competitors appeared, and schisms sometimes menaced *Nacionalista* ranks, but prodigals of every persuasion were always permitted to return to the party fold. In 1935, an American newspaper editor lamented the absence of a loyal opposition and characterized insular political history as a disheartening "record of mergers, consolidations, coalitions, and reconciliations."[12] For all practical purposes, a one-party system had emerged in the Philippines.

American displeasure with the development ignored a fundamental reality. The Philippines—no matter how benevolent its government— was a colony. Filipino politicians were acutely aware of that fact. They believed—probably correctly—that independence could only be

11. M. M. Kalaw, *The Development of Philippine Politics, 1887–1920* (Manila, 1925), 309.
12. *Manila Daily Bulletin,* April 30, 1935.

achieved via united political action. Sergio Osmeña and Manuel Quezon, the leaders of the *Nacionalistas* from 1907 to 1942, wove dissimilar elements into an uneasy but effective popular front. Differences between prominent members—including Quezon and Osmeña —often threatened the alliance's delicate fabric; but splits were repaired before the party could be torn asunder.

Nacionalista success rested on a cold appraisal of political actualities. Power emanated from contradictory sources: although the party drew its leadership and financial support from the upper echelons of Philippine society,[13] most of its votes came increasingly from the inhabitants of rural municipalities. The coalition's internal logic dictated *Nacionalista* tactics. Party spokesmen advocated conventional economic programs to retain the allegiance of conservative landowners. At the same time, they issued stirring calls for immediate and complete independence to placate the radical yearnings of tenant farmers. The party, in short, became all things to all men.

Quezon and Osmeña conducted the performance skillfully.[14] By constantly stressing the desirability of political freedom, they avoided a variety of serious questions. To *Nacionalista* regulars the only debatable issue was independence. Beside it, all other unresolved problems paled into insignificance. When forced to comment on obvious imperfections in Philippine society, party leaders attributed them directly or indirectly to the pernicious influences of foreign domination. Rich and poor alike rallied to the integrating cause. Urbane Filipinos recognized the superficiality of the technique, but tended to regard it as a necessary evil. Villagers accepted party slogans as fundamental truths. In the minds of many peasants, independence took on miraculous connotations. Some barrio dwellers even began to view the anticipated condition as a panacea for everything from landed proprietors to hookworms. The awkward alliance between sophisticates and rustics worked. Its ingenious designers, however, had devised an unstable and potentially volatile political mixture.

13. In 1923 only eight of ninety-three members in the House of Representatives were not classified as landowners or lawyers. In 1938 the ratio in the National Assembly was sixteen out of ninety-eight. See R. P. Stephens, "The Prospects for Social Progress in the Philippines," *Pacific Affairs*, XXII (1950), 149.

14. Quezon and his career were brilliantly analyzed by Friend, *Between Two Empires*.

The economic programs initiated by the United States did not achieve comparable results.[15] The first blunder occurred in the sensitive area of trade relations. In 1909, over vigorous objections by Filipino assemblymen, the Philippine Commission removed the remaining barriers between the Islands and the United States. Advocates of the measure maintained that free trade would shower material blessings on the archipelago's population. Rapid growth and steady diversification, together with soaring prosperity levels, were among the predicted benefits. Proponents, however, failed to recognize the dangers inherent in the unequal relationship. The arrangement tied an underdeveloped and relatively stable agrarian system to the world's most elaborate and dynamic industrial complex. Disparities between the linked economies determined the ensuing course of Philippine affairs.

Long-range results of the trade revision were predominantly negative.[16] Above all, it provoked an uneven growth of export agriculture. Sugar, copra, and abaca yields rose almost geometrically in an effort to meet the American market's seemingly insatiable demands.[17] Other commodities did not fare so well. Tobacco—owing largely to European and domestic consumption—managed to retain a position of importance; cotton and coffee output, however, sagged dangerously. Even food production experienced a comparative contraction. The amount of land devoted to rice cultivation, for example, increased slowly, but the staple's place in the hierarchy of cash crops declined. Under the influence of the trade policy, a previously specialized economy became perilously overspecialized. By 1938, Filipinos were shipping 85 per cent of their exports to, and receiving 65 per cent of their imports from, the United States.[18] A dismayed High Commissioner complained that the archipelago relied on American consumers and manufacturers "to a greater degree than any single state

15. For the best over-all assessment of economic developments see F. H. Golay, *The Philippines: Public Policies and National Economic Development* (Ithaca, N.Y., 1961).

16. A detailed discussion can be found in P. E. Abelard, *American Tariff Policy toward the Philippines, 1898–1946* (New York, 1947).

17. Sugar production rose from 135,000 metric tons in 1920 to 1,450,000 metric tons in 1934. See Philippine Commonwealth, Department of Agriculture and Commerce, *Atlas of Philippine Statistics* (Manila, 1939), 7.

18. Hayden, 789.

in the Union" depended economically "on the rest of the United States."[19]

Less apparent but equally significant results of the trade policy were agricultural inefficiency and industrial paralysis. On the one hand, unlimited access to high-priced markets removed competitive pressures from the agrarian sector of the Philippine economy. Landowners soon discovered that conventional farming methods would suffice —most of them increased output by expanding the boundaries of their estates rather than by adopting new techniques.[20] On the other hand, unrestricted availability of relatively low-price manufactured goods hindered the emergence of consumer industries. While processing and extractive enterprises—designed primarily to facilitate export operations—were established on a limited scale, other types of manufacturing failed to materialize. As a consequence, many of the necessities and most of the luxuries of life continued to be imported.[21] The relationship fostered a period of hectic activity, one that created illusions of growth, change, and prosperity. In reality, however, it perpetuated the defects of an established colonial economy.

Among those primary weaknesses were a number of perplexing conditions related to landownership. American administrators recognized the centrality of the issue. As early as 1902 they attempted to overhaul an antiquated registration system. One year later complex negotiations for the purchase of church estates were brought to a successful conclusion, and the insular government embarked upon an ambitious redistribution program. Over the years other, if less sweeping, efforts were made to resolve the persistent problem. None of them succeeded. The final American record on the crucial land question added up to an unbroken series of failures.

The unenviable performance grew out of cultural and political miscalculations. In the first place, the approaches adopted by the United States were ill suited to Philippine conditions. Administrators attempted to apply techniques derived from the American frontier to the inhospitable milieu of Southeast Asia. Homestead laws, survey pro-

19. Abraham Chapman, "American Policy in the Philippines," *Far Eastern Survey*, XV (1946), 167.
20. In 1940, per hectare sugar yields were less than half of those prevailing in Java. See Cressey, 544.
21. Shirley Jenkins, *American Economic Policy toward the Philippines* (Stanford, Calif., 1954).

cedures, and registration machinery which had worked relatively well in Kansas and Colorado broke down completely in Nueva Ecija and Pangasinan. A second cause of failure grew out of the Filipinization process. Almost from the outset of American rule, most provincial and municipal officials came from prominent families with vested interests in maintaining or expanding the traditional landholding system. Like their ancestors, many local leaders used their positions to serve selfish purposes. Political and social realities, therefore, combined to shatter effective implementation of the land policy. Instead of creating a nation of free farmers, the United States unintentionally fostered the formation of a society composed primarily of landlords and tenants.

American land policy began as a twofold effort to right ancient wrongs: in oversimplified terms, it sought to protect and expand the prerogatives of small farmers while restricting and reducing the role of estate owners. The original purpose was to create an agricultural system based on family farms. For all practical purposes, the program's slogan might have been "forty acres and a carabao for every *tao* in the Philippines."

The first step toward achieving that Jeffersonian objective came early. The Land Act of 1902 attempted to alter property patterns by regulating the disposal of a vast public domain.[22] Under its provisions individual acquisitions were limited to 16 hectares (approximately 40 acres), while corporation purchases were restricted to 1,024 hectares (approximately 2,500 acres). The statute also simplified registration procedures and established uncomplicated methods for resolving land disputes. Settlers could acquire title to 16-hectare frontier plots by homesteading them for a period of five years and by paying the government a 20-peso fee. Unappropriated land in established municipalities which had been tilled continuously by a villager before or after 1898 could be obtained by applying to the government for a free patent.

While the measure incorporated the conventional wisdom gleaned from an alien heritage, it completely ignored the experiences and traditions of Filipino hamlet dwellers. Colonial officials—beguiled by the spell of the American West—believed the land law would provoke mass migrations into the Philippine wilderness. They also hoped the

22. Land policy and its implementation were discussed by a former Director of the Department of the Interior. See Worcester and Hayden, 589–598.

exodus would provide a safety valve for the pent-up populations of central Luzon and the western Visayas. Neither expectation materialized. Most villagers were either unwilling or unable to leave their birthplaces for distant opportunities.[23] Ignorance of the law, abiding family ties, stultifying indebtedness, ancestral animosities toward primitive tribesmen, and deep-seated fears of the unknown combined to restrict the scale of movement.

The legislation, consequently, generated a discouraging trickle rather than an inspiring trek toward the heralded lands of promise. Those who did manage to extricate themselves from the emotional and economic encumbrances of barrio life encountered unforeseen difficulties in the forested interior.[24] Physically and psychologically they may have been equal to the demands of pioneering, but politically and legally they lacked the shrewdness essential to successful homesteading. Frontier officials blocked individual and collective efforts to acquire titles; legitimate requests for decisions were ignored; essential surveys were not conducted; and approved applications were pigeonholed. Land grabbers took advantage of the orchestrated delays to file precisely executed counterclaims which were favorably received by the courts—all too often peasants carved out homesteads and produced first crops only to discover that their stump-strewn farms were located on land owned by cunning townsmen. Many accepted the cruel reverses with passive fatalism. Others refused to abide by rulings they considered to be essentially unjust. The defiant minority was brought into line either by threat of expensive litigation or by outright force.[25]

23. Philippine Islands, Office of the Governor General, *The Friar Land Inquiry* (Manila, 1910), 10. For statistics on the immobility of village populations, see E. D. Hester and P. N. Mabbun, "Some Economic and Social Aspects of Philippine Rice Tenancies," *Philippine Agriculturist*, XXI (1924), 399.

24. Much of Nueva Ecija province was settled under the provisions of the Land Law of 1902. By 1939, however, the province had the highest tenancy rates in the Philippines. A partial explanation for the discouraging outcome was provided by a witness to the migration. Observing Ilocano pioneers in 1918, he said, "They come in groups of from five to twenty [families] . . . under a headman who takes possession of a certain amount of public land. When . . . cleared and put in a state suitable for cultivation, it is distributed among . . . the community, but the title remains with the headman." See H. H. Miller, *Economic Conditions in the Philippines* (Boston, 1920), 69.

25. In Pangasinan province, a prominent land grabber said, "It was immaterial to him what decision was made by the Director of Lands . . . since if

The resettlement program, therefore, failed to gain momentum during the first decade of American rule. After 1910, popular awareness of the land law and its potential benefits, together with official efforts to eliminate inequities, increased the flow of homesteaders to respectable dimensions. But, again, aspiring peasant proprietors encountered disappointments. Title applications from the growing wave of settlers overwhelmed the limited capacities of the Bureau of Lands. Chronic surveyor shortages slowed the registration process. Clerks and judges in understaffed Land Courts also found it impossible to keep pace with demands for their services. A dismaying backlog of unresolved disputes developed. By 1926, fewer than 10 per cent of the claims accumulated since 1902 had been adjudicated.[26] Instead of alleviating a critical problem, inept policy implementation contributed additional sources of stress to the circumstances surrounding village life.

The land redistribution program suffered a similar fate. In 1903, after delicate bargaining with the Vatican, Governor General Taft announced that 410,000 acres had been purchased from the Religious Orders for $7,239,000. The outlay was to be redeemed via resales to cultivators who had labored on ecclesiastical estates. Administrators believed the intricate reform would reduce or eliminate a prime source of discontent in restless barrios. Another article of their official faith was that the "Friar Land" experiment would provide a possible solution for the problem of private latifundia throughout the archipelago. The course of events, however, again shattered government optimism.

Failure grew from several sources. For one thing, the much-publicized transaction did not encompass the total holdings of the Catholic church.[27] Many *taos*, a majority perhaps, continued to toil for the proprietors they had traditionally served. Discontent, accordingly, persisted on ecclesiastical estates. During the 1930's, in fact, American administrators were confronted with the same disturbing conditions that had faced their predecessors.[28] For another, all the

---

he lost [the legal dispute] he and others would burn the houses of the entry-men and if necessary kill them." Worcester and Hayden, 587.

26. By 1926, 127,256 homestead applications for 4,593,403 acres had been filed, but only 10,150 titles covering 284,654 acres had been issued. See Forbes, I, 327.

27. Worcester and Hayden, 592.

28. After the Sakdal Uprising of 1935, the colonial government purchased

land purchased by the insular government was not turned over to tenants. Villagers received priority, and parcels worked by them were transferred as quickly as possible. After the redistribution, however, titles for more than 200,000 virgin acres remained with the insular Department of the Interior. On the twin altars of fiscal responsibility and economic development the holdings were sacrificed by sale or lease to private American and Filipino interests. One exchange, for instance, involved a single block equal to one-eighth of the area originally acquired from the church.[29] A third and critical deficiency of the program was its failure to devise local machinery to assure long-range success. Legal facilities, rural credit associations, marketing cooperatives, and modern agricultural methods should have been developed to complement redistribution. None appeared. Peasants were given a tantalizing glimpse of freedom and abandoned to find their own way out of the agrarian wilderness.[30]

Few achieved proprietor status. Short on money, seed, and work animals, most former tenants turned to local patrons for financial support and agricultural assistance. Entrenched custom, village naiveté, usury, and other sharp practices by real or aspiring landlords, combined to undermine the program's purposes. The redistribution of ecclesiastical estates soon became an exercise in futility. The Friar Lands, wrote Manuel Quezon, "seldom got into the hands of those who worked them and lived on them."[31] Private *hacenderos* (large landowners) eventually achieved control of most of the parcels. Some even reverted to the church.[32]

Census statistics revealed the land policy's fluctuating results. Between 1903 and 1918, the number of farms increased from 815,000 to 1,955,000—of which 1,520,000 were operated by owners.[33] By 1939, both aggregates had fallen sharply. Farm totals slumped to 1,634,726, and the number of owner-operators plummeted to

---

four estates covering 95,000 acres in the vicinity of Manila for $2,814,789. The properties and their values were listed in the *Manila Daily Bulletin*, Sept. 4, 1935.

29. Worcester and Hayden, 594.
30. H. H. Miller, *Principles of Economics*, 412.
31. Manuel Quezon, *The Good Fight* (New York, 1946), 167.
32. Karl Pelzer, *Population and Land Utilization* (Shanghai, 1941), 131.
33. E. H. Jacoby, *Agrarian Unrest in Southeast Asia*, 197. The figures, particularly those for 1903, have been questioned. See LeRoy, *Philippine Life in Town and Country*, 71; and Pelzer, 131.

804,786.[34] During the same interval, the insular population soared from approximately ten to sixteen million. Peasant proprietorship, quite obviously, was a contracting statistical category. Owners by scores of thousands were falling into the ranks of sharecroppers and migratory workers. By the eve of World War II tenancy rates in the populous provinces of Luzon and the Visayas had reached ominous levels, and 3,500,000 people were classified as agricultural day laborers.[35]

The discouraging reversal undermined a variety of promising projects. Living levels for most of the population remained low. A 1939 study, for example, gauged per capita income at 80 pesos and estimated the per capita cost of "bare subsistence" at 75 pesos.[36] Monetary returns, of course, were not equally distributed: 10 per cent of the population received 40 per cent of the national income; the remainder shared the balance.[37] Among other things, the deplorable conditions of peasant life drained momentum from public health and education programs. Like their ancestors, most villagers continued to suffer from the debilitating by-products of poverty—malnutrition, intestinal parasites, and tuberculosis.[38] All too few of them, furthermore, could afford to send their numerous progeny to municipal elementary schools. As late as 1936 fewer than 40 per cent of all rural children were attending classes.[39] If a generation of American rule improved the political climate in the Philippines, it did not alter the dreary lot of the peasantry. Most hamlet dwellers, as one observer remarked, continued to live in a "warm, fertile, friendly, rural slum."[40]

While villagers eked out a marginal existence under circumstances

34. *Yearbook of Philippine Statistics, 1946* (Manila, 1947), 138.
35. Jacoby, 117.
36. K. K. Kurihara, *Labor in the Philippine Economy* (Stanford, Calif., 1945), 37.
37. Stephens, 117.
38. Annually, 15,000 people died of beriberi; 85 per cent of the rural population suffered from hookworm and roundworm; and the death rate from tuberculosis ran at an awesomely consistent 275 per 100,000. See O. L. Dawson, "Philippine Agriculture: A Problem of Adjustment," *Foreign Agriculture*, IV (1940), 396.
39. F. M. Keesing, *The Philippines: A Nation in the Making* (Shanghai, 1937), 45.
40. Bernstein, 117.

comparable to those endured by their forebears, the gentry reaped a harvest of affluence and influence. United States economic and political policies created unparalleled profits and opportunities for well-established rural families. The same programs, however, dovetailed to the disadvantage of barrio people. During the revolutionary era, wealthy *provincianos* had begun to leave the countryside; under American jurisdiction, their migration took on the character of a gathering exodus. As more proprietors abandoned rustic settings for careers in provincial capitals or Manila, the gap between *hacenderos* and tenants became even more pronounced. Most significantly, the social and cultural distinctions which formerly divided *ilustrados* and *taos* were reinforced by physical separation.

Absentee ownership created a kind of emotional vacuum in agricultural hamlets. Historically, effective rural relationships had been based upon face-to-face associations, with sentimental ties between superiors and inferiors constituting the essential element in conventional reciprocity systems. The urban gravitation by elitists removed the last vestiges of compassionate leadership from many villages. To operate vacated latifundia most *hacenderos* hired professional managers, under whose direction impersonal efficiency replaced paternalism.[41] Overseers pressed tenants for repayment of long-standing loans, charged them for services which had been previously extended gratis, and required them to perform extra labor without the recompense of fiestas. The depersonalized atmosphere destroyed the worn emotional links which had connected estate owners and *taos*. Traditional symbiosis gave way to an unhealthy condition verging on parasitism.

In the emerging social context, an ancient term took on fresh connotations. At the time of the conquest, Spaniards applied the West Indian appellation *cacique,* or chief, to insular *datus*. The label stuck. In village vernacular *cacique* became synonymous with *principal*. By 1850, the word incorporated all the varied roles and responsibilities gradually accumulated by gentry families. The growth of absentee ownership during the late nineteenth and early twentieth centuries, however, provoked a dramatic semantic shift. In popular parlance *cacique* became a term of opprobrium. Under the laissez-faire approaches of the American era, "caciquism" came to mean economic

41. Henry Wells, "Communism in the Philippines," *American Perspective,* IV (1950), 82.

exploitation without a corresponding responsibility for material or psychic sustenance.[42]

The growing sense of deprivation in the villages was heightened by rising aspiration levels. The United States unleashed ferment by creating expectations beyond the reach of most Filipinos. Half-a-world away from home, Manila's small American community pursued the "good life" with uncommon fervor. Comfortable homes, glittering automobiles, attentive servants, and exclusive clubs eased the daily burden of imperial responsibility.[43] Elaborate parties, polo matches, the race track, golf and tennis tournaments dispelled the monotony of weekends. Summer seasons in Baguio and its temperate mountain environs eliminated even the problem of heat. The living patterns evolved by resident Americans provided standards which insular elitists found irresistible. Affluent Filipinos were soon involved in a race to emulate or exceed the life styles of their mentors. Conspicuous success by a few pacesetters intensified the privation felt by cognizant villagers.

Under more traditional colonial circumstances the abrasive problem might have been confined to tolerable limits. But the unorthodox nature of American rule made restrictions on popular awareness impossible. Stress on public education created unprecedented material wants throughout the archipelago. Transportation improvements also broke down barrio isolation to reveal glimpses of creature comforts and luxuries beyond the dreams of humble *provincianos*. During the 1920's, furthermore, the mass culture burgeoning in the United States began to exert new pressures on Filipinos. Hollywood films, in particular, altered established attitudes and aspirations. In the cinemas that appeared wherever electric current was generated, standing-room-only crowds viewed the productions with unabashed wonder and enthusiasm. To impoverished members of the audience stark contrasts in ways of life suddenly became blatantly apparent. Peasant exposure to the other world—no matter how brief—made the grim realities of daily existence well-nigh unbearable.

In the years before Pearl Harbor, relationships between the classes

42. Fred Eggan, "The Philippines and the Bell Report," *Human Organization*, X (1951), 16.
43. For a discussion of the racial implications of recreation patterns, see Friend, 36–69.

deteriorated rapidly. An expanding bourgeoisie might have eased social tensions. But the middle-class opportunities that materialized tended to be restricted by the archipelago's colonial status: elitists monopolized the higher echelons of the *Nacionalista* Party, the bureaucracy, and the professions; and aliens—particularly Americans, Spaniards, Chinese and Japanese—continued to dominate the insular economy.[44] Teaching positions in public and private schools absorbed large numbers of university graduates. Other degree holders filled available openings in law, medicine, journalism, and the civil service, or occupied occasional vacancies in the clerical ranks of the small business community. Beyond those narrow boundaries, significant vocational alternatives dwindled toward the vanishing point. The dynamism which developed, furthermore, was primarily an urban phenomenon. For the most part, upward mobility was confined to the vital currents coursing through Manila and its regional counterparts, while something akin to stagnation prevailed in the economic and social backwaters of the countryside.

The cumulative effects of the changes inaugurated by the United States were devastating to peasant morale. Mired down in poverty on the fringe of plenty, villagers saw no way to bridge the frustrating gap. Feelings of alienation spread through large segments of the provincial population. Specific antipathies toward callous *caciques* grew. General animosities toward the prosperous minority intensified. In the final analysis, however, the transmutations swirling around barrio people were completely beyond their comprehension or control. As the incidence of depersonalizing alterations increased, discouragement gave way to hopelessness, and a condition verging on anomie began to characterize the rural climate.

The prewar disequilibrium which threatened society emanated, in part, from the goals of American colonialism. Without considering the suitability of the objective, the United States attempted to create a bourgeois republic in its Pacific dependency. But it failed to initiate broad policies which might have assured the rapid growth of middle-class elements. Inadvertently, the United States strengthened the social legacy of Spain: elitists derived augmented powers; peasants inherited mounting squalor. The outcome might have been

---

44. Foreign control of the economy was surveyed by Jenkins, 39. The growth of Japanese interests is traced by G. K. Goodman, *Davao: A Case Study in Japanese-Philippine Relations* (New York, 1967).

avoided if Americans had heeded Henry George's warning: "To edu-
cate men who must be condemned to poverty, is but to make them
restive; to base on a state of glaring social inequality political institutions under which men are theoretically equal, is to stand a pyramid
on its apex."[45]

45. Henry George, *Progress and Poverty* (New York, 1883), 9.

CHAPTER 3

Tenants and Laborers

By 1940 the elaborate edifice constructed after 1898 had begun to topple. Outwardly, it appeared stable. Particularly against the somber political horizons of colonial Southeast Asia, the Commonwealth government emerged as a seemingly unshakable monument to American sagacity and Filipino adaptability. Closer inspection, however, revealed internal flaws. Uneven social development constituted the primary weakness. At best, no more than 20 per cent of the population derived tangible benefits from American sovereignty. The rest of the archipelago's inhabitants, especially the overwhelming village majority, gained little more than mounting awareness of their collective plight. After Manuel Quezon's presidential inauguration in 1935, conventional nationalism lost some of its emotional and intellectual charm. Observers of Philippine affairs began to redirect their attention from the superficialities of trans-Pacific relations toward fundamental domestic issues. Because of its pervasive character, the "rural question" captured the interest of *avant-garde* scholars and journalists, whose inquiries stripped away the insular regime's impressive façade and exposed its ramshackle foundations.

In a decade beset by material problems, investigators inevitably concentrated on the economic forces that victimized barrio people.[1] Inequities growing out of complex tenancy systems provoked liberal

1. The most comprehensive investigation was conducted in 1936. For comparative information on tenants and rural laborers in eighteen provinces, see Philippine Commonwealth, Department of Labor, *Report of the Fact-Finding Survey of Rural Problems in the Philippines Submitted to the Secretary of Labor and to the President of the Philippines* (Manila, Jan. 21, 1937). Cited hereafter as *Fact Finding Report;* authors and pertinent sections of the report are referred to in individual citations. This chapter is in part based on material presented in my dissertation, "Philippine Social Structure and its Relation to Agrarian Unrest," copyrighted by David Reeves Steartevant, Stanford, 1959.

indignation. Exploitation of migratory workers generated radical out-rage. Righteous rumbles from Americans and Filipinos on the urban left, however, wrought no transformations in the countryside's tradi-tional ways. The institutions under attack had developed gradually over more than three centuries and were simply too well established —too ingrained in the thick fabric of provincial life—to give way under a sudden barrage of words.

If nothing else, studies conducted during the 1930's revealed the intricacy of rural problems. Probers uncovered endless variations in tenant and labor patterns. In almost every instance, however, local forms represented off-shoots of the *kasama* (share tenancy) or *inquilinato* (cash tenancy) systems. Linked to the dominant models were a series of robber-baron techniques utilized by the sugar planters of central Luzon and the western Visayas. By 1939, at least 50 per cent of the village population in both regions worked spasmodically under one of the configurations or, in extreme cases, under bewilder-ing combinations of all three.[2]

While the *kasama* or *aparceria* system prevailed throughout the Philippines, it was most deeply embedded in rice growing regions. According to customary arrangements, landowners furnished the pad-dies and the seed together with the cash necessary for transplanting and harvesting, while tenants (*kasamas* or *apaceros*) provided labor, tools, and work animals. The *apacero* also assumed liability for half the costs involved in *palay* (unhusked rice) production. After ex-penses had been deducted from the tenant's portion of the crop, the remainder was divided equally between the contracting parties.

Fifty-fifty divisions were normal in most areas, but other share arrangements were sometimes negotiated under the *kasama* system.[3] In frontier regions scarcity of labor forced proprietors to grant attrac-tive terms as incentives for prospective tenants. Hard-pressed owners frequently supplied everything—including draft animals and work implements—while permitting *apaceros* to retain half of the total

2. High tenancy rates, paradoxically, prevailed even where peasant propri-etorship predominated. In Ilocos Norte and Ilocos Sur, 90 per cent of the pop-ulation owned land, but 80 per cent of the parcels were cultivated by *kasamas*. Villagers rented distant holdings and became tenants on more conveniently situated plots. Similar interleasing systems were also common in Batangas and Pangasinan. Miller, *Principles of Economics*, 339–400.

3. A. M. Dalisay, "Types of Tenancy Contracts on the Rice Farms of Nueva Ecija," *Philippine Agriculturist*, XXVI (1937), 159–191.

crop. In more densely settled districts, relatively prosperous *kasamas* were sometimes able to carry all the expenses connected with transplanting and harvesting. Often, they received two-thirds of the rice yield. A fourth form of "partnership" developed in the teeming municipalities of the central plan. There, intense competition for fertile land permitted *hacenderos* to charge standard fees for access to superior parcels. Known as the *pamata* in Bulacan and the *postura* in Pangasinan, the annual levies ranged from 50 to 200 pesos in the years prior to World War II.[4]

Access payments probably materialized as intervening steps toward the *inquilinato* system prevalent on the well-established estates dotting Manila's hinterland. Under cash tenancy sections of great *haciendas* were leased to *inquilinos* for stipulated amounts in money or in kind. Annual rent, called *canon,* varied by regions. Before the war it ranged from 25 to 50 pesos per hectare. Seed, implements, and work animals were provided by the *inquilino,* who bore all the risks that have plagued farmers in both temperate and tropical climes from time immemorial. His yearly income, in large part, depended on unpredictable market conditions and the whims of nature.

Kasamas often became involved in the leaseholding process. A few successful *inquilinos* (with no intention of dirtying their immaculate fingernails) acquired extensive holdings. Big operators arranged contracts with share tenants and settled back to supervise bookkeeping procedures. Larger proprietors, particularly absentee owners such as religious corporations, preferred dealing with a handful of *inquilinos* rather than hundreds of *apaceros.* Under the system no managerial responsibilities were required of *hacenderos,* and they usually received guaranteed payments at the beginning of the agricultural year.[5] In some instances, well-to-do *inquilinos* made no effort to live on, or near, rented farms. Instead, they turned over lands and dependents to hired overseers. The practice compounded *kasama* miseries. Thrice-removed from their *proprietario,* affected *taos* received ever-diminishing shares from the picked-over remains of harvests.[6] Previously

4. Andres Castillo, *Philippine Economics* (Manila, 1949), 180.
5. K. J. Pelzer, *Pioneer Settlement in the Asiatic Tropics* (New York, 1945), 92.
6. Illegal rice manipulations by estate managers became a major problem during the 1930's. "The palay," declared the Secretary of Labor, "is either sold or held for speculation, and as a result almost nothing is left for the tenants." Ramon Torres, "Summary of Findings," *Fact Finding Report,* 14.

forgotten by the departed *cacique, apaceros* were victimized further by "absentee leaseholders."[7]

Some *inquilinos* commanded sufficient resources to become involved in large-scale farming. The vast majority, however, rented family-sized holding and devoted all their energies to retaining them. Demand for fertile hectares in central Luzon was so intense that estate owners enjoyed an on-going seller's market. Cash tenants, accordingly, made every effort to satisfy managers or *hacenderos*. Among other things, they were required to improve their farms constantly even though each betterment tended to increase annual rental fees. Many *inquilinos,* moreover, were forced to make regular outlays toward the completion of large-scale *hacienda* projects such as roads, bridges, dams, and irrigation systems. Those who refused to contribute money or labor were expelled from the estate.[8] For an owner the expulsion process was simple. He merely placed the parcels farmed by insubordinate *inquilinos* on the block at the next public auction and leased the land to the highest bidder.

Most dependent villagers existed under variations of the *kasama* or *inquilinato* systems, but some hamlet dwellers—particularly adventurous younger sons of share farmers—attempted to supplement meager family earnings by migratory labor. Seasonal workers seldom traveled great distances. The chief demand for their services was on the sugar estates of Pampanga, Tarlac, and Laguna in Luzon, and of Negros Occidental and Oriental in the Visayas. Most of the main island's wage laborers, for instance, came from towns and provinces close to the cane fields. Hands for Negros' lush crop were acquired primarily from the overcrowded municipalities of neighboring Panay. Itinerant recruiters, paid on a commission basis, signed up the workers and provided third-class transportation to and from the *haciendas* of their employers. Planters supplied living quarters for the temporary work force over the contract's duration. Wages varied—they were usually calculated according to amounts of cane cut and loaded; for example, during the late thirties, a proficient bolo-wielder's daily compensation ranged from 50 to 60 centavos.[9]

7. Castillo, 179.
8. Pelzer, *Pioneer Settlement,* 93.
9. For detailed information on Negros, see R. N. Severino, "Agrarian Problems and Labor Conditions in Negros Occidental"; and P. L. Solidum, "Labor Conditions in Oriental Negros," *Fact Finding Report,* 197–206; 207–16.

In addition to migrants, who were employed only during the harvest and milling seasons, large sugar estates retained sizable labor contingents of a permanent nature. Regular employees were usually born on the *hacienda,* married there, and remained within its confines throughout their lives. As a general rule, resident wages were lower than those of transients. But fringe benefits, in the form of better housing, together with access to elementary schools and rudimentary medical facilities, eased their burdens to tolerable levels. Paternalism, unfortunately, again tended to prevail only on estates where landowners lived among their dependents.

Under the best of circumstances, living and working conditions fell short of those generally associated with garden communities. In the prewar Philippines, where big sugar and big money were synonymous, even the most enlightened planters were far more concerned with collecting profits than accumulating good works. According to conventional insular wisdom, respectable balance sheets depended upon docile workers. Major growers, therefore, evolved elaborate techniques to control labor. Employees, for example, were forbidden to buy commodities beyond estate boundaries. Purchases of any kind— those of transients and residents alike—came from the *cantina,* or *hacienda* store. Owned by the *hacendero* and managed customarily by his wife, the establishment handled all the necessities and minor luxuries of rural life. Its prices, however, exceeded those of retail businesses on the outside.[10] Seasonal workers often received their pay in the form of costly *cantina* goods, and permanent laborers too were encouraged to charge items throughout the year. After the harvest, final tabulations by the proprietress usually revealed debits in employee accounts. Chronic indebtedness, as all employers knew, proved highly conducive to worker tractability.

Sharp practices, furthermore, were not limited to the *cantinas.* Required by the terms of their contract to remain within *hacienda* limits —a confinement enforced by armed guards—workers were compelled to rely on *hacenderos* for recreation and entertainment. Gambling dens, offering *jueteng* (lotteries), *monte,* blackjack, and other popular diversions, operated every weekend, and laborers who managed to avoid the appeal of cards or dice found it almost impossible to resist the cockpit. Each Sabbath, fighting birds drew *aficionados* to the

10. Harlan Crippen, "Philippine Agrarian Unrest," 344.

hacienda arena. By evening most spectators had been converted into wagerers and separated from their weekly earnings. Winners encountered no difficulties in sharing their good fortune: proprietors provided dance halls and prostitutes for celebrating cane-cutters, and rude cabarets and cribs gathered in cash missed by the estate's other subsidiary enterprises.[11] The *haciendas,* in short, were throughly efficient institutions. Six months of backbreaking toil produced little in the way of take-home pay. The treatment accorded migrant workers by planters, said one incensed labor investigator, was "as crude as the sugar they produced."[12]

Inquilinos and transients grew accustomed to exploitation, but *kasamas* were weaned on involuntary servitude. By 1940 most of central Luzon's villagers had been legally subjected to share tenancy. Outwardly, the expanding system appeared to revolve around legitimate partnerships between proprietors and *apaceros* in which responsibilities and compensations were equally shared. In reality the relationship was weighted heavily toward landowners. A *kasama* who received 50 per cent of the harvest was the rare exception rather than the rule. *Cacique* practices—carefully camouflaged to soothe the authorities—deprived the tenant of his contractual allotment and extracted extra services from him and his family. The endless inequities crushed rural aspirations and produced fatalistic resignation on a massive scale.

The rules of the game were determined by the marginal character of village existence. Few *apaceros* possessed either money or food at the beginning of an agricultural year. They had no alternative other than to apply to the landlord for advances in money—ranging from 25 to 125 pesos—or in rice to tide their families over the lean months before the planting season.[13] Rice was customarily loaned without interest up to the time of sowing, but rations extended after the seedlings were in the ground were subject to usurious charges varying from 50 to 500 per cent.[14]

Three common interest rates prevailed in rice provinces: *takipan,*

---

11. Organized gambling and prostitution were not limited to sugar *haciendas.* A labor investigator who examined the practices reported them to be particularly widespread on "large private estates owned by religious corporations." D. D. Paguia, "Common Vices in the Rural Districts," *Fact Finding Report,* 71.

12. Pablo Manlapit, "Conditions in Pangasinan," *Fact Finding Report,* 264.

13. Pelzer, *Pioneer Settlement,* 94.

14. Miller, *Principles of Economics,* 394.

takalanan, and *terciahan.* The *takipan* required the tenant to pay back two *cavans* of rice (one *cavan* equaled slightly more than two bushels) for every *cavan* borrowed. The *takalanan* demanded three for two, and the *terciahan* four for three. Loans were usually extended on a six-month basis. If principal and interest were not repaid immediately after the threshing season, rates doubled. Under the *takipan,* for example, tenants unable to return two *cavans* at harvest time for every one advanced during the growing season experienced twofold increases in their debts. Compound annual interest, in other words, amounted to 400 per cent.[15]

Indebtedness constituted the keystone of the *kasama* system. Landowners, accordingly, went to great lengths to deepen *apacero* obligations: more money or rice than requested was sometimes graciously extended to tenants; dubious weights and measures tipped scales in the *hacendero*'s favor; contract terms, which might have benefited share farmers, were forgotten or carefully concealed; and half-remembered loans were permitted to go unmentioned until accumulated interest reached astronomical levels. Ignorant of their legal rights, befuddled by the inscrutable ways of moneychangers, and cowed by generations of subordination, *kasamas* were forced to rely on proprietary mercies. A flagrant case described by Theodore Roosevelt, Jr., illustrated the all-too-frequent outcome. "A small farmer," wrote the Governor General, "borrowed 300 pesos. He never obtained any more cash. When the time came to pay his interest each year, the usurer offered him remission if he would sign a document substituted for the original contract. This document was in a language he did not understand. At the end of four years he owed 3,000 pesos."[16]

Debts of individual apaceros reached impossible totals. In 1924—before the tenancy problem achieved its prewar proportions—authorities estimated that it would take at least 163 years of uninterrupted toil and frugality for members of an average tenant family to pay off their outstanding obligations and acquire title to the land they cultivated for the *cacique.*[17] Predictably, *kasamas* seldom made the

15. Dalisay, 165.
16. Theodore Roosevelt, "Land Problems in Puerto Rico and the Philippines," *Geographic Review,* XXIV (1934), 200.
17. E. D. Hester and P. N. Mabbun, "Some Economic and Social Aspects," 405.

effort. In the Philippines—unlike the preindustrial, northern or western United States—tenancy was not the first rung on the ladder to farm ownership. It was the final step into perpetual peonage. If debt bondage had been terminated by death, eventual escape might have seemed feasible. Indebtedness, however, was normally transferred to the deceased debtor's children. Wayward youths who attempted to repudiate parental obligations felt the ire of entire villages and often experienced ostracism from friends and neighbors.[18]

For obvious reasons, the transferrable nature of debts was difficult to document. But a child labor contract, dated 1899, exposed the operation of the system:

I, Maximina Capistrano, widow and of advanced age, native of this pueblo of Angat, having Cedula No. 240121, declare before those present . . . that I owe Dña. Filomena Vergel de Dios . . . the sum of forty pesos . . . and as I have no means of paying . . . I have agreed to hire to . . . Vergel that one of my children, named Florentina, for which [Vergel] will allow four pesos the first year . . . and for the second year . . . an increase of half a peso. The third year she will allow five pesos, and the fourth year six . . . until the debt is cancelled. But . . . if the girl dies, then I may pay in money what remains of the debt; or . . . dispose of another child of mine. . . . But if God should take my life, then [Vergel] or anyone authorized by her, may at once levy upon my effects, and should there be none, then others of my children will be obliged to serve her or pay the money conjointly, as for them the money was spent.[19]

The likelihood of being reduced to peonage was also compounded by chronic underemployment. The dry season's stupefying heat spanned a seemingly interminable period of lethargy during which most villagers had nothing better to do than watch dust devils swirling crazily through vacant barrio streets. The size of tenant farms in central Luzon ranged from only 2.6 to 3.4 hectares.[20] Labor requirements on parcels of that size seldom exceeded 75 to 80 man-days a year.[21] Discounting weekends and holidays, consequently, many *apaceros*

18. Miller, *Principles of Economics*, 396.
19. Philippine Islands, Department of the Interior, *Slavery and Peonage in the Philippine Islands* (Manila, 1913), 66. All the field reports and documents underlying the study are available in two large folio volumes in the Dean C. Worcester Collection at the University of Michigan.
20. J. E. Velmonte, "Farm Security for the Tenant," *Philippine Agriculturist*, XXVI (1937), 396.
21. Miller, *Principles of Economics*, 174.

were idle at least 180 days out of every 365. Access to profitable secondary occupations might have eased the *kasamas'* plight, for Filipino farmers were willing and able to perform a variety of manual activities, but during the parched months there was little demand for jack-of-all-trades skills. Since inadequate reservoir and irrigation systems made round-the-year farming impossible, entire populations in the rural regions began and ended their agricultural activities at approximately the same time. Job openings that materialized after the harvest were soon occupied. Unemployed *taos* had no choice other than to stretch out in the shade and regather their limited strength for the bone-draining labors of the planting season. Occasionally they performed menial tasks to remain in the good graces of *hacenderos* or estate managers. In addition to voluntary services, *apaceros* were usually required to carry out a number of activities within *hacienda* precincts. Written contracts normally contained clauses which defined specific duties. An American radical uncovered one document that obliged tenants to work gratis on road maintenance and bamboo-cutting projects. It also provided for compulsory attendance at the town's Catholic church, and forbade *kasamas* to receive visitors from the outside world. Individual violation of any requirement called for fines ranging from two to four *cavans* or rice.[22]

Where written contracts did not exist, as was most often the case, obligatory services and penalities took on a manorial character. *Apaceros* were compelled to perform chores in or around the *proprietario*'s home. Certain occasions also called for expensive gifts. On the *hacendero*'s birthday, for instance, *taos* delivered treasured fowls and animals or badly needed sacks of rice to the great house. Demeaning rules abounded. Estate operators extracted five *cavans* of rice from insubordinate *kasamas* who fished without permission, gathered fruit or cut bamboo for personal use, or permitted hungry animals to wander into growing crops. *Cacique* approval had to be won to arrange marriages between dependent villagers. It also had to be secured before a tenant appeared as a witness in court proceedings. Failure to abide by any regulation resulted in heavy fines which, if unpaid, were again subject to usurious charges.[23]

Since debts were a family concern, tenant offspring assumed partial responsibility for long-standing deficits. Adolescents generally labored

22. J. S. Allen, "Agrarian Tendencies," 62.
23. Miller, *Principles of Economics*, 390.

in the fields, while younger children, sometimes counter to parental desires, were pressed into service within the landowner's household. Minors who served paternalistic *hacenderos* were usually well treated. Their assigned responsibilities were not demanding, and they frequently received better food and clothing than their brothers and sisters. Where absentee ownership prevailed, sentiment seldom played a role. In extreme cases, profit-seeking overseers transferred younger children of badly strapped tenants to employment agencies operating out of Manila. Recipient concerns paid their small charges' expenses to the capital and supported them indifferently until employers could be found. The urban segment of the undercover transaction was completely heartless. Furtive employers paid the recruiting agency a set fee—prewar rates for servants of eight to ten years averaged 20 pesos—and agreed to retire connected transportation and maintenance costs in small monthly installments. "Until the entire sum is repaid," wrote a scandalized investigator, "the children do not receive one centavo in wages, though they work hard, as a rule without any education and often without adequate food or clothing."[24]

The wretchedness of peasant existence deserved the descriptive powers of a tropical Dickens. None came forth. One Filipino writer, however, managed to convey a portion of his less fortunate countrymen's agony. His short sketch—uncut to retain its impact—reads as follows:

The Nueva Ecija peasant knows that he is a peasant—*paraluman*. He does not regret that he is a paraluman, [only] that he is a paraluman in Nueva Ecija. But here he was born and here he must stay for he has no money to take him to kinder lands—like the Cagayan [a frontier province].

He lives with his family of five or six on a corner of a piece of land he cultivates—big or small as it has pleased the *Hacendero* to apportion him. No matter how industrious and thrifty he may be, he cannot hope ever to own the land he labors on, nor any other piece of land in the province, for in Nueva Ecija and other Central Luzon provinces, the agricultural lands are owned by a few rich Hacenderos and no tenant's money can buy such land.

He usually hires his work animals from the Hacendero. He keeps them in a small enclosure at night, and gets up at four or five o'clock in the morning to let them graze under his watchful eye, for there are no pasture lands in the *Hacienda* during the growing season from August to February, and if he turned them loose, they would feed on the *palay*. If a tenant's carabao is even found in the rice field of another tenant,

24. Jacoby, *Agrarian Unrest in Southeast Asia*, 63.

whether or not the animal has done any damage, the tenant pays a fine of ten cavans of palay . . . to the Hacendero—according to the so-called "laws of the Hacienda"—made by the Hacendero himself.

The Hacendero furnishes half of the *binhi* (seed); the other half comes from the tenant. It is sown in the seed-beds in June. When the seedlings are large enough, and the paddies . . . ready, the transplanting begins. The tenant does not do this alone, but invites his neighbors to help him. He pays them [a traditional fee], half of which comes from him and half from the landowner.

For whatever amount the tenant borrows for other purposes, the Hacendero charges him fifty per cent interest. The Hacendero will deny this because it is against the law, but it is true nevertheless. If a tenant borrows a sum of money equivalent in value at the time to twenty cavans of palay, the Hacendero makes it appear in his book, the item signed or thumb-marked by the tenant, that the latter owes him thirty cavans. Such is the easy escape from the so-called usury laws of the Philippines! And on his part, the tenant takes the money at any cost and keeps mum about it. He has no other source of income than farming and no one but the Hacendero would lend him the money he needs.

From the time the transplanting is finished in early August, up to the harvest time, which comes in February, the farmer has practically nothing to do but see that his fields are well supplied with water. He sits at home most of the day, giving his finger- and toe-nails—lost in the mud during the plowing and harrowing season—a chance to regrow, or patches his tumble-down house.

When the grain has matured, he makes another trip to the Hacendero's office for money to pay those who will help him cut the palay and gather it in bundles for the threshing. The *trilladora* (threshing machine) hums in field after field. Sometimes when the farmer has no more rice to eat, he will himself thresh a small part of the still-undivided harvest, but this is prohibited by the Hacendero who sends out his *katiwales* (private guards) at night to detect violators. If the farmer is caught, he either forefeits the whole harvest to the landowner or is hauled to court, whence he goes straight to jail for theft though he may plead (honestly) that he intended to report to the Hacendero the exact amount he had threshed to save his family from starvation.

Some years ago the tenant still threshed his palay by spreading it beneath the feet of two or three horses driven side by side in a circle around a bamboo pole. The farmer liked to do this, he was paid for threshing the Hacendero's share, and his children got a good deal of fun out of it, but in this day of the machine, the tenant is not allowed to thresh in this manner. The Hacendero's huge trilladora must do the job, and for every hundred cavans of palay threshed, the tenant pays the landlord ten cavans.

The palay pouring out of the threshing machine is put in sacks. After it has been weighed, the farmer hauls it to the provincial road, alongside of which it is piled up and watched day and night until the Hacendero's truck comes along and brings it to the hacienda *camarin* [storehouse]. Then the tenant goes to the landlord once more for his clearance.

Generally, the farmer has had no schooling and even if he has learned a little reading from his mother or a grey-haired neighbor who taught the *Caton* [primer], he is weak at figures. So before he goes to the office he fills his pockets with small pebbles or grains of corn with which to count. Each grain represents a cavan of palay. If he has to represent a half cavan, he divides the corn grain into two equal parts. If a fourth of a cavan is to be represented, he goes to the pains of cutting the grain into four equal parts.

One half of the harvest goes to the Hacendero. Then from his share, the tenant pays the landlord his part of the [expenses]. Then he pays his personal accounts with interest, these often amounting to thirty or forty cavans. Hence it often happens that even if the harvest comes to a hundred or more cavans only one of two cavans remain for him and his family in payment for a year of labor.

What about the twelve months until the next harvest? There is no other way: he borrows from the Hacendero at the same usurious rate of interest. And so it comes about that the tenant's life on the haciendas of Nueva Ecija is reduced to a state of perpetual dependence and indebtedness.[25]

Rural penury provided scant opportunities for levity. Once a year, however, the peasantry cast off restraint. After the harvest, fiestas erupted throughout the countryside. The celebrations—staged one after another in every Philippine municipality to honor local patron saints —created ephemeral illusions of abundance.[26] Individual and collective efforts to banish gloom led villagers to throw normal caution to the winds. Impoverished farmers frequently sold prized carabaos or mortgaged remaining property to attend and participate in the festivities. Rounds of feasting, brass bands, parades, reunions with distant relatives, string orchestras, street dancing, cockfights, fireworks, religious processions, passion plays, and political oratory—to mention only the more obvious attractions—drew entire barrio populations into municipal centers. The carnival atmosphere lasted from three to seven days. For once, everyone had more than enough. Villagers remained in the *municipio* until the celebration concluded or until their stamina and money were gone.

25. M. D. Manawis, "The Life of a Nueva Ecija Peasant," *Philippine Magazine*, XXXI (1934), 12, 42. Labor Department findings confirmed Manawis's message. Secretary Ramon Torres estimated daily per capita income for *kasama* families in Nueva Ecija at slightly less than 2 centavos. See *Fact Finding Report*, 5.

26. For a brief account, see Quezon, *The Good Fight*, 2–4.

For all too many tenants, unfortunately, fiesta excesses completed the rural economy's elaborate ensnarement. The festivities consumed whatever surpluses share farmers gleaned from a year of labor. After the municipal fêtes most of them returned home to conditions of deepened dependence. Psychologically purged, they had little or nothing to anticipate. Occasions honoring marriage, birth, and death constituted the only conceivable interruptions to barrio routines. Wedding and funeral ceremonies, receptions and wakes were occasions that called again for emotional and material displays involving major family expenditures.

The peasantry's apparent impulsiveness angered many observers. Middle-class Manileños, in particular, railed against the "thriftless" irresponsibility of their country cousins. A Tagalog labor investigator, for example, denounced improvident Visayan villagers:

> By nature an Iloilo laborer is a vicious . . . being. Generally speaking, a majority of them [cannot resist] the lure of gambling. It is not surprising that a month or two after the harvest . . . , when he has no other profitable work to do, he frequents again his landlord's house for an *alili* [advance] on the coming rice crop.
>
> Several factors conspire to make an ordinary Iloilo . . . tenant a spendthrift. The outstanding one is his love of ostentation. He will go to the extreme of selling or mortgaging his only patrimony or selling or pledging his only work animal that his son Juan may have the same, if not a bigger, marriage celebration [than] that given when his neighbor's son Pedro got married. And when we consider that among barrio people a dowry in the form of a house is generally asked of the bridegroom-to-be by the parents of the girl, and a certain sum of money, ranging usually from P50.00 to P100.00 is paid to her parents [as] a marriage settlement, it is not [strange that] an Iloilo farm tenant sinks deeper and deeper into the mire of poverty and indebtedness. . . .
>
> If the God of Misfortune be not satisfied with the above, and the Grim Reaper visits, . . . the debt-encumbered tenant, because of traditional precepts, must see to it that the [departed] is buried with all pomp and solemnity, the cadaver taken from the family house with the local curate and brass band to accompany it and impart into the air an atmosphere of general sadness. Add to this a concrete panteon [tomb] and nine nights of velacion [mourning], when tuba [fermented coconut milk] flows freely and . . . tables [groan] with food—no wonder many of the best rice lands in Iloilo are in *manos mortis*.
>
> And to crown the above factors . . . is the chain of never-ending church fiestas, celebrated . . . when abundance reigns supreme—harvest period. The children must have new clothes and pairs of shoes and the

girls must have their hair [done] . . . indeed it must be a wonderful family pouch if it does not run empty.[27]

Critics conveniently ignored the harsh realities confronting barrio dwellers. Above all, many of them overlooked the insidious influences growing out of chronic frustration. Peasant responses to oppressive living conditions followed active and passive patterns. Rural gamblers, for instance, were not afflicted with a perverse idiosyncrasy. Like other victimized but still hopeful people, they were committed to get-rich-quick avocations. The dominant reaction of their less optimistic peers, however, was one of easy-going acceptance. Prewar observers usually portrayed Filipino villagers as fun-loving and reckless or languid and unambitious—in either case, too wasteful for their own good. But such behavior, as one scholar pointed out, "can hide deep wells of feeling."[28] To thoughtful inquirers the peasantry's apparent indifference to its grim fate represented a highly developed defense mechanism. By the eve of Pearl Harbor most tenants had simply given up. They had retreated from the demands of a hostile world to take refuge in carefree indolence.

Some *provincianos*, however, refused to surrender. Defiant individuals and groups occasionally challenged local representatives of central authority. Rebels, for the most part, relied on tried and tested harassing techniques. Bandits, secret societies, unorthodox sects, and mutual aid associations disputed the impersonal claims of institutions and laws emanating from Manila. Insular and municipal officials, consequently, were faced by periodic contagions of violence. Conservative urban diagnosticians customarily attributed the flare-ups to naiveté and to the delusions of "self-styled" leaders, while liberal journalists and politicians generally traced the outbreaks to social or economic grievances. Townsmen of both persuasions, however, were hard put to explain the bizarre forms assumed by peasant movements. Their confusion was an indication of the depth of the cultural chasm separating city and countryside. The fundamental tension between the little and great traditions survived three and a half centuries of accelerating acculturation. The resulting strains produced a stormy heritage.

27. C. I. Lim, "Conditions in Iloilo," *Fact Finding Report*, 173–74.
28. Bruno Laskar, *Human Bondage in Southeast Asia* (Chapel Hill, N.C., 1950), 5.

PART II

THE TURBULENT TRADITION

And in the last days it shall be, God declares, that I will pour
out my spirit upon all flesh, and your sons and your daughters
shall prophesy, and your young men shall see visions, and your
old men shall dream dreams.

Acts 2 : 17

PART II

THE TURBULENT TRADITION

Religious Rebellions

Throughout the Spanish era tranquility rather than turbulence characterized life in the countryside. Humbled by constricting birthrights and the necessity for making constant adjustments to the demands of indigenous and alien authorities, most villagers dedicated themselves to passive survival. Occasionally, collective violence erupted, but militant challenges to the prevailing order tended to be short-lived and isolated. A few gathered sufficient momentum to assume the dimensions of regional insurrections. One only—the complex upheaval which began in 1896—took on the qualities of a general rebellion. Scattered agrarian protests, however, did not add up to a revolutionary heritage. Their sporadic nature, in fact, demonstrated that aggressive popular responses were the exceptions that proved the submissive rule.[1]

The barrio population's normal tractability created illusions of harmony. European visitors often carried away impressions of amiable farmers and friendly fishermen attending to undemanding duties in a land of equatorial abundance. One Victorian traveler, for example, described evening domestic routines in idyllic terms:

Very pretty do the village maidens look, as lightly clad in almost diaphanous garments, they stand beside the mortars plying the pestle, alternately rising on tiptoe, stretching the lithe figure to its full height and reach, then bending swiftly to give force to the blow. No attitude could display to more advantage the symmetry of form which is the Tagal maiden's heritage, and few sights are more pleasing than a group of these tawny damsels husking paddy midst chat and laughter, while a tropical moon pours its effulgence on their glistening tresses and rounded arms.[2]

1. The same condition prevailed throughout the village world of Southeast Asia. John Bastin and H. J. Benda, *A History of Modern Southeast Asia* (Englewood Cliffs, N.J., 1968), 92.
2. Sawyer, *The Inhabitants of the Philippines*, 218–219.

Familiarity, of course, dissolved attractive images. The normal civility of *provincianos*—like the placid slopes of dormant Philippine volcanoes—disguised pent-up forces of terrifying potential. Resident Westerners were not deceived by the peasantry's meekness. Individual outbursts occurred too often and too unpredictably to be ignored. The fact that apparently complacent hamlet dwellers occasionally went berserk led some Spaniards to conclude they were dealing with treacherous people. An official revealed common Iberian stereotypes in his portrayal of the *"indio":*

> I consider the moral picture of the Indian as very difficult to draw, for frequently one finds united in him abjectness and ferocity, timidity and a wonderful fearlessness . . . in danger, and slovenliness combined with industry and avaricious self interest. It is impossible to represent . . . all the phases of their contradictory character. But in general the Indian is pacific, superstitious, indolent, respectful to authority, heedless, distrustful, and deceitful. . . . The natives are also spiteful and revengeful when they believe themselves offended; and at such times, hiding their [anger] under the veil of . . . humility, they await the opportunity for satisfying it and generally give rein suddenly to their ill-will with perfidy and ferocity.[3]

Chronic worry—verging at times on fear—lurked behind such characterizations. Despite the colony's over-all stability, Spaniards felt threatened. The tendency of distraught peasants to "run amok," linked to their inclination to participate in isolated insurgencies, caused administrators to infer that they were sitting on Krakatoa. Realistic Spaniards, furthermore, compared conditions in the nineteenth-century Philippines with those existing in prerevolutionary Latin America. All that was needed to ignite a similar holocaust, they believed, was sophisticated leadership.

Iberian anxieties were not groundless. Since the inception of Spanish rule, intermittent unrest had harried ecclesiastical and secular authorities. Uprisings occurred somewhere in the archipelago on the average of once every twenty years,[4] but none got out of hand. Like

---

3. Juan Manuel de la Matta, "Communication from the Intendant of the Army and Treasury of the Philippine Islands, to the Governor and Captain General Don Marcelino de Oraa, in Regard to the Moral Condition of the Country after the Insurrection of a Portion of the Troops of the Twenty-First Regiment of the Line," Manila, Feb. 25, 1843, *BR,* LII, 99. Cited hereafter as de la Matta, "Confidential Report."

4. John Foreman, *The Philippine Islands* (London, 1899), 133. A survey of

their analogues in the New World, they broke out unexpectedly, reached frenzied climaxes, and subsided just as suddenly, leaving little more than tangled corpses and traumatic memories to mark their fury. Churchmen and administrators in the Pacific dependency dignified the upheavals by labeling them rebellions, though few deserved the title. Most of them, in fact, resembled large-scale riots. In the outmoded vice-regal vocabularies of Peru or New Spain they would have been dismissed as *"tumultos."*

Until the mid-nineteenth century, the flare-ups reflected stresses growing out of Spanish imperialism. Excluding Manila and its environs, the colony had developed as a mission enterprise. Originally, emphasis on conversion and insistence on orthodoxy exerted profound pressures on the population. Restlessness, as a consequence, usually revolved around religious factors. Forced to deny traditional deities, villagers evolved covert means to satisfy spiritual longings. Some dissenters dedicated themselves to restoring indigenous beliefs and practices. Others attempted to combine native and Catholic elements into acceptable new formulations. Both responses drew the ire of missionaries. Churchmen, however, were never able to eradicate the "heresies." In the face of constant surveillance, revivalistic and syncretistic undercurrents persisted. From time to time they surfaced in mystery-permeated violence.

Symptoms of cultural alienation appeared early. Seventeenth-century tumults, in fact, exposed the supernaturalistic themes which were to dominate popular uprisings. In 1622 "nativism" swept through the coastal communities of Bohol.[5] The antifriar mass movement materialized abruptly. Lulled by the ostensible devotion of their charges, many missionaries had left the island to attend commemorative services in Cebu, but ominous circumstances soon confronted the remaining Jesuits. Outlawed *babailanes* (priests) and *catalonans* (mediums) returned from the mountains to spread apostasy among former neighbors. Their spokesman, a spellbinder named Tamblot, called upon villagers to reject the Spaniards and their faith. Those willing to return to ancient ways were promised lives of plenty in upland retreats.

---

uprisings in the seventeenth and eighteenth centuries appears in Phelan, *The Hispanization of the Philippines*, 136–157.

5. Nativism has been defined "as any conscious, organized attempt . . . to revive or perpetuate selected aspects of a culture." Ralph Linton, "Nativistic Movements," *American Anthropologist*, XLV (1943), 230.

More importantly, potential disciples were guaranteed invulnerability against Spanish reprisals.[6] Tamblot's message shattered clerical handiwork. Four villages rebelled. Others threatened to erupt in xenophobic excesses, and a general exodus toward the high country began. Before startled Spaniards could react, the contagion leaped the straits to infect Christian hamlets in neighboring Leyte. Fearing a regional uprising, the Governor of Cebu recruited a force of several hundred "loyal Indians" and led them against mountain strongholds on both islands. Spanish and Cebuano ruthlessness quickly restored order. Disheartened churchmen, however, had to devote years to the repair of spiritual and emotional wreckage.

Four decades later a similar eruption interrupted Visayan peace. Like the Bohol-Leyte episode, the Panay tumult of 1663 originated in nativistic yearnings. Unlike its forthright predecessor, it rapidly took on eclectic elements. Calling for the revival of pre-Spanish religion, a proficient sorcerer named Tapar won a small but devoted following among Catholic parishioners. Over missionary protests, some villagers began to participate in traditional rites. Although resident friars warned their superiors in Cebu of impending trouble, church authorities—fearful perhaps of another Bohol—were reluctant to initiate punitive measures. Tapar refused to be ignored. The defiant leader finally took an inspired step which routed hamlet opposition and outraged the ecclesiastical establishment. Proclaiming himself "God Almighty," he labeled one of his aides "Jesus Christ," another the "Holy Ghost," and added insult to injury by designating a female associate *"Maria Santísima."* To that charismatic assemblage he appended a roster of "popes" and "bishops" until all his lieutenants carried divine or semidivine titles. The conglomeration of sacred and sacerdotal types demolished the orthodoxy of Panay's villagers. Almost overnight Tapar's small following blossomed into a mass movement. When the dissenters launched attacks on mission compounds, Spaniards responded with predictable fury. Cebuano contingents again overwhelmed and scattered the religious rebels. They also hunted down Tapar and his retinue. The last vestiges of the "diaboli-

---

6. According to a contemporary Spanish account, Tamblot promised that the "mountains would rise against their foe; that the muskets of the latter would not go off, or rebound on those who fired them; that if any Indian should die, the [gods] would resuscitate him." "Extract from Murillo Velarde's *Historia de Philipinas*," *BR*, XXXVIII, 88.

cal farce" vanished after a series of grotesque public executions.[7] By 1664, subservience, if not serenity, had returned to Panay.

While neither uprising constituted a serious challenge to Spanish sovereignty, their disruptive courses established the broad boundaries of barrio opposition to the Hispanic tradition. Between 1620 and 1820, discord emanated from a variety of sources. Some outbreaks were stimulated by economic policies. Others were generated by inept local administration. Regardless of their secular origins, however, many militant movements took on sacred characteristics. Like Tamblot and Tapar, popular redeemers usually claimed miraculous powers. They won and retained supporters by portraying themselves as prophets or deities in regular communication with a "supernatural pseudo-community."[8] They also expanded the ranks of their adherents through apocalyptic pronouncements linked to assurances of collective invulnerability. Sooner or later, leaders and followers alike experienced delusions of limitless power. At that juncture they frequently attacked available symbols—usually clerical—of Spanish authority. Village violence in turn provoked metropolitan vengeance. Sorely outnumbered Spaniards, in fact, tended to overreact to challenges from scattered segments of the rural population. The repetitive pattern—religious insurgency followed by Spanish repression—produced a series of miniature Armageddons in Luzon and the Visayas. Iberian churchmen and administrators, however, never grasped the significance of the rhythmic phenomena. More importantly, they refused to accept the upheavals as manifestations of profound cultural stress or deep-seated social tension. Instead, they regarded them as

7. The "Trinity," wrote a chronicler, "was fed to crocodiles," the woman labeled "Mary most Holy" was beheaded. "Extracts from Diaz' *Conquistas*," *BR*, XXXVIII, 219.

8. The phrase was coined by Anthony F. C. Wallace, "Revitalization Movements," *American Anthropologist*, LVIII (1956), 273. Wallace's effort to "structure" the ubiquitous phenomena is but one of many endeavors. For broad treatments of the subject see Sylvia L. Thrupp, ed., *Millennial Dreams in Action: Essays in Comparative Study* (The Hague, 1962); Norman Cohn, *The Pursuit of the Millennium: Revolutionary Messianism in Medieval and Reformation Europe and Its Bearing on Modern Totalitarian Movements* (London, 1962); E. J. Hobsbawm, *Primitive Rebels: Studies in Archaic Forms of Social Movement in the 19th and 20th Centuries* (New York, 1963); and V. Lanternari, *The Religions of the Oppressed: A Study of Modern Messianic Cults*, trans. by Liza Sergio (New York, 1963); for further information see the bibliography appended to "Book Review: The Religions of the Oppressed," *Current Anthropology*, VI (1965), 464–465.

outlandish examples of provincial perversity. Devotees of native messiahs, moreover, were dismissed as naive and superstitious *"fanáticos"* deserving neither curiosity nor compassion.

Spanish contempt for the peasantry contributed to the misinterpretations. Within conventional mission perspectives villagers emerged as inferior and immature beings. "They are great children," said one friar, "and must be treated as if they were very little ones."[9] His paternalism underscored the analytical problem. Spaniards refused to take peasant unrest seriously and tended to view local uprisings as petulant outbursts against legitimate authority. Accordingly, the flare-ups assumed the character of infantile tantrums. Since the expressions could be traced to passing anger, there was no need to seek more fundamental explanations nor to examine possible relationships between tumults. Each upheaval came to be looked upon as an isolated event which had no particular bearing on larger religious and political issues.

Contrary to Iberian impressions, the eruptions were not without rhyme or reason. The scattered insurrections took place too often to be discounted completely. They also represented something far more complex than simple sequences of frustration and aggression. Subtle connections existed between apparently unrelated outbreaks. Local continuities should have exposed the little tradition's remarkable tenacity, but Spanish disdain for village leaders and their otherworldly protests prevented colonial authorities from comprehending the importance of the periodic insurgencies. In their ultimate reckonings, church and state officials were concerned with elitist activities and aspirations. Manila's foremost dread was the formation of a working coalition involving disgruntled *principales* and discontented peasants. In 1841 Hispanic fears were confirmed by the first coordinated religious rebellion in Philippine history.

The challenge incorporated elements of greater magnitude, diversity, and persistence than those customarily associated with rural discord. Villagers again constituted the majority of the dissident movement's membership. Converts were won from municipalities ranging across three populous provinces south of Manila. When violence flared, it quickly took on the spectacular character of a regional insurrection. Leadership for the disruption, however, came from a new

9. P. P. de la Gironier, *Twenty Years in the Philippines* (New York, 1854), 82.

source. Filipino priests, lawyers, *gobernadorcillos,* and other alienated individuals from the higher echelons of provincial society played important roles in the disturbance. The fact that gentrymen rather than unlettered barrio dwellers directed the enterprise proved dismaying to Spaniards. Menaced by real and imagined symptoms of protonationalism, they responded to the upheaval with unusual ferocity. Like its less sophisticated precursors, the offending religious brotherhood was wiped from the face of the earth. But its ramifications could not be completely erased. Urban aftershocks shook Manila and its Tagalog suburbs for several years. Rural reverberations, moreover, echoed through the affected countryside for more than a century.

The instigator of the far-reaching affair was a devout young *provinciano* named Apolinario de la Cruz.[10] An unlikely candidate for notoriety, he was born of peasant parents on July 31, 1815. His law-abiding family had resided for generations in barrio Pandak, Lucban town, Tayabas province. During his youth Apolinario displayed intelligence and Christian convictions. Local churchmen, consequently, introduced him to scholarship and encouraged him to pursue a clerical career. All went well until 1839, when he traveled to Manila to embark upon monastic training. Reactionary church policies, however, frustrated his ambitions. Ecclesiastical authorities in the capital had begun to enforce stringent bans on the recruitment of Filipino friars. Forbidden to enter one of the influential orders, Apolinario swallowed his pride and became a lay brother at the Hospital of San Juan de Dios. There, he served his superiors unobtrusively. In his spare time he attended sermons by prominent priests, continued his inquiries into the Bible, and began to study theological works. The conscientious layman caused no problems. A Spanish resident at the hospital described the future "incendiary" as an unassuming individual: "He was a young man of *mestizo* features, modest, reserved, and without appearance of talent or mischief. Several times

10. Information on the uprising of 1841 was drawn primarily from José Montero y Vidal, *Historia general de Filipinas,* III (Madrid, 1895), 37–56; and from the contemporary account by Manuel Sancho, "Relaciónes expresivas de los principales acontecimientos de la titulada Cofradía del Señor San José," Aug. 16, 1843, 1–189. A microfilm copy of Sancho's unpublished manuscript was obtained from the Newberry Library, courtesy of the Edward E. Ayer Collection, The Newberry Library, Chicago. To avoid repetitious references, citations will be appended only to quotations or to statements requiring fuller explanations.

he . . . entered my room to deliver medicine for my use, while I studied or read to myself. I would tell him to place the medicine on the table, and he would do so, retiring without a word."[11]

Silence on Apolinario's part, however, did not signify submission He appealed his exclusion to higher authorities and awaited vindication. In the meantime he began to formulate possible countermoves. With other lay brothers he discussed the feasibility of establishing a religious organization open only to *indios*. Pleasant dormitory theorizing concerning the merits of "Filipinos of heart and face" came to an abrupt halt in June 1840 when Apolinario was notified that his appeal had been denied; he was also informed that his services were no longer required at the hospital. He promptly abandoned Manila's rigid religious atmosphere and returned to the flexible spiritual milieu of his boyhood.

The provinces proved hospitable to both Apolinario and his unorthodox ideas. Shortly after his arrival in Lucban he founded the Cofradía de San José. Apolinario's saintly demeanor and captivating eloquence rapidly won a loyal following in the municipality's barrios. That initial success led him to extend his proselytizing activities across the beautiful tilting landscapes where Tayabas, Batangas, and Laguna tumbled together. Within weeks the confraternity was a flouishing organization. Converts began to attend weekly prayer meetings in nearby municipalities. On the nineteenth of each month many of them converged on Lucban town to attend a sung mass and to enjoy a convivial meal presided over by their youthful leader. The benign tone of both events drew acolytes from all social strata. Confraternity assemblies were soon characterized by communal shoulder-rubbing between reverent *principales* and pious *taos*. The charm and Christian fellowship of the get-togethers soothed even the suspicions of Spanish clerics.

The era of good feeling, unfortunately, was extremely brief. Apolinario's success proved unsettling to friars throughout the southern Tagalog region. Four months after his return, he had initiated hundreds of dues-paying members into the movement. When the special masses were performed, Lucban overflowed with faithful *confreres* and ardent proselytes. The organization's geometric growth rate, moreover, appeared to be irreversible. Circumspect clerical inquiries revealed Spartan-like internal discipline. Dissent in any form led to expulsion and ostracism. Try as they might, anxious churchmen could not evolve

11. Montero, 54.

techniques to influence Cofradía decisions. *Indios* dominated the society. Spaniards and *mestizos* were forbidden to enroll in the organization and were excluded from its esoteric functions.[12] Spanish sensitivities were further assaulted by the pretensions of the leader and his principal aides. Apolinario, for example, had assumed the title "Brother Puli." His chief lieutenant—a dynamic young man christened Octavio Ignacio de San Jorge—had appropriated the even more distasteful sobriquet "Purgatorio." October 1840, however, brought the most disturbing development. Resident clerics learned that Cofradía directors had forwarded a petition to the Archbishop in Manila requesting ecclesiastical recognition. Iberian tolerance immediately gave way to persecution.

Manuel Sancho, the Vicar of Tayabas province, soon emerged as the Cofradía's chief antagonist. At his behest, the previously cooperative priest of Lucban parish notified Apolinario that special masses would no longer be performed. When 600 devotees of the confraternity assembled in the plaza on schedule, they were ordered to disperse. Refusal led to the arrest of 243 worshipers.[13] At that point Lucban's sympathetic *gobernadorcillo* intervened to bring about their release, but before he could obtain the required order from provincial governor Juan Ortego, two male prisoners received thirty-one lashes, and an incarcerated woman was spanked for defying clerical authority. The public degradations convinced Apolinario that the confraternity's only hope resided with diocesan officials in Manila.

After their release from jail he comforted his reassembled flock and suggested they return to their homes to await developments. He then collected a few trusted advisers and fled Tayabas. From a new headquarters in Majayjay, Laguna, he continued his recruiting campaign and doubled his efforts to achieve ecclesiastical recognition. Anticipating the latter move, Fray Manuel Sancho sent explicit warnings to his superiors concerning the society.[14] His letters advised them to abolish the confraternity before its membership became involved in religious or political heresy. Forewarned, the Archbishop rejected the Cofradía's application but mystifyingly refused to order action against the movement or its leaders. Convinced that prominent churchmen

12. De la Matta, "Confidential Report," 211.
13. Sinibaldo de Mas y Sanz, *Secret Report on the Condition of the Philippines in 1842* (Manila, 1963), 115.
14. Sancho, 64–71.

could still be swayed by personal pleas, Apolinario returned to Manila to challenge the ruling. His persistence stiffened diocesan antagonism. The Archibishop's mounting hostility forced Apolinario to consider other approaches. On the advice of leading *confreres* he petitioned the Royal Audiencia for redress of grievances. The expedient represented the penultimate step toward bitter conflict.

Resort to secular authority came at the suggestion of a Filipino priest and four lawyers.[15] Apolinario's councilors believed their approach offered several possibilities for resolving confraternity difficulties. They realized church officials could ignore governmental intervention, but they insisted there were no legal barriers against state recognition. Judicial consideration of a well-prepared case might absorb several months. During that interval, energetic recruiting could transform the Cofradía into a majority movement in Tayabas, Laguna, and Batangas. If, under those circumstances, recognition was still withheld, one alternative remained open. Members of the society, declared an outspoken attorney, could resort to *"cortar cabezas"* (beheading).[16] The strategy's intricacies were never tested. Infuriated by Apolinario's actions, Governor General Marcelino de Oraa ended the jurisdictional dispute. He also ordered the offending Cofradía leader to appear at the *Ayuntamiento* (city hall). Urban confederates saved Apolinario by spiriting him to one of the capital's crowded *indio* quarters.

The debacle in Manila was matched by a series of equally disturbing developments in the provinces. During Apolinario's absence, Manuel Sancho's friars took the offensive. Their tactics confronted Purgatorio with additional problems. He continued holding clandestine meeting and buoyed demoralized *confreres* by reading epistles from Apolinario. He even exploited the Cofradía's last slim hope. Provincial secular authorities had not become involved in the controversy. Governor Ortega's refusal to uphold Sancho during the Lucban episode. Purgatorio maintained, had been instrumental in achieving the jailed *cofrades'* release. Arguing that governmental neutrality was tantamount to support, he used the point to shore up

15. *Ilustrado* involvement in the upheaval proved so unsettling to the Royal Intendant that he railed against "vicious secular priests" and "pettifogging lawyers," and recommended the elimination of university training in law and theology. De la Matta, "Confidential Report," p. 105.

16. Montero, 53.

the disintegrating society. Secretly discouraged, however, he informed Apolinario of the grim situation and urged him to return before "all was lost."[17]

Manuel Sancho was not to be denied. Recognizing that limited persecutions often stimulate rather than eliminate heresies, he sought means to annihilate the Cofradía. A good opportunity came on October 19, 1841. That evening Majayjay's parish priest led a raid on the confraternity's nerve center. Purgatorio, several aides, and documents were seized. Confiscated articles included letters from Apolinario, membership rolls, dues collections for the month of September, and two "sacrilegious" paintings.[18] The jubilant parson ordered militiamen to escort his prisoners to Lucban jail. After their departure, he transferred the evidence to the Governor of Laguna, who then yielded to priestly demands by outlawing the society in his own and adjoining provinces. Manuel Sancho's clerical cup ran over.

Inadvertently, however, Sancho and his friars had committed a serious blunder. Governor Ortega was not in Tayabas. Caught between contentious clerics and *confreres,* he had gone to Manila to seek executive guidance on the troublesome issue. In his absence, political responsibilities devolved upon the *gobernadorcillo* of Lucban. At the request of his wife, who was a member of the Cofradía, the compliant official released the prisoners upon their arrival from Majayjay. Purgatorio and his aides left Lucban before their castoff shackles had cooled and headed for Laguna. En route they learned that Apolinario had extricated himself from the manhunt in Manila and was on his way toward a rendezvous with armed supporters in the *pueblo* of Bay. Purgatorio rallied additional followers and hurried to the lakeside community. Shortly after sunset on October 21, 1841, a tumultuous reunion took place in the normally sedate *municipio.* Forty-eight hours had witnessed a miraculous reversal of confraternity fortunes. Propelled by a growing sense of omnipotence, Apolinario and his irregulars marched on Lucban town.

The milling host paused on the outskirts of the municipality and established a rude base at barrio Igsabang.[19] Bolo-toting *provincianos*

17. Montero, 52.
18. Sancho, 83.
19. According to a twentieth-century account, Igsabang became Tayabas province headquarters for the Cofradía after the expulsion from Lucban. R. G. Woods, "The Strange Story of the Colorum Sect," *Asia,* XXXII (1932), 450.

from Laguna, Batangas, and Tayabas quickly converged on the hamlet. Reinforcements, however, were not limited to alerted villagers. Bands of Negrito headhunters from the mountains also began to drift into Igsabang. "In a matter of hours," wrote a badly shaken Manuel Sancho, "the solitary place became a vast and animated camp."[20] On the afternoon of October 22, a delegation of armed *confreres* appeared at Lucban's *convento* and called for a mass in honor of their patron saint. The parish priest rejected their demand. Denouncing the Cofradía as a nefarious racket, he ordered the spokesmen to abandon Apolinario and to lead their assorted followers home. They returned, instead, to Igsabang. By nightfall, the campsite was overflowing with dissenters. Many of the insurgents, furthermore, had acquired muskets. The time for talk and legal maneuvers had clearly come to an end.

With all the fatal pieces falling into place, Governor Juan Ortega reappeared, equipped with authorizations from Governor General Oraa to dissolve the confraternity. He promptly issued an ultimatum ordering Igsabang's occupants to disperse within twenty-four hours or suffer the consequences. Supremely confident, the rebels remained in place. On the afternoon of October 23, Ortega led 300 men, supported by three small artillery pieces, toward the Cofradía's position. Composed of militiamen, municipal policemen, and retired reservists under the command of *cabezas de barangays* and a tremulous rent administrator, Ortega's motley force straggled into Igsabang around 3:00 P.M. More than 3,000 dissenters waited behind hastily prepared earthworks for the Governor's assault. Hoping to demoralize the peasants and tribesmen, Ortega fired several ragged salvos into their midst. Disorder ensued, but it ravaged the attackers rather than the defenders. Answering musket fire and arrow volleys poured from behind the barricades. Within minutes, the Governor's polyglot troops discarded their firearms and broke. Abandoned on the disintegrating firing line, Ortega was cut down in a bolo charge led by Purgatorio.[21] Surging *confreres* also overran the artillery position capturing guns and ammunition intact. Without realizing it, the insurgents had won more than a skirmish. Confronted by a determined rebel army,

20. Sancho, 18.
21. Prior to the skirmish Ortega had been criticized by Sancho for indecisiveness and warned, "You will be the first victim." Mas, 202.

Manuel Sancho gathered up his stunned friars and abandoned Tayabas province to Apolinario de la Cruz.

At dawn the victorious Cofradía streamed out of Igsabang and marched to the remote *sitio* of Ipilan on the Alitao plain. Roughly ten kilometers beyond Tayabas town, the new location offered natural advantages. A treeless expanse at the foot of forested Mount San Cristobal, it was flanked by rain-swollen streams. Alitao required only minor modifications to withstand a heavy attack. Assuming responsibility for preparing the redoubt, Purgatorio worked round the clock. He supervised the construction of a timber palisade across the position's front, engineered the placement of captured cannons, oversaw the erection of lean-to shelters for the *cofrades* and their numerous dependents, and initiated the collection of provisions from villagers in the surrounding countryside. By October 28, his 4,000-man force was ready to defend Alitao. Hoisting a white signal flag over the encampment, Purgatorio settled back to await developments.

While his subaltern improvised defenses, Apolinario communed with God. Under his detached guidance, Alitao took on the qualities of an impromptu theocracy. The ramshackle compound developed around a large structure called "Santo Camarin." Hung with allegorical paintings, the shrine became the scene of continuous services dedicated to San José. Apolinario resided near the chapel in a small bamboo house. Daily councils with Cofradía commanders were held in the residence. Occasionally, Apolinario emerged from seclusion to inspire his followers. He guaranteed that the Lord was with the confraternity. At the appointed hour, he assured them, divine intervention would cause the earth to open and swallow their adversaries.[22]

The spiritual leader's rare appearances produced confusing reports concerning his behavior. Spaniards patrolling the trouble zone heard that Apolinario was living in "ridiculous majesty" surrounded by attractive maidens who "attended to his needs and pleasures."[23] Less earthy rumors also indicated he was experiencing delusions of grandeur. Some maintained he had declared himself "king of the Tagalogs." Others alleged he had named five bishops who reciprocated the honor by electing him "Supreme Pontiff." Gossip concerning an "indigenous Pope" caused an abundance of righteous comment in

22. Montero, 45.
23. Sancho, 39.

Manila. Incensed friars, said a French observer, "responded to the
sacrilege by accusing Apolinario of worse heresies than Luther."[24]

Rebellion in the south, linked to growing restlessness in the capital,
led Marcelino de Oraa to proceed cautiously. Fearing Tagalog defections, the Governor General selected men for his punitive expedition
with Machiavellian insight. Reliability and professionalism became
the key criteria. Regular Pampangan detachments met both tests. The
veteran soldiers from central Luzon were regarded as the cream of
the colonial military establishment.[25] Commanded by Spanish officers,
and conveniently quartered in Manila, they were also locally infamous for their hostility toward Tagalogs. Oraa, accordingly, ordered
two infantry companies, a cavalry troop, and an artillery battery
composed of Pampangueños to march on Tayabas under the command of Lieutenant Colonel Joaquin Huet. Advancing with great
difficulty through both mounting anarchy and monsoon squalls, the
400-man force reached Tayabas town on October 29. There, they
merged with provincial units totaling 600. Huet rested his drenched
troops and began preparations for a decisive encounter at Alitao.

While his men recovered from their hundred-kilometer ordeal, the
Spanish colonel completed the prescribed political course of action.
On October 30 he issued a degree offering amnesty to all who would
renounce the Cofradía and threatening extermination to all who
remained loyal. Translated into Tagalog and circulated through surrounding *poblaciones,* the ultimatum granted *confreres* twenty-four
hours to make individual decisions. Twelve copies of Huet's proclamation were carried under a flag of truce to the rebel bastion. Before
a cheering assembly, Apolinario mocked the documents, ripped them
to shreds, and cast the crumpled remnants into a campfire. His performance so impressed Huet's *indio* messengers that they denounced
Spain and joined Alitao's defenders. Their minor defection demonstrated the critical state of provincial affairs. A tense Sabbath passed
without one penitent rebel appearing in Tayabas town.

Huet, consequently, moved to make good his threat. Fully informed
of Ortega's fiasco on the preceding Sunday, the experienced cam-

24. Montero, 42.
25. Pampanga provided more troops for the colonial army than any other
province in the Islands. Phelan, 149. A maxim testified to Iberian faith in the
volunteers from central Luzon: "One Spaniard and nine Pampangueños are
more than a match for ten men from any nation."

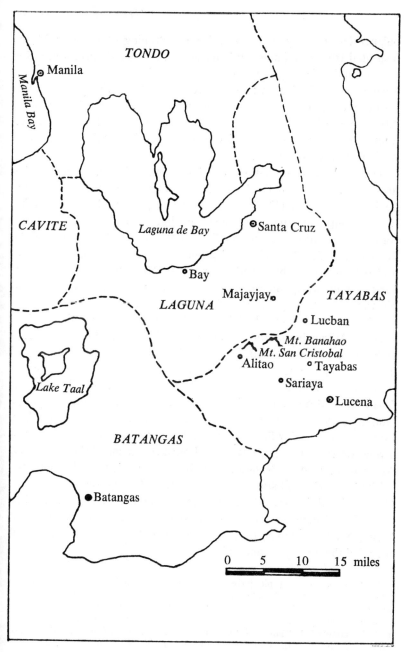

2. The Southern Tagalog Provinces of Luzon, 1841

paigner left nothing to chance. On the evening of October 31, he
inspected troops, animals, and equipment, examined current scouting
reports, and ordered patrols to occupy strategic positions along Alitao's
escape routes. At 4:00 A.M. on November 1, the main force marched
on the rebel stronghold. Two hours later, alert *confreres* sighted the
1,000-man column. Certain of victory and reassured by comforting
four-to-one odds, they pulled down Purgatorio's white banner and
ran up a scarlet battle flag.

The fratricidal conflict began almost immediately. Concentrating
artillery fire on the palisade, Huet attempted to soften the target for
an infantry attack. His first assault was repulsed with discouraging
losses. Continuing the cannonade, he directed heavy shot on Purgatorio's gun positions. By noon Alitao's defenses had begun to crumble.
Huet then ordered cavalry and infantry forward. Pampangan sabers
and bayonets soon breached the parapet. Hand-to-hand fighting ensued behind the splintered barricade. With his cannons silenced and
his wavering men dying around him, Purgatorio rushed to the bamboo house and demanded of Apolinario that he produce the promised
miracle. Advancing skirmishers interrupted the heated interchange. It
ended when aides dragged their shouting leaders from the threatened
dwelling. They emerged into chaos. Calvalrymen were turning the
smoldering redoubt into a charnel house. Riding down fleeing *confreres,* they drove confused survivors toward certain death on the
inundated flanks. Purgatorio tried to steady his wilting defenders.
Forming an irregular line with fierce Negritos, he unleashed waves of
arrows on the attackers. Disciplined musket fire ended the brief rally.
At 3:00 P.M. Alitao's tattered emblem came down. The 600 dis-
spirited *cofrades* still standing were herded into a makeshift stockade.
Huet ordered his men to apply torches to the fallen stronghold's
remaining structures. By nightfall preliminary casualty reports had
been tabulated. Spanish officers reported that 1,000 dead rebels still
occupied the muddy compound.[26]

26. Writers on the topic have customarily calculated the Cofradía's death
rate at between 800 and 1,000. The Vicar of Tayabas made no effort to tabu-
late human costs. His final statement, however, revealed the size of the encampment and the battle's possibly staggering outcome. Absolving his countrymen, he concluded, "There were at maximum 11,000 *cofrades* at El Alitao.
How shall we repair the damage done to the credulous followers? . . . If they
died, it was purely their own fault. . . . Blame the crazy mothers who took
their children to suffering and death." Sancho, 189.

Steadfast bodyguards enabled Apolinario to avoid capture or death. Miraculously escaping the well-patrolled massacre site, he picked his way through chaotic municipalities to the peaceful *pueblo* of Sariaya. Late on the evening of November 2, he stumbled into the community and gratefully accepted an offer of refuge from a sympathetic couple. While Apolinario attempted to relax and the woman prepared food, her husband—a disillusioned member of the Cofradía—slipped from the dwelling and informed neighboring *confreres* of their discredited leader's presence. Bent on gaining vengeance for slaughtered comrades, they fell on the fugitive. Over wifely protests, the defectors escorted Apolinario to surprised municipal officials. Early the next morning he was transferred to Huet's command post in Tayabas town. Several hours later, military judges tried him and handed down a death sentence. Shortly before dawn on November 4, 1841, the contrite rebel delivered his final confession to a Spanish priest. At daybreak, a firing squad executed Apolinario de la Cruz.

The violence appeared to be over. Huet restored Tayabas to the friars and officials and led his boastful Pampangueños back to the capital.[27] Spanish courts also hastened to dispense heavy-handed justice in Laguna and Batangas. But the tried and tested Iberian pacification drill failed to produce stability. Manila and its predominantly Tagalog hinterland remained restless. Recurrent rumors concerning new and larger rebellions cropped up constantly. At every opportunity pamphleteers reminded Manileños of the mass "assassinations" at Alitao. They called simultaneously for a vendetta against Spaniards and their Pampangan lackeys.[28] On January 21, 1843, regular Tayaban troops stationed in the capital's Malate district rebelled. Under the command of an alienated career sergeant, they advanced through pre-dawn darkness on the Walled City. With the aid of *coprovincianos* quartered in the bastion, they seized Fort Santiago and lifted the standard of rebellion. Spaniards quelled the mutiny before Manila's startled populace could react. The abortive effort to redeem Tagalog pride ended in a new round of public executions in Bagumbayang Field. After the setback, disgrunted city dwellers avoided armed confrontations. The next thirty years, however, witnessed intensifying

27. Upon their return, the soldiers proclaimed that all the people at Alitao, regardless of "sex or age, had been slain, beheaded, and dismembered for having followed Hermano Puli's preachings." Woods, 451.

28. De la Matta, "Confidential Report," 96.

campaigns to Filipinize the clergy. Long-range results of Apolinario's career included the poignant deaths of Fathers Gomez, Burgos, and Zamorra in 1872.[29] The religious issue exposed by his tragic movement became, in time, a *cause célèbre* for *ilustrado* nationalists.

While politically aware city dwellers began to compile a revolutionary martyrology, Apolinario's provincial followers were gradually forgotten. Obscurity, however, did not denote passivity. Survivors of the blood bath at Alitao continued to be defiant. Abandoning the valleys and lowlands to their Iberian and *mestizo* overlords, they scaled Mount San Cristobal and its imposing neighbor Banahao. The slumbering volcanoes exercised a dual attraction over Apolinario's former disciples. Settings for pre-Spanish religious rites, the awe-inspiring slopes also reminded the refugees of Christianity's fabled shrines. Draped with brooks and waterfalls, honeycombed with caves, and covered by lush vegetation, the mountains became a "Holy Land" for devotees of San José. Precipices, grottoes, and streams received appropriate titles. Caverns were named in honor of the "Trinity" and the "Saints." A crystalline creek was classified the "River Jordan," a vermilion-tinged spring was designated "Blood of Christ," and an opaque pool was labeled "Milk of the Virgin." Freed from friar surveillance, the exiles fashioned a spiritual milieu perfectly attuned to village aspirations. San Cristobal and Banahao, consequently, became the destinations for regular pilgrimages from the sullen lowlands.[30]

Slowly but surely subtle transformations occurred in the sect's ill-defined doctrines and practices. By 1870 inhabitants of tiny communities dotting the mountain sides had dropped the name Cofradía de San José and had begun to call themselves "Colorums."[31] Priests and priestesses left the heights periodically to convey the developing gospel to their countrymen or to dispense healing waters and relics

29. The three Filipino priests were publicly executed by garrote in Bagumbayang Field for alleged complicity in a military mutiny at the Cavite Arsenal. Many historians believe the cruel spectacle marked the real birth of Philippine nationalism. See, for example, Agoncillo and Alfonso, 155–157.

30. The shrines were described by Woods, 452. During Holy Week 1966, the author visited the area on a field trip. Thousands of pilgrims from the surrounding countryside had come to barrio Kinabuhayan (Place of the Resurrection) to participate in sacred ceremonies.

31. The origins of the word are usually traced to the Latin phrase *"per omnia secular seculorum,"* used by Catholic priests to terminate prayers. The last three syllables appear to have been corrupted by peasant religious leaders and applied to the mountain sects.

from San Cristobal's shrines. They won converts throughout the region where Apolinario had briefly reigned. Emulating Old Testament prophets, lank-haired true believers also carried the liberating creeds southward into the Bicol provinces and northward into central Luzon. By 1890 the folk cults were firmly rooted among the main island's peasantry. The expanding Colorum movements, however, did not restrict disciples to peaceful quests for followers. Still defiant, their members carried on clandestine activities against Spaniards and *principales:* bandits and rustlers used San Cristobal and Banahao as secure bases for depredations on valley towns and *haciendas;* fugitives from municipal police or the Guardia Civil, moreover, always found sanctuary under the enveloping clouds. Lawlessness and spirituality, in short, mingled pleasantly beside the "River Jordan." The mountains became an informal headquarters for class warfare of mounting intensity. When the decade of discord erupted in 1892, the heights emerged as a staging area for anarchy.[32] Apolinario's dissident heritage, furthermore, lingered on to plague American colonial officials and Filipino administrators well into the twentieth century.

32. An American officer responsible for maintaining order in the area where Laguna, Batangas, and Tayabas met, referred to the mountainous border region as "one of the worst holes in southern Luzon." *Report of the Philippine Commission, 1904* (Washington, D.C.), III, 87.

CHAPTER 5

Guardia de Honor

Religious uprisings were not restricted to the Tagalog provinces or the Visayas. Comparable protests erupted in the Ilocos region.[1] During the late nineteenth century enthusiasm for an intricate chiliastic doctrine swept through the villages of northwestern Luzon. Devotees belonged to the Guardia de Honor, an organization less well known than the Cofradía de San José, although the Guardia manifested some similarities to the earlier movement. Peasants again made up most of the organization's membership. *Principales* also provided initial leadership. The society's local directors, moreover, gradually became involved with the authorities in disputes which became sufficiently acrimonious to spark a regional insurrection. There, however, the resemblances ended. Unlike Apolinario's confraternity, which began its existence as a direct challenge to the ecclesiastical status quo, Guardia de Honor was founded to uphold orthodox Catholicism. The transition to spiritual and political anarchy took more than a quarter century. When the process ended, the original sodality had undergone a metamorphosis: millennial ethics replaced Christian values; and violent rejection of all external authority supplanted passive acceptance of traditional control systems. Utterly indiscriminate in their religious, social, and ethnic antipathies, the sectarians were equally hostile to *hacenderos,* Spaniards, Filipino revolutionaries, and Ameri-

1. Ilocos Norte alone gave birth to three rebellions between 1807 and 1815. In 1811, villagers attempted to restore worship of the pre-Spanish deity Lungao. "A fanatic . . . styling himself a new Christ," wrote a contemporary Spaniard, "appeared to the fishermen and announced to them their true redemption——freedom from monopolies and tributes. . . . This fanatic and more than seventy of his following called 'apostles' were seized, with their gowns, litters, flags, and other articles with which 'the new god' [planned to] make himself manifest." *BR,* LI, 32.

cans. Nationalism, in short, played no role in the disruption. Instead, it developed as a revealing example of rustic utopianism.

Under more prosaic circumstances, the confraternity might not have experienced such a transformation. The movement, however, emerged during an era of mounting stress. In 1850 accelerating economic changes began to refashion the fabric of Ilocano society. Improving transportation facilities stimulated export agriculture and provoked spectacular increases in property values.[2] Like their counterparts elsewhere in the archipelago, gentrymen began to accumulate farms. Legal or illegal land-grabbing dispossessed many villagers and confronted others with unprecedented problems. After 1892, political discord contributed additional uncertainties to the northwest's troubled atmosphere. The revolutionary currents of 1896–1897 undermined the traditional order's foundations, and in 1898, it collapsed. During the Filipino-American War something akin to chaos descended on the populous strand of provinces stretching from Tarlac to Ilocos Sur. Reflecting the kaleidoscopic transmutations of that time of trouble, Guardia de Honor underwent continuous alterations. Ultimately, the peasant association expired in quixotic quests for a vanishing millennium.

Despite the movement's turbulent history it was established to achieve three commonplace purposes. Inaugurated in 1872 at Santo Domingo Convent in Manila, the lay organization was designed to promote Christian virtues (particularly chastity), foster devotion for the Blessed Virgin, and increase popular participation in church functions. Referred to interchangeably as Guardia de Honor de Maria (Mary's Honor Guard) or Guardias de Honor de Nuestra Señora del Rosario (Honor Guards for Our Lady of the Rosary), the sodality generated intense interest among urban and rural parishioners.[3] Requirements for joining were minimal. Initiates swore to abide by the Guardia's regulations and had their names added to authorized rolls. They then received certificates and colorful scapularies. To remain in good standing, members demonstrated their reverence by reciting the rosary at assigned hours each day and by escorting the Virgin's image

2. For information on the region's economic development during the late nineteenth century, see *Census of the Philippine Islands, 1918,* I (Manila, 1920), 235.

3. J. Y. Mason Blunt, *An Army Officer's Philippine Studies* (Manila, 1912), 87.

during processions. Humdrum activities notwithstanding, the confraternity enjoyed immediate popularity. Thousands of Manileños
and *provincianos* affiliated themselves with the association. Amazed
Dominicans were soon hard put to control the burgeoning institution.
In stern Manila, clerical restraints limited enthusiasts to acceptable
practices,[4] but in the more permissive provinces lax supervision produced unforeseen problems.

The shortage of secular clergymen that plagued Philippine church
officials created conditions favorable to unchecked growth. Already
overburdened with spiritual duties, harried pastors in the Ilocos region had little time to shepherd Guardia de Honor. They saw to the
compilation of membership rosters and selected prominent townsmen
to serve as local *cabecillas* (subleaders). After attending to essentials,
they left the organization to its own devices. Clerical neglect did not
dampen popular enthusiasms. Multihued scapularies quickly became
fashionable. Wherever the garments appeared, parish priests were
confronted by sharp increases in the frequency and fervency of
Marian devotions. By 1880 the movement threatened to get out of
hand. Hundreds of villagers were proclaiming themselves Guardias de
Honor without clerical sanction. Many began to incorporate pagan
rites into their daily worship. Disturbed Spanish clergymen, accordingly, recommended abandonment of the experiment. In 1882 their
superiors complied by withdrawing recognition from the Ilocano
chapters.[5]

Canonical displeasure brought no improvement to the situation. If
anything, it produced contrary results. Freed from constraint, the
sodality acquired additional momentum. Pagasinan province—the site
of a famous shrine to the Blessed Virgin—became the center for
confraternity activities. Julian Baltasar, a long-term resident of Urdaneta town, soon emerged as the organization's titular leader.

4. The organization's ceremonial function survived in Manila. For a captivating short story concerning its role, see Nick Joaquin, "Guardia de Honor,"
Prose and Poems (Manila, 1963), 112–127.
5. Most of the information on Guardia de Honor between 1882 and 1896
was drawn from an unpublished manuscript in the Dominican Archives. Father
Pablo Fernández, curator of the extensive collection, granted permission to
use the handwritten account but requested that it not be quoted. Unless indicated otherwise, information on the sodality during those years is drawn
from Cipriano Pampliego, "Documento curioso sobre los guardias de honor de
Pangasinan y otras cosas curiosas de los katipuneros" (Dominican Archives,
Manila), 19 pp.

Notorious in church circles as a powerful *anitero* (animist) and an accomplished faith healer, he was called "Apo Laqui" (literally Mister Grandfather) by his disciples.[6] Hamlet devotees were equally impressed by the reputed powers of Baltasar's blind wife. Known quite simply as the "goddess," the sightless woman had attracted a loyal following of her own. Under the sway of the charismatic couple, Guardia de Honor became a millenarian movement.

The dramatic shift was signaled by an apocalyptic pronouncement. Early in 1886, Baltasar proclaimed the approach of Judgment Day: a deluge would descend on the earth; the ensuing floods would wipe out corrupt mankind, though the virtuous might hope to escape the raging waters. Salvation for the select few, according to Baltasar, could only be achieved through migration to Santa Ana, a small island in the Agno River near Asingan town. Accepting his warning as divine revelation, Ilocano villagers abandoned their farms and fishing boats and fled toward safety. By the end of the dry season thousands of prayerful peasants were camped along the Agno. Fearing a spiritual explosion or a temporal disaster such as cholera, provincial authorities took action.[7] Pangasinan's governor ordered the *Guardia Civil* to evacuate newcomers from the area. Accompanied by parish priests from San Manuel, Tayug, and Asingan towns, guardsmen gradually disbanded Baltasar's followers. The dispersal proceeded without bloodshed or arrests. When normal rains came, and a new dry season arrived on schedule, Iberian churchmen and officials heaved a collective sigh of relief and hoped they had seen the last of Guardia de Honor.

The deflating experience failed to daunt Baltasar. Undismayed by the interruption to their plans, Apo Laqui and the goddess returned to Urdaneta. Continuing their self-ordained ministry to Honor Guards, their home soon became the center of a reanimated movement. Between 1886 and 1896 a constant stream of villagers visited the Baltasar residence. At times Urdaneta resembled a gypsy encampment overflowing with foot-loose *provincianos,* scampering children, creaking carts, and raucous animals. The peasant caravans arrived and departed according to rhythms beyond the ken of curious outsiders. Most of the pilgrims, however, paused at the Baltasar's house to pay

6. Figuratively, "Apo Laqui" meant "male deity." In the same context, "Apo Bae"—Mrs. Baltasar's title—meant "female deity." Blunt, 94.
7. Ulpanio Herrero y Sampedro, O.P., *Nuestra Prisión* (Manila, 1900), 273.

homage on their way to or from the Dominican shrine in neighboring Manaoag. There, overworked clerical residents found it almost impossible to keep pace with demands for special masses. Once more scapularies and rosaries began to appear in unprecedented numbers. The Guardia's resurgence, linked to rumors concerning Mrs. Baltasar's growing powers, convinced Pangasinan's churchmen that the time had come to reassert ecclesiastical control.

Father Cipriano Pampliega, Urdaneta's parish priest, assumed command of the effort. He first requested information on the sodality's Ilocano chapters. Dominican record keepers in Manila provided approximately 16,000 names from the original rosters.[8] When conferences with several listed *cabecillas* revealed they were no longer affiliated with the confraternity, Pampliega concluded that Baltasar had forged a fraudulent society larger by far than anyone in authority realized. Fearing the movement's potential, Pampliega offered his stabilizing counsel to the Guardia's Urdaneta directorate, but it was courteously rejected. The curate then conveyed his anxieties to the Chaplain of Santo Domingo Convent and urged secular officials to take action before Baltasar provoked another Santa Ana episode. Plagued by growing reports of nationalistic conspiracies, Pangasinan's governor was reluctant to become involved in what appeared to be tangential issues. Nevertheless, he summoned Baltasar to Lingayen. Convinced after cursory interrogations that he had been drawn into a purely religious question, he advised the aging *anitero* to behave and released him to the custody of the Honor Guards. Baltasar's successful brush with officialdom refurbished his image. Inadvertently, however, the governor's tolerant gesture had opened the way for a successful new round of Guardia recruiting.

Father Pampliega, whose advice had been spurned, gathered small solace from the advanced years of his spiritual adversaries. Certain that the infirm couple were not long for the world, he prayed their deaths would mark an end to the society. In November 1896, the goddess quietly passed away. At the widower's request, Pampliega conducted the funeral service, presided over a Catholic interment, and

8. Rosters indicated that most of the original members resided in La Union, Ilocos Sur, and Zambales. Pangasinan contained relatively few. The parishes of Urdaneta and Santa Maria, however, had listed more than 600 Guardias. Dom Remualdo Santos, O.S.B., "The Guards of Honor, 1872–1910" (unpublished seminar paper, Ateneo de Manila University, 1966), 5–6.

mingled with grief-stricken mourners. But his cooperation did not produce a rapprochement. Before long, word spread through Urdaneta that Mrs. Baltasar's disembodied form had materialized over several watering places. Her spirit, according to Pampliega's animated parishioners, was imparting curative powers to the town's most popular wells and fountains. The weary curate attempted to evolve new methods to meet his ethereal challenger.

While Father Pampliega wrestled with Mrs. Baltasar's ubiquitous ghost, Apo Laqui sought new worlds to conquer. Early in 1897 he remarried. After a short honeymoon he led his bride and a few advisers to the remote *sitio* of Montiel. He ordered assembling followers to clear large sections of the surrounding forest and began preparations for his own demise. The sixty-seven-year-old redeemer renamed the community "Cabaruan" (Renewal) and initiated a thorough reorganization of Guardia de Honor. From among the experienced *cabecillas* he also selected an heir apparent. Antonio Valdes—a magnetic, ex-barrio lieutenant from Manaoag—became Baltasar's aide-de-camp. Under his prodding, subleaders and proselytizers increased efforts to strengthen the sodality. In a matter of weeks Cabaruan emerged as the de facto capital of an expanding state within a state.

The feverish activity indicated more than anxiety over Baltasar's longevity. External pressures of a new variety had begun to affect the Honor Guards. For more than two years local members of the Katipunan (the revolutionary secret society founded in Manila in 1892) had been courting Guardia de Honor. Like their fellow conspirators in the south, Pangasinan's Katipuneros advocated cooperative actions against Spain. But Apo Laqui, disturbed by the Katipunan's Tagalog leadership and repelled by its secularism, kept the revolutionaries at a safe distance. The fragmenting political situation, however, demanded action. Determining to pursue a neutral course, he commissioned Valdes to form military units for the protection of Guardia interests. While his subaltern molded bolo companies, Baltasar attempted to guide his followers along a perilous path between the contending parties.

The effort failed. Abrasive relations with both camps forced Valdes to seek firearms. His amateurish raids on Spanish outposts provoked reprisals from the Bishop of Vigan, who classified Guardia de Honor as a dangerous heresy, and from the governor of Pangasinan, who issued orders outlawing the sodality's leaders. Civil guards occupied Cabaruan. They arrested Baltasar and forcibly dispersed the community's sizable population. Valdes, however, remained at large. Rallying Apo Laqui's followers, he dedicated the confraternity to a vendetta against all outsiders. The dissenters soon became proficient guerrillas. When the Truce of Biyak-na-bato temporarily terminated the indecisive contest between Spaniards and Katipuneros, Guardia de Honor continued its private war.

Baltasar's fate reinforced Valdes' resolution. The general amnesty of December 1897 brought about the release of Apo Laqui. Ravaged by seven months in Lingayen's *carcel,* the failing leader returned to Cabaruan where he died before the end of the year. Valdes blamed meddling outlanders for his death; and, pronouncing equal anathema on Spanish administrators and *ilustrado* agitators, he led his most experienced fighters into the mountains. Early in 1898, they launched hit-and-run attacks on lowland towns and *haciendas.* Pummeled *principales* and civil guards called the elusive raiders bandits. Valdes rejected the derogatory label and, with the flair of an experienced filibuster, named his growing army *los agraviados* (the oppressed). In Pangasinan, the unresolved revolution had set the stage for bitter civil strife.

Intricacy marked the initial stages of the struggle. Elsewhere— particularly in Tagalog-speaking areas—the events of 1896–1897 tended to simplify complex political equations. Revolutionary dialectics, in fact, drove large segments of the insular population into polarized positions. Pangasinan and neighboring provinces did not experience a similar division, since Guardia de Honor provided villagers with an acceptable alternative to the secular goals set forth by more sophisticated contenders. A three-cornered rivalry between Spaniards, Katipuneros, and Agraviados ensued. Spanish endurance was not equal to the test. Iberian power in the northwest, consequently, began to atrophy before Commodore Dewey's appearance in Manila Bay. The American naval victory, and the return of Aguinaldo, signaled the death of Spanish sovereignty. Nationalists quickly filled the administrative void. By late June 1898 they had gained control of municipalities throughout the vast region beyond Pampanga. But their triumph proved short-lived. Within weeks, the outlines of new jurisdictional disputes had become apparent: Katipuneros, or their allies, governed the towns; Guardia de Honor, however, ruled the barrios.

Sensing a possible stalemate, Antonio Valdes resorted to an ingenious tactical device: he stepped forth as Catholicism's champion.[9] Unwittingly, nationalists had provided an opportunity for the expedient. Released from centuries of bondage, many Filipinos turned on their clerical masters, and persecutions of both the mild and vicious varieties—winked at or provoked by Katipuneros—immediately swept the provinces. Valdes ordered his followers to aid Spanish curates wherever they came under attack. His mandate generated liberating raids on *municipios* from Tarlac to Ilocos Sur.[10] Priests and friars undeniably profited from the rampage; scores of churchmen were released from captivity, while others were respectfully and efficiently escorted to safety.[11] The northern *principalia,* however, suffered a series of embarrassing setbacks. Their declining prestige strengthened Valdes' standing in the countryside. Peasants rushed to join Guardia de Honor. Even a few respected opponents defected to the ballooning sodality.[12] Valdes' ploy, in short, broke the emerging stand-off. By September 1898, he controlled an impressive military force. In the border zone uniting Pangasinan, Tarlac, and Nueva Ecija, the Agraviado commander could deploy more than 5,000 armed men.[13] They were, furthermore, equal or superior to any contingents local gentrymen might send against them. Valdes, accordingly, decided to test the mettle of Aguinaldo's embryonic regime.

For the revolutionary government, the unforeseen challenge mate-

9. Herrero, 274.

10. Early American students of the revolutionary era believed Dominicans provoked the countermovement in the Ilocos. See, for example, J. R. M. Taylor's observations, United States, War Department, Bureau of Insular Affairs, *Compilation of Philippine Insurgent Records: Telegraphic Correspondence of Emilio Aguinaldo, July 15, 1898, to February 28, 1899,* Annotated (Washington, D.C., 1902), 36; cited hereafter as BIA, *Compilation.*

11. Most of the liberated churchmen were taken to coastal towns, from which they made their way to Hong Kong. A beneficiary, who castigated Valdes for "superstitious tricks," paid a grudging tribute to the confraternity: "What a special providence of God who made use of those pseudo guards of honor to improve our condition!" Herrero, 639.

12. One of the most important recruits was a Guardia Civil sergeant named Pedroche, who emerged as the Agraviado leader in Tarlac province. For a short account of his career in Guardia de Honor, see Joaquin Duran, *Episodios de la revolución filipina* (Manila, 1900), 71–72.

13. Blunt, 89.

rialized at a most inappropriate time. Harassed by political vicissi-
tudes, Aguinaldo and his aides were also beset by military pressures
from the United States.[14] The Guardia's *Jacquerie* compounded their
agonies. During October and November 1898, disturbing reports concerning the area north of Pampanga began to accumulate at Aguinaldo's
headquarters. Information on the spreading disorder made it clear
that highwaymen, brigands, and irregular military units were operating throughout the region. Prominent families, together with barrios
and administrative centers loyal to the new government, came under
probing attack.[15] By early December, law and order in Tarlac, Pangasinan, and La Union had almost disappeared. Nationalist leaders
in the provinces began to rage against counterrevolutionary tendencies and complained to Aguinaldo of "treason on the part of our
troops and civilians."[16]

Christmas brought the gift of chaos. Coordinated uprisings plunged
Tarlac into near anarchy.[17] Telegrams jamming southbound wires
described widespread "criminal" activities by bands of *tulisanes*
(bandits).[18] In an attempt to isolate the infection, Aguinaldo tried to
throw a *cordon sanitaire* around the province. He also rushed military
reinforcements north by rail to initiate martial law, and Tarlaqueños
remained under a state of seige throughout January 1899. Conditions
in Tarlac were such that efforts by the revolutionary government to
withdraw detachments for strategic redeployment against the Americans proved futile. Within hours after the abandonment of a *pobla-
cion,* guerrillas fell upon the town to sack government buildings,
destroy records, and attack leading citizens. The conflict quickly took
on the character of class warfare. A message from the administrative
head of Tarlac revealed the *principalia*'s growing anxiety. "Many

14. Disorder was so prevalent in the Philippines during July and August
1898 that Aguinaldo had to appoint delegates to represent some important regions at the Malolos constitutional convention. Agoncillo and Alfonso, *A Short
History,* 248–249.

15. General Macabulos to Aguinaldo, November 30, 1898, BIA, *Compilation,* 31.

16. General Pio del Pilar to Aguinaldo, Dec. 4, 1898, *ibid.,* 31.

17. Pedroche, who led the upheaval in Tarlac province, briefly gained control of four *municipios.* His operations were brought to a halt in Camiling
town. Posing as an ally, the municipal *presidente* lured the ex-sergeant to a
banquet. During the course of the meal, Katipunero assassins killed Pedroche
and several of his aides. Duran, 72.

18. See telegrams to Aguinaldo, BIA, *Compilation,* 35–37.

rich people here," he telegraphed Aguinaldo, "urgently ask the creation of a . . . body of volunteers . . . formed of trustworthy and prominent persons . . . for the pursuit of robbers and to fight the Americans if necessary. We have the money," he concluded optimistically, "and only need rifles."[19]

Aguinaldo, confronted by powerful American army units disembarking in Manila Bay, was unwilling to become involved in distant encounters between *hacenderos* and *taos*. He ordered municipal administrators and provincial military commanders to proceed cautiously and attempted to stabilize conditions through a balanced policy of attraction and coercion. Neither approach worked. When amnesties failed to reduce the discord, peasant rebels were proscribed, hunted down, and killed.[20] But the countermovement continued to grow. Recognizing that religious motives propelled the dissenters, one government troubleshooter recommended that Gregorio Aglipay be sent "to quiet Tarlac."[21] Villagers, however, could not be stopped by either nationalistic bishops or bullets. Agraviado leaders, furthermore, instigated terroristic campaigns that blocked government efforts to drain away their reservoir of popular support. The results met the pragmatic test: Guardia de Honor won additional supporters. Sectarian field commanders began to refer to one another as "brigadier generals." It was not an idle boast. By the end of February 1899, the crosscurrents in the north had assumed the dimensions of an apparently irresistible tidal wave. Residents of major *municipios* found themselves besieged. The important railroad town of San Carlos, Pangasinan, for instance, requested government detachments to defend its 23,000 inhabitants from the assaults of "those who call themselves the discontented or oppressed and Guards of Honor."[22]

The Dominicans' carelessly embedded plant had borne bitter fruit. Within a year, mutations produced a self-propagating specimen which even the friars came to regard as a noxious weed. After the outbreak of Filipino-American hostilities on Feburary 4, 1899, revolutionary authorities turned from abortive peacemaking in the north to the

19. Provincial Chief of Tarlac to Aguinaldo, Dec. 29, 1898, *ibid.*, 41–42.
20. J. R. M. Taylor, comp., "The Philippine Insurrection against the United States" (microfilmed galley proofs in 5 vols.; National Archives, Washington, D.C., 1906), I, 45; cited hereafter as Taylor, *Insurgent Records*.
21. Secretary of Agriculture to Aguinaldo, Dec. 28, 1898, BIA, *Compilation*, 37.
22. Taylor, *Insurgent Records*, 45.

more perilous problems created by advancing aliens. Concentrating on Aguinaldo's ragged but defiant legions, United States troops paid little heed to the religious peculiarities multiplying around them. Late in 1899, however, when forward elements reached Pangasinan, the issue could no longer be ignored. From the thriving seedbed, thick runners of discord twisted north, east, and south into La Union, Ilocos Sur, Nueva Ecija, Zambales, and Tarlac.

The contagion caused the Americans as much difficulty, if not more, than it had Aguinaldo. Major General Elwell S. Otis, the commander of "pacification" forces in the Philippines, grasped neither the military nor social realities confronting his field officers. Weaned on the Anglo-Saxon sportsmanship of the War between the States and shaped by the primitive clarities of Indian campaigns on the frontier, he regarded the "strange fanaticism" swirling through Luzon as but another example of oriental perversity. "Self-declared prophets," the impatient general grumbled, "were proclaiming new creeds . . . quite markedly variable in origin and nature." Since Otis considered the malady to be essentially inexplicable, he fell back on a conventional American approach. Assuming that the activities of the sects were based upon the pecuniary motives of their leaders, the general ordered a crackdown. Subordinates wrestled an established redeemer from the arms of his followers in Bulacan province and threw him behind bars for "illegal money exactions from the more ignorant natives." After taking a first step toward confining the pestilence, Otis consulted urban observers. Manila's "educated Filipinos" proved to be uneasy. They spoke apprehensively about the increase of "fanatical sects," and warned the general that difficulty might be experienced "in handling them if they were permitted to follow their inclinations." Otis, in brief, found no answers. But he concluded his report to Washington with a provocative observation, "Whatever the cause, the fact disturbed the Roman Catholic clergy and was the subject of much animated discussion."[23]

While Otis conducted opinion surveys, and priests buzzed over his findings, General Arthur MacArthur sought the focus of dissent. Patrols reconnoitering Pangasinan's intricate village network encountered a variety of secular and sacred eccentricities, but their strangest discovery was a community of 10,000 people where a *sitio* was supposed

23. United States, War Department, *Report of Major General E. S. Otis: Sept. 1899 to May 5, 1900* (Washington, D.C., 1900), 142–143.

to be. Cabaruan, which one American labeled an "ill-starred town of religious fanatics and vulgar thieves," had been uncovered by the newcomers.[24] With a tactician's directness, MacArthur moved to eradicate the cultists. Hastily concentrated infantry companies occupied the place after a brief and practically bloodless skirmish. Shortly thereafter, General Otis received a lengthy telegram on the action's objective:

> Cabaruan is . . . located some eight miles east of Malasiqui. . . . It has been selected as the rendezvous of a fanatical religious organization of some kind and people from surrounding towns and barrios forced to assemble there. . . . The fanatics are also robbers and murderers, and have recently committed the most cruel depredations on surrounding towns, especially Malasiqui, where nine murders have been committed within the last few weeks. . . . The . . . people there have been ordered home and in a few days it is hoped that the excitement that has kept this part of Pangasinan in an uproar . . . will subside. Precisely how the religious and robber elements are combined I have not been able to ascertain, but it is a fact . . . that this part of Pangasinan has been terrorized by these people—the large town of Malasiqui being almost entirely depopulated. . . . The importance of this day's work cannot be overestimated.[25]

General MacArthur's conclusion proved wrong. The "day's work" exerted about as much influence over the course of affairs in Pangasinan as Aguinaldo's proclamation of martial law had worked the year before in Tarlac.

When MacArthur departed the area, regimental officers were left to grapple with the complexities of Cabaruan. Early in 1900, they stationed an infantry company in the town to oversee the gradual dispersal of its residents. While the inhabitants did not fade away, the "uproar" subsided. Sectarians devoted more energy to marathon prayer sessions and correspondingly less to plaguing inhabitants of neighboring settlements.[26] Even the population leveled off around the 10,000 mark. With peace seemingly restored, the small garrison was withdrawn. Officers at headquarters in Dagupan instituted a wary surveillance over the community. Any belief that stability might develop evaporated quickly, for the soldiers' departure signaled a fresh outburst of growth. Within a year, 10,000 more people migrated to

24. LeRoy, *Americans in the Philippines*, II, 302.
25. Otis, 143.
26. Worcester and Hayden, *Philippines Past and Present*, II, 945.

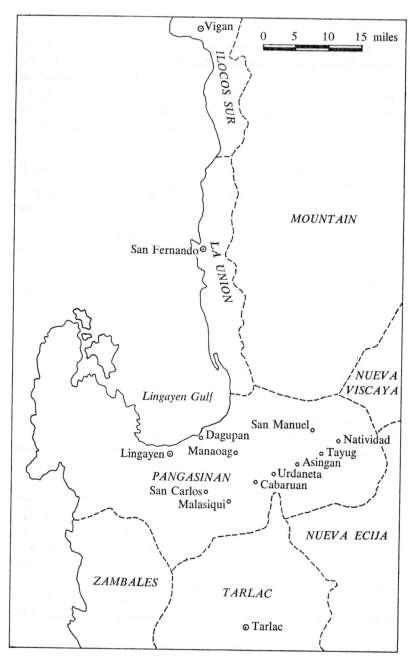

3. Northwestern Luzon, 1900

Cabaruan.[27] A new and heartier variety of religious dissent had apparently sprung up in Pangasinan.

The revival constituted an additional irritation to military personnel already overburdened with occupation duties. Unaware of the town's stormy history, American officers and enlisted men could not fathom Cabaruan's significance. Antonio Valdes did everything he could to deepen their confusion. Respecting American manpower, equipment, and mobility, he fell back on the guerrilla's ultimate weapon: duplicity. Three years of irregular warfare had converted the *Agraviado supremo* into a masterful dissembler. Posing as a responsible *presidente,* he continued to direct the Guardia's clandestine activities. His performance, linked to the efficient secret operations of his followers, kept the outlanders at bay for more than a year.

What the Americans lacked in insight, they made up for in persistence. Patrols visited Cabaruan regularly. Their reports revealed a series of mystifying contradictions. The community was orderly to a fault; it was also unusually clean and well laid out. Major streets radiated from the plaza like spokes on a wagon wheel. Each thoroughfare, together with the section through which it passed, was named after one of the twelve apostles.[28] Valdes—known only as a personable administrator addicted to gleaming top boots and ornate uniforms—presided over the destinies of the devout inhabitants. He was ably assisted by a dozen lieutenants. The town's admirable traits, however, were canceled out by some dubious features. While Cabaruan's exploding population manifested all the trappings of prosperity, the town lacked any visible means of support.[29] Few if any people worked. They made little effort, for example, to cultivate the surrounding countryside. Scouting detachments returning to Dagupan, furthermore, inevitably picked up disturbing rumors concerning Caba-

27. Katherine Mayo, *The Isles of Fear: Truth about the Philippines* (New York, 1925), 181. Miss Mayo's book was probably the most objectionable collection of "objective" observations written during the 1920's. But her short description of Cabaruan was based on the account of an American army officer stationed in Dagupan during the years 1899–1902. Stripped of their patronizing veneer, her remarks revealed interesting details on Guardia de Honor.

28. United States, War Department, *Report, 1900* (Washington, D.C., 1901). See I, Part 8, "Reports from Colonel J. F. Bell, Commander, Thirty-Sixth Infantry, U.S.V. to Adjutant-General Second Division, Eighth Army Corps," 331–335. Cited hereafter as Bell, "Reports."

29. Mayo, 183.

ruan. Inhabitants of surrounding communities regarded the place with ill-concealed terror. They complained of chronic criminality and whispered of sadistic rites.[30]

Doubling their efforts to unravel the enigma, headquarters personnel attempted to surprise the town's leaders. The new approaches produced no proof of wrongdoing, but they led to a cat-and-mouse game between the Agraviados and the United States Army. Reconnaissance patterns were constantly changed. When that technique failed, veteran squads made their way to the community via the most devious routes. Residents of Cabaruan's extensive environs, however, were vigilant and always discovered the interlopers. They notified messengers who, in turn, set into motion a unique alarm system. Within moments after receiving word of an approaching patrol, the Cabaruan brass band—drums rolling, cymbals clashing, and trumpets blaring—marched out to meet the invaders. When musicians and military met, the bandsmen wheeled smartly and led the abashed Americans through throngs of smiling residents to the plaza where they were welcomed by hamlet officials.[31] Repeated embarrassments of that type led some Americans in Manila to chide the Pangasinan regiment for the "Cabaruan fiasco."[32]

Intelligence and legal officers in Dagupan, however, were not as naive as their superiors and Valdes believed. While awaiting the accumulation of irrefutable testimony, they compiled information on the town and concluded that the manifestation confronting them represented something far more complex than popular superstition or religious racketeering. By 1900, Guardia de Honor had become an amorphous and seemingly all-pervasive hysteria which threatened to eliminate everything associated with stable village behavior. The seizure has unleashed lemminglike population movements in the north. Peasant families from nearby provinces—particularly La Union and Ilocos Sur, arrived every day in Cabaruan. For a people conditioned to servile conduct, the migrations added up to insubordination on a colossal scale. Emboldened by Agraviado successes, Ilocano villagers had evolved a simple, yet devastatingly effective, pattern of rebellion. When the harvest was gathered, farm couples packed up children, belongings, and poultry; seized the landowner's *palay,* live-

30. Bell, "Reports," 332.
31. Mayo, 181.
32. Worcester and Hayden, II, 944.

stock, and carabao; joined like-minded neighbors; and began the liberating trek to the promised land. On arrival, they deposited confiscated rice and animals in communal granaries and pens. The bounty, united with booty collected by raiders, produced an atmosphere verging on perpetual fiesta. Cabaruan, in short, was living parasitically on the agricultural yield of at least three provinces.[33] The place was virtually permeated with the aroma of social revolution.

The town's peculiar political organization posed greater problems for its martial analysts. Ostensibly anarchistic, Cabaruan was not chaotic. Opposition to external power—whether clerical, national, or colonial—was balanced by internal subjection to authoritarian figures. The uniformed headman and his resplendent aides were more than polite dandies. They directed an unyielding, *pure* theocracy. Two and a half years of turmoil had exerted apocalyptic pressures upon Guardia de Honor. The deceased Julian Baltasar had been elevated to the status of a living deity. Many residents regarded him as "God Almighty." The *supremo* Antonio Valdes, his principal adviser Gregorio Claveria, and their constant companion Maria de la Cruz, were worshiped respectively as "Jesus Christ," the "Holy Ghost," and the "Virgin Mary." The twelve lieutenants, perhaps inevitably, were believed to be the "Savior's Apostles."[34] Such an assemblage made anything seem possible.

Observers recorded no pronouncements comparable to Baltasar's "revelation" of 1896, but the behavior of Cabaruan's inhabitants indicated the millennium was at hand. They were experiencing the elation of the elect on the eve of a final reckoning when the corrupt universe would be transformed and justice would replace oppression. If they conceived of redemption in terms utterly incomprehensible to their more sophisticated contemporaries, it was because they were simple men and women. Like other pre-political dissenters elsewhere in the world, they did not aspire to an affluent utopia. They conceived of "the good society as a just sharing of austerity rather than a dream of riches for all."[35] While awaiting divine retribution, it was their responsibility to strike down perpetrators of evil. Blacklists of sinners, particularly *hacenderos* and apostates, were compiled. Agraviados convinced themselves that when the great day dawned, lands of

33. Bell, "Reports," 333.
34. Mayo, 182.
35. Hobsbawm, *Primitive Rebels*, 82.

those marked for extinction would be divided among the righteous. Cabaruan's wide-ranging raiders, accordingly, did not strike in a hit-or-miss fashion. They preyed specifically on those obviously unfit to enter what an American general called "the chosen kingdom" of Guardia de Honor.[36]

The town's impossible "economy," however, bothered regimental officers in Dagupan more than its unorthodox "theology." Ever-accumulating immigrants quickly consumed the provisions confiscated from Cabaruan's thatched *bodegas* and bamboo corrals. The sustenance crisis produced two equilibrium-shattering results. On the one hand, disputes over food shook the doctrinal unity of the leaders. A disgruntled lesser prophet led a minor hegira to Santa Ana— Baltasar's old Mecca.[37] There, he established an independent spiritual refuge. Ilocanos fleeing personal wildernesses could now choose between rival lands of milk and honey. Santa Ana rapidly became a reflection of the original "city of God." By March 1, 1901, 10,000 people had collected in the "New Jerusalem." On the other hand, Cabaruan passed the economic point of no return. Still absorbing pilgrims, it achieved a peak population of 25,000 early in 1901. The frenzied search for rations forced Agraviado raiders to modify their tactics. Attacks on selected *principales* were supplemented with random assaults on humble outsiders. Small farmers, who had tacitly supported and secretly enjoyed Guardia activities when they were directed at the rich, turned against the movement when it unleashed its fury on the poor.[38]

At this point, with terror sweeping Pangasinan, Dagupan's commander moved to still the turbulence. Judgment Day came, but not in the vague fraternal form envisioned by the Agraviados. It materialized suddenly and overpowingly in khaki uniforms, bristling bayonets, and a provost marshal. On March 3, 1901, American infantry battalions occupied Cabaruan and Santa Ana. Efficient platoons sought out Valdez, Claveria, and Maria de la Cruz. The trio was arrested, shackled, and marched off to an army stockade in Urdaneta. Within

36. United States, War Department, *Report, 1901* (Washington, D.C., 1902), I, Part 3, "Report of Brigadier General J. H. Smith, U.S.A.," 114. Cited hereafter as Smith, "Reports."
37. Bell, "Reports," 334.
38. Formerly silent villagers became vocal early in 1901. They provided incontestable evidence to Americans in Dagupan concerning murder and terrorism by members of the confraternity. Mayo, 182–183.

hours, they were joined by twelve dispirited apostles. With their redeemers in chains, the self-confidence of Cabaruan's inhabitants vanished. By nightfall, the first crestfallen *taos* were preparing to return to their old communities.

The diaspora took several months. March and April saw the countermigration reach its peak under the prodding of American soldiers, although a hardcore of the faithful remained in Cabaruan to await the military tribunal's decision. The court declared Antonio Valdes and Gregorio Claveria culpable on multiple counts of murder and terrorism and sentenced them to death. Other leaders, found guilty of aiding or abetting the illegal activities of the headmen, received long prison terms. On June 1, 1901, in Urdaneta, Pangasinan, Valdes and Claveria were publicly hanged.[39] "Jesus" and the "Holy Ghost" were dead. So, apparently, was Guardia de Honor.

It all seemed over. Cabaruan and Santa Ana dwindled back to sleepy settlements dreaming fitfully of bygone notoriety. Ilocanos went home, or—if that grim alternative was too unbearable—joined their peripatetic *coprovincianos* in other parts of the archipelago. Except for those who had felt its wrath, or those who had been transformed by its aspirations, the contagion was forgotten almost as quickly as it had appeared. Manila, in particular, transferred its attention to other problems. Administrators consigned the Agraviados to the official limbo of lunatics and lost causes. Time, they were certain, would erase memories of Guardia de Honor.

But urban civil servants and politicians had failed to take account of the countryside's turbulent tradition. Like Apolinario's Cofradía, Baltasar's Guardia lingered on. Irreconcilable Agraviados formed secret societies which kept the spark of rebellion alive. When the United States Army withdrew from Pangasinan, neophyte provincial authorities had to deal with an undercurrent of anarchism that surfaced periodically in violent upheavals. A minor uprising occurred in Natividad in 1903.[40] Similar incidents of diminishing intensity continued for another six years.[41] Governors, mayors, and constables, however, kept a tight lid on the province. Reports on Pangasinan's most notorious organization finally dropped away to naught. After

39. Smith, "Reports," 118.
40. See "Report of the Governor of the Province of Pangasinan," in *Report of the Philippine Commission, 1904,* Part I, 583.
41. *Annual Report of the Director of Constabulary, 1909* (Manila, 1910), 6.

1910, the dossiers of the Philippine Constabulary received no more entries on Guardia de Honor. But anonymity did not mean extinction. Hearty offshoots of the movement sprang up in neighboring regions.[42] The dissident heritage survived even in Pangasinan. Peasant associations, operating under deceptive new titles, perpetuated the legacy of Antonio Valdes. During the late 1920's and early 1930's they ignited fresh conflagrations in the Guardia's former heartland.

42. Guardia de Honor gave birth to several millennial movements. Its most violent offspring, the Santa Iglesia, will be dealt with in the next chapter. Less apparent outgrowths materialized in the nearby highlands. For an intriguing discussion of offshoots in the Mountain Province, see Fred Eggan and Alfredo Pacyaya. "The Sapilada Religion: Reformation and Accommodation among the Igorots of Northern Luzon," *Southwestern Journal of Anthropology,* XVIII (1962), 95–113.

CHAPTER 6

Bandits and Popes

Millenarian outbursts were but one way of demonstrating opposition to authority. Other responses ranged from indolence on the part of amenable majorities, to harassment and flight on the part of recalcitrant minorities. From the outset of Spanish rule, individuals and groups had demonstrated their hostility to domination by refusing to accept Iberian spiritual or temporal restrictions. Many discontented hamlet dwellers "fled from the hells" to the bracing atmosphere and comparative freedom of the mountains. Known as *"montestas"* or *"remontados,"* the fugitives flourished in sparsely settled uplands or on out-of-the-way islands such as Palawan.[1] They constituted no problem to the Spaniards so long as they were left alone. Any effort to force them to accept either Christianity or Western legal codes, however, led to bitter resistance.

In the more densely populated lowlands of Luzon and the Visayas, few villagers could escape the local ramifications of Spanish power. Most barrio people accepted subordination with fatalistic grace; others refused to be cowed. Defiant individuals evolved a variety of techniques to torment the authorities. Of those, the most effective was banditry. Known as *tulisanes* or *ladrones,* outlaws disrupted the countryside throughout the Spanish era. The problem, however, became acute during the developmental sequence of the late nineteenth century. After 1850, lawlessness of a new type started to disturb provincial officials. Depredations could no longer be attributed to ancient blood feuds. Solitary murders and assaults, moreover, could not be dismissed as tragic results of frustrated passions. Rural crime began to take on class connotations. Rustlers, highwaymen, extor-

1. The terms *montesta* and *remontado* were sometimes used as synonyms for bandit. LeRoy, *Philippine Life in Town and Country,* 29–30.

tionists, and cutthroats preyed increasingly upon estate owners, lawyers, usurers, friars, and itinerant Chinese merchants—all the emerging
enemies, in short, of the troubled peasantry.

Violence, furthermore, became perversely logical. Under favorable
circumstances, small *tulisan* bands merged with like-minded groups to
form coalitions. Celebrated filibusters occasionally employed the combined desperadoes to execute raids on *municipios,* terrorizing prominent townsmen in the process, and wreaking vengeance on Spaniards
or "Sangleys" who fell into their hands.[2] Brigandage of that magnitude sometimes assumed proportions and characteristics verging on
those of irregular warfare. Eliminating it proved equally difficult. Few
bandits, after all, victimized the poor. Fewer still operated in the
vicinity of their homes. Attacks on well-to-do strangers and affluent
foreigners, or onslaughts against distant *poblaciones* and their prosperous inhabitants, were regarded by most villagers as rewarding, if
not legitimate, pursuits. Relatives, neighbors, and friends provided
sanctuary and sustenance to outlaws. Informers seldom appeared.
Tulisanes, consequently, tended to vanish into the rural background
as quickly as they had materialized. Villagers came to look upon the
largess-dispensing outlaws as defenders and frequently elevated them
to the status of folk heroes. Their exploits, embellished and romanti-
cized to swashbuckling heights by admirers, created persistent Robin
Hood myths in the barrios.[3] Spain, accordingly, found it impossible
to eradicate banditry. The Guardia Civil—formed specifically to
counter *tulisanismo*—merely attempted to limit it to bearable levels.

Filipino practitioners of the demanding art unconsciously followed
time-honored precedents. Like their reckless counterparts elsewhere

2. The town of Tayug, Pangasinan, for example, was overrun by outlaws in
1876. The brigands burned the houses of Tayug's *principales* and murdered six
prominent citizens. Led by a famous bandit named Tancad, the band of sixty
desperadoes had operated successfully for several years in the provinces of
Bulacan, Pampanga, Nueva Ecija, and Pangasinan. Civil Guards and Spanish
Army units cornered Tancad and his followers early in 1877. Twenty-two of
the captured *tulisanes*—including Tancad—were publicly executed by garrote
in Bagumbayan Field. A brief account of the group's "exploits," together with
newspaper descriptions of the executions, is contained in a short manuscript
in the Ayer Collection of Newberry Library: José Maria Maurin. "Recuerdos
de una expedición a la Pampanga . . . Antecedentes acerca del célebre tulisan
conocido con el nombre de Tancad" (August 1877), 5 pp.
3. See the observations of William Howard Taft in *Report of the Philippine
Commission, 1902* (Washington, D.C.), I, 17.

on the great tradition's frontiers, they attempted to turn back or resist unwelcome change. The unequal struggle between emotion and reason was lost before it was joined. But village protagonists did not know that. Cataclysmic events, completely beyond their comprehension or control, propelled them to self-destructive extremes. The most that can be said for the *tulisanes* is that they went down fighting. Their suicidal activities, nevertheless, bore the familiar stamp of "social banditry," of which a careful student of the phenomenon said that it was

little more than endemic peasant protest against oppression and poverty, a cry for vengeance on the rich and the oppressors, a vague dream of some curb upon them, a righting of individual wrongs. Its ambitions are modest: a traditional world in which men are justly dealt with, not a new and perfect world. It becomes epidemic rather than endemic when a peasant society which knows of no better means of self-defense is in a condition of abnormal tension and disruption. Social banditry has next to no organization or ideology. . . . Its most highly developed forms, which skirt national guerrilla warfare, are rare and, by themselves, ineffective.[4]

In the Philippines, its ultimate expressions were not uncommon. Telescoping calamities at the turn of the century produced them in bargain lots.

Operational patterns were not the only parallels to appear among provincial outlaws. Like their posturing brethren in other parts of the world, Filipino social bandits exuded a rude charisma. Almost without exception, brigands claimed miraculous attributes. Outstanding chieftains were widely reputed to be protected by potent *antinganting*. The wonder-working talismans—ranging from simple amulets and charms to elaborate uniforms bearing mystical designs or quasi-Latin formulas—allegedly shielded their owners from malign sorcery and physical misfortunes. Famous *ladrones* often maintained they were immune to death. Some even averred they possessed the capacity to extend invulnerability to followers. Less pretentious *tulisanes* asserted they could resurrect dead comrades. The most influential outlaws, however, posed as reincarnations of divine beings or deceased popular champions. On a limited scale, their appeal was comparable

4. Hobsbawm, *Primitive Rebels*, 5.

to that exercised by prophets of old and new religions. Bandit leaders, in brief, gained prestige among their supporters, and notoriety among their adversaries, by surrounding themselves with supernatural auras.

Brigandage of both the mercenary and social varieties flourished as never before between 1890 and 1910. Revolutionary turmoil and the chaos emanating from Filipino-American hostilities created conditions favorable to its growth. Famine, pestilence, and death—riding hard on warfare's bloody heels—created a contagion of lawlessness. In many areas banditry became almost as prevalent as ruination. Exact statistics on the era's ghastly toll have never been tabulated. Political and military convulsions, however, led directly or indirectly to the deaths of at least 200,000 Filipinos. Those not consumed by battle perished in its aftermath. Cholera, diphtheria, tuberculosis, dysentery, typhoid, and other medical nightmares cut terrifying swaths through the hamlet population. Work animals overlooked by marauding soldiers fell by the scores of thousands to anthrax and rinderpest.[5] Intense hunger—verging, at times, on wholesale starvation—compounded the agonies of peasant survivors. In many districts, food became a far more precious commodity than human life. Desperate times, in short, made outlaws; outlaws made the times more desperate.

The devastaing interaction became particularly pronounced following Aguinaldo's capture. Concerted opposition ended with his reluctant oath of allegiance to the United States. Resistance of sorts continued, but it quickly deteriorated to the level of fragmenting irregular warfare. After April 1901, irreconcilable Filipino patriots found themselves operating in a demoralizing half-world of fading guerrillas and jaded bandits. The remaining armed opponents of the new metropolitan power, furthermore, were labeled *tulisanes* and treated like common criminals. While American military commanders concentrated on obliterating nationalist pockets in the southern Tagalog provinces and the eastern Visayas, Manila's civil administrators created an instrument to establish law and order throughout the archipelago. On June 18, 1901, the Philippine Commission authorized the formation of a binational police force to be deployed in the provinces. Unlike the defunct *Guardia Civil*—on which it was partially pat-

5. According to some students, 90 per cent of the carabao population was wiped out between 1896 and 1902; this figure, together with preceding casualty estimates, is taken from Leon Wolff, *Little Brown Brothers* (New York, 1961), 360.

terned—the Philippine Constabulary was designed to eradicate brigandage by winning the confidence of insular civilians.[6]

Within a year the militarized enforcement agency had begun to earn its keep. During 1901 and 1902, *tulisanismo* erupted everywhere. Forced to grapple continually with the hydra-headed monster, American and Filipino officers soon became aware of its characteristics. Constabulary analysts even evolved a series of categories to identify their furtive opponents. Under the genus "outlaw" they established three distinct subspecies: (1) *ladrones,* (2) *ladrones políticos,* and (3) *ladrones fanáticos.*[7] The first two yielded relatively easily to systematic force.[8] By late 1903, most of the "flotsam and jetsam from the wreck of the insurrection" had been cleared away.[9] The third variety, however, manifested extraordinary regenerative capacities. Instead of disappearing, seditious religious creeds tended to proliferate. Ferreting out the leaders of secret congregations posed unanticipated difficulties and often provoked violent peasant responses. The disruptive outcome of clandestine spiritual associations prompted one Constabulary realist to predict "frequent local uprisings for a long term of years."[10]

His gloomy prognosis proved accurate. Between 1902 and 1906, militant sects surfaced from northeastern Mindanao to northwestern Luzon. In addition to troublesome Colorums and anarchistic Guardias de Honor, toiling constabularymen faced Pulajanes and Colorados (Reds), Cazadores (Hunters), Babailanes (Priests), Santos Niños (Holy Children), and Hermanos del Tercero Orden (Brothers of the Third Order). They were also confronted by crusaders who called themselves Soldados Militantes de la Iglesia (Militant Soldiers of the Church), and by numerous converts to underground cults with redun-

6. For a detailed discussion of the origins and early development of the organization see George Y. Coats, "The Philippine Constabulary, 1901–1917" (Doctoral dissertation, History, The Ohio State University, 1968), 410 pp.
7. The classifications were used by General Henry T. Allen in *Report of the Philippine Commission, 1903* (Washington, D.C.), III, 100.
8. Constabulary casualty reports for the first year of field operations exposed the effectiveness of police tactics: "Insurgents killed, 11; captured, 35; surrendered, 360; ladrones killed, 663; captured, 2,802; surrendered, 707." Constabulary losses for the same period were: "Inspectors killed, 2; enlisted men killed, 20; inspectors wounded, 1; enlisted men wounded, 40." *Report of the Philippine Commission, 1902,* I, 180.
9. The metaphor, which became a Constabulary favorite, was first used by Colonel J. F. Bell in reference to Pangasinan. Bell, "Reports," 331.
10. H. T. Allen, *Report of the Philippine Commission, 1903,* III, 37.

dant names such as *Dios-Dios, Cruz-Cruz,* or *Anting-Anting.* District inspectors found the grandiose titles delightful. That, however, was all. Without exception, the esoteric societies instigated—or were linked to—terroristic upheavals in the municipalities that severely taxed Constabulary resources. Responsible officers, therefore, learned to fear the implications of village mysticism. "These spasmodic up-risings," warned an assistant chief, "may be put down as long as they come one at a time, but in the event that they should become general, the civil government might be sorely embarrassed to cope effectively with the situation."[11]

Colonial officials could not unravel the enigmatic movements. They understood most lawbreakers. Intransigent nationalists and profes-sional rustlers, for example, were comprehensible felons. In Ameri-can terms, their activities were similar to those of recalcitrant Con-federates or defiant Western-style "bad men." Peasant religious rebels, however, were another matter. Their otherworldly behavior went well beyond the pale of conventional American experience. Baffled admin-istrators, consequently, fell back on the superficial explanations and repressive techniques of their Spanish predecessors. They dismissed militant sects as unfortunate outgrowths of "native superstition" and ordered the Constabulary to keep them under tight rein. It was easier said than done. Despite close police surveillance spiritual tumults continued to disrupt the countryside. In 1906, an involved American official expressed private aggravation. "It seems impossible," confided W. Cameron Forbes to his journal, "for these people not to be drawn by misguided leaders into a sort of religious frenzy."[12]

Constabulary efforts to end the seizures followed predictable pat-terns. Tacticians in the organization's Manila headquarters determined to reduce the problem to manageable proportions by apprehending the instigators of violence. While the expedient worked, success required a decade of remorseless police activity. Provincial com-manders gradually identified the peasantry's charismatic *supremos* and arrested or killed them one by one. Since many of the cult lead-ers called themselves *papas* (popes), constabularymen appropriated the title to designate their most resolute foes. If nothing else, the

11. W. C. Taylor, *ibid.,* 122.
12. W. C. Forbes, "Journal" (typescript, Manuscript Division, Library of Congress), II, 3.

campaign to eradicate village pontiffs exposed a limited number of Americans to the inequities of Philippine life.[13]

Skirmishes between constables and devout brigands quickly took on the quality of miniature civil wars. Prominent *provincianos*, particularly *hacenderos*, merchants, and municipal property owners, affiliated themselves with the drive to wipe out *tulisanes*. "Educated Filipinos," as one American put it, were "extremely desirous to see thorough and consistent order maintained."[14] Impoverished barrio dwellers, for the most part, aligned themselves with the religious Robin Hoods. The running conflict had little or nothing to do with yearnings to free the Philippines from foreign domination. Peasant belligerents were dedicated to more basic objectives. They sought an ill-defined utopia, observed a district inspector, in which "there would be no more labor, no taxes, no jails, and no constabulary."[15] Internecine strife emanating from the divergent goals raged across the archipelago until 1911. While scores of popes rallied sizable village followings to their liberating creeds, three persistent movements instigated profound discord: Babailanes in Negros, Pulajanes in Samar, and Santa Iglesia devotees in central Luzon.

Like other rural upheavals, Babailan difficulties antedated the revolutionary era. Between 1850 and 1900, Negros became one of the richest islands in the Philippines. Sugar production rose from 4,000 to 2,000,000 *piculs* per year, and population soared from 18,000 to more than 200,000.[16] The transformation enabled a few *hacenderos* to accumulate Midas-like fortunes. Staggering wealth in the hands of a few, unfortunately, was not the only outcome of economic development. Social antipathies spread in the wake of rapid technological change. Following the course of their ancestors, disinherited farmers and disgruntled field hands abandoned lowland estates to live in the mountains. The refugees joined freebooting *montestas* who were dedicated to folk rites and committed to banditry. In 1887, a young mystic named Dionisio Sigobela took over the leadership of the exiles.

13. See, for example, the revealing social commentary in J. R. White, *Bullets and Bolos* (New York, 1928), 108–119.
14. H. T. Allen, *Report of the Philippine Commission, 1902*, III, 38.
15. *Ibid.*, 100.
16. Figures on sugar production were drawn from *Census of the Philippine Islands, 1918*, I, 219; those on population from *Census of the Philippine Islands, 1903*, III, 123.

Proclaiming himself an emissary of God, he accumulated pontifical paraphernalia and adopted the title "Papa Isio." Sigobela instilled unquestioning obedience among his followers. He also converted them into disciplined raiders. Under his direction piecemeal thievery gave way to coordinated attacks on major plantations and municipal centers. The brigands forced *hacenderos* and *Guardia Civil* detachments to adopt defensive postures. Bandit lairs in the highlands, however, remained inviolate. By 1895, Pope Isio and his Babailanes had become "undisputed masters of the mountains."[17]

Political turmoil thrust Sigobela into a larger role. Wealthy Negrenses skillfully avoided direct involvement in the upheavals of 1896–1897. Primarily concerned with property rights and their perpetuation, the island's elitists wanted nothing to do with Katipunan-style radicalism. Threats of local disorder growing out of America's Luzon intervention finally forced them into action. In early November 1898, hastily organized forces led by estate owners accepted the surrender of Spanish troops and officials. Forty-five delegates then assembled in Bacolod town. Within twenty-four hours they wrote a constitution, elected a president, and established a provisional government. The sham revolution took three days. The Negros Republic —affiliated with, but not part of, Aguinaldo's regime—lived for less than three months. It quietly passed away on February 2, 1899, when American ships and men appeared off Bacolod. President Aniceto Lacson immediately arranged a conference with the flotilla's commander and agreed to cooperate with the new colonial power. His conservative statesmanship, according to a blunt Filipino journalist, saved "sugar estates owned by the rich people of Negros from the ravages of an unnecessary war."[18]

If the charade preserved property, it failed to maintain domestic tranquillity.[19] Lacson's transparent opportunism alienated sizable segments of the island's restless population. Some villagers, many sugar workers, and practically all of Negros' small but growing middle class were repelled by the provisional government's blatant expediency. Expecting reforms, they had supported *hacenderos* in the effort to

17. LeRoy, *The Americans in the Philippines,* II, 108.
18. Sol H. Gwekoh, *Manila Times,* Feb. 7, 1966.
19. According to a Constabulary officer, "Negros suffered less from the insurrection and more from subsequent brigandage than any other island." White, 25.

throw off the Iberian yoke. When eighty-five days of "independence" brought no perceptible change, agrarian radicals and municipal nationalists recognized the hollow nature of their victory. Most of them were unwilling to accept a permanent administration dominated by "Spanish or half-Spanish landed proprietors."[20] Negros, consequently, teetered on the brink of anarchy when the Americans began their debarkation. The presence of United States troops in the *poblaciones* checked the revolutionary inclinations of bourgeois elements. Their appearance in the countryside, however, drove many villagers over the edge. Aside from *hacenderos,* Papa Isio and lesser *tulisanes* were the chief beneficiaries of the new political arrangement.[21]

Sigobela reaped his first harvest of plunder and converts following the November coup. The elimination of Spanish authorities enabled him to increase the intensity and frequency of Babailan raids on plantations. Successful pillage won additional recruits. By February 1899, Isio controlled several thousand experienced marauders—some of whom were *Guardia Civil* veterans. Elitist collaboration with the Americans completed the alienation process. The warm welcome received by the invaders, in effect, made allegiance to Sigobela the only available alternative to capitulation. Sensing the favorable shift in peasant opinion, he began to stress the glories of independence—a highly desirable condition which would usher in a "communistic paradise."[22] To underline his intentions, he also used an official seal carrying the legend *Gobierno Revolucionario de Negros.*[23] Papa Isio's spiritual and political appeal proved attractive to many humble Negrenses. During the first six months of 1899, he won the overt or covert support of poor people all over Negros.

Popular sympathy shielded Isio for the next eight years. Between 1899 and 1902, American occupation forces attempted to eliminate brigandage. Their field-manual campaign subjected Babailanes to unprecedented pressures. Municipalities and large estates were gar-

20. LeRoy, *The Americans in the Philippines,* II, 106.
21. Elitist collaboration with the United States made Sigobela the leader of nationalist forces in Negros. He received a colonel's commission from Aguinaldo's revolutionary government and occasional support from Katipuneros in neighboring Panay. For a brief account of his activities from 1899 to 1902, together with some of his official correspondence, see Chap. 7 of Taylor, *Insurgent Records,* II; and Exhibits 1315, 1316, and 1317.
22. LeRoy, *The Americans in the Philippines,* II, 107.
23. White, 85.

risoned to meet surprise attacks. Brash company commanders then penetrated mountain regions to destroy rebel food supplies and bases. Areas which had never been reconnoitered by Spanish patrols became familiar ground to the newcomers, whose tactics curtailed, but did not crush, Sigobela's movement. Compassionate villagers continued to provide cover, information, and provisions to the harried outlaws. Pope Isio and his disciplined followers finally yielded before obviously superior force and went underground to await auspicious developments.

In 1902, the United States Army's departure and the Philippine Constabulary's arrival convinced Sigobela that the moment of truth was at hand. In early October, scattered Babailan bands converged on mountain assembly points. Like most of his predecessors and many of his successors, the peasant leader believed that one spectacular act of terror could ignite a conflagration. He therefore commissioned his most reliable aid—a veteran brigand named Delmacio—to lead their followers in an all-out assault on Bacolod. Flames from the burning provincial capital—according to Sigobela's straightforward scenario —would signal a general uprising. Popular rebellion would topple the hated planters and mark the dawn of a new day for oppressed Negrenses. The liberation effort began on schedule. Delmacio advanced toward Bacolod in a righteous orgy of arson and pillage. Scores of villagers and field hands along his line of march joined the rebels. On October 30, however, Constabulary detachments intercepted the triumphant procession ten miles from its objective. Insular policemen not only routed the ragtag army, they also managed to capture Delmacio alive.[24] Two months later, he was tried for sedition, convicted, and publicly hanged. Isio and his followers never recovered from the defeat.

After 1902, Bacolod's defenders turned the tables on Papa Isio. Farsighted Constabulary officers exploited the organization's local renown by inaugurating a drive to earn the peasantry's respect. Slowly but surely the goal was achieved. Alert foot patrols checked rustling and petty thievery in the countryside. More importantly, company commanders stressed impartial law enforcement. For the first time in the history of Negros, villagers received something akin to justice

24. For an account of the uprising see *Report of the Philippine Commission, 1903,* III, 115.

from men in authority.[25] The subtle approach proved far more effective than a regiment of American soldiers. Khaki-and-red Constabulary uniforms gradually became welcome sights in the barrios. The personal relationship that developed between constables and hamlet people won over or neutralized Sigobela's secret sympathizers. When the lowlands were secure, American officers initiated a relentless manhunt for Pope Isio. In 1907, the worn-out brigand surrendered to his chief nemesis, Captain John White. His apprehension marked the demise of organized banditry on the island. Two years later a humane governor general commuted the pontiff's inevitable death sentence to life imprisonment. The grounds for clemency spoke volumes on a tragic era. Governor James Smith granted the reprieve to Dionisio Sigobela "because it appears that his mind is somewhat unbalanced."[26]

Isio's fate was less grim than that accorded most of his papal contemporaries. Elsewhere in the archiepelgo compassion played a minor role in the drive to stamp out religious brigands. Spiritual convulsions, together with government repressive measures, reached their violent apogee in Samar. Economically, the island represented the antithesis of Negros. Cursed by typhoons, fevers, mountains, rain forests, and swamps, the forbidding place defied nineteenth-century technology. Third-largest land mass in the Philippines, Samar in 1900 boasted fewer than ten kilometers of barely passable roads.[27] Horse trails to the interior were nonexistent. Footpaths, known only to primitive hunters and adventurous *remontados,* were the sole means of crossing the island. Communications between widely spaced coastal towns took place via fishing boats and occasional interisland vessels. Physically, Samar added up to little more than an ideal refuge for fugitives from the law.

The island was also blighted by social discord. Long before the revolutionary decade, linguistic and religious distinctions divided lowlanders and mountain people.[28] Economic friction intensified the

25. Wealth ceased to provide legal immunity. For a description of an intricate murder case which ended with the imprisonment of a prominent citizen, see White, 112–113.
26. National Archives of the United States, Bureau of Insular Affairs, File Enclosure 19077. Materials from the National Archives will be cited hereafter as N.A., B.I.A., F.E.
27. Worcester and Hayden, *Philippines Past and Present,* I, 394.
28. For a provocative discussion of conditions on the island together with the

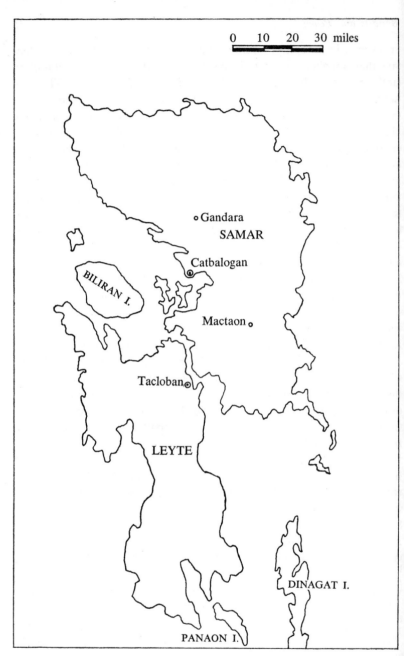

4. The Eastern Visayas, 1900

incipient feud. Cebuano-speaking landowners and tradesmen, conversant with Catholicism and other elements of Iberian culture, dominated seaside towns. *Kaingin* (slash and burn) cultivators, fluent only in Waray-Waray and devoutly loyal to syncretistic folk cults, presided over inhabitable portions of the rugged interior. A kind of no-man's land, occupied primarily by voracious leeches and anemic wild hogs, separated the competing cultures. Inlanders seldom traversed it. When sufficient *abaca* had been accumulated, however, back-country farmers tediously packed the cash crop to coastal markets. Their sojourns in the *municipios* were seldom rewarding. Fast-talking hemp merchants usually fleeced the deliberate peasants, while rice retailers and other townspeople cheated or humiliated them at every turn. A tropical cold war of sorts, characterized by wary coexistence, developed. Occasionally, it exploded into individual or collective acts of violence. Sporadic brigandage became the hill man's favorite weapon against his coastal tormentors. The *pueblos* responded with increasing reliance on policemen, civil guards, criminal courts, jails, and penal colonies. By 1896, the escalating conflict had transformed Samar into a breeding ground for social bandits.

The Filipino-American War converted the hill people into implacable guerrillas. Until 1901, Samar remained a political and military backwater. Remoteness, in fact, determined its fate. Retreating General Vicente Lukban selected the trackless interior as his final redoubt. Organized hostilities in the Visayas, consequently, reached their frenzied, no-quarter climax on the "evil-looking humpbacked island."[29] Driven to savagery, cornered revolutionaries and anxious invaders both resorted to unspeakable atrocities. Lukban did not surrender until February 1902. In the meantime, United States Marines, sailors, and soldiers—proceeding on explicit orders—attempted to turn Samar into a "howling wilderness."[30] Punished to the breaking point,

---

uprising which grew out of them see Richard Arens, S.V.D., "The Early Pulahan Movement in Samar and Leyte," *Journal of History*, VII (1959), 303–371. For a description of folk beliefs in the region see also his "Witches and Witchcraft in Leyte and Samar Islands, Philippines."

29. The description came from Major L. W. T. Waller, who commanded the marine force on Samar. J. L. Schott, *The Ordeal of Samar* (Indianapolis, Ind., 1964), 4.

30. Brigadier General Jacob Smith coined the infamous phrase. For an analysis of American military strategy and tactics in the Islands, see John Gates, *Schoolbooks and Krags: The U.S. Army in the Philippines, 1898–1902* (Westport, Conn., 1973).

coastal inhabitants accepted American sovereignty and attempted to refashion their shattered world. Back-country residents, however, continued to resist. Mauled beyond rational responses, they resorted to mysticism.[31] A bizarre peasant uprising—shot through with supernaturalistic impulses—broke out in 1902. The spectacular eruption brought additional notoriety to the wracked island. In Manila, it became known as "Bloody Samar."

Symptoms of the new rebellion had been disguised by the Revolution's death agonies. Late in 1902, armed bands began to raid coastal *sitios* and barrios. American authorities classified the depredations as banditry and traced them to scavengers from Lukban's defunct army. Eager to rid the island of martial law and occupation troops, colonial officials established a civilian administration headed by Filipino personnel. As quickly as possible, they also replaced hard-bitten American combat units with locally recruited constabularymen. The ameliorative gestures did not pacify Samar. If anything, Filipinization promoted greater discord. Manila's assessment of the situation, in short, had been grossly inaccurate. A few intransigent *"insurrectos"* commanded small groups of foragers, but most of the raiders— leaders and followers alike—came from seething mountain villages. The unrest represented the opening skirmishes of a local civil war.

The conflict's patterns bore little if any resemblance to Lukban's final effort. Prominent citizens, for example, played no role in the dissident movement. *Principales,* in fact, soon became its primary targets.[32] Bandits, never-say-die common soldiers, ex-convicts, and Dios-Dios divines directed the rebels. Communal governments—of, by, and for the poor—appeared throughout the interior. The *barangay*-like regimes acted as semiautonomous units in larger, less formal coalitions. Neither national independence nor republicanism was a unifying motive. Back-country *supremos* did not emulate elitist patriots by calling themselves *presidentes* and *coronels;* rather, hearkening back to prerevolutionary clarities, they appropriated sacred titles such as "First Teacher" or "Pope,"[33] and rallied the hill people to a holy crusade against their coastal exploiters. They built unity around spiri-

---

31. A revealing fictional account of the uprising was written by an American schoolteacher who served on Samar. Elinor Chamberlain, *The Far Command* (New York, 1952).
32. *Report of the Philippine Commission, 1903,* III, 115.
33. *Ibid.,* 121.

tual themes. Thatched *iglesias,* accordingly, became the developing insurrection's command posts. Militant preachers used the chapels to disseminate anarchistic doctrines, to distribute *anting-anting,* and to arouse congregations to martial heights. Dedicated *"soldados"* left the services to march against lowland towns. Wearing nondescript red uniforms emblazoned with white crosses and fighting with the ferocity of men convinced of their own invulnerability,[34] the marauders dismayed the constables and townspeople, who tagged the gaudy terrorists "Pulajanes." The scarlet label stuck. It soon became a catchall category for peasant religious rebels throughout the eastern Visayas.

There was no dearth of claimants to the contemptuous designation. Pulajan successes encouraged similar movements in Leyte and Bohol. By late 1903, Samar's pontiffs commanded 7,000 disciplined bolomen. Across San Juanico Strait spreading discord produced comparable results. By the same date, Leyte's rising popes controlled roughly half that number. Sorely outnumbered Constabulary companies could not keep pace with caroming violence on either side of the narrow strip of water. Requests for assistance brought sizable police reinforcements to both islands, but the additional contingents were unable to contain the sprawling rebellion. Pulajan pyromania reached its zenith in 1904. During a harrowing two months, roving incendiaries burned out fifty-three communities in Samar alone and kidnapped many of the fleeing survivors. When red-garbed arsonists began to threaten the provincial capital, Manila concluded the time had come for concerted action. Late in 1904, Filipinization was reluctantly cast aside. An American governor, an American general, and United States Army regulars landed at Catbalogan. Their arrival marked the formal beginning of the "Pulajan Campaign."

It raged for two years. American officers stationed troops in threatened municipalities and ordered mobile Constabulary and Army units to take the offensive. Ambushes, counterambushes, and hand-to-hand combat characterized the primitive war of attrition. Both sides suffered frightfully. By late 1905, Constabulary casualty rates had soared. Grim statistics from Samar led United States life insurance companies to refuse policies to junior officers bound for the eastern Visayas, and enlisted recruiting dipped below replacement levels. But the Pulajanes found themselves in worse straits. Patrols from the coast combed the

---

34. Pulajan tactics were discussed in Victor Hurley, *Jungle Patrol: The Story of the Philippine Constabulary* (New York, 1938), 123–151.

interior. Remote villages and *sitios,* together with their *iglesias* and rice hoards, went up in flames. Hill residents, furthermore, were subjected to reconcentration in lowland centers. With women, children, and infirm old people forcibly removed, constables and soldiers shot or arrested every adult male they encountered in the back country. By early 1906, hundreds of Pulajanes had been killed, and thousands had been thrown into improvised stockades.[35] Government tactics, in short, reduced the once robust revitalization effort to a rattling skeleton.

With the movement apparently broken, Governor George Curry took steps to end the carnage. Ordered to establish a "firm and just" provincial administration, the emergency executive began to stress amelioration. Pulajan prisoners were given land and relocated in new communities. Efforts were also made to improve relations between linguistic and economic groups. In March 1906, Curry opened peace negotiations with the remaining dissidents. The delicate diplomacy led to an armistice agreement. On March 24, constabularymen, soldiers, and provincial dignitaries assembled in the mountain *sitio* of Mactaon. Samar's last organized Pulajan band also arrived on schedule. Since everything was proceeding satisfactorily, Curry and his companions relaxed. One relieved American even set up a camera to record the historic moment. When the long file of xenophobes turned to face the victors something went wrong. Brandishing razor-sharp bolos, the *soldados militantes* let out a bloodcurdling battle cry and attacked. The melee was over in minutes. An incredulous governor surveyed the bloodsoaked surrender site and issued orders to renew hostilities. Aside from dead and wounded, the only tangible result of Curry's bargaining was a blurred photograph of charging Pulajanes.[36]

The "Mactaon Massacre" demolished any hopes that internecine strife might be peacefully resolved. Constables and soldiers scoured the back country of Samar and Leyte for fleeing pontiffs. Pope Pablo and most of his exhausted followers—participants in the bloodbath at Mactaon—were killed in November 1906. Papa Faustino, Leyte's

35. According to Constabulary statistics, 300 Pulajanes were killed and 6,400 were captured; of the latter, five received death sentences, forty drew long prison terms, and fifty were assigned to provincial jails. The remainder were released after taking oaths of allegiance to the United States. Many were resettled in new communities. *Report of the Philippine Commission, 1906* (Washington, D.C.), II, 434.

36. For a Constabulary account of the incident, see the organization's monthly journal, *Khaki and Red* (Manila), July 1931, 40–41.

chief redeemer, fell in 1907. Their demise ended organized resistance in the eastern Visayas. With the islands pacified, Curry and American regulars returned to Manila. The Constabulary stayed in the field. Remorseless constables tracked down Otoy, Samar's last pope, in 1911. His arrest eradicated the remaining tendencies toward banditry. Nothing of lasting significance came out of the tragic decade: the fighting ended; watered-down reforms trickled from Catbalogan; order, of sorts, prevailed. In reality, however, the tranquillity that settled over Samar and Leyte was akin to the peace of death.

Babailan and Pulajan upheavals soon degenerated into savage struggles. In each instance, social antipathies became so pronounced that innocent villagers suffered grievously. Sectarian sadism gradually turned hamlet dwellers against both movements.[37] In oversimplified terms, Visayan peasants accepted the colonial government because it represented a lesser evil. North of Manila religious unrest developed along more discriminating lines. Santa Iglesia outbursts never deteriorated to the level of promiscuous cruelty. The organization's only foes were Americans, *hacenderos,* Filipino officials, constables, and municipal policemen. Loving the church for the enemies it made, barrio people throughout central Luzon gave wholehearted support to the sect. Dissident spiritual and military leaders, furthermore, retained *tao* loyalties to the bitter end. The lengthy conflict between provincial authorities and the Santa Iglesia, accordingly, took on many of the qualities of a regional folk epic.

Again, the movement sprang from prerevolutionary undercurrents. Around 1890, a devout bandit named Gabino won a loyal following among the villagers of Pampanga.[38] Operating from Mount Arayat's graceful slopes, the cult leader challenged Iberian authority from San Fernando town to southern Tarlac. In 1893, *Guardia Civil* detachments caught up with the elusive *supremo.* Shortly after his arrest he was executed by a Spanish firing squad. Gabinastas went into hiding but remained loyal to their leader's egalitarian principles. Late in 1894 the movement reemerged under the name Santa Iglesia. Gabino's

37. Babailanes and Pulajanes both resorted to extreme cruelty in their campaigns to influence uncommitted villagers. W. Cameron Forbes recorded the punishment of peasants who cooperated with the Constabulary. People who led government patrols had their Achilles tendons severed; those who gave information to an American officer had their "lips . . . cut off." Forbes, "Journal," I, 139.

38. Hurley, 121.

former disciples dominated hamlet congregations. Members carried crosses and rosaries and followed daily rituals similar to those of Guardia de Honor. During the Revolution and the Filipino-American War branches of the heterodox spiritual associations apparently mingled. When the United States Army cracked down on Cabaruan and Santa Ana, some Honor Guards—particularly in Nueva Ecija— affiliated themselves with the Holy Church. The organization would probably have escaped official notice if a charismatic figure had not materialized.

Felipe Salvador, who took over direction of the Santa Iglesia in 1902, was no ordinary *provinciano*. By his own admission, he lived as an outlaw during the decade before 1896.[39] The conflict with Spain permitted him to achieve a measure of respectability. Among other things, he carried out a successful raid on the Spanish garrison at Dagupan, Pangasinan, a feat that yielded 100 Mauser rifles.[40] It also supplied Salvador with a heroic reputation and led directly to a colonel's commission in the revolutionary army. The former bandit served as a guerrilla officer until late 1901, when he was captured by an American unit in Nueva Ecija. Fortunately for Salvador, his provincial jailers recognized neither the rank nor the significance of their prisoner. Early the next year, while being marched with other *insurrectos* to Bilibid Prison, he slipped away from the straggling column and evaded Constabulary guards. The daring escape added a new dimension to his swashbuckling image.

Salvador's regional fame made him the natural rallying point for a popular movement. With unerring insight into peasant ways and aspirations, he exploited every opening.[41] He first returned to his pre-revolutionary haunts in Pampanga province. After establishing a base on Mount Arayat and recuperating from the physical ravages of five strife-filled years, he began to circulate through the villages of central Luzon. Half a decade of uninterrupted stress had transformed Salvador. Dropping the guise of a dashing filibuster, he strode forth armed with the moral rectitude and righteous fury of an Old Testament prophet. Displaying shoulder-length hair, Biblical attire, and an impressive crucifix, he was accompanied by twenty-four similarly ap-

39. Salvador was interviewed shortly before his death. See Luther Parker, "Why Colorums?" *Philippines Free Press,* Feb., 7, 1931, 21.

40. Hurley, 122.

41. For interesting insights into Salvador's activities see Ignacio Villamor, *Criminality in the Philippine Islands* (Manila, 1909), 51–52.

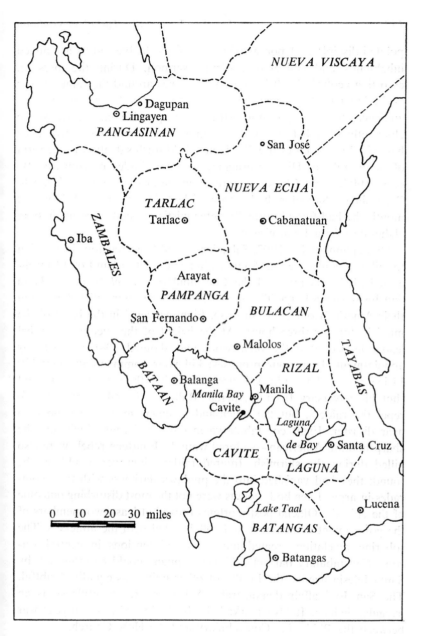

5. Central Luzon, 1900

pointed disciples.[42] Upon arriving in a barrio he blessed its assembled
inhabitants and delivered a stirring sermon. During the message,
escorting acolytes knelt in concentric circles around the saintly figure
—the inner twelve facing the speaker, the outer dozen staring at his
audience. Salvador's oratory struck a responsive chord. He spoke
eloquently of a better world—an imminent utopia which would be
heralded by a "rain of fire."[43] He also held forth salvation in the form
of Santa Iglesia. His performance won multitudes of converts. By
early 1903, Holy Church congregations flourished from Bulacan to
Pangasinan. Salvador had accomplished his purpose. Within six
months he had forged normally antagonistic peasant elements into an
elaborate spiritual conspiracy.

On September 16, 1903, Salvador moved from religious inspiration
to military confrontation. Shortly after midnight, a band of 140 well-
armed dissidents attacked the Constabulary *cuartel* (compound) in
San José, Nueva Ecija. The assault caught forty-four enlisted men and
their American officer by surprise. Fighting raged in the heart of the
municipality for three hours. At the height of the encounter a rebel
leader leaped atop the breastwork and shouted, "We are here by
appointment; keep your promises; kill your commanding officer!"[44]
Firing ceased. The sudden silence ended when the menaced lieutenant
shot his adversary from his perch. Rallying constables managed to
repel the raiders, but the touch-and-go engagement added up to a
near disaster. Eight constabularymen died, and four—including the
sharpshooting American—suffered wounds. Fourteen rebels were also
killed during the skirmish. Injured raiders, however, could not be
found; they had vanished into the predawn darkness with their comrades-in-arms. Even body counts were not the most disturbing outcome
of the episode. Official post-mortems proved at least two members of
the government detachment had collaborated with the attackers. The
sobering revelation created unprecedented tensions in central Luzon's Constabulary barracks. If one company could be infiltrated by
Santa Iglesia agents, the loyalty of other units was equally doubtful.
The San José affair demonstrated Salvador's resourcefulness as an
irregular fighter. It also marked the beginning of a seven-year war
between the Philippine Constabulary and the Holy Church.

42. Proselytizing techniques are discussed in Coats, 201–202.
43. Hurley, 122.
44. *Report of the Philippine Commission, 1904*, III, 71.

Neither side violated the rules of the game. While constables labored to win the peasantry's confidence, Salvador and his aides played their Robin Hood parts to the hilt. Armed forays were restricted to symbols of law and order. Systematic robbery complemented attacks on constabularymen and municipal police. Wealth confiscated from privileged people, furthermore, was frequently redistributed to needy *taos*.[45] Villagers in Bulacan, Pampanga, Tarlac, Nueva Ecija, and Pangasinan, therefore, aligned themselves with Santa Iglesia. "All the population," lamented a district inspector, "are in sympathy and the majority in some manner connected with this movement."[46] Salvador's performance kept the Constabulary in the unenviable position of the sheriff of Nottingham. Try as they might, men in khaki and red could not extricate themselves from villainous roles. Peasants, peculiarly enough, derived benefits from the competition, since logic compelled both constables and cultists to vie for the affections of barrio people. Central Luzon's inhabitants, in all likelihood, were the only rural citizens in the archipelago to profit from religious insurgency.

More than any other factor Salvador's furtive tactics insured Santa Iglesia's longevity. He avoided large-scale challenges comparable to those of the Pulajanes. Instead, he waged a classic "little war." By restraining the omnipotent delusions of his followers, he restricted the level of government reaction. Brief, intense fighting around carefully selected targets was followed by long periods of relative inactivity. When the Constabulary had been lulled into a false sense of security, Salvador would strike again. The pattern of harassment was utterly unpredictable. It ranged from carefully planned expeditions for firearms and ammunition to devious tactics such as poisoning the food of celebrating constabularymen.[47] The clandestine nature of the operation exacted a psychological toll among beleaguered provincial administrators. American Constabulary officers, for example, frequently opened their annual report on the district with the phrase, "Felipe Salvador, the well-known bandit leader . . . has been lurking . . . in the low and swampy regions of Nueva Ecija . . . and around Mount Arayat."[48]

45. John B. Devins, *An Observer in the Philippines* (New York, 1905), 83.
46. *Report of the Philippine Commission, 1904*, III, 72.
47. In 1903, a patrol was poisoned while dining in a barrio lieutenant's home. Asked, "Why did you poison the soldiers?" He replied, "Salvador told me to do it." Devins, 169.
48. *Annual Report of the Director of Constabulary, 1909* (Manila, 1910), 5.

Salvador, however, did not waste his time lying in wait for the authorities. He carried on his religious activities quite openly. Friendly villagers simply screened his presence from prying officials. Moving regularly between southern Bulacan and northern Pangasinan, Salvador provided the peasantry with constant inspiration. His recommendations pertained to a vast range of topics. In addition to dispensing wisdom on spiritual and domestic matters, he supplied advice on farming, together with uncannily accurate information on tropical storms.[49] The weather forecasts convinced doubting Thomases of his near-divinity. Hamlet dwellers believed the prognostications were derived from regular conversations with God. Barrio people, consequently, gave their all to the *supremo,* who, like other charismatic leaders, acquired an honorific title, "Apong Ipe." According to Constabulary records, many farm couples offered their daughters to the peregrinating mystic: the gesture originated in a belief that sexual unions involving Salvador and village maidens would produce a Malayan messiah to lead "Filipinos of heart and face" out of the alien wilderness. Periodically, the prophet returned to Mount Arayat. Large groups of *taos* from surrounding plains sometimes assembled there for elaborate rites. The pilgrimages usually signaled a fresh outburst of sectarian militancy.

After the San José affair, Felipe Salvador no longer took part in Santa Iglesia forays. He helped plan the military ventures, but that was the extent of his personal involvement. Holy Church marauders marched to battle under the authority of a veteran freebooter named Manuel García. Known to admiring cultists as "Capitán Tui," the strutting field commander personified rustic conceptions of courage. Friend and foe alike, for example, referred to him as a *juramentado.*[50] He specialized in witty taunts and vocal challenges to his enemies. Like other *ladrones fanáticos,* García possessed total faith in personal *anting-anting.* The lank-haired Capitán wore a bronze medal of the Holy Trinity on his forehead and carried an enchanted cross. When action was joined, García ignored government volleys. Completely fearless, he stood erect, chest bared to the opposition, and directed his

49. The Constabulary was convinced that Salvador's meteorological data came from the old Spanish Weather Bureau in Manila. *Report of the Philippine Commission, 1906,* III, 55.

50. The Spanish term was usually applied to amuck Moslems who carried out suicidal attacks on Christians. Its application to García revealed his martial qualities. His bellicose style is described in Coats, 208–209.

soldados militantes with the flair of a tribal chieftain. He was, by all testimony, an extremely good man in a fight. Seldom, if ever, did he return to Arayat without achieving his purpose. Peasants, naturally enough, concluded that Salvador and García constituted an unbeatable combination. Privately, many enlisted constables must have held the same opinion.

In 1906, popular illusions concerning the leadership's invulnerability were shattered. Salvador and his aides committed their first—and last—strategic blunder. On April 16, Manuel García led eighty bolomen in a twilight assault on the Constabulary *cuartel* in Malolos, Bulacan.[51] Capitán Tui captured his objective and made off with the detachment's arms and ammunition. Similar attacks in other provinces occurred the same night, though none achieved its goal. The coordinated offensive—designed again to provoke a general uprising—stimulated massive government responses. Constabulary headquarters in Manila threw every available man into the field. Instead of fading away, as they had always done in the past, the long-haired rebels chose to fight. For the next eight weeks, running battles flared across the length and breadth of seven provinces.[52] The struggle ended in a sectarian catastrophe. Out-gunned "fuzzy-wuzzies"—as the dissenters were labeled by Manila's Kiplingesque journalists—fell by the score. Fate even caught up with García and his band. On July 9, 1906, an encounter across Bulacan's rain-drenched rice paddies enabled constabularymen to kill Capitán Tui and many of his followers. García's death terminated the uprising. It also brought an end to Santa Iglesia depredations in central Luzon.

To the constables who pursued him, Felipe Salvador seemed to have nine lives. He remained at large for the next four years. As in the past, sympathetic villagers shielded the aging *supremo* from inquisitive authorities. The best measure of hamlet loyalty was the fact that a two-thousand-peso reward for information leading to his arrest went unclaimed. Now and then rumors of Santa Iglesia plots spread through the region's municipalities. The Holy Church, however, had suffered an irreversible defeat. Hard-pressed *soldados militantes* broke

51. *Report of the Philippine Commission, 1906*, II, 240.
52. Skirmishes broke out in Cavite, Rizal, Bulacan, Pampanga, Tarlac, Nueva Ecija, and Pangasinan. The fact that Salvador was able to attract followers from four distinct dialect groups demonstrated the universality of his appeal. The uprising is discussed in Coats, 209–213.

up into smaller and smaller bands, but Constabulary patrols rounded them up one by one. Salvador became an isolated symbol of defiance in a pacified Philippines. The times—if not the people—turned against him. On July 24, 1910, he and his remaining acolytes were surprised by constabularymen near barrio San Isidro, Pampanga.[53] He made no effort to resist. Tried and convicted for murder and sedition, Salvador was transferred to Bilibid Prison to await execution. Appeals to Malacañan Palace for commutation of the death sentence fell on deaf ears. Late in 1911, the greatest of the religious brigands ascended a scaffold. Reverent and resilient to the end, he clutched a worn Bible until the trap was sprung.

Salvador's demise marked the close of a stormy era. After 1910, *tulisanismo* dwindled to manageable proportions. Rural lawlessness, in fact, returned to thoroughly prosaic patterns. Between 1911 and 1920, occasional rustling, thievery, and crimes of passion constituted the most significant interruptions of provincial peace. Many Americans and urban Filipinos convinced themselves that an age of tranquillity was at hand. Official optimism, unfortunately, was unjustified. It rested on a superficial belief that agrarian unrest emanated from circumstances peculiar to the revolutionary epoch. It also stemmed from the comfortable assumption that local uprisings were by-products of peasant ignorance. Filipinization and public education were expected to eradicate both sources of discord. Time and progress, according to Washington's colonial scenario, would eliminate "the bandit microbe in the system of the ordinary 'tao.' "[54]

Manila's diagnosis ignored the countryside's turbulent history. American administrators and Filipino politicians confused fatigue with popular concurrence. Despite crushing defeats and the annihilation of local champions, the heritage of spiritual dissent was not dead. Babailanes, Pulajanes, Salvadoristas, and less persistent religious rebels had responded to stress in the manner of their ancestors. Like the seventeenth-century hamlet dwellers who rallied to Tamblot and Tapar, many turn-of-the-century villagers sought supernatural answers to the problems of barrio life. Between 1923 and 1931, some of their sons and daughters resorted to similar solutions. The otherworldly renaissance again demonstrated the little tradition's tenacity.

53. N.A., B.I.A., F.E. 4865-51.
54. *Report of the Philippine Commission, 1904*, III, 87.

PART III

MYSTICISM REVISITED

And every one who was in distress, and every one who was in debt, and every one who was discontented, gathered to him; and he became captain over them. And there were with him about four hundred men.

I Samuel 22 : 2

CHAPTER 7

Colorumism

After 1911 relative peace prevailed in the provinces. Many Americans attributed improving circumstances to the delayed impact of enlightened colonial policies. Developing public health and education programs, the effects of the "Friar Land" liquidations, and an increase in the number of pioneer settlements, unquestionably helped to calm the rural scene.[1] More significantly perhaps, general exhaustion, disillusionment among barrio nonconformists, and effective police work by the Philippine Constabulary combined to reduce levels of disorder. Comparative stability, however, did not signal an end to discord. Unlike the Westernized elite and the emerging middle class, peasant dissenters refused to capitulate. An irreconcilable minority shifted from overt to covert rebellion. Between 1911 and 1920, accordingly, esoteric societies and conspiratorial sects proliferated in the countryside. The underground organizations prolonged the heritage of peasant resistance to external authority and provided protective covering for a new generation of potential redeemers committed to violent rectification efforts. After 1923 the movements surfaced in a series of abortive tumults. The unforeseen rebirth of agrarian unrest destroyed official delusions of evolving tranquillity and inaugurated a new era of turbulence.

The recrudescence worried colonial administrators and irritated prominent *Nacionalistas*. Spokesmen for both groups stressed the obvious advantages of Filipino-American collaboration and tended to dismiss rural rebellions as unimportant local phenomena attributable

---

1. One scholar saw a connection between land policy and rural protests. Noting a decline by 1919 in the disposal of former church holdings, he observed, "The year in which there was a sudden slump in the sale of friar lands marked . . . . the beginning of the present agrarian unrest," Macaraig, *Social Problems*, 249.

in large part to peasant naiveté or to the nefarious activities of a few self-styled leaders. Manila's attempt to denigrate the aims and techniques of dissenters led to serious misinterpretations concerning the course of provincial affairs. Discord was traced to malcontented minorities. Uprisings were ascribed to mass fantasies invented by hamlet demagogues. Dissident village movements of all persuasions, moreover, were lumped together in a category far beyond the limits of the evolutionary political style then current in the insular capital. Responsible Americans and Filipinos, in brief, failed to recognize either the depth or the diversity of hamlet alienation.

The first indication of continuing tension appeared in an unlikely location. A sparsely settled, and theretofore socially untroubled, corner of Mindanao erupted in antigovernment violence. The origins of the flare-up were neither political nor economic but emanated, instead, from religious friction. Rivalry between Catholics, Aglipayans, and Colorums split the village populations of Surigao and Agusan provinces into contending camps. Factional competition gradually intensified to the point where secular authorities became involved. Efforts by municipal police and the Constabulary to curtail sectarian activities—particularly the folk rites of the Colorum group—led to clashes between cultists and representatives of the state. In 1924 accumulated frustrations exploded into bloody insurrection.

As was the case with previous rural difficulties, the roots of the conflict ran back into earlier times. Between 1910 and 1920 the islands of Siargao and Bucas Grande off the northeastern tip of Mindanao became the focal points of a popular challenge to the religious status quo. Abrasiveness occurred first in the Bucas Grande community of Socorro. Displeasure with the parish priest provoked a large portion of the population to abandon Catholicism.[2] By 1917 energetic Aglipayan missionaries had won over 90 per cent of Bucas Grande's people. Before the Independent Churchmen could consolidate their gains, however, they were confronted by an unexpected

2. For primary materials on the Colorum uprising of 1924, gratitude must be extended to John and Maria Miller. During 1965–1967, Mr. Miller served as a Peace Corps Volunteer in Surigao del Norte province. Interested in the local history, the couple talked with residents, read reports of past events, and collected pertinent documents from Constabulary officers. Much of the credit for this account, therefore, belongs to the Millers and to the hospitable people of Surigao who talked freely with them. Information from the file will be cited as Miller Papers (New Concord, O.).

rival for peasant affections. Learning of wholesale defections from the Church of Rome, Laureano Solamo—the *supremo* of Visayan Colorums—sent a group of emissaries to Bucas Grande. Their reports convinced him that the situation was ideally suited to a major conversion effort. Late in 1918, consequently, *halens* (Colorum immigrants) from Bohol, Leyte, Samar, and Cebu began to arrive on both the mainland and the offshore islands.[3] Within two years the newcomers had established enclaves in Misamis, Agusan, and Surigao provinces. But Solamo's lieutenants enjoyed their greatest success on Bucas Grande. By early 1921 all the island's Catholic defectors had affiliated themselves with the folk faith.

While provincial authorities regarded the sect as an outlandish religious expression, its original activities provided no ground for intervention. Organized for devotions to the "Sacred Heart of Jesus and the Immaculate Heart of Mary," the cult subjected converts to rigid discipline. Initiates were required to rid themselves of personal property and were urged to settle in tightly organized villages. On Bucas Grande, for example, the barrios of Socorro and Pamosaingan became self-sufficient Colorum settlements.[4] Spiritual leaders assembled residents for compulsory prayers at 4:00 A.M. and 6:00 P.M. Between morning and evening devotions, inhabitants labored at assigned tasks—primarily farming, fishing, and lumbering. Yields from the communal enterprises were divided equally among villagers. One month out of each year, moreover, was set aside for mutual-assistance projects such as house construction. Dwellings were identical in size and shape. In every way the hamlets added up to intriguing examples of peasant utopianism.

Asceticism reinformed Colorum egalitarianism. Prohibitions developed against smoking, drinking, dancing, cursing, and gambling. Elaborate restrictions also regulated sexual activities. Segregated labor and housing patterns, in fact, reflected antipathy toward all fleshly pleasures. Contacts between men and women occurred only occasionally. Single males and females lived in supervised dormitories at

3. The Constabulary traced later difficulties to "unstable elements" who migrated from Pulajan areas in Samar and Leyte. H. H. Elarth, *The Story of the Philippine Constabulary* (Los Angeles, 1949), 60.
4. Miller Papers, "An Interview with Mr. Pablo Cosigna," Surigao, Jan. 24, 1966, 1. Mr. Cosigna and his father were residents of Socorro and were forced to accept Colorumism. Unless otherwise indicated, information on religious and social practices will be drawn from the "Cosigna Interview."

opposite ends of Colorum communities. Married couples and their younger offspring occupied intervening structures. Courtship of either the formal or informal variety was forbidden. *Pators,* as congregation leaders were called, completed all marital arrangements with parents of potential brides and grooms. Frequently, young people were not even consulted about prospective mates. When negotiations had been concluded the *pator* conducted wedding services and assigned the united couples to domiciles in the married quarter.

Spiritual relationships were as stringently governed as social and economic conduct. Colorums throughout the eastern Visayas and northern Mindanano recognized the ultimate authority of Laureano Solamo. From his ornate headquarters near Cebu City, the *supremo* controlled far-flung sectarians via a hierarchical chain of command.[5] A veteran revivalist named Felix Bernales directed Solamo's Mindanao followers.[6] Known as "Lantayug." Bernales demanded and received total devotion. Juan Bajao, another Cebuano, acted as liaison between the regional leader and local lieutenants. *Pators* oversaw the destinies of individual congregations, which were composed ideally of 156 adults. Church groups, in turn, broke down into twelve smaller units, called *decorians,* each consisting of a headman and twelve disciples.

Mystery bound the complicated structure together. Like other Colorum sects in southern and central Luzon. Solamo's followers abided by intricate creeds derived directly or indirectly from the confused legacies of Apolinario de la Cruz and his charismatic successors. The revolutionary era, however, had added some distinctly new features to the syncretistic faiths. During the quarter-century since 1896, village cultists had elevated a group of fallen patriots—particularly

5. Solamo claimed 180,000 peasant followers. He owned real estate and several houses in Carmen, a suburb of Cebu City, together with a well-patronized dance hall and a popular cockpit. He based his varied operations in a palatial three-story structure in Carmen, which devotees believed would survive the deluge. An interviewer described Solamo as a "short, stout, sissylooking fellow who seeks the company of the fair sex rather than men." Known to his Visayan disciples as "Tatang" (Father), he was usually escorted by two brawny female bodyguards. For further details on the cult leader, see Pablo N. Pimentel, "Tatang," *Philippines Free Press,* July 2, 1927, 2, 8.

6. Bernales, who was sixty-three years old when he arrived in Socorro, had been involved in several scrapes with the authorities. Among other entries on his crowded police records was an arrest for posing with his mistress as "King and Queen of the Philippines." *Manila Daily Bulletin,* April 25, 1924.

José Rizal and Andres Bonifacio—to the status of divine or semi-divine beings.[7] In the minds of many barrio people, Rizal exerted a heavenly influence comparable to that of Jesus Christ. The revolutionary martyr's "Second Coming," according to hamlet believers, would initiate a final struggle to achieve social equity. His imminent return, furthermore, constituted the major premise in their articles of faith.

Bernales, or Lantayug, personified the myth. Ignoring conventional designations such as "Papa," he proclaimed himself a reincarnation of José Rizal.[8] Under any circumstances, the "Malayan Messiah's" alleged reappearance would have been enough to cause profound unrest. Lantayug, however, did not limit his performance to dramatic poses. He reinforced peasant credulity with predictions of universal calamity. The earth and its occupants, Bernales said, teetered on the brink of disaster. Epidemics, flame, floods, and fratricidal war would scourge mankind. Only Bucas Grande's most dedicated inhabitants could hope to escape unscathed. Survivors would be called upon to construct a new order on corruption's sodden ashes. Socorro, Lantayug promised, would emerge as the "Eternal City" of a theocratic paradise. Within its shining precincts, José Rizal, sovereign over all, would dispense justice and well-being from a golden throne.[9]

Visions of the approaching apocalypse exerted a growing influence over Colorum behavior. Preparations for doomsday, in fact, soon absorbed most sectarian energies. Lantayug's followers began to coerce acquaintances and relatives into the expanding movement. By 1922 forced conversions were occurring regularly throughout northeastern Mindanao. Reluctant initiates, called "Judases," were subjected to the same worldly asceticism and spiritual discipline endured by volunteers. Devotees who did not live on Bucas Grande were required to make pilgrimages to the sacred isle. There, visitors joined residents in nightly ablutions. Candlelit bathing tanks, fed by "divine springs" and equipped with powerful *anting-anting,* received the faithful between

7. For information on the origins and development of "Rizalism" see Marcelino Foronda, "The Canonization of Rizal," *Journal of History,* VIII (1960), 1–48; and *Cults Honoring Rizal* (Manila, 1961).
8. Many of his followers, however, addressed him as "Papa Indong." N.A., B.I.A., F.E. 4865-A-57.
9. For an unsympathetic account of the prophecies and the uprising, see Mayo, *Isles of Fear,* 189–195.

dusk and dawn.[10] Baptismal functionaries, called *tapales,* presided over the eerie ceremony. They immersed pilgrims in holy waters and anointed them with oils. The process, Colorums believed, washed away illness and sin. It also assured safe passage into Lantayug's brave new world.

Until 1922, the sect attracted scant attention from provincial or insular authorities. In that year, however, several factors combined to arouse official suspicions. The cult's rapid growth was a primary source of worry. Surigao's Catholic politicians and civil servants became uneasy over the widespread acceptance of Lantayug's eschatological doctrines. Fearing his "theology's" social implications and leery of his outspoken anti-Catholicism, they began to pry into Colorum practices. Municipal administrators quickly discovered a perceptible decline in annual revenues. They attributed the decrease, quite legitimately, to sectarian refusal to pay taxes. Public health officers also registered formal complaints concerning the unsanitary and potentially hazardous state of Bucas Grande's bathing facilities. Landowners railed against confiscatory views on property and expressed alarm regarding the number of forced conversions in Surigao and Agusan. Policemen, perhaps inevitably, concluded that Lantayug's operation was little more than a transparent extortion racket. Early in 1923, therefore, town prosecutors began to seek evidence linking the regional leader to *estafa* (swindling) or some other form of subtle criminality.

Surveillance provoked Colorum resistance. Small Constabulary patrols from provincial headquarters in Surigao town started to reconnoiter Bucas Grande. The irregular visits generated concern in Socorro and Pamosaingan. Some constables, according to hamlet dwellers, abused their authority by insulting residents; others stole pigs and chickens. On at least one occasion, a scuffle broke out between an autocratic trooper and an enraged villager. The brawl convinced islanders that men in khaki and red were as untrustworthy as their less resplendent municipal counterparts.[11] Members of the sect, consequently, equipped themselves with crude weapons and prepared to battle the authorities.

10. The favorite talismans were small bottles containing powdered kneecaps suspended in oil. Quests for the ingredient caused problems with the authorities. Infant bones were preferred. Several Colorums were arrested in 1923 for grave robbing. *Manila Daily Bulletin,* Feb. 3, 1924.
11. Miller Papers, "Cosigna Interview," 3.

In October 1923 relations between the Colorums and officialdom reached their nadir. Acting on orders from the Provincial Health Department, Surigao's Constabulary commander led a well-armed detachment to Socorro. After reminding Lantayug of repeated violations of public sanitation standards, Captain Valentin Juan demolished the bathing tanks.[12] Oddly enough, fighting did not break out. Stunned residents observed the sacrilegious act passively. Juan and his riflemen, however, marched through ominous silence to the beach and a waiting launch. The troopers' departure was the last peaceful sailing from Bucas Grande. After the incident, official visitors to the island were fortunate to get away in one piece.

Convinced that Lantayug and his followers were up to no good, Captain Juan sought evidence of sedition. During November he visited other Colorum barrios.[13] The survey uncovered nothing of an incriminating nature. Early in December, therefore, Juan resorted to cloak-and-dagger tactics. Posing as *halen* converts, two Constabulary agents tried to infiltrate one of Socorro's emerging *decorians*. Both men disappeared. Three plainclothesmen sent to Bucas Grande to find them also vanished. Unwilling to risk more of his under-strength company, the provincial commander requested assistance from municipal authorities. Shortly before the New Year, two policemen from Dapa town crossed the strait on a similar mission. They, too, failed to return. The outcome of all three operations soon became public knowledge. Surigao and Augusan began to buzz with grotesque reports. Among other tales, it was bruited about that Lantayug's "fanatics" had dissected the government men and dined triumphantly on their victims' raw hearts.[14] Hoping to squelch the rumors before panic set in, Valentin Juan ordered his men to prepare for action.

Activity was not restricted to Surigao town. Since October, Bucas Grande's residents had lived in a state of gathering anxiety. The destruction of Socorro's bathing tanks convinced Lantayug that the moment of truth was at hand. Proclaiming 1924 the year of Divine Retribution, he called upon his followers to make final spiritual and temporal arrangements. Aides trained Colorum males in bolo handling; women and children evacuated coastal villages for the safety of upland retreats; and toiling peasants transformed barrio Pamosaingan

12. Woods, "Strange Story of the Colorum Sect," 454.
13. *Khaki and Red,* July 1931, 203.
14. Woods, 454.

into a Pulajan-style redoubt. By January 1, the Colorums of Bucas Grande were ready to withstand either the deluge or a Constabulary attack.

The long-awaited encounter occurred in early January. Throughout the holiday season, warnings of impending natural calamities and imminent peasant uprisings swept over the provincial capital. Harried by requests for armed detachments from distraught municipalities, Valentin Juan decided to end Lantayug's war of nerves. On the morning of January 7, he assembled his tiny command.[15] Designating three constables to guard the *cuartel* until a patrol returned from the south, he issued 375 rounds of rifle ammunition to each of the remaining troopers and ordered his executive officer, Lieutenant Juan Guillermo, to outfit the eighteen-man force for an expedition to Bucas Grande. Promptly at 4:00 p.m., the contingent marched from their post. Juan's abbreviated display of force created the desired affect. After reassuring Surigao's population, the captain led his riflemen down the town wharf. Shortly before 4:30, the constabularymen piled aboard the company steam launch and churned away toward the offshore islands. The commander, of course, was not as self-assured as he appeared. Uncertain of what lay beyond the choppy strait, he quartered his men that night in Gigaquit on the mainland. They sailed to Siargao the next morning. Juan picked up Numancia's police chief, who was informed of current conditions on the neighboring island, and ordered his helmsman to steer for Pamosaingan. Around 3:00 P.M. on January 8, the expedition dropped anchor 100 meters off the barrio.

Sensing trouble, Juan and Guillermo surveyed the quiet hamlet. Pamosaingan resembled a typhoon's eye. Nothing moved. The distorted world beyond the officers' binoculars—empty paddies, sealed houses, and vacant streets—seemed totally unreal. After several tense moments, a figure emerged from one of the thatched dwellings. The villager strolled to the water's edge, leaned against a convenient coconut palm, and silently studied the astonished constables. Lieutenant Guillermo hailed the man and ordered him to ferry the troopers

15. Details on the expedition are drawn from the account of a Constabulary participant. Miller Papers, "The Colorum Uprising in Surigao as Told by a Surviving P.C. Hero, Sergeant Leonardo Tecson, to José Navallo Eñano," Gigaquit, Surigao del Norte, 1966.

ashore. He refused. "If you wish to land," he shouted, "do it yourself! We have no houseboys here!"[16] The barb shattered Valentin Juan's composure. Grabbing a rifle, he fired on Guillermo's heckler. Unharmed, the man raced back to the sheltering line of houses. Juan, Guillermo, and their men stormed the beach. Forming skirmish lines, they unleashed volleys on the village and advanced to its outskirts. Guillermo's squad paused at the first structure, and the lieutenant called on its occupants to surrender. When no one emerged, he told a sergeant to burn the house. Before the command could be executed, an elderly man stepped from the threatened dwelling. "Your guns are useless," he announced. "You are our victims. Comrades come out!"[17] As though to disprove the claim, Guillermo shot the speaker. Five hundred bolo-wielding Colorums leaped from concealed trenches and fell on the constables. Despite deadly rifle fire, Juan and his men were quickly overwhelmed. Only two badly slashed troopers managed to survive the ambush. Paddling toward the launch under covering fire from the helmsman, they left the dismembered bodies of Captain Juan, Lieutenant Guillermo, Numancia's police chief, and sixteen enlisted men in the village. Eighty dead or dying peasants lay beside the remains of their government adversaries.[18] After hauling the bleeding troopers aboard his boat, the helmsman circled into the west. Shortly after dusk, he and his stricken passengers eased alongside Surigao's darkened pier.

Word of the "Pamosaingan massacre" raced through the provincial capital and near-panic immediately set in. By midnight the town was shuttered, barred, and silent. Throughout the hours of darkness, the most persistent sound was the staccato click of telegraph keys. While messengers informed distant officials of Surigao's plight, townsmen, expecting attack from the countryside or an assault from Bucas Grande, waited through the night. Shortly before daybreak, a few people left their dark houses. All appeared well. Within minutes, streets and byways teemed with people. When dawn finally came, an

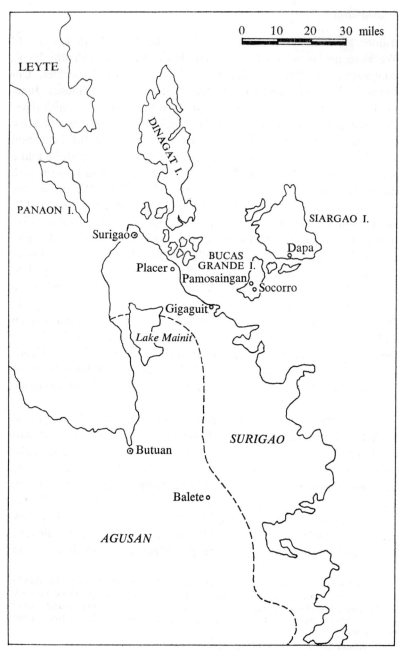

LEYTE

DINAGAT I.

PANAON I.

SIARGAO I.

Surigao

Dapa

Placer

BUCAS
GRANDE I.

Pamosaingan

Socorro

Gigaguit

Lake Mainit

SURIGAO

Butuan

Balete

AGUSAN

6. Northeastern Mindanao, 1923

exhausted resident wrote, "a prayer went up to God thanking Him for having permitted [us] to live to see a new day."[19]

Collective gratitude, unfortunately, was extremely short-lived. Sunlight exposed the precarious state of Surigao's defenses. Eight subdued troopers and a worn lieutenant manned the Constabulary barracks. Fatigued by a night march from Lake Mainit, the patrol leader said he and his men would protect "townspeople as long as they could."[20] Not reassured, Surigao's inhabitants gathered hopefully outside the telegraph office. Posted cables from Manila, Cebu City, and Zamboango proclaimed reinforcements were on their way. Until they arrived, the town would have to rely on its own resources. All afternoon refugees from inland barrios and east-coast municipalities swarmed into the provincial capital. Without exception, the newcomers carried reports of massing Colorums. By moonrise on January 10, insomnia had become a general condition. Two more days and one more night passed before the tension broke. On the morning of January 12, Governor Pedro Coleto received a harrowing piece of information. Captain Juan's decomposing cadaver—dressed in a cleanly pressed uniform and funereally arranged in a fishing boat— had been run aground the preceding evening along an uninhabited mainland beach.[21] Before the jittery populace heard the bad news, twenty-five constables from Butuan debarked in Surigao. That afternoon the gunboat U.S.S. *Sacramento* steamed into the empty harbor. At the eleventh hour, Coleto's capital had been saved from itself.

While Surigao's people withstood their ordeal, Manila remained calm. Cooled by sea breezes and secure behind the colonial regime's elaborate political and military machinery, American administrators viewed the distant disorder with detachment. Governor General Leonard Wood disputed Governor Coleto's claim that his province was threatened by more than a thousand armed "fanatics." Labeling the report an exaggeration, Wood reduced the menace to manageable dimensions. Rebel strength, he said, "could be safely estimated at about 500."[22] Malacañan Palace nevertheless, ordered 150 constabulary troopers to depart for the trouble zone aboard the Coast Guard

19. The statement, plus details on Surigao town's reaction to the events on Bucas Grande, were drawn from a contemporary letter to the editor (see José Farolan, "Panic in Surigao," *Philippines Free Press*, March 1, 1924, 28).

20. *Ibid.*

21. Miller Papers, "Consigna Interview," 3.

22. *Manila Daily Bulletin*, Jan. 10, 1924.

cutter *Polillo*. The Executive Mansion also detailed a veteran campaigner, Colonel C. H. Bowers, to assume command of the expedition.

Landing in Surigao town on January 13, Bowers immediately recognized the serious nature of the outbreak. Preliminary assessments revealed that Coleto's evaluation of the situation was more accurate than Wood's. Surigao province alone—mainland and offshore islands—sheltered at least 3,000 aroused sectarians.[23] Intelligence from neighboring Agusan and Misamis indicated growing disturbances in and around Colorum enclaves. Even more ominous was news that reliable officers stationed in Leyte and Samar had filed reports of burgeoning unrest among former Pulajanes.[24] Confronted by the specter of chain reactions involving cultists throughout the region, Bowers requested additional time and supplementary reinforcement. Within a week, he had 300 Constabulary officers and men at his disposal and 200 more en route. The *Polillo* and *Sacramento,* together with their American seamen, were also placed under Bower's jurisdiction. Unwilling to tempt fate, the Colonel asked for and received a battery of field artillery. Before the affair ended, every man and every gun had been put to use.

While Bowers assembled forces, Lantayug and his aides schemed. Buoyed by their victory over Captain Juan, they prepared for the government's next move. Socorro's defenses were strengthened. When the men in khaki and red waded ashore on Bucas Grande, according to elaborate Colorum strategy, mainland coreligionists would converge on the provincial capital. Their assault was designed to provoke more than confusion. Underground *decorians* in the city would carry out a simultaneous uprising. Constabulary headquarters and other government buildings were to be seized, captured troopers and officials were to be put to death, and Surigao province was to be proclaimed the first state in a Rizalist theocracy.[25] Events proved the inherent madness of Lantayug's method.

The first of several unequal engagements occurred on January 23, 1924. Bowers attempted to disperse the religious rebels by a show of force. Ordering the *Sacramento* to maneuver off Socorro, he trans-

23. Of these, 1,000 were reported to be residents of the provincial capital. *Manila Daily Bulletin,* Feb. 19, 1924.

24. To prevent outbreaks in restless Samar, the Constabulary made arrests in Gandara and other Pulajan communities. *Manila Daily Bulletin,* Feb. 1, 1924.

25. According to urban newspapers, details on the plot were revealed by captured rebels. *Manila Daily Bulletin,* Feb. 7, 1924.

ferred 300 constabularymen to Siargao Island aboard the *Polillo*. Unfortunately, neither demonstration impressed Lantayug. Secure in the embrace of an ostensibly friendly deity, the Colorums refused to capitulate. Instead, they braced themselves for a repetition of the Pamosaingan episode. Bowers refused to cooperate. Accurate salvos from the gunboat pulverized Socorro's trenches and breastworks. The *Sacramento*'s machine gunners then covered a landing by 100 troopers. The invaders did not linger but put Socorro's ruins to the torch and returned immediately to the *Polillo*. With the initial phase of his strategy reduced to rubble, Lantayug and his aides led their demoralized followers beyond the range of naval artillery. Two days later, Bowers returned with a larger force. Constabulary patrols—assisted by defectors—quickly located the rebels' inland base at the foot of Lobo Mountain.[26] The Colonel, three artillery pieces, and 300 troopers soon had Lantayug's 400 intransigents cornered.

Phase two of the complex plot produced equally disastrous results. Early in February, mainland Colorums tried to deliver the finishing stroke. With Bowers and most of his command involved on Bucas Grande, two hundred confident dissidents collected outside Placer town. They planned to overrun the *municipio* as a prelude to the coordinated assault on Surigao's thin defenses. Neither objective was achieved. Veteran Constabulary detachments just in from Zamboango intercepted advancing bolomen on the Mainit Road. A nightmarish encounter ensued. When it ended, fifty-four Colorums lay dead, twenty-two had suffered grievous wounds, and a majority of the survivors found themselves trudging toward the provincial jail.[27] Rebels who managed to escape carried news of the debacle to coreligionists in neighboring barrios.

For all practical purposes, the uprising was over. On February 12 a bloody, if anticlimactic, skirmish occurred in Agusan province. One hundred fleeing dissidents ambushed a pursuing Constabulary platoon near barrio Balete. An officer and nine troopers died during the brief encounter, but thirty-five rebels lost their lives.[28] One week later,

26. *Manila Daily Bulletin,* Feb. 9, 1924.
27. *Khaki and Red,* July 1931, 203. A local resident maintains the death toll was much higher. Near the site of the skirmish a mass grave contains the remains of sixty-four Colorums. Miller Papers, "Records of Miguel G. Calderon, Municipal Secretary (Ret.), Surigao, Surigao del Norte," January 1966, 3 pp.
28. Woods, 459.

Lantayug and 285 followers, still reeling from an artillery barrage, staggered down Lobo Mountain.[29] Bowers accepted their surrender. It had been an incredible two months. Since mid-December, when the first government agents disappeared on Bucas Grande, thirty-seven officers and men had been hacked to death. During the same interval, approximately 200 Colorums died violently. How many religious rebels were wounded will never be known. Both sides, in short, paid a terrible price. The whole affair, moreover, might have been avoided. Instead, it grew senselessly from an aging madman's visions and an ambitious Constabulary captain's meddling.

Uneasy peace returned slowly to the region. By late March, the wheels of justice were ready to grind. Lantayug, his *querida* (mistress) Eusebia Puyo, Juan Bahao, and other leaders, together with 190 ragged Colorums, appeared before the Court of First Instance in Surigao town. Charged with murder, sedition, and brigandage, they pleaded innocent. Contrary to local rumors, the prisoners proved to be destitute. Judge Ricardo Jalbuena, therefore, appointed several reluctant attorneys to speak for the accused. The mass trial opened on April 3, 1924. It closed seven days later. Lantayug and his principal aides were found guilty on multiple murder counts. Jalbuena sentenced them to Bilibid Prison for life. Six Colorums were acquitted. The remaining rebels were held accountable for sedition and received lesser punishments: 190 were ordered to the insular penitentiary for ten years; Eusebia Puyo, largely due to her gender, was sent back to Surigao jail for a three-year term.[30] Summing up the peremptory proceedings, Judge Jalbuena declared, "Were it not for the fact that . . . all [of them] are uneducated and ignorant, each would have been sentenced to capital punishment."[31] Legal niceties demonstrated the validity of the magistrate's contention. Laureano Solamo, who was the instigator of the macabre affair, went scot-free. Secure behind a phalanx of Cebuano lawyers, the Colorum *supremo* continued to operate in a lucrative realm above and beyond the law.[32]

29. *Manila Daily Bulletin*, Feb. 16, 1924.
30. *Manila Daily Bulletin*, April 10, 1924.
31. *Manila Daily Bulletin*, April 25, 1924.
32. Unable to prove complicity in the Surigao uprising, constabularymen arrested Solamo in 1927 and convicted him on extortion charges. He began an eight-year prison sentence in August of that year and was forced to pay a P20,000 fine. *Report of the Governor General of the Philippines, 1927* (in ms.; National Archives, Washington, D.C.), I, 718.

An objective appraisal of the flare-up was hard to come by. Like Judge Jalbuena, colonial authorities, and prominent American residents dismissed the rebellion as a throwback to less sophisticated times. They categorized Solamo, probably correctly, as a profit-seeking charlatan. They also relegated his followers, quite incorrectly, to the historical ash heap reserved for witless pawns. Two patronizing statements summed up metropolitan reactions. Colonel C. E. Nathorst, an old Constabulary hand and a participant in the campaign to suppress the outbreak, ascribed events in Surigao to lust and greed. "The whole question as to the formation of this fanatical sect." he observed wryly, "is that of women and money—for the leader."[33] Less pungent, if more graceful, responses appeared in American newspapers. "These religious fanatics," editorialized the *Manila Daily Bulletin,* "are to be pitied. . . . But when we reach a point where they feel it necessary to oppose openly the forces of the government, pity cannot be the guiding sentiment." Warming to his righteous theme, the editor concluded "opposition to constituted authority will under no circumstances be tolerated."[34] Both observations expressed the tenor of the times. Unconsciously, insular Americans had fallen into the same psychological pitfall that had engulfed their Spanish predecessors. Official and unofficial attitudes toward the Colorum trouble, in fact, coincided almost exactly with the friars' responses to similar upheavals during the nineteenth century.

If the uprising had provoked Americans and Filipinos to hard thoughts concerning the growing disequilibrium within Philippine society, something of value might have emerged. It did not. No one, apparenlty, asked why the uprising had occurred. Official post-mortems were of the hasty and confidential variety. Cautious criticism of Captain Juan disappeared from legislative chambers and the press before the rebellion terminated.[35] The dead company commander, as a matter of fact, was accorded the respect reserved for martyred heroes. One Filipino senator, who had the temerity to challenge Colonel Bowers' punitive measures against Socorro, was squelched by colleagues.[36] American

33. N.A., B.I.A., F.E. 4865-A-57.

34. *Manila Daily Bulletin,* Jan. 26, 1924.

35. A conference of provincial administrators discussed Constabulary activities on Bucas Grande. Participants concluded: "had the religious zealots been handled more tactfully the trouble might have been avoided." *Philippines Free Press,* Feb. 16, 1924, 8.

36. Senator José A Clarin of the Eleventh District, which included Surigao

administrators and leading *Nacionalistas* even set aside constitutional differences temporarily to endorse government actions. Their consensus denied any merit or meaning to the defunct rebel cause. Excluding transitory compassion for the families of deceased peasants, about all the Colorums received from urban politicos and journalists was ridicule. The entire episode, in short, became another exercise in futility.

The only significant result was deep distrust in official circles concerning the motives and methods of agrarian dissenters. After January 8, 1924, Constabulary officers brought heterodox peasant leaders under close surveillance. Rumors of apocalyptic pronouncements or reports of secret gatherings were enough to generate preventive action.[37] Any spiritual association with unorthodox political or economic objectives, moreover, received a "Colorum" designation. Newspapers and periodicals picked up the theme. Within weeks Colorumism had become synonymous with fanaticism and criminality. Indiscriminate use of the term rapidly created a Colorum scare. Uneasy politicians and reporters prone to exaggeration convinced many people that conspirators dedicated to sedition or to terrorism populated the countryside. In time, even authoritative United States publications accepted the myth. *The New York Times,* for example, printed the story, ascribing 13,000 political murders (mostly unsolved) to Colorum assassins.[38]

Actuality differed radically from journalistic fancy. Offbeat cults existed in most, if not all, Philippine provinces; some even thrived in Manila. Most village dissenters, however, were pacifistic and law-abiding.[39] Few rural religious leaders—no matter how grandiose their

province, maintained the destruction of Socorro was "wholly unjustified and an unnecessary measure;" he also declared there was "no law that empowered Colonel Bowers to burn the town." *Manila Daily Bulletin,* Jan. 26, 1924.

37. Retired General Guillermo Francisco granted an interview to the author in 1966. Entering the Constabulary as a third lieutenant in 1904, he rose to the rank of lieutenant colonel by 1924. He and other senior officers recognized the dangerous potential of peasant religious movements. As district commander of the Visayas during the Colorum years, he said, "Things were tense. If I heard there was a popular faith healer in my district, I had him kept under close surveillance. If I heard that a prophet was predicting natural disasters, I either had him arrested or shipped out to another island."

38. *The New York Times,* Dec. 6, 1931, Section IX, 10. The alleged killings occurred between 1872 and 1923.

39. The leader of a utopian barrio in Comarines Sur summed up the real situation. When asked if his 150 followers had any connections with other

delusions—claimed more than several thousand followers. The vast majority, furthermore, operated independently of one another.[40] Despite Constabulary anxieties, there was no coordinated plot to topple the government. Fears of a general uprising emanated primarily from insecurity concerning the inequitable state of provincial affairs. In large part, the much-publicized Colorum threat was a joint figment of elitist guilt and police suspicion.

The real tragedy of Surigao was that its underlying importance went unnoticed. No one in authority sought a fundamental explanation of the upheaval. Like its precursors elsewhere in the Philippines, it was traced to ignorance and fanaticism. Like its forerunners, also, it was regarded as an isolated event. The fact that the flare-up represented an ingrained peasant response to incomprehensible change was never apparent to Manila. Urban denunciations of the movement's impossible goals, moreover, prevented metropolitan administrators and Filipino politicians from recognizing a significant new element in sectarian behavior. Unlike its historical analogues, the Mindanao revitalization effort incorporated patriotic aspirations into its liberating doctrines. With all their otherworldly proclivities, the Colorums represented a rude form of hamlet nationalism. Emphasis on José Rizal constituted the key to understanding the countryside's evolving climate. Two decades of American rule had altered peasant aspirations. In the emerging universe of village true believers, millennium and independence had come to mean one and the same thing.

Colorum sects, he said, "they did not know . . . there were other Colorums in other places." *Philippines Free Press,* July 30, 1927, 15.

40. Bishop Isabelo de los Reyes of the Philippine Independent Church testified to the parochialism of sect leaders. During the 1920's, while acting as Gregorio Aglipay's personal secretary, he was commissioned to organize the folk cults into a semblance of unity. The task proved impossible. "Individual leaders were such megalomaniacs," he said, "they were incapable of anything resembling either rational or coordinated action." Isabelo de los Reyes, interview, 1966.

CHAPTER 8

The Millennial Empire of Florencio I

The Surigao uprising was the opening installment of a disturbing trilogy. In the Mindanao episode, popular nationalism played a minor role in a predominantly religious drama. The second act took place on a different stage. Negros and Panay—two of the most developed islands in the Visayan group—provided lush settings for a new cast of players with highly original, if unsophisticated, aspirations. Secret societies committed to improving the lot of humble Negrenses and Ilongos initiated the plot. Their efforts to better working conditions, unfortunately, quickly gave way to more grandiose designs. An eccentric visionary—unusual even to the milieu that had produced Dionisio Sigobela—formulated an impossible plan for the renovation of insular society. Essentially political, his revitalization scheme derived much of its impact from traditional mysticism. Once unleashed, supernaturalism became the driving force, again leading to violence. In 1927 brief insurrections broke out on both islands. Cautious action by authorities, however, prevented a repetition of the Surigao affair. What began with the dire propensities of Greek tragedy, in fact, degenerated at its climax into comic opera.

The upheaval's farcical outcome diverted most observers from its grim origins. By 1925, the provinces of the Western Visayas—particularly Negros Occidental—were rife with discord. World War I multiplied severalfold the conditions that had given birth to Babailanismo. Soaring American sugar prices—and seemingly limitless demands for the commodity—generated an unprecedented boom in Bacolod and its municipal satellites. The ascending economic spiral persisted into the postwar era. But the prosperity of Negros continued to be severely restricted. Wealth, like land, remained the near-monopoly of a few prominent families.[1] Nowhere in the Philippines were the differences between rich and poor so starkly apparent. Rising expectations and improving public education, together with mounting population pressure and intensifying class antipathies, combined to produce a social atmosphere heavy with violent implications.

The first symptoms of stress became apparent in 1923. Peasant secret societies—which had been organized around 1920—began to compete openly for the loyalty of destitute field hands and impoverished mill workers. Two associations, Kusug Sang Imol (Power to the People) and Mainawaon (Merciful), acquired large followings.[2] Dedicated at the outset to mutual-assistance projects and higher wages, the organizations attempted to use bloc voting, political influence, and, when necessary, terror to achieve their objectives.[3] Intensifying rivalry for members, however, undermined the goals of both societies. In February 1923, Mafia-style disputes erupted in the towns and cane fields of Negros Occidental. Arbitration efforts, by no less a figure than General Emilio Aguinaldo, failed to resolve the parochial conflict.[4] Within a year, confrontations between armed factions were absorbing more energy than challenges to planters or sugar centrals. In March 1924, consequently, the Philippine Constabulary assumed control of several troubled municipalities and restricted Kusug Sang Imol and Mainawaon activities.

Intervention by the insular police did not bring peace to Negros. Tensions persisted between contract laborers and planters. During 1925 and 1926 wage disputes produced a round of indecisive strikes on several major *haciendas*. Agricultural workers in Negros Oriental and Iloilo also began to affiliate themselves with the embryonic union movement. On March 1, 1927, a showdown between labor and capital on the Bais Estate in Negros Oriental ended with widespread

1. By 1936 approximately 5 per cent of Negros Occidental's population (25,930 people out of roughly 500,000) controlled all of the province's agriculture properties. Those possessing more than 500 hectares numbered only 61. *Fact Finding Report*, 206.

2. For brief discussions of these and other mutual-aid societies in that period, see Macaraig, *Social Problems*, 407–410.

3. Several murders, including that of a justice of the peace, were traced to the organizations. *Manila Daily Bulletin*, March 28, 1924.

4. *Manila Daily Bulletin*, March 31, 1924. The edition also contains a summary of Constabulary findings on the societies over a six-month period.

sabotage and property destruction.[5] Called in to restore order, a Constabulary officer won the appreciation of liberal Manileños by siding publicly with the strikers.[6] His statement encouraged a few urban progressives to conclude that an acceptable technique had become available for the resolution of village grievances.

Unforeseen events interrupted the development. While inexperienced organizers struggled to achieve the support of contract laborers, a more conventional redeemer began to attract the loyalties of migratory workers in Negros and Panay. During 1926, Florencio Natividad —alias Prudencio Zarada, alias Flor de Entrecherado (in the Constabulary's customary jargon)—assumed leadership of many dispossessed Negrenses and Ilongos.[7] Before anyone in or out of authority recognized what was happening, the magnetic former fish merchant plunged both islands into near-anarchy.

Judged by barrio standards, Entrencherado was no run-of-the-mill prophet. The son of a wayward seaman by a wife he soon deserted, Entrencherado was born on Corregidor in 1871. While playing alone one day under the sentinel island's watchtower, young Florencio was approached by what appeared to be two dignified old men. He recognized them immediately: one was God; the other was Padre Burgos. The Lord, Entrencherado said, pointed to Father Burgos and declared, "This child is good . . . he will replace you."[8] After a brief interchange along similar lines, the heavenly figures departed. Florencio told his mother of the incident. Shortly thereafter, the young woman moved with her child of destiny to Cavite.

Placing Florencio in the hands of her parents, Mrs. Natividad left

5. Striking workers burned three cane fields and damaged five locomotives. *Manila Daily Bulletin,* March 3, 1927.

6. *Ibid.,* March 6, 1927.

7. Newspapers and official reports used a variety of spellings to render the Emperor's chosen name. Intrencherado and Yntrencherado cropped up as frequently as Entrencherado. For purposes of consistency the latter form will be employed. Appreciation must be extended to Anne T. Hall. During 1966, while enrolled in a graduate seminar at the Institute of Asian Studies of the University of the Philippines, she tracked down a great deal of unpublished biographical data on Entrencherado's childhood and youth. She also conducted a series of interviews with Dr. José A. Fernández, psychiatrist, with regard to his celebrated patient's case. Materials from her files, together with other pertinent primary documents, will be labeled: Hall Papers.

8. Hall Papers, "Fernández Interview." The quote, along with other statements from the Emperor, comes from the "personal history" compiled by Dr. Fernández in May and June 1927.

the provincial port town for Manila. Entrencherado spent the next nine years in the shadow of his grandfather, Captain Luis de la Cruz, master of the interisland steamer *San Pedro,* who introduced his grandson to the ways of the sea. Rope-sorting and caulking work, however, did not end Florencio's messianic inclinations, for in 1885 he had another vision. Gently awakened one night by an apparition in red, the fourteen-year-old peered sleepily from his bedroom window. His visitor immediately put Entrencherado at ease. Squatting comfortably by a lamppost, the Lord asked, "Young man, what are you doing here?" Confused by the question, Florencio replied vaguely. The Lord then said, "This is not yet your work. There are still many works that you are going to do. Someday you will be taken by your mother and then you will go to Jolo. Your father is there, and there you will fight the Moros." Entrencherado agreed. "Yes," he said, "I believe you are right." His pronouncement understood, the apparition disappeared into the night.[9]

A year later, Entrencherado set forth on his own. Following the course charted by his nautical elders, he became a ship's steward on the S.S. *Mayon.* Over the next four years he acquired a sailor's respect for the intricate straits connecting the South China Sea and the Pacific. In 1890 he left the freighter when she dropped anchor off Iloilo. Confused recollections shrouded his ensuing activities. He apparently worked briefly, if conspiratorially, as an assistant in a Chinese *tienda* (shop). Florencio performed the storekeeper's chores, as he said later, "because there is no book by which we will learn their secret deeds against . . . the government."[10] Repelled by the devious techniques of "Sangleys," he returned to the straightforward sea. He lived for several years as a fisherman on Isla de Gigante. Around 1896 he landed in Iloilo town with enough money to marry and to buy a small business.

By the time the revolution against Spain erupted, Entrencherado had established himself as a man of some substance. Ilongo patriots, consequently, tried to persuade Florencio to join the Katipunan. He refused. His devout Catholicism, in fact, let him to conclude that the war against Spain was an unmitigated evil. On the advice of the Holy Spirit, he later told his psychiatrist, he fled Iloilo and went into hiding

9. See J. A. Fernández, "Florencio Natividad, alias Flor Intrencherado," *Journal of the Philippine Islands Medical Association,* XII (1932), 627–634.
10. Hall Papers, "Fernández Interview."

near a *municipio* named Jordan on Guimaras Island. The conflict with the United States lured Entrencherado from his self-imposed exile. During 1899, he fought the Americans "to avenge the wrong done my country."[11] But his service in the revolutionary army was extremely brief. Chronic disputes with superiors led him to abandon the cause. Late in 1901 he turned full political circle to become an undercover agent for the newly formed Philippine Constabulary. For roughly the next half-decade, he worked quietly and efficiently in the campaign against Papa Isio.[12]

About 1905, Entrencherado took up a less perilous vocation. He and his wife bought a *sari-sari,* or neighborhood, store in barrio Payao, Binalbagan town, Negros Occidental. Over the next few years nothing of moment occurred. Around 1915, however, Florencio was shocked to find himself losing heavily at *monte.* An inveterate and normally successful gambler, he found the experience mind-shattering. Stalking back to his house, he raised a red-and-black flag and pronounced anathema on the entire village.[13] Neighbors attempted to have Entrencherado put away. Local authorities—perhaps because of his past service to the provincial government—rejected community pressures and classified him as a harmless crank. Aside from occasional deviations of a mildly paranoid variety, Florencio caused no problems. Most of the time he devoted himself to the quiet study of books or pamphlets on prophecy, cosmology, and comparative government. Whether due to neighborhood animosities of the mandates of another vision, he pulled stakes again in 1921. Back on Gigante Island he established a dried-fish business. Blessed by bountiful catches and aided by the commercial sense of his wife, Entrencherado prospered as never before. In 1925, ready to challenge a corrupt world, the self-assured fifty-four-year-old returned to Iloilo province.

Entrencherado purchased a rambling thatched structure on the outskirts of Jaro town. After brief exposure to the thick Ilongo political climate, he launched a private crusade to liberate the archipelago. His approach to the problem created quite a stir. To the amazement or delight of practically everyone in the vicinity, he proclaimed himself "Emperor of the Philippines." The spacious house—made more

11. Hall Papers, "Fernández Interview," March 23, 1966.
12. *Khaki and Red,* July 1931, 200.
13. Hall Papers, "Fernández Interview."

impressive by wide verandas and bamboo towers—was transformed into a "royal palace." Local carpenters also constructed separate quarters for liveried servants and uniformed guards who soon populated the compound. Entrencherado, however, was the most striking figure in the household. Jaro's cooperative tailors, hatters, and metalsmiths fashioned for him the wardrobe and accouterments of an imperial personage. Immaculate in pith helmet, pigskin leggings, and colorful uniforms of his own design, or formally attired in purple robe and jewel-encrusted crown, with sceptor, sword, and dagger accessories, Florencio I presided over his domain from a baroque rattan throne.

An overnight celebrity, Entrencherado did not confine himself to the creature comforts of his residence. Erect, bewhiskered, and articulate, the aspiring liberator strode confidently into the Visayan political arena. Late in 1925, to the amusement of *Nacionalista* professionals, he entered the race for governor of Iloilo province.[14] While he failed to win the executive's chair, his unique approach to campaigning made Entrencherado famous throughout the region. Undismayed by the setback, he extended his itinerary and his organizational endeavors across Panay and Negros. Rural response to his unorthodox programs, moreover, could only be classified as enthusiastic. By the end of the year Entrencherado had ceased to be a joke in the political circles of Bacolod and Iloilo town.

Peasants, for the most part, did not laugh at Florencio I. Entrencherado's logic hit a responsive chord among poor people. His issues were their issues. First and foremost, he spoke out against taxes. Reduction of the annual *cedula* from two pesos to twenty centavos was the main plank in the Emperor's platform. He also railed against the activities of alien merchants. Classifying Chinese and Japanese storekeepers as parasitic interlopers, he accused them of sucking life from the Philippine economy. Last, but not least, he labeled insular elitists collaborators and castigated the *Nacionalista* Party for a profitable sell-out to the United States. The Americans, interestingly enough, came out of Entrencherado's diatribes quite well. Praising the metropolitan power for its enlightened policies, he called for independence via monetary arrangements. Filipinos, he maintained, could demon-

14. *Khaki and Red,* July 1931, 200.

strate their collective appreciation by literally paying a debt of gratitude to Calvin Coolidge's America.[15]

After describing the ills of Philippine society and diagnosing their causes, Entrencherado outlined his remedies.[16] Immediate independence represented the solution. Once sovereignty had been purchased, all property would be transferred to the new imperial regime. Aliens, particularly the hated "Sangleys," would be driven from the archipelago. The entire population would then be divided into paramilitary syndicates, each of which would assume responsibility for an essential national service. The rapacious rich would be replaced by an aristocracy of merit. Headed by the Emperor and made up of kings, counts, generals, brigadiers, colonels, and the like, Entrencherado's compassionate leaders would direct Filipinos toward unparalleled prosperity. Magnanimous to a fault, Florencio I even offered hope to some popular *Nacionalistas*. Under the right circumstances, he said, he would be willing to share governmental powers with Manuel Quezon and Sergio Osmeña.[17]

While few villagers understood the impossible implications of Entrencherado's political design, they thoroughly enjoyed his autocratic antiauthoritarianism. They also shared his aversion toward taxes and Chinese merchants. The Emperor's undeniable appeal, however, emanated from another source. He was—as even his urban detractors admitted—an arresting individual. More significantly, to barrio dwellers he represented a living mystery. Florencio I, quite unblinkingly, claimed control over the elements. His omnipotent capacities, he said, were derived directly from Padre Burgos, José Rizal, and the Holy Ghost. A friendly "Spiritual Guide" directed his daily activities. In addition, his crown and imperial dagger represented deadly devices. The regal head covering, for example, contained a hidden magnet which could drive adversaries insane. The stiletto possessed qualities of a more terrifying nature. "When I get mad and saturated

15. In 1926, Entrencherado demonstrated his loyalty to the metropolitan power by writing a friendly letter to the President of the United States. The communication was deposited in the National Archives. See N.A., B.I.A., Personal Name Information File.

16. Entrencherado published his plans for the future in a variety of pamphlets. For a translation of one of the documents see Appendix A of this volume.

17. *Manila Tribune*, April 24, 1927.

with the evils that are happening in the world," he declared, "I stick the dagger in the ground, and something happens to those who made mistakes."[18] Human error, furthermore, was about to come to an end. Unless Filipinos joined Entrencherado's effort to refashion insular society, the world would be destroyed on February 4, 1929. On doomsday, the Emperor warned, typhoon gales of 4,000 kilometers per hour would roar over the Islands, and fire storms would erupt in their wake, setting the stage for a deluge of mountain-swallowing dimensions.[19] Field hands and mill workers, impressed by his prophecies, affiliated themselves with the liberation movement.

By late 1926, Entrencherado had become a force to be reckoned with. At least 10,000 peasants in six Visayan provinces had sworn allegiance to the aspiring monarch.[20] A group of young advisers, wise in the rough-and-tumble techniques of labor organization, had also gravitated to the "palace" in Jaro. Concerned by the Emperor's instantaneous success and fearful of his expanding organization's potential, *hacenderos,* municipal politicians, and union leaders began to express alarm. Their collective complaints provoked a Constabulary investigation.

It was easy to accumulate damning evidence against Entrencherado. Provincial Constabulary commanders had already compiled a great deal of information on the Emperor and his liberation movement. Municipal police departments, too, had begun to take preventive action. During the first half of the year, local authorities in Panay expelled Florencio I from three municipalities for incendiary statements. He had also been jailed for five days in Estancia town on charges of carrying concealed weapons.[21] Weaving facts or allegations from scattered sources into extortion and sedition indictments, the provincial attorney general summoned Entrencherado to appear before the Iloilo Court of First Instance.[22]

18. Hall Papers, "Fernández Interview."
19. *Washington Star,* April 8, 1928, N.A., B.I.A., Personal Name Information File.
20. Followers could be found in Iloilo, Capiz, Antigua, Negros Occidental, Negros Oriental, and Cebu. The greatest number resided in the first two provinces. *Report of the Governor General of the Philippines, 1926* (in ms.; National Archives, Washington, D.C.), I, 591.
21. *Khaki and Red,* July 1931, 200.
22. Sedition charges emanated from incendiary statements such as, "I am an anarchist with nothing but a dagger for the blood of the earth and a bomb

The validity of the accusations was never tested. Entrencherado's
trial, however, constituted the high point of the judicial season. To the
captivation of newspapermen, the proceedings opened against a backdrop of pomp and circumstance. Escorted by several hundred subjects, the Emperor arrived on schedule. One attendant sheltered
Florencio I from the sun with a "royal umbrella," while a second aide
daubed away "kingly sweat" with imperial handkerchiefs. When
Entrencherado settled in the witness chair, a valet rearranged the
sovereign's carefully pressed uniform to prevent unsightly creases.[23]
Finding it impossible to maintain decorum in the face of the Byzan-
tine displays, an unamused magistrate ended testimony after three
days. Transcripts and evidence were transferred to Doctor Kahili, a
local mental specialist famous for crisp diagnoses. Examination of the
Emperor's remarks and writings convinced Kahili the accused man
was unbalanced. Entrencherado, the physician declared under oath,
suffered from "mental alienation, *sesada* [fried brains], and foolishness."[24] His opinion terminated the trial. Judge Salas declared Entrencherado insane and ordered him to the insular mental hospital.
Prepared for such an eventuality, the Emperor's lawyers immediately
appealed Salas' decision to the Supreme Court of the Philippines.
Pending review, Florencio I was released on his own recognizance.

The outcome, strangely enough, satisfied everyone. Law-enforcement officers and provincial administrators concluded that a potentially dangerous situation had been resolved by recourse to the courts.
Florencio I, safely ensconced in Jaro, believed higher authority would
attest to both his sanity and his innocence. The Emperor's provincial
followers interpreted his liberation as proof of their leader's omnipotence. Instead of undermining Entrencherado, the trial strengthened
him and everything he stood for. By the end of February 1927, the
Entrencheradista movement had acquired an ominous momentum
comparable to that of Colorumism following the death of Captain Juan.

Tension mounted throughout March and April. During March, Entrencherado's stock in the countryside reached its zenith.[25] For several

---

of nitroglycerine to blow up what hinders my way." *Philippines Free Press,*
May 21, 1927, 28.
23. *Mindanao Herald* (Zamboango, P.I.), June 4, 1927; N.A., B.I.A., Personal Name Information File.
24. *Manila Tribune,* Dec. 8, 1927.
25. By the end of March, more than 26,000 people had affiliated themselves

years he had been predicting that Mount Kanlaon would erupt on March 19, 1927. When the dormant volcano spewed smoke and fire exactly on schedule, few Visayans had the temerity to dispute the Emperor's omniscience. With converts flocking to his standard, Florencio I issued a special circular for the edification of Negrenses and Ilongos. Distributed secretly, it read in part: "You who are poor are the many, you must unite with Flor Yntrencherado. Do not obey the orders of the rich, think of your body, of your wife, of your children, who will be swept by the flood, because of the rich. Therefore do the Natural Defense, that all unite with Flor Yntrencherado, for the hour will come when the poor will be ordered to kill all the rich, who did not unite to free the poor."[26]

Unaware of the document, insular officialdom awaited definitive action by the Supreme Court. It came on April 23, 1927. Assembled in Baguio for the "summer session," the Justices unanimously upheld Judge Salas' decision. Entrencherado and his aides, in full regalia, had journeyed to the mountain capital for the hearing. Taken aback by the high tribunal's ruling, Florencio I managed to retain his poise. After agreeing to confinement in Manila's San Lazaro Asylum, Entrencherado requested time to set his affairs in order. The court granted him three weeks. Released on bail, the Emperor returned to Jaro in the custody of his attorney. He was scheduled to sail for Manila on the evening of May 13, 1927. Developments delayed his departure.

The uprising began at 7:00 A.M. Telegraphers in Bacolod reported that wires north and south of the provincial capital had suddenly gone dead.[27] While policemen and constables sought an explanation, municipal authorities grappled with more pressing problems. By 7:15 A.M., 300 armed Entrencheradistas, led by Policarpio Montarde and his four brothers, had assembled in the plaza of Victorias town. Two local policemen manned the square. Policarpio confronted the law officers with an impressive document (Montarde maintained it was a new law from Paris), and demanded an emergency conference with community officials. The policemen said their superiors were not yet available. Policarpio cut them down and led the triumphant rebels into the vacant *presidencia*. For the next two and a half hours, field

---

with the Emperor. The Constabulary also estimated they had contributed at least P34,000 to Entrencherado's cause. *Khaki and Red,* July 1931, 200.

26. *Philippines Free Press,* June 25, 1927, 8.

27. *Manila Daily Bulletin,* May 14, 1927.

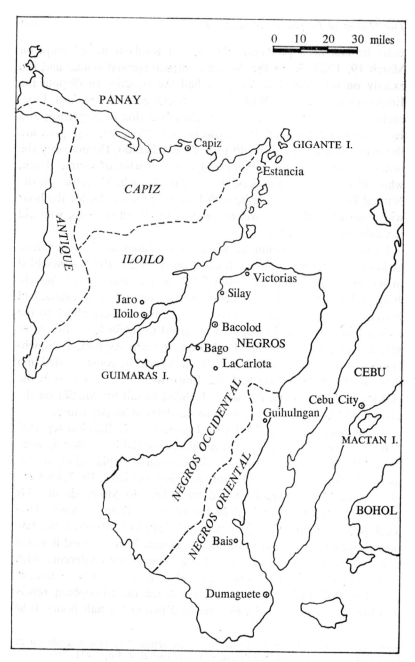

7. The Central Visayas, 1927

hands destroyed land deeds and tax records. By 10:00 A.M., they were ready to extend their rampage to Chinese *tiendas* and the property of prominent citizens. In the meantime, most of Victorias' 15,000 inhabitants had fled. Milling refugees hindered the arrival of a Constabulary platoon. The troopers, however, pushed their way into the abandoned coastal town around 10:30 A.M. A short skirmish followed. Disciplined, if desultory, rifle fire by constabularymen quickly brought about a rebel surrender. Casualties were kept to a mimimum. By 3:00 P.M. order had been restored: fifty-six Entrencheradistas occupied cells in the municipal jail, and residents had begun to return to Victorias.[28]

Elsewhere in Negros Occidental, the Emperor's subjects initiated similar actions. Rioters took over La Carlota's municipal building and engaged in the same type of destruction the Montarde brothers had unleased in Victorias. One policeman was killed, one was injured, and four civilians suffered superficial wounds before constables subdued the town's conquerors. In Silay, Entrencheradistas also tried to burn the houses of wealthy residents. The arrival of another Constabulary detachment prevented widespread arson. On the outskirts of La Castellano, a mob seized three Spanish *hacenderos,* lashed them to posts, and flogged them into unconsciousness.[29] The tumult's climax came in Bago town. When 200 cane-cutters occupied the plaza, an adaptable municipal official invited them to inspect the *presidencia.* After the last curious insurgent had filed into the building, the administrator stepped outside and locked the door. Forty-five minutes later he turned over the key and his abashed prisoners to a pleased Constabulary lieutenant. In Bago, no one was even bruised. By nightfall of May 13, a semblance of order had been restored to Negros Occidental.[30]

But the uprising was not over. Panay, particularly Iloilo province, remained explosive. Defying orders to turn himself in to colonial authorities, Entrencherado refused to leave Jaro. By dawn of May 14,

28. *Report of the Governor General of the Philippines, 1927,* I, 721.
29. *Philippines Free Press,* May 21, 1927, 25.
30. Given the extensive nature of the disturbance, casualties were few. Three municipal policemen and three rebels were killed, one policeman and thirteen Entrencheradistas were wounded, and only five civilians suffered injuries. By the evening of May 13, 363 insurgents were behind bars. More surrendered voluntarily elsewhere in Negros during the next few days. Unlike the Surigao affair, not a single constable was injured. *Report of the Governor General of the Philippines, 1927,* I, 721.

100 followers had gathered around the royal palace. During the next twenty-four hours, 300 more peasants slipped through Constabulary cordons to join the garrison. Coils of barbed wire materialized from one of the outbuildings. Deep entanglements—manned by Entrencheradistas armed with axes, bolos, clubs, knives, homemade pistols, and ancient shotguns—soon surrounded the compound.[31] Hoping to avoid further bloodshed, Colonel Guillermo Francisco (commander of the Visayan District) sent a Constabulary squad into the municipality to keep a wary eye on Florencio I and his aroused subjects. Jaro's more sensible citizens abandoned their town to representatives of the contending governments. By the morning of May 16, only two alternatives were left: war or diplomacy.

Both regimes, fortunately, decided to negotiate. Entrencherado's wife, Rosalia, and Colonel Francisco inaugurated the conciliation effort. On May 15, they discussed means to resolve the confrontation. Pending discovery of a way out, Colonel Francisco promised to keep the Constabulary at a distance. Impressive assistance arrived on May 16. Representative Tomas Confesor and Attorney General Alva Hill drove to Jero through hostile crowds to lend their voices to the moderating cause. Late that afternoon, Governor General Leonard Wood sailed into Iloilo harbor aboard the executive yacht *Apo*. Apprised of the situation, he offered to discuss mutual problems with the Emperor.[32]

Wood's gesture defused the political time bomb. On the morning of May 17, Major Burton Read (the Governor General's aide-de-camp), Francisco, Confesor, and Hill met with Entrencherado, his relieved wife, and suspicious imperial advisers in Jaro's thatched palace. Due largely to Confesor's creative skills as an interpreter, persuasion broke the deadlock, and the Emperor agreed to discuss affairs of state with his American counterpart. Shortly after noon, Florencio I boarded the *Apo*. Kissing the Governor General's hand, he said, "Spain is the mother and the United States is the father of the Philippines."[33] Anchor noises drowned out Wood's reply. While the gleaming yacht steamed down Panay's coast, her passengers exchanged pleasantries and practicalities. Soothed by the nautical atmosphere

31. *Mindanao Herald*, June 4, 1927; N.A., B.I.A., Personal Name Information File.

32. *Manila Tribune*, May 17, 1927.

33. *Manila Tribune*, May 26, 1927.

and spoiled by the Governor General's stewards, Entrencherado's anxieties seemed to fade. When mealtime came, however, he refused to sample the fare. Confesor again resolved an embarrassing situation. Volunteering to act as food-taster, he painstakingly introduced Florencio I to a repast worthy of Malacañan Palace.[34] Remaining imperial animosities evaporated in the smoke of fine after-dinner cigars. By sunset, the Emperor had capitulated to kindness. When the *Apo* hove to off Iloilo town, he issued a proclamation ordering his subjects to disperse and voluntarily boarded an interisland steamer outbound for Manila. Wood and his Filipino-American negotiating team had every reason to feel satisfied with the day's work.

Entrencherado landed in the colonial capital on May 19. After a brief interview with journalists, he was driven to San Lazaro. Two weeks later, psychiatrists certified his precarious mental condition. In 1929, he was transferred to spacious quarters in the new Insular Psychopathic Hospital. Accorded royal treatment by order of the Governor General, he received daily visits from his wife, Rosalia Entrencherado, and her niece, who lived in a small house beyond the hospital grounds. Neither woman worked. They apparently maintained themselves by selling the "crown jewels" and other imperial artifacts.[35] Mrs. Entrencherado prepared her husband's meals, perfumed his cigars, and proofread his voluminous writings until her death in 1933.[36] Florencio I quietly passed away two years later. Without question, he enjoyed the most civilized fate ever meted out to an aspiring peasant redeemer.

His followers were less fortunate. During June 1927, Courts of First Instance in Bacolod and Iloilo worked overtime to relieve the strain on provincial jails. Most Entrencheradistas were released with reprimands from trial judges, probably because it was planting time. Intransigent rebels, particularly those known as insubordinate employees, were ordered to municipal *carcels* for terms ranging from six

34. *Philippines Free Press*, June 4, 1927, 44.
35. Hall Papers, "Fernández Interview."
36. Hall Papers, Anne T. Hall, "The Entrencherado Revolt," unpublished seminar paper, Institute of Asian Studies, University of the Philippines, April 19, 1966, 15. During his years at San Lazaro and the Insular Psychopathic Hospital, Entrencherado wrote a series of lengthy letters to newspapers, some of which were published in the Spanish-language *El Debate*. He also composed a two-volume autobiography which was handed over to his heirs after his death.

months to two years. Men who led attacks on the towns of Negros Occidental received maximum sentences; one of the captured Montarde brothers went to Bilibid for life; the other three were imprisoned for twenty years. Similar punishments were handed down to instigators of the assault on La Carlota.[37] By the end of the month, Negrense authorities had efficiently rid themselves of a host of real and potential troublemakers. The central Visayas, consequently, became remarkably orderly.

One prominent incendiary remained at large. Policarpio Montarde, the leader of the raid on Victorias, managed to evade Constabulary pursuers and make his way to the mountains. Equipped with two pistols and surrounded by an aura of invincibility, he was welcomed as a natural leader by small outlaw bands. Policarpio seized his opportunity. Within weeks he forged the latter-day Babailanes into an irregular military force and launched a private guerrilla war against his pursuers.[38] The Constabulary, however, refused to be placed on the defensive. Fighting one desperate little rearguard action after another, Montarde fled across Negros, Cebu, Bohol, and northern Mindanao. His followers were killed or arrested by ones or twos, but Policarpio always managed to escape. Early in 1929, the apparently charmed *pistolero* slipped back into Negros. Several weeks later, municipal police surprised and arrested him in Guihulngan town, Negros Oriental. On August 29, 1929, the provincial Court of First Instance found him guilty on multiple counts. He was sentenced conclusively to Bilibid Prison: ten years for sedition; fourteen years, one month, and one day for second-degree homicide; and life for double murder.[39] The trial marked the end, chortled the Philippine Constabulary, of "one of the most notorious characters ever developed in the Visayas."[40] It also represented the dying gasp of the Entrencheradistas.

Long before Montarde's imprisonment, however, the uprising had passed from public attention. Official and unofficial reactions again followed time-honored precedents. Jocular or angry references to peasant ignorance and fanaticism shouldered aside impartial efforts to uncover the eruption's origin. Leonard Wood, who had handled the crisis with such delicacy, regarded the upheaval as a minor affair.

37. *Philippines Free Press*, June 25, 1927, 8.
38. *Manila Tribune*, April 25, 1929.
39. *Report of the Philippine Constabulary, 1929* (Manila), 11.
40. *Manila Tribune*, April 25, 1929.

"Whole incident," he cabled Washington, "is one of those fantastical quasi-religious outbreaks similar in general character to colorum outbreak although not so extensive."[41] Malacañan Palace, consequently, was quite willing to permit the tumult to be dismissed on gales of laughter. The Governor General even contributed to the light-hearted responses: three weeks after the rebellion he referred to it as an "imperialistic movement."[42]

Resident American publishers, however, saw nothing funny in the disturbances. Castigating the villagers who permitted an "insane fanatic" to provoke them into a "miniature revolution," the *Manila Daily Bulletin* pontificated:

The sincerity of the fanatics is no justification for their acts. If it were not for their sincerity they would be less dangerous. In their blind devotion to and excited defense of their leader, they are objects of pity. However, there is a limit to coddling and pampering them. When their misguided devotion carries them to the point where they constitute a public danger, where they defy authority, only unyielding severity will stop them.[43]

The *Philippines Free Press* took an identical stand:

The courts have labeled Intrencherado "mentally unbalanced" which is a diplomatic way of calling the man crazy, yet his hollow promises continue to attract credulous liegemen, believers who are ready to lay down their lives for him if need be. Nearly all of those followers, it is safe to say, are of the lowest stratum of society, men who have not received the benefit of an education, who very likely do not know the meaning of the printed page. They are more to be pitied than blamed, but for the sake of maintaining the prestige of our government, an example must be made of them.[44]

One Filipino daily viewed the uprising from a more perceptive angle. Admitting the humble origins and lack of education of Entrencherado's subjects, the *Manila Tribune* pointed to more complex motives:

Some enlisted from ignorance. They believed that under him, they would enjoy complete immunity from evils resulting from floods, earthquakes, lightning, etc., and would pay less taxes to the government. They were dazzled by the garb of the Emperor. Another small portion joined

41. *Philippines Free Press*, May 21, 1927, 40.
42. *Philippines Free Press*, June 4, 1927, 8.
43. *Manila Daily Bulletin*, May 16, 1927.
44. *Philippines Free Press*, May 21, 1927, 30.

for plunder and power. . . . The greater portion [however] joined for
revenge of accumulated wrongs and pent-up grievances . . . between the
rich and the poor.[45]

While unrecognized at the time, the *Tribune*'s observations represented the fuzzy shape of future reactions. The Entrencheradista
uprising constituted the last agrarian rebellion to be chronicled by
cliché. After 1927 the focus of rustic violence shifted from the southern islands to Manila's hinterland. Discord's proximity altered conventional editorial attitudes. City observers began to look upon peasant upheavals as manifestations of something other than primitive
superstition. In the search for explanations of the recurring protests,
"poverty" and "landlessness" replaced "fanaticism" and "ignorance."
By 1930, sophisticated Manileños increasingly interpreted provincial
insurrections, no matter how outlandish their goals, as calls for help.

45. *Manila Tribune,* May 28, 1927.

CHAPTER 9

San José to Tayug

Incipient nationalism notwithstanding, the Colorum and Entrencheradista episodes followed established patterns. Emphasis on the glories of independence characterized both discordant expressions; in reality, however, neither Lantayug nor Florencio I gained converts by their ostensible patriotism. Their undeniable attraction rested instead on direct appeals to the religious beliefs and ethical yearnings of Filipino villagers. Dire prophecies linked to alleged communication with divine or semidivine beings won and retained hamlet loyalties. In each instance, supernaturalism provided the unifying element. The fact that both manifestations occurred in the third decade of the twentieth century was purely coincidental. Similar efforts to create a moral order had surfaced repeatedly during the preceding three hundred years. Propelled by the little tradition's turbulent undercurrents, Colorumism and Entrencheradism broke forth as modern variations on ancient themes.

Popular upheavals also erupted in north-central Luzon. Between 1924 and 1931, new secret associations arose that were dedicated to social reorganization. Insular authorities—conditioned by events in Surigao—labeled the dissidents "Colorums" and tried to connect their activities with real or imagined religious conspiracies elsewhere in the archipelago. But the Ilocano dissenters of Nueva Ecija and Pangasinan knew little or nothing of their southern counterparts. Vicitimized by land-grabbers and practically excluded from the colonial regime's political processes, they considered themselves worldly innovators. Utopianism characterized their collective strivings. While mysticism played a contributing role, in the final analysis Luzon's hamlet insurgents did not rely on heavenly intervention. Drawing strength from their own violent heritage, they launched relatively down-to-earth struggles to right secular wrongs.

Without question, grievances abounded. Since the days of Guardia de Honor and Santa Iglesia, conditions in eastern Pangasinan and northern Nueva Ecija had worsened. Laissez-faire land policies contributed to the social debacle. After 1900, Ilocano pioneers poured through the territory seeking unclaimed hectares. By 1920 their vanguard had spilled over into the Cagayan Valley and begun to clear its forested precincts. The migration, unfortunately, failed to satisfy basic land hungers. The same lamentable agrarian conditions that existed in central Luzon's more developed sectors soon prevailed in the Iloko-speaking districts of both provinces.[1] Diligent farmers who originally aspired to become self-sustaining citizens suddenly found themselves in the degrading position of share tenants. Hope died hard. Despairing of assistance from callous elitists or indifferent Americans, a desperate minority turned to defiant *co-provincianos* for solace and solutions.

In the context of peasant history, Luzon's rebel leaders represented transitional types. Maturing under United States jurisdiction, their attitudes toward insurgency combined old and new ingredients. Like the *tulisanes* and *papas* of bygone days, they won popular respect by challenging the prevailing order. They also attracted hamlet supporters by personal charisma. Their purposes, however, differed radically from those of the past. Unlike most of their predecessors, they believed salvation of sorts could be achieved on earth. Patriotic secret societies, rather than revitalizing religions, constituted their answer to the peasantry's plight. Ultimately, they were dedicated to fomenting spontaneous revolutions. They sought, therefore, to strike the terroristic spark which would ignite a general uprising.

The romantic expedient's first advocate was Pedro Kabola.[2] A wiry

---

1. Statistics on tenancy rates in Nueva Ecija and Pangasinan for the 1920's were never published. By 1939, however, Nueva Ecija had the highest percenttage (67.8) in the Philippines. See Pelzer, *Pioneer Settlement*, 92. Pangasinan's rate for the same year was 33.8. But the figure failed to reveal conditions in the eastern third of the province. Tenancy figures in several *municipios* verged on 99 per cent. In 1936 investigators said of Tayug, "There are three outstanding hacenderos, Messrs. Mariano Lichauco, Luis Lichauco and Macario Lichauco . . . there are no other private landowners in the entire municipality." *Fact Finding Report*, 256.

2. The most detailed account of Kabola and the abortive San José uprising of 1925 appears in R. M. Stubbs, "Philippine Radicalism: The Central Luzon Uprisings, 1925–1935" (Doctoral dissertation, History, University of California, Berkeley, 1951), 24–53.

field hand with an affinity for trouble, he was born during the last decade of the nineteenth century in Narvacan, Ilocos Sur. Around 1910, he left his crowded birthplace and, joining other land-seekers, moved down the narrow coast to settle temporarily in eastern Pangasinan. While fellow settlers carved out homesteads, Kabola followed less mundane interests. Footloose by nature, he traveled from barrio to barrio and from odd job to odd job, lingering only long enough to accumulate a few centavos and to absorb a locality's stormy legends. Fired by tales of daring bandits and swashbuckling religious rebels, he formulated impractical plans to carry on the insubordinate tradition. His amateurish attempts to establish underground societies led to repeated difficulties with municipal authorities. Late in 1918, consequently, he shifted his operational base to Nueva Ecija.

The move brought no improvement in Kabola's relationships with officialdom. By 1921, Constabulary records listed a series of alleged crimes under his name. Among other things, he had been arrested on five separate occasions for sedition, extortion, conspiracy, horse thievery, and attempted rape.[3] In each instance—to the frustration of the police—provincial courts released Kabola on grounds of insufficient evidence. Notoriety in the *presidencias* of Pangasinan and Nueva Ecija, however, added up to celebrity status in the region's villages. In the view of many barrio people, Kabola's successful circumventions of the law contributed an aura of invincibility to his reputation. By 1923, he was ready to parlay his fame and his knowledge of the countryside into a revolutionary movement.

Early that year, Kabola and a few friends founded the Kapisanan Makabola Makasinag (Association of the Worthy Kabola). Peasant interest in the covert organization was stimulated by a variety of ingenious techniques. Kabola, for example, let it be known that he was in regular communication with the living personalities of José Rizal and Felipe Salvador.[4] The martyred heroes, he told potential recruits, had commissioned him to lead a popular struggle for the liberation of the Philippines. True to the miraculous tradition, Kabola also guaranteed invulnerability to villagers who affiliated themselves with the Kapisanan. At that point, his appeals diverged sharply from

3. *Philippines Free Press,* March 14, 1925, 5.
4. Macaraig, *Social Problems,* 410.

rustic precedents. Kabola did not advocate spiritual means to accomplish temporal ends. He called instead for the establishment of a secret people's army. When enough contingents had been formed, he maintained, surprise attacks on strategic municipalities would throw insular authorities into disarray. Successful local uprisings would provoke the masses to action. Decisive aid of terrestrial origin would then materialize. The Emperor of Japan, Kabola assured his listeners, approved Kapisanan goals.[5] Widespread disorder in the Islands would signal intervention by the Imperial Fleet. Outmaneuvered, outmanned, and outgunned, Americans and *caciques* would flee the Philippines. Wholesale property redistributions would then follow, setting the stage for an era of unbroken peace and plenty.[6]

The proposition was enough to seduce almost any hamlet dweller into sedition. But Kabola added further lures to his message. Fully aware of the peasantry's fascination with conspiratorial fraternities, he evolved elaborate initiation rites and intricate symbolism for the Kapisanan's membership. Entrants were required to pay a 3.20 peso enrollment fee, to endure inoculation with a diluted mercury solution, to take a solemn, Katipunan-style oath, and to abide by complex regulations designed to maintain the organization's secrecy. They were also ordered to acquire weapons and to prepare colorful uniforms for the impending struggle for liberation.[7]

Initially, at least, Kabola's caution yielded dividends. He and his aides began to sport the trappings of prosperity. Despite mounting suspicion, provincial authorities remained in the dark concerning both the society and its violent goals. Lengthening Kapisanan membership rolls testified to the *supremo*'s success. Within a year, 1,500 farmers in four provinces had joined the patriotic movement and approximately ten times that number had become covert sympathizers.[8] Assuming the title "General-in-Chief," Kabola—splendid in military shirt, riding breeches, cavalry boots, and side arms—inspired his followers with periodic inspection trips to remote barrios.[9] By mid-1924,

5. *Philippines Free Press*, March 14, 1925, 5.
6. *Report of the Governor General of the Philippines, 1925* (in ms.; National Archives, Washington, D.C.), 565.
7. For initiation procedures and membership requirements, see Stubbs, 34–36.
8. *Report of the Governor General of the Philippines, 1925*, 565.
9. Kabola sold ranks in his liberation army to members of the organization. The P3.20 initiation fee assured a classification of "private"; higher categories

many of his village adherents were convinced they represented the tide of the future.

Their confidence was misplaced. Kabola's sudden affluence piqued the curiosity of Nueva Ecija's politicians and policemen. When surveillance failed to produce evidence of illegalities, they resorted to more subtle detection methods. In December 1924, paid informers learned of the Kapisanan and notified their official benefactors. Determined to avoid another Surigao, Constabulary officers developed a consuming interest in their old adversary. By the end of January 1925, they had collected a body of information on Kabola and his society. At roughly the same time, government agents infiltrated the supposedly secret organization.[10] Intrigue, in short, produced counterintrigue. Before Kabola recognized what was happening, he had been outplayed at his own game.

The battle of wits ended abruptly in early March. Driven to premature action by his impatient followers, Kabola laid plans for an insurrection. The uprising was to take place on the night of March 5–6, 1925. San José town—Felipe Salvador's initial objective—was to be the primary target. When the municipality had been overrun, victorious Kapisananes would punish official malefactors, redistribute land, and proclaim independence. The plot, oddly enough, outlined nothing in the way of follow-up operations. Kabola and his aides probably assumed that one dramatic success would provoke similar triumphs everywhere.

The strategy's demerits were never tested. Fully aware of Kabola's intentions, the Constabulary bided its time. Opportunity for a crackdown came on insurrection eve. At nightfall on March 4, Kabola met his followers to issue final instructions. Two hundred society members from San José's barrios and several government agents attended the conclave.[11] A six-man Constabulary squad, led to the forest clearing

---

and their respective prices were: corporal, P5.20; sergeant, P8.20; lieutenant, P10.20; captain, P15.20; major, P20.20; colonel, P30.20; and general, P50.20. The 20-centavo charge covered the cost of the diluted mercury inoculation which supposedly granted invulnerability to its recipient. *Philippines Free Press,* March 14, 1925, 8.

10. Stubbs, 43.

11. The account of the incident is drawn from Stubbs. Newspaper versions indicated the troopers were attacked by Kapisananes. See *Manila Daily Bulletin,* March 5, 1925. Published Constabulary summaries also maintained that the patrol acted in self-defense. *Khaki and Red,* July, 1931, 203.

by informers, also slipped into a concealed position near the site. The patrol leader quickly sized up the martial capacity of the rebels and decided to employ an ancient ruse. While Kabola spoke, individual troopers crawled to dispersed points around the gathering. The *supremo*'s peroration signaled the moment for organized pandemonium. Firing rifles, shouting commands, and scurrying noisily through tinder-dry underbrush, the constables first generated panic and then charged. Kabola and his aides tried to rally their confused subordinates. Before anything resembling order could be established, troopers killed the "General-in-Chief" and five "staff officers." Kabola's death unleashed a stampede into the enveloping darkness. Too frightened to run, seventy-two Kapisananes discarded weapons and lifted their hands. Resignation gave way to dejection when they realized they had capitulated to six constables—three of whom were bleeding profusely from deep bolo wounds.

The demoralizing reversal set the tone for the ensuing days. By dawn of March 5, constabularymen and municipal police had rounded up Kapisanan suspects throughout the region. News of the engagement, however, spread across neighboring municipalities even more rapidly than mobile government patrols. Exaggerated reports of the conspiracy created furors in Nueva Ecija and Pangasinan. While peasants abandoned barrios for the comparative safety of the countryside, overseers and *hacenderos* evacuated great houses for the security of the provincial capital. The simultaneous counterflights exposed the north's hidden torment. Kapisananes, quite obviously, were not the only residents thinking in violent terms. Practically the entire population—rich and poor alike—was concerned about class conflict.

Within two weeks, the affair had taken on less ominous implications. Governmental interrogators questioned 1,053 Kapisananes—most of whom had surrendered voluntarily—and released all but eighty-five.[12] When the small scope of the flare-up became known, urban journalists relegated the episode to the status of a tempest in a teapot. The *Philippines Free Press,* Manila's bellwether journal, summed up majority opinion:

And now in the grey dawn of "the morning after," the truth is seeping in; the army of 12,000 men dwindling to a few groups of ignorant, deluded, superstitious peasants; the principal "plot" being that concocted

12. *Report of the Governor General of the Philippines, 1925,* 566.

by the leader of the band to collect as many pesos and young women from the members as possible; and the weapons of revolution being found to consist of wooden spears, a few rusty pistols and some two dozen cartridges.[13]

Justice proceeded despite editorial ridicule. Late in March, forty-four conspiracy and forty-one sedition indictments were filed in Nueva Ecija's Court of First Instance. Public passions received scant opportunity to cool. The mass trial began on April 10; nineteen days later the judge handed down his decisions. Given the hubbub of the preceding month, punishments were exceptionally light. Nine Kapisananes were granted acquittals. Thirty-five were found guilty on conspiracy charges and sentenced to jail terms ranging from one to eight months. Those accused of sedition encountered greater severity. The magistrate declared all forty-one culpable and consigned them to Bilibid for sentences of two to four years.[14] Compared to the treatment accorded peasant rebels in the past, the result constituted a humanitarian milestone.

Judicial leniency in the case, however, emanated from factors other than compassion. At least two extenuating circumstances influenced the outcome. In the first place, Kabola and his principal aides were dead. Their demise placed the ostensible villains of the piece well beyond government jurisdiction. Provincial authorities tended to regard surviving Kapisananes as representatives of that unwieldy social segment normally called the "ignorant masses." As such, they were not held completely accountable for their misdeeds. One prisoner's confession, for example, revealed a touching guilelessness. When asked what the purposes of the association were, he replied:

All I was told was that Apo Lakai [Kabola] was going to the United States last Tuesday morning, to return the night of the same day, and would carry with him the Philippine flag of independence. The flag was to be inaugurated last Wednesday, and there was a general convocation called for that day. We were to wear our uniforms and carry with us rice and money. I was not told what we were to do next, but I was made to understand that we were to swear to defend at all cost our flag of independence.[15]

The second influence in the jailed Kapisananes' favor came from

13. *Philippines Free Press*, March 14, 1925, 4.
14. Stubbs, 48.
15. *Philippines Free Press*, March 14, 1925, 6.

Manila. If the *Free Press* spouted conventional wisdom on the San José incident, rival publications avoided superficial treatment. Several newspapers, including the *Daily Bulletin,* abandoned reliance on "ignorance" and "fanaticism" and traced the abortive uprising to land-grabbers.[16] Malacañan Palace joined the swelling chorus. Governor General Wood ascribed the difficulties in Nueva Ecija to unhealthy agrarian conditions. "Behind the revolt," he declared, "were homesteaders who lost their farms and tenants with grievances against landlords."[17] Few provincial judges could ignore such voices. Cabanatuan's chief magistrate, accordingly, ended the awkward proceedings as quickly as possible and handed down what amounted to token punishments.

Official post-mortems, unfortunately, failed to reflect the moderate trend. An investigating committee made up of Filipino Cabinet members discounted economic arguments and attributed the outbreak to Kabola's pernicious influence. The dead incendiary, their report maintained, had undermined the traditional symbiosis between *hacenderos* and *taos*. Villagers, also, bore partial responsibility for the sad state of affairs. "Relations . . . between the proprietors and farm tenants, the homesteaders and the government are not what they should be," complained Manila's department heads, "because tenants and home-seekers are very unreasonable in many of their demands."[18] The Constabulary came to a similar conclusion. Leaving interpretive subtleties to his civilian superiors, central Luzon's district commander blamed the entire episode on Kabola. Colonel José de los Reyes predicted peace in Nueva Ecija "unless . . . the slain chieftain of the San José 'colorum' uprising, as generally believed by his followers and the ignorant masses, should come back to life and renew his attempt to establish a communistic government."[19]

The colonel's tongue-in-cheek observation was far more prescient than he realized. Kabola did not rise again. In short order, however, his followers emerged from the insular penitentiary. Older, wiser, and immeasurably tougher, some of the parolees harbored longings for a return match with the Constabulary. Kindred spirits—they soon discovered—dwelled in villages throughout the north. By early 1927,

16. *Manila Daily Bulletin,* March 17, 1925.
17. Stubbs, 48.
18. *Ibid.,* 50.
19. *Manila Daily Bulletin,* March 19, 1925.

pent-up hatreds had become devouring passions. All that was needed to spark new violence was dedicated leadership. Before the year ended, Kabola's rugged successor disembarked on one of Manila's piers.

Pedro Calosa, the returning traveler, had been molded by some of the same influences that shaped Kabola.[20] Both men were Ilocanos. Calosa was born near the turn of the century in Bauang, La Union. He too participated in the gathering migration from the Ilocos region, for early in the American period, his family had moved to Tayug, Pangasinan. Like Kabola, therefore, he was influenced by the diminishing shadows of Guardia de Honor and Santa Iglesia. There, however, biographical similarities ended. Unlike Kabola, Calosa grew to manhood under cosmopolitan circumstances. Orphaned by cholera, he and an older brother left the Philippines during the second decade of United States rule. For roughly the next ten years, he worked in Hawaii's sugar and pineapple fields, where backbreaking drudgery put the finishing touches on his dissident personality. In 1926, he forged Filipino contract laborers into an agricultural union and attempted to foment strikes for better wages and working conditions. When the effort failed, Calosa wound up behind bars. Labeled a dangerous agitator, he was released after serving time in the territorial prison and was deported to his homeland. The rebellious components of Calosa's character, consequently, added up to much more than the sum of Kabola's intransigent parts.

His Philippine activities reflected that complexity. At the first opportunity, Calosa left Manila's hostile environs and returned to eastern Pangasinan. The oppressive social atmosphere of the province depressed him even more than its primitive economy. Within six months, he was drawn—voluntarily in some instances, involuntarily in others—toward a number of seditious schemes. Forewarned of his record, the Constabulary kept Calosa under surveillance. Try as they might, however, men in khaki and red could not gather enough hard evidence to jail the ex-convict.[21] Harassed by the insular police and applauded secretly by peasant rebels, Calosa soon realized he was a

20. For biographical information on Calosa, see Appendix B of this volume.
21. Calosa and two former Kapisananes were arrested in January 1929 for planning an attack on the municipio of Rizal, Nueva Ecija. For a brief account of the incident, see *Report of the Governor General of the Philippines, 1929* (in ms.; National Archives, Washington, D.C.), 7.

marked man. In 1930 he accepted the situation's grim logic and became involved in what could only be classified as a revolutionary gesture.

Calosa's conspiracy avoided the artless errors that ruined Kabola's plot. Conditioned to circumspection by hard-handed experts in Hawaii and the Philippines, he moved cautiously toward ill-defined goals. Late in 1928 he formed an underground society called the P.N.A. (Philippine National Association). Membership in the religious organization did not come easily. Surrounded by informers and Constabulary agents, Calosa insisted that aides sound out potential converts thoroughly before alerting them to the association. Once inducted, proselytes were required to maintain absolute secrecy.[22] Calosa held up his end of the bargain by prohibiting anything resembling mass meetings. Communication was usually restricted to face-to-face encounters. Detailed instructions, when necessary, were dispensed through small congregations in back-country *iglesias*. The techniques worked. By mid-1930, more than a thousand peasants in Pangasinan and Nueva Ecija had been initiated into the patriotic faith. Municipal authorities and the insular police, furthermore, remained unaware of the organization.

Calosa's accomplishment created problems. His followers—particularly a handful of vindictive former Kapisananes—pressed him to implement Kabola's strategy. Alive to the impracticalities of the scheme, Calosa urged patience. His lieutenants listened but did not hear. Differences between the leaders sprang from contrary experiences. Calosa was the only P.N.A. director who had seen America's Pacific Fleet riding at its Pearl Harbor moorings. He was also the only one who had witnessed dedicated men crumble under overwhelming odds. His provincial associates failed to grasp either reality. To them, military power and the Constabulary were one and the same. They believed, moreover, that *taos* all over the Philippines were eager to strike down their oppressors. Naiveté and frustration led them to advocate violence. Warned finally that the P.N.A. would inaugurate its insurrection with or without him, Calosa reluctantly endorsed the quixotic exercise. He undoubtedly hoped to influence the venture toward partial success.

To an astonishing degree, he attained his purpose. Late in 1930,

22. For society oaths, see *Manila Tribune,* Jan. 13, 1931.

Calosa and Cesario Abé (a former aide to Kabola) decided to carry out a surprise attack on a northern municipality. Both men concluded outside assistance would be beneficial. During November and December they felt out *supremos* of other secret societies in neighboring provinces. Some dissident leaders endorsed the idea[23] but refused to commit their organizations to coordinated uprisings. Throwing caution to the winds, Calosa and Abé resolved to make the attack at the end of the holiday season. If all went well, the P.N.A. would: (1) wreak vengeance on the Constabulary; (2) plunder the property of municipal officials and prominent families; (3) dramatize the problems of tenant farmers; and (4) set off a spontaneous revolution. Incredibly, three of the goals were achieved.

The assault was carried out with a precision that would have gladdened the heart of Felipe Salvador.[24] Calosa and Abé kept their intentions to themselves until the eleventh hour. On the afternoon of January 10, 1931, they notified subordinates to prepare for action against Tayug, Pangasinan. The municipality's residents were still gripped by the post-New Year malaise. Dusty crepe paper and tattered tissue reminders of Christmas and Rizal Day drooped along the *municipio*'s quiet streets. Most citizens that Saturday felt as dull as the town's weathered decorations. Community officials and members of Tayug's understrength Constabulary detachment, like their spent fellow townsmen, retired early. The place—as Calosa and Abé had anticipated—was ripe for the taking.

The uprising began shortly after midnight. Rebels set fire to the houses of two municipal policemen in neighboring San Nicolas. With the community diverted by the flames, forty farmers equipped with bolos and a few vintage shotguns commandeered two provincial buses bound for Tayug ten kilometers away. While the vehicles lurched toward town, twenty or thirty more villagers—some on foot, others

---

23. The most powerful secret society in the region was the Tangulan led by Patricio Dionisio. The Constabulary regarded Calosa's organization as a branch of the Tangulan. Several authorities on the prewar decade perpetuated the error. See, for example, Hayden, *The Philippines,* 379. In interviews with the author, both Calosa and Dionisio denied the Constabulary's contention. The Tangulan and its controversial *supremo* will be discussed in Chapter 10.

24. The account of the uprising was drawn from Stubbs, 60–87, from the *Manila Daily Bulletin,* the *Manila Tribune,* and the *Philippines Free Press* of January 1931; and from Pedro Calosa's recollections. Since details of the engagement are relatively well known, repetitious citations will be avoided.

on horseback—converged on the *municipio*. Around 1:00 A.M., sixty or seventy peasants (including fourteen young women) assembled quietly near the Constabulary barracks. One of the girls lured the lone sentry from his post. Her male compatriots promptly hacked him to death and plunged him into the *cuartel*. Some of the insurgents attacked sleeping constables, others confiscated the company's racked rifles, broke open ammunition boxes, and set the structure ablaze. In the confusion, eight of eleven enlisted men escaped. Their superiors were less fortunate. Awakened by the commotion, the commander and his executive officer rushed toward the flaming barracks. Both men fell in the street under withering rifle fire. By 1:30 A.M. Tayug belonged to the insurgents. With their defenders dead or in headlong retreat, townspeople joined a pell-mell flight toward the countryside.

For the next five and a half hours the raiders dominated Tayug. During that chaotic interval, their activities bore the ambivalent stamp of most Philippine peasant uprisings. After routing the Constabulary they turned to assaults on other authority symbols. The *presidencia*, together with its hated land records, went up in flames, as did the post office. Looters broke into thirty-five houses—including several belonging to prominent citizens—stripped them of valuables, and put the torch to them. By daybreak the vendetta was over. When first light appeared behind the cordillera, the rebels reassembled in the littered streets and moved silently under charred Christmas decorations and a pall of smoke toward the deserted plaza. They halted beneath the bells of Tayug's old church. There, a spirit appropriate to the dawning Sabbath swept their ranks. Pounding and shouting finally brought a priest to the *convento* door. To his astonishment, he was greeted respectfully by the grimy company, which filed into the fortresslike edifice. While weary raiders entered the adjoining church to sprawl on ancient pews, their leaders requested mass and breakfast. The clergyman and his servants obliged. For their services they received expressions of gratitude. Spokesmen for the group also recommended that the pastor and his staff leave the buildings. After they left, members of the band settled down with satisfied souls and bellies to await developments.

Retribution came swiftly. An hour and a half after the attack on the Constabulary barracks, a survivor jogged into San Quentin town twelve kilometers to the southeast. He informed a telegrapher of events in Tayug. Immediately messages were sent to Manila and

Dagupan. The alarms contained exaggerated details on a massacre perpetrated by hundreds of "Colorums." Authorities in the colonial capital responded accordingly. Well before sunrise they ordered overwhelming forces into eastern Pangasinan. While police reinforcements hurried by road and rail toward the trouble zone, the Philippine Division of the United States Army (maneuvering on nearby Lingayen Gulf) was placed on standby alert. Around 6:30 A.M., the first Constabulary contingent—fifteen steel-helmeted troopers and two junior officers from Dagupan—arrived in Tayug. Thirty minutes later, carefully deployed riflemen opened fire on the *convento*. Secure behind massive walls, the rebels answered with a defiant fusilade.

The strange skirmish raged for twelve hours. Until late afternoon, the outcome remained in doubt. Accurate fire from besiegers kept the insurgents in their bastion. But random volleys from the church and *convento* also pinned down the assailants. By 4:00 P.M., ammunition supplies on both sides were almost gone. Developing uncertainties vanished when one hundred Constabulary reinforcements from Manila darted into the square. The tragic Sabbath soon reached its climax. Suddenly and inexplicably the *convento* door swung open. Firing ceased. A young woman stepped from the building. While disbelieving troopers stared, she lifted a Philippine flag over her head. Waving the emblem slowly, her bare feet moving to its cadence, she marched across the sun-splashed plaza. When she reached the statue of José Rizal, Constabulary rifles shattered the hypnotic spectacle. The woman's body crumpled beneath her banner at the monument's base. After that, both sides lost their zest for fratricide. Collective agonies ended when a storming party broke through bullet-splintered church doors into the dim nave. Rebels threw down their empty firearms and gave up the fight. By 7:00 P.M., Tayug town was quiet.

In the gathering darkness, officers moved through columns of smoke from Constabulary cooking fires and attempted to count the costs. Forty-four rebels had been captured. Six of the raiders—including the once-stately flag bearer and another woman—were dead. Twenty members of the determined band had suffered injuries. Somehow, fifteen or twenty more had managed to escape before troopers forced their way into the church. On the government side, five members of Tayug's scattered company had been killed. A captain from Manila, together with a lieutenant and three enlisted men from Dagupan's contingent, had been wounded. Property losses were extensive. Spiritual and psychological damages, however, were beyond calculation. Years later a Filipina novelist came close. "When it was over," wrote Kerima Polotan, "many things were gone. Not just relatives dead, and houses burned and important papers missing from the municipio, but something else again: a certain innocence, a graciousness, gone from the town."[25]

To the Constabulary's dismay, Calosa could be found among neither casualities nor captives. Interrogations failed to uncover any leads. Tight-lipped prisoners—emulating the still-defiant Abé—refused to disclose their chieftain's whereabouts. Fearing further attacks, officers ordered squad leaders to track down the *supremo*. Wide-ranging patrols discovered several cases of attempted arson but did not flush Calosa.[26] By sunrise of January 12, the subject of the manhunt appeared to have vanished. Around 10:00 A.M., a sergeant led his weary detachment as a last resort to the rebel leader's house. Calosa—the proud father of a newborn infant—was there. He maintained, furthermore, that he had devoted the preceding thirty-six hours to an exhausting paternal vigil.[27] Unable to dispute the squalling evidence, the disconcerted constables insisted that Calosa accompany them. He surrendered peacefully. Shortly after noon, Calosa and twelve other suspects—all women, arrested in or near their homes—were en route to Dagupan jail.

Shock waves from the episode rumbled across Luzon for several months. Before they subsided, customary urban attitudes toward agrarian unrest had received a series of unsettling jolts. The incarcerated peasants proved far more articulate than any of their predecessors. Many of them, moreover, were relatively well educated.[28] The

25. Kerima Polotan, *The Hand of the Enemy* (Manila, 1963), 12. The novelist's father, then a Constabulary lieutenant, led the Dagupan detachment into Tayug. Her fictional account of the incident captures the terror of an agrarian uprising to a greater degree than any other source.

26. The Constabulary maintained that Calosa left Tayug after the assault on the barracks and attempted to burn outbuildings of *"El Porvinir,"* the Lichauco family's 4,000-hectare estate. Stubbs, 78.

27. Until his death, Calosa insisted he was not in Tayug during the uprising. Testimony from participants (constables and raiders), however, indicated otherwise. *Manila Tribune*, Feb. 13, 1931.

28. The most disturbing aspect of the insurrection to Manileños was the prominent role played by Filipinas. Most of the female participants, furthermore, were young and had attended—or were attending—high school. See

combination brought village grievances to the fore in a dramatic fashion. Manila's newspapers, for example, quoted Cesario Abé extensively. He insisted the uprising had been staged "to secure a redistribution of wealth in order to help poor people free themselves from oppression."[29] Other dissidents spoke out against ecclesiastical persecution, saying they desired "the Independent Church to be the supreme religion in the Islands."[30] Another group held they had acted for patriotic reasons and "wanted only the Filipino flag to fly over government buildings."[31] All of them, furthermore, repudiated "Colorum" labels. The enunciation of compelling material, spiritual, and national goals, linked to the rejection of supernaturalism, reached sympathetic ears in Manila. Almost overnight, influential defenders rallied to the prisoners.

The mass trial—which began one month after the uprising—took place in a glare of publicity. Opposition politicians, led by Alejo Mabanag, *Democrata* candidate for the Senate, directed the defense. Calosa and Abé received additional assistance from prominent lawyers in Lingayen. The proceedings, consequently, consumed two and a half months. Mabanag established his argument early: appealing to the social consciences of his countrymen, he read rebel confessions into the record. One of the raiders, Benito Allas, declared, "Many of us, including myself, were formerly owners of big pieces of land in Tayug and Santa Maria. We have been driven from our lands by the *hacenderos,* from the lands which our fathers and grandfathers cleared [or] have occupied since time immemorial. Because of this grievance we have long planned . . . to drive away the *hacenderos* and get our lands back."[32]

Throughout February, March, and April, defense attorneys whittled down prosecution charges. They did not dispute the fact that a secret society had come into being. Nor did they deny that the organization had planned and executed an attack on Tayug. They contended, nevertheless, that their clients had been driven by lofty desires to

---

Aleko E. Lilius "The Women of Tayug," *Philippines Free Press,* Jan. 17, 1931, 41, 44.
29. *Philippines Free Press,* Jan. 17, 1931, 44.
30. *Manila Tribune,* Jan. 13, 1931.
31. *Manila Tribune,* Jan. 15, 1931.
32. *Philippines Free Press,* Feb. 14, 1931, 30.

correct accumulated evils. The real culprits were "caciquism," colonialism, and Catholicism. Behind the rebellion, they insisted, lurked a series of chronic irritants which produced only persecuted tenants, anxious nationalists, and frustrated Aglipayans. The insurrection, Mabanag and his men concluded, would never have occurred in a just society.

An equally determined prosecutor was unmoved. Pointing doggedly to the grisly results of peasant reform impulses, he demanded the maximum penalities due murderers and seditionists. The trial ended on April 20, 1931, with partial victory for both sides. No one received the death sentence. All of the women were released on grounds of insufficient evidence. The judge found most of the men guilty, but assigned them to only five years in prison. Ex-convicts Pedro Calosa and Cesario Abé emerged as the scapegoats. Both men were ordered to Bilibid for forty years. The Pangasinan Court of First Instance also required the convicted parties to pay 1,000 pesos in damages to the heirs of each of their Constabulary victims.[33]

It soon became apparent that Tayug's rebels had been heard. High-echelon responses to Mabanag's indictment of the system, however, left much to be desired. Newspapermen questioned Governor General Dwight F. Davis concerning conditions in Pangasinan. Davis admitted that there were many areas in the Philippines where tenants had just grievances but said he did not believe Tayug was one of them.[34] Secretary of the Interior Honorio Ventura fell back on more conventional interpretations. "The Colorums," he declared, "had no definite purpose in what they did. The spirit behind the movement was a hash of religion, politics, fanaticism and a little of everything else that can serve to enflame them." Ventura ended his statement on a hard note: "If the government could afford it there would be no problem. It is just a matter of adding some 10,000 men to the Constabulary and distributing the force in all the municipalities."[35]

His opinion did not go unchallenged. Tomas Confesor—who had ably assisted Leonard Wood toward a peaceful resolution of the

33. Decision: Criminal Case No. 11885, Lingayen Court of First Instance. Cited in Alejandro R. Tauli, "The 'Colorums' of Tayug" (Unpublished paper, Institute of Asian Studies, University of the Philippines, 1966), 16.
34. *New York Times*, Jan. 22, 1931.
35. H. E. Fey, "Farmers' Revolt in the Philippines," *Christian Century*, XLVIII (1931), 1004.

Entrecherado affair—disputed Ventura's reasoning. As the outspoken new Director of Commerce and Industry, he traced Tayug to "caciquism." Confesor, moreover, went further and ascribed the growth of aggressive religious sects throughout the Philippines to economic inequities. Most "colorums," he said, "are in reality nothing but discontented tenants who have been mercilessly exploited and who seek revenge through acts of violence."[36]

Influential American residents echoed Confesor's theme. Speaking for the American Chamber of Commerce in the Islands, Walter Robb criticized the Constabulary for its trigger-happy performance. "Of what to do there may have been doubt," he grumbled, "but never a doubt of willingness to do it."[37] Tayug's troopers received similar castigations from A. V. H. Hartendorp, the editor of *Philippine Magazine*. Men in khaki and red, he suggested, "instead of striding along with guns on their shoulders, might well get a little closer to the people." Hartendorp also warned his readers that a dangerous cleavage was developing between classes: "Our legislators should think more about the common people—at other times than just before elections. We should be on our guard in this country against the government becoming an *ilustrado* government out of touch with the people and unsympathetic to their needs, leaving them ready to turn to men of the type of Pedro Calusa [*sic*] for leadership."[38] The most startling statement, however, came from the editorial office of the *Philippines Free Press*. After years of crusading against fanaticism, the weekly proclaimed a new gospel:

Let's get over the ridiculous idea that every manifestation of unrest rises from colorum activities. . . . No nation can be founded on a downtrodden peasantry which is constantly in debt to landowners. Any attempt to blame religious fanaticism for the effort of an oppressed peasantry to achieve some measure of economic independence is ridiculous and dangerous—ridiculous because it sows the seed for more widespread manifestations of that discontent.

36. *Philippines Free Press,* Jan. 24, 1931, 30.
37. Walter Robb, "What Ho, the Guard," *American Chamber of Commerce Journal,* XL (1931), 18.
38. A. V. H. Hartendorp. "The Tayug 'Colorums,'" *Philippine Magazine,* XXVII (1931), 567. Editorial heat led to official inquiries into Constabulary conduct prior to and during the uprising. Lieutenant Colonel Ramon Ochoa, the provincial commander, was reprimanded and dropped to the bottom of the seniority list. *Manila Daily Bulletin,* April 16, 1931.

It's about time that some facts were looked in the face, and that the *laissez-faire* theory of doing nothing be thrown out of our government.[39]

The "facts," unfortunately, were not faced. Three peasant rebellions and one abortive conspiracy in seven years wrought no change in Philippine life. Some editors and a handful of politicians called for reforms. Their appeals went unheeded. Social distance between villagers and elitists, consequently, continued to grow. Few insular Americans or Filipino administrators comprehended the significance of the gap. It had existed too long—become so much a part of daily routine that its potential was no longer discernible. The Constabulary, for instance, regarded the Tayug incident as an inexplicable event. On the organization's thirtieth anniversary, an official chronicler revealed his inability to perceive the obvious: "The officers and soldiers . . . in this municipality were Filipinos who had been stationed there for years. They met the town folk . . . at parties, and the officers stood high . . . with the cream of society. They all spoke the . . . local dialect. Many of them spoke English and Spanish, and yet one of the most unexpected surprises—a massacre—occured [*sic*]."[40]

Americans—fresh from the depression-threatened United States—grasped the situation immediately.[41] Social tensions in the Philippines struck them with an initial impact comparable to Manila's heat. Above all, Tayug brought the message to Malacañan Palace. Calosa's uprising was not dismissed as an isolated or unimportant event: Surigao in 1924, Nueva Ecija in 1925, Negros and Panay in 1927, Pangasinan in 1931; however viewed, the sequence foreshadowed trouble. A new Governor General, John C. Early, expressed private concern and began confidential inquiries into the state of provincial affairs. At his behest, peasant leaders visited the Palace. Most of them spoke frankly. General Teodoro Sandiko, a fiery old Katipunero, held nothing back. "The Americans," he said, "have too much respect for property and property rights. Let the United States get out, and the oppressed will soon right things with the bolo."[42]

39. *Philippines Free Press*, Jan. 17, 1931, 30.
40. *Khaki and Red*, July 1931, 204.
41. See, for example, the comments of Joseph R. Hayden, "Cooperation in the Philippines Found to Carry Its Penalties," in *Christian Science Monitor*, Sept. 12, 1931.
42. Hayden, *The Philippines*, 410.

PART IV

SECULAR MOVEMENTS

And Jesus said,
Beware of false prophets
For they will appear in sheep's clothing
But they are like ravening wolves
And ye shall know them by their works

Matthew 7 : 15, 16

CHAPTER 10

Urban Conspiracies

Teodoro Sandiko's rhetoric summed up the unexpressed feelings of many Filipinos. Dissatisfaction, after all, was not a purely rural phenomenon. The peasantry, furthermore, was not the only discontented element in Philippine society. With the inauguration of Filipinization, old-school revolutionaries—especially Emilio Aguinaldo's confidants —found themselves excluded from the developing *Nacionalista* oligarchy. Cut off from the centers of power, some of them flirted with plots to topple the American regime. During the late 1920's and early 1930's members of emerging social groups also began to experience disaffection. Unlike the aging patriots, bourgeois and proletarian dissenters abandoned their nostalgic notions concerning what might have been. Alienated segments of the new urban classes—particularly after the onset of the Great Depression—encountered economic complexities of an unprecedented nature. A minority sought radical solutions to their problems. Like General Sandiko, some city dwellers concluded that American power constituted the primary obstacle to effective reform. They concentrated, therefore, on achieving early or immediate independence as the first step toward social rectification. A few extremists even made plans to achieve the goal through popular uprisings. On a lesser scale, then, Manila became a source for political conspiracies comparable in many respects to the millennial undercurrents flowing through the provinces. After the Tayug uprising, the separate streams of protest began to merge.

Faint outlines of rural-urban coalition appeared first in the Ricartista movement. Artemio Ricarte y García, the focal point of a decade and a half of plotting against the American regime, was the only prominent nationalist who refused to accept the outcome of the Filipino-American War.[1] While more adaptable leaders adjusted to

---

1. The best accounts of Ricarte are G. K. Goodman, "General Artemio

the advantages and disadvantages of United States sovereignty, Ricarte remained loyal to the "spirit of '96."[2] Rather than compromise his principles, he endured exile, solitary confinement, and expatriation. Predictably, he became a symbol of selfless patriotism to chauvinistic islanders of the postrevolutionary generation. Ricarte, unfortunately, outlived his reputation for gallantry. In early 1942, after a thirty-year absence, the venerable general returned to his homeland in the company of Japanese conquerors. Ricarte's association with the invaders during the Occupation shattered his heroic image. Equally despised by collaborating oligarchs and resisting commoners, he experienced a fall from nationalistic grace.[3] By the time World War II ended and the seventy-nine-year-old Ricarte expired, both in 1945, insular opinion had consigned him temporarily to the status of a Filipino Marshal Petain. Of all the irreconcilables at the century's turn, only Artemio Ricarte y García suffered a fate akin to that meted out in Greek tragedy.

Nothing in Ricarte's early life indicated its Aeschylean outcome. Born on October 20, 1866, of reasonably well-to-do parents in Batac town, Ilocos Norte, he had profited from the expanding educational system. Trained to read, write, and calculate in Batac's Dominican primary school, he completed a college preparatory course at the Order's Manila academy, San Juan de Letran. In 1886 he enrolled in Santo Tomas. Like many of his student contemporaries, however, Ricarte rebelled against the political and intellectual constraints of the Pontifical University. Financially unable to acquire a European education, he transferred to the new Escuela Normal in the capital's

---

Ricarte and Japan," *Journal of Southeast Asian History,* VII (1960), 48–60; and Amando J. Malaya's Introduction to the *Memoirs of General Artemio Ricarte* (Manila, 1963), xv–xxv. Unless otherwise indicated, details on the General's career through 1915 are drawn from Malaya's profile; those after 1915 are based on Goodman's article.

2. Ricarte recommended the substitution of "Rizalines" for "Philippines." He also advocated patriotic names for children. His grandson, for example, was christened Bislumino ("Bis" for Bisayans, "lu" for Luzon, and "mino" for Mindanao). F. A. Reel, *The Case of General Yamashita* (Chicago, 1949), 135.

3. Ricarte was damned as a traitor by both sides in the postwar collaboration dispute. See, for example, H. J. Abaya, *Betrayal in the Philippines* (New York, 1946), 50; and C. M. Recto, *Three Years of Enemy Occupation* (Manila, 1946), 19. For a provocative recent discussion of the issue see D. J. Steinberg, *Philippine Collaboration in World War II* (Ann Arbor, Mich., 1967). Another view is provided by T. A. Agoncillo, *The Fateful Years,* 2 vols. (Quezon City, 1965).

Ermita district. In 1888 he received an elementary teaching certificate. That same year, he began his brief career as a provincial schoolmaster in San Francisco del Malabon, Cavite.

Bright, ambitious, and ideologically inclined, Ricarte soon tired of classroom routine. In 1893 he found a more challenging outlet for his energies. Teacher by day, conspirator by night, he became a leading architect of the revolutionary infrastructure spreading through Manila's hinterland. Adopting the alias "Vibora" (Viper), he achieved a responsible position in one of the Katipunan's influential Cavite councils.[4] When fighting erupted in 1896, Ricarte threw himself into the struggle. The Viper's spirited leadership quickly demonstrated the appropriateness of his *nom de guerre*. By the end of 1897 he had risen to the rank of captain general in the Revolutionary Army. After the truce of Biyak-na-Bato and the appearance of Commodore Dewey's squadron in Manila Bay, Ricarte returned confidently to his earlier activities. His elation however, proved short-lived. Early doubts concerning America's intentions led him to warn Aguinaldo of an imperialist coup.[5] Ricarte's realistic political assessment and unblemished martial record again won him a strategic post. When fighting broke out between the United States and the embryonic Philippine government, Vibora was serving as operations chief of the Second Military Zone around Manila. He remained in similar command positions throughout 1899. Despite all the reverses of those years, for Ricarte they must have been a heady experience. Events had transformed an outwardly reticent pedagogue into a decisive man of action.

The dawn of the twentieth century, however, marked an end to Ricarte's record of accomplishment. With Aguinaldo's army crumbling and its remnants resorting to guerrilla warfare, Vibora evolved a daring scheme to shore up the disintegrating cause. Manila, he believed, constituted the key to the precarious military and political situation.[6] If the colonial capital could be wrested from the enemy, American supply lines might be disrupted, and in the United States the Republican Party's comfortable majority might be dissolved. A frontal as-

4. Inspiration for the alias came from Matthew 10:16. Leopoldo Serrano, "Vibora, the Misunderstood Patriot," *Philippine Herald Magazine* (July 26, 1958), 4.
5. T. A. Agoncillo, *Malolos: The Crisis of the Republic*, 179.
6. See Appendix D, "Unsigned Draft of a Letter in Regard to Attack on Manila, January 1900, Found in Papers of General Ricarte y Vibora," in *Memoirs of General Artemio Ricarte*, 100–101.

sault, quite obviously, was beyond question. But a clandestine attack offered remote possibilities for success. On the night of July 3–4, 1900, therefore, Ricarte and members of his civilian-clad Viper Regiment attempted to infiltrate the colonial capital. They hoped to occupy strategic points in the metropolis from which they could provoke an insurrection against the occupying power. The gamble failed. American patrols, in fact, captured Ricarte and most of his dispersed raiders on their way into the city. A few scattered and easily extinguished fires ignited by arsonists revealed the conspiracy's picayune outcome. When the sun rose on the one hundred twenty-fourth birthday of the United States, Artemio Ricarte had no reason to celebrate. "Independence Day" 1900 marked the end of his freedom.

From then on, liberty became an elusive commodity in Ricarte's life. Offered amnesty by his captors in return for an oath of allegiance, the general declined. Not to be outdone, the Americans followed through on their threat. Six months later, Ricarte and other recalcitrant nationalists—including Apolinario Mabini and Gregorio Aglipay —were unceremoniously transported to a penal colony on Guam. The isolation technique achieved its purpose. One by one the homesick exiles compromised with the inevitable, took the required oath, and returned to their native land. By 1903, only Ricarte and the ailing Mabini remained in Agaña. In February the Americans closed the camp on Guam and shipped both of its inmates back to Manila. Officials in the Philippines, however, were in no mood to let bygones be bygones. Before permitting either man to disembark, port authorities demanded indications of allegiance to the new regime. Mabini— paralyzed and mortally ill with tuberculosis—complied. Ricarte, hale, hearty, and still haughty, refused. He was immediately escorted to the customshouse and given a final opportunity to recant. When he again declined, he was hurried aboard a steamer bound for Hong Kong. The unnecessary little melodrama on Manila's waterfront probably sealed Ricarte's fate. Penniless, alone, and completely embittered, Vibora committed himself to a one-man crusade against the Americans in the Philippines.[7]

His second involuntary absence from the archipelago was of shorter duration. Die-hard Filipinos in the British Crown Colony came to

7. Ricarte's views toward the United States were made clear by his revolutionary superior. Emilio Aguinaldo and V. A. Pacis, *A Second Look at America* (New York, 1957), 185–186.

Ricarte's aid. By May 1903 he had become the leader of a government-in-exile which was busily engaged in formulating plans to renew hostilities. Rumors of an impending conflict between Japan and Russia provoked dreams among Hong Kong's polyglot exiles of sympathetic explosions throughout colonial Asia. In December 1903, consequently, Ricarte slipped back into Manila bent upon igniting a local conflagration. His effort came to naught. Old comrades-in-arms and fellow internees tried to convince Vibora that the times were no longer ripe for political or military intrigues.[8] Never-say-die anti-Americans such as Macario Sakay and Felipe Salvador, moreover, either rejected or ignored Ricarte's requests for assistance. Undeterred, he pressed on. He won the support of a few obscure hyperpatriots and provoked a minor Constabulary defection in Ilocos Sur, but he did not set off a popular upheaval.[9] All Ricarte really accomplished was to renew American interests in his activities. In May 1904, constables arrested him in Mariveles, Bataan. Tried and convicted for subversion, he was sentenced to Bilibid Prison. Ricarte entered the penitentiary on June 7, 1904, where he remained in solitary confinement for six years.

During his imprisonment, Ricarte's only contacts were jailors, ants, cockroaches, and occasional American officials requesting acceptance of their infernal oath. Divested of everything but his life, Vibora rejected their threats and blandishments. A sympathetic English journalist finally won minor concessions for the prisoner.[10] Supplied with pen and paper, Ricarte retained his sanity by compiling a sketchy memoir of the revolution against Spain. When the general completed his sentence in June 1910 and stepped through Bilibid's heavy gate, waiting Americans apprehended him and transferred him to the port area. At the customshouse, he was subjected to the same procedures he had been resisting for a decade. Confronted with the usual choice, allegiance or banishment, he responded in the customary manner. By evening, he was on another ship destined for Hong Kong. The calendar read June 26, 1910. For all practical purposes, however, to

8. Appendix L, "Police Record of Artemio Ricarte," in *Memoirs of General Artemio Ricarte*, 132–133.
9. For an account of the Constabulary mutiny in Vigan, Ilocos Sur, see *Report of the Philippine Commission, 1904*, IV, 101–105.
10. William Watson of the Manila *Cablenews* compiled an extensive collection on the Revolutionary and early American period in the Philippines. The papers are available for the use of researchers at the American Embassy in Manila.

Ricarte and his bureaucratic tormentors it might as well have been July 4, 1900.

In a very real sense, Vibora never recovered from the trauma of his original capture. He devoted the next four and a half years to a variety of activities designed to weaken or bring down Spain's successor. Oblivious to the growing pro-American consensus in the Philippines, he continued to scheme with the dedication of a belligerent. Association with extremist groups in Hong Kong accentuated his desire for vengeance. Soon ostracized by conservative Filipino residents, Ricarte found his way into the Crown Colony's *demimonde* of colonial refugees, political eccentrics, and free-lance espionage agents. In conjunction with twenty or so like-minded Filipinos, he hoped to harass the United States into abandoning its imperial experiment. In cooperation with Usa Onkihiko, proprietor of a Hong Kong house of prostitution and self-anointed Japanese spy, he also worked to accumulate intelligence on American defenses in the Philippines. Ricarte's activities from 1910 to 1915, in short, established the affiliations which eventually destroyed him.

None of his endeavors succeeded. He first initiated a propaganda campaign through *El Grito de Presente,* a Spanish-language fortnightly that advocated boycott of American goods and antimetropolitan violence. In its pages, Ricarte called constantly for immediate independence. To the standard nationalist demand, however, he added fervent appeals for redistribution of insular wealth. Neither the tabloid nor its publisher-editor created much enthusiasm. Short on subscribers in Hong Kong and the Philippines, *El Grito* went out of business. Ricarte simultaneously sought to maintain himself and his patriotic vendetta through a variety of questionable activities. Among other things, he conducted long-distance recruiting campaigns for a Luzon liberation army. Income from the sale of commissions helped defray the costs of his private crusade. In 1913, probably in collaboration with Usa or other Japanese nationals, Vibora masterminded the theft of secret documents on Corregidor's Coast Artillery positions. Eleventh-hour intervention by Constabulary agents prevented delivery of the plans to Ricartista liaison men.[11] Alert again to his machinations, American authorities placed Ricarte's Philippine supporters under surveillance and pondered means to neutralize his "Oriental

11. N.A., B.I.A., F.E. 4865-77.

cunning." Convinced he was a profiteer, they offered indirectly to buy off the general, a proposition which Ricarte rejected.[12] Early in 1914, his alternatives for trouble-making almost exhausted, Vibora returned to his favorite project: a holiday conspiracy to capture Manila.

Improbable in 1900, the plot was utterly impossible fourteen years after its original failure. Ricarte, however, had never been restrained by practicalities. He ordered lieutenants in the Philippines to engineer an urban insurrection. Except for the season, the strategy was an exact duplication of the ill-fated July 4 affair. On the evening of December 24, 1914, Ricartistas were to assemble at key locations in and around Manila. Their initial objectives were to be police stations, Constabulary *cuartels,* and small military posts. After detachments had seized the regime's minor bastions and appropriated arms and ammunition, they were to merge for a collective assault on Fort William McKinley. Reinforced, it was assumed, by thousands of Manileños and *provincianos,* the rebels would then overrun the capital's American garrison. With the city and its suburbs in Ricartista hands, everything else was expected to fall into place automatically. Independence, according to Vibora's Hong Kong prognosis, could be achieved with ease.

The intrigue, however, never got off the ground. Ricarte's followers in 1914 bore little or no resemblance to their guerrilla predecessors. Composed primarily of "domestics, cooks, *cocheros* [coachmen] and *muchachos* [houseboys]" (many of whom cared deeply for their employers and were uneasy over their safety) the Manila liberation army blundered its way into a debacle.[13] Twenty-four hours before Christmas morning, policemen, constabularymen, and American military units were placed on full alert. Forewarned of the conspiracy by informers and agents, the only question bothering official circles concerned Ricartista assembly points. By mid-afternoon of December 24, Filipino and American authorities possessed that information. Around 7:00 P.M., small groups of men, some wearing bright uniforms, began to gather near the Manila Botanical Gardens. Similar bands collected on the Luneta, at a Paco baseball park, at several Tondo intersections,

12. Goodman, "Ricarte and Japan," 51.
13. The plot, its discovery, and its suppression are discussed in Appendix N, "The Christmas Eve Fiasco and a Brief Outline of the Ricarte and Other Similar Movements from the Time of the Breaking Up of the Insurrection of 1899–1901," in *Memoirs of General Artemio Ricarte,* 157–170.

and at various plazas in the suburbs. With one or two exceptions, the assemblies took place under the watchful eyes of plainsclothesmen. At 8:00 P.M., waiting police squads converged on the stunned Ricartistas. Few leaders escaped the roundup. By midnight many of Vibora's aides were behind bars. One suburban *presidencia* (Navotas, Rizal) fell to an insurgent crowd. Local police, however, reoccupied the vacant and unharmed government building several hours later. The sun rose over a serene city, most of whose celebrating residents were unaware of the abortive "revolution." Constabulary officers completed preliminary reports on the night's events and left their Spartan *cuartels* to enjoy the holiday. Clerk-typists filed their superiors' accounts in Ricarte's dossier under the heading: "Christmas Eve Fiasco."

Vibora's day as a nationalistic agitator was almost done. Irritated by the seditious enterprises emanating either directly or indirectly from the "arch plotter," American authorities determined to apprehend Ricarte.[14] Early in 1915 they brought pressure to bear on their British counterparts in Hong Kong. Under the guise of wartime emergency measures, the forty-nine-year-old incendiary was ordered to leave the Crown Colony. His departure triggered a chase up the China coast worthy of a dime-novel thriller. Pursued by Constabulary agents (and shielded by their Japanese rivals), Ricarte found temporary refuge in Shanghai's French Settlement. His Filipino and American shadows, led by Detective Lieutenant Edwin C. Bopp of the Manila Police, filed extradition papers with the consular officials. The long-awaited legal showdown, however, did not occur.[15] Bopp's quarry again evaded his pursuers and boarded a Japanese freighter. When the *Kasuga Maru* weighed anchor the following morning, Vibora stood triumphantly free on her stern. Delighted Filipino journalists recorded his parting message, "Good-bye, Shanghai!"[16] Crestfallen, Bopp returned to Manila, while in Yokahama Ricarte disembarked to

14. For a summation of Ricartista plots between 1911 and 1914, see *Report of the Philippine Commission, 1914* (Washington, D.C.), 108–110. The file of one secret service man (Constabulary Agent 26) on his surveillance over a Ricarte lieutenant in Manila between 1910 and 1914, is also available in N.A., B.I.A., F.E. 4865-106C.

15. For Governor General Francis Burton Harrison's views on Ricarte, see N.A., B.I.A., F.E. 4865-106C.

16. One of the more detailed accounts appeared in *Taliba,* the city's leading Tagalog newspaper. The article was translated and forwarded to Washington; see N.A., B.I.A., Personal Name Information File.

the plaudits of Japanese admirers. The outcome restored some of Vibora's prestige. The Shanghai incident, in fact, would have been a fitting conclusion to Ricarte's eventful career.

For a long while, that appeared to be the case. Ricarte's conduct from 1915 to 1941 seemed above reproach. Exhausted by a quarter century of unproductive plotting, Vibora drew martyrdom's comforting mantle about his shoulders and settled down to the life of a revolutionary elder. He acquired a teaching position at a mission school in Tokyo. While Ricarte commuted daily to Spanish classes in the capital, his wife operated a little restaurant called "Cafe Karihan" at their Yokohama home. The tea house became a Mecca for traveling Filipinos. Whenever liners bound to or from Manila docked at the bustling port, students, tourists, and politicians paid courtesy calls on the couple. Affluent guests left tips to ease their hosts' genteel poverty. In return, the Ricartes dispensed tropical hospitality, green tea, and temperate advice. Still thoroughly anti-American, Vibora gradually mellowed. Increasingly, he advocated evolution rather than revolution and cautioned young crusaders to operate within the law. Time, he seemed to imply, would resolve most problems. A *detente* of sorts even took place between Ricarte and the United States. Throughout the long residence in Yokohama, Vibora regularly received his mail from a solicitous clerk at the American Consulate. By 1935, the *rapprochement* between former enemies was so well advanced that colonial administrators vied with prominent *Nacionalistas* in extending Ricarte cordial invitations to attend the Commonwealth Inaugural. Rigid as ever, the old soldier declined.[17] Unwittingly, Vibora had committed his penultimate political error.

Ricarte's retirement from the world of intrigue did not end his influence over Filipino dissidents. If anything, time and distance added imposing new dimensions to the Viper's image. Without question, his exploits provided material for several reams of hyperbolic folklore. During the 1920's and early 1930's legends concerning Ricarte's feats accorded him all the attributes of a popular champion. A few urbane Filipinos wondered whether Vibora was "hero or unreconstructed nuisance," but many of their less-fortunate countrymen regarded the

17. For correspondence on the issue, see N.A., B.I.A., Personal Name Information File.

general as a potential deliverer.[18] His alias, his idea of urban insurgency, his share-the-wealth schemes, and his reputed connections with Japanese leaders constituted an attractive combination for the new generation of aspiring rebels. Ricarte and his conspiracies might have been gone, but the Viper's reputation continued to cause problems for law-enforcement officers in the Philippines.

Most of the plots, identified in one way or another with Ricarte's legacy, were rural affairs. Between 1915 and 1930, Constabulary commanders in north-central Luzon uncovered a variety of small secret societies dedicated to fomenting insurrection. None of the organizations represented a serious threat to the status quo. Pedro Kabola's awkward venture of 1925 was, in fact, typical. Similar patriotic movements—backed primarily by dissatisfied Ilocano villagers—occasionally surfaced in Pangasinan, La Union, and Ilocos Sur. Little if any relationship existed between the covert associations, but all of them used Ricarte's regional fame to rally the peasantry. All of them, furthermore, promised Japanese naval and military assistance when the revolutionary moment of truth arrived. In each instance, local authorities were able to head off trouble without bloodshed.[19] Irritating as the recurrent rumors of uprisings might have been, American and Filipino officials took consolation from the apparent demise of urban conspiracies. After the onset of the Great Depression, however, insular administrators were confronted with efforts to resurrect Vibora's Manila strategy.

Advocates of the discredited technique represented a different breed of extremist. Unlike their predecessors, the new dissident leaders tended to be middle-class professionals with grievances against the *Nacionalista* oligarchy. Disgruntled lawyers, unsuccessful union organizers, disappointed office-seekers, and frustrated journalists attempted to assume control of popular movements in both the city and the countryside. Amateurish as their initial endeavors were, they brought a measure of sophistication to the uncoordinated activities of alienated commoners. Above all, they tried to forge rural and urban poor people into disciplined movements dedicated to secular goals. While they failed to achieve that objective, their efforts provided organizational models for a handful of attentive contemporaries.

18. *Memoirs of General Artemio Ricarte*, xv.
19. *Annual Report of the Philippine Constabulary, 1930* (Manila), 7–8.

Patricio Dionisio exemplified the evolving style.[20] He was born on March 15, 1890, in barrio San Augustin, Hagonoy town, Bulacan. Since his parents were relatively well off, Dionisio encountered no difficulties in acquiring formal education. He attended elementary and high school in his native *municipio* and completed a liberal-arts curriculum in the colonial capital. Around 1915, he began his career as a newspaperman with the influential T.V.T. combine (*Tribune, Vanguardia, Taliba*). Dionisio's Tagalog eloquence and intense nationalism quickly won him a comfortable niche in the publishing network. By 1922 he had become a member of *Taliba*'s editorial board. Politics, however, beckoned Dionisio far more than journalism. Devoting a portion of his expanding income and growing leisure to self-improvement, he enrolled in law school. In 1925 he passed the bar. As a recognized columnist and practicing attorney, he had every reason to expect a challenging future.

Scaling the governmental heights proved far more difficult than Dionisio had anticipated. By 1926 the *Nacionalista* Party no longer provided easy access to the summits of insular society. Controlled by vigorous men in their forties and staffed on the central and provincial levels by Dionisio's contemporaries, the hardening political hierarchy offered few opportunities for yet another ambitious lawyer. Ten or fifteen years earlier, a man of Dionisio's caliber would have been courted by influential patrons. If fortune smiled, he might have made his way into the upper echelons of the emerging establishment. But that was no longer the case. The education system which benefited Dionisio had produced hundreds of individuals with comparable attainments. Senior *Nacionalistas* could not find places for all of them in the party or in the bureaucracy. Unable to acquire power in the conventional manner, Dionisio sought it via unorthodox means.

Early in 1927 he formed a secret society called Katipunan ng Bayan (National Association). Like scores of similar groups in the city and the countryside, the organization espoused patriotic goals. More importantly, it also stood for revolutionary social and economic objectives. Its purpose, Dionisio later declared, was to propagate "the

20. Patricio Dionisio was gracious enough to grant the author two lengthy interviews in March 1966. Biographical details for the years 1915 to 1935 are drawn primarily from his recollections. To avoid repetition, only quotations and statements requiring elaboration will be cited. Material from the conversations will be listed as Dionisio interview.

radical ideas of Andres Bonifacio . . . among the laboring classes."[21] Dionisio, however, conceived of "workers" in broader terms than most urban nationalists—everyone who toiled with his hands fit into his category. Proletarian and peasant followers, consequently, were equally desired by the innovative *supremo*. He established his first chapter in the squalid waterfront precincts of Manila's Tondo quarter. His second branch drew its membership from farming and fishing villages in Bulacan. With small bases secured, Dionisio pondered methods to transform his creation into an effective mass movement.[22]

At the onset, the effort altered only Dionisio. Adapting whole-heartedly to the conspiratorial milieu he had penetrated, he took on a disarming alias, "Prudencio Noble," and plunged into recruiting activities. For several months he encountered little success. On August 13, 1927, however, Dionisio met two like-minded Tagalogs from the provinces. The trio—all operating under assumed names—gathered at a run-down *sitio* on Manila's outskirts.[23] Satisfied with one another's political views, they agreed to combine their embryonic associations in a determined membership drive. They also decided to reassemble on November 30, 1927, to evaluate the results. When the three convened as scheduled, individual reports revealed 31,000 initiates. The experiment, quite obviously, had been a success. Its outcome, moreover, suggested some staggering possibilities.

Dionisio devoted most of 1928 to contemplating attractive alternatives. Uncertain which way to move, he considered converting the growing patriotic movement into either a labor union or an opposition political force. Before he could resolve the quandary, familial difficulties intervened. An older brother, who had migrated to California and reportedly accumulated a fortune, died suddenly. Relatives pressured Dionisio into making a time-consuming voyage to America, where he spent six weeks sorting out the tangled legal strands in Los Angeles, San Francisco, and Stockton. When the estate—disappointingly small—was finally settled, he booked passage for Manila. Free

21. *Fact Finding Report,* 93. The lengthy statement in the survey on radical societies—including the *Tangulan*—was written by Dionisio.

22. For the Constabulary version of Dionisio's career, see Stubbs, "Philippine Radicalism," 94–125.

23. One of the men was Vicente Almazar, a lawyer and a leader of tenant unions in Bulacan. For the names of other middle-class leaders who became involved in the movement, see Hayden, *The Philippines,* 915.

again to concentrate on the Katipunan ng Bayan, he looked up Artemio Ricarte during a three-day layover in Yokahama. Conversations with Vibora and four Japanese associates, who remain anonymous, convinced Dionisio he could rely on them should the need arise. Ricarte, however, recommended he solicit the advice of Emilio Aguinaldo concerning future strategy. Shortly after his return to the Philippines, he paid a courtesy call at the big house in Kawit, Cavite. Aguinaldo proved far less sanguine than Vibora. Reminding Dionisio of his own "unfortunate experiences," he counseled against violence and urged the novice *supremo* "to exercise caution."[24] Still unsure of the Katipunan's destiny, Dionisio went back to his law practice.

Events occurred that made the decision for him. A round of conferences with fellow organizers and their aides revealed some surprising developments. During Dionisio's absence, recruiting had continued unabated. Ten thousand additional laborers had affiliated themselves with the society. While many of the recent initiates resided in Manila, the majority came from the belt of populous provinces stretching between southern Tayabas and Ilocos Norte.[25] The accomplishment exceeded Dionisio's most optimistic expectations, but it also created problems. The movement, his advisers warned, threatened to become unwieldy. Impatience also characterized the new Katipuneros, who lacked discipline and a clear sense of direction. Dionisio vowed to provide both ingredients.

It was easier said than done. His first effort to create order came before the year's end. On December 30, 1928, Dionisio convened a secret assembly in Manila. Organization received top priority on the abbreviated agenda. Enthusiastic representatives from provincial and municipal chapters approved the formation of executive bodies to oversee Katipunan affairs.[26] They also listened attentively to an im-

24. Dionisio interview.
25. Dionisio regarded the 40,000 members enrolled by late 1928 as the organization's hard core. He estimated their approximate numbers and distribution as follows: Manila, 5,000 to 7,500; Bulacan, 5,000 to 7,500; Batangas, 5,000 to 7,500; Cavite, 2,000 to 3,000; Laguna, 2,000 to 3,000; Rizal, 2,000 to 3,000; Pangasinan, 2,000 to 2,500; La Union, 1,500 to 2,000; Ilocos Sur, 1,000 to 1,500; Nueva Ecija, 1,000 to 1,500; Tarlac, 500 to 1,000; Pampanga, 500 to 1,000. Followers accumulated between 1929 and 1931 were, from Dionisio's viewpoint, less reliable. He tended to look upon the later recruits as "sympathizers." Dionisio interview.
26. The convention approved the formation of a Supreme Council in Manila,

passioned speech by their *supremo*. Dionisio advocated tighter control over the far-flung membership and set forth what he hoped would be inspiring social and economic objectives. His remarks were well received. When the delegates adjourned, Dionisio and his principal associates believed they had taken several firm steps toward directed democracy.

The belief proved illusory. Throughout 1929, regional and local branches continued to record spectacular growth rates. Each accumulation of converts placed additional strain on the fragile links connecting leaders and followers. By the end of the year, 97,000 members had been inducted into the movement.[27] Impending mergers with comparable groups in Manila and the countryside, furthermore, promised to produce another expansion of geometric proportions. Under the circumstances, any resemblance between the Katipunan ng Bayan and a secret society became purely coincidental. When Constabulary and police agents began to infiltrate some of the more obvious chapters, Dionisio tried to allay official suspicions by registering the association as a mutual-aid agency. Early in 1930, Treasury Department personnel approved the *supremo*'s tentative charter but insisted that he change its historically controversial title. Dionisio substituted Kapatiran Tangulang Malayang Mamamayan (Association for an Offensive for Our Future Freedom). Inexplicably, his revision calmed the civil servants. After normal bureaucratic delays, they certified the organization.

Legal recognition did not eliminate Dionisio's difficulties. If anything, the transition from covert to overt operations compounded them, for public awareness of the Tangulan (Offensive), as the new society was known, promoted further growth. Manifesting little or no interest in "future freedom," chauvinistic recruits called instead for militant action to achieve immediate independence. Inevitably, the contagion infected members of the supreme council. Buffeted between belligerent local chapters and overconfident advisers, Dionisio was hard put to restrain his followers. By mid-1931, the *supremo* found himself in the position of the legendary Jacobin who complained, "Which way are the people going? I am their leader."

---

and the creation of Provincial Councils and Municipal Federations in rural areas. *Fact Finding Report,* 93.

27. *Ibid.,* 94.

To Dionisio's dismay, segments of the Tangulan were moving simultaneously toward several different destinations. Strained by disputes over objectives and priorities, the movement split into radical, moderate, and opportunistic factions. Dionisio tried to mediate between the contending camps. He failed. During the last six months of 1931, extremists took command. Two letters, purportedly written by General Artemio Ricarte, began to circulate among the membership.[28] The first portrayed the Tangulan as the ideal instrument to achieve Philippine freedom. It also held forth promises of Japanese arms and air support for revolutionary endeavors. The second acknowledged receipt of 10,000 pesos from Tangulan leaders and promised secret delivery of modern rifles to that amount. The fictitious correspondence convinced many fence-sitters. By late September 1931, Dionisio was fighting a desperate rearguard action against his more aggressive followers.

The *supremo* was not the only individual shaken by developments in the unruly society. Constabulary headquarters—still smarting from criticism over the Tayug affair—also became concerned about Tangulan intentions. Fearing another uprising, superior officers ordered the Intelligence Section to compile data on the association. Real and pseudo information was not difficult to accumulate. Local commanders had been interested in Tangulan activities for some time. Strategic chapters of the society, accordingly, had been penetrated by informers and plainsclothesmen.[29] In some instance, infiltration had been so thorough it was difficult to sort out government agents from nationalistic agitators. When the results of all that activity descended on the Santa Lucia Barracks (Constabulary headquarters), a threatening picture emerged. Rumors of rebellion were rife across Luzon. Regional intelligence officers spoke of furtive gatherings and mentioned reports of armed bands drilling for a martial confrontation. They also linked Pedro Calosa's defunct society to Dionisio's movement and traced the Tayug uprising to Tangulan machinations. Ricarte's alleged letters completed the ominous impression. With Japan's Imperial Army units overrunning Manchuria on the thinnest of pretexts, no responsible American or Filipino wished to test Japanese designs on the Philippines. By late October, Constabulary Commander Charles

28. Stubbs, 100–101.
29. *Fact Finding Report,* 94.

Nathorst had concluded that a coordinated insurrection involving urban and rural elements was imminent. Vibora's apparent involvement in the conspiracy also led him to believe the outbreak might erupt during the Christmas season.

By December 1, 1931, both sides believed their opponents were ready to strike. Dionisio and Nathorst launched separate efforts to prevent armed clashes. Instead of slowing the race toward a head-on collision, their endeavors accelerated it. Nathorst acted first. Proclaiming an earnest desire to avoid bloodshed, he warned the governor of Nueva Ecija to be on guard against a Christmas Eve uprising.[30] On December 7, the General's letter appeared on the front pages of Manila's leading newspapers. Sandwiched between sensational stories of blood compacts, secret oaths, and Tangulan plots, Nathorst's communication created incipient panic in the city and the countryside. An anxious Dionisio tried to track down the sources of the ubiquitous rumors. With all their loose talk about rebellion, none of the Tangulan's supreme councillors appeared to have issued orders to begin hostilities. Superficial checks with chapter officials, however, revealed many of their followers were preparing for action on December 24. Some of them had even been alerted to the revolution's signal: an electric-power shutdown in Manila. Fearing his organization had been victimized by provocateurs, Dionisio summoned provincial and municipal leaders to warn them of his suspicions.[31] Their December 9 convergence on the city confirmed the authorities' worst fears. Constabulary and police officers concluded the meeting had been called for the express purpose of advancing zero hour.

Senior law enforcers, accordingly, decided to pre-empt the offensive. Shortly after nightfall on December 10 they ordered special detachments to round up Tangulan functionaries in Manila and Bulacan. By midnight, Patricio Dionisio and most of his aides had been jailed. Within twenty-four hours, the *supremo*'s provincial associates experienced a similar fate.[32] Elsewhere in Luzon, *Nacionalista* administrators called mass meetings to inform citizens of governmental actions and to warn them against irresponsible conduct. Constabulary squads also collected sufficient evidence to nail down criminal indictments. On December 14, 1931, Dionisio and his advisers were formally

30. *Manila Daily Bulletin*, Dec. 7, 1931.
31. *Fact Finding Report*, 95.
32. *New York Times*, Dec. 11, 1931, 10.

charged with conspiracy. The operation encountered few obstacles. Resisting arrest, an angry Tangulan cut one Manila policeman. Other than that, the dragnet added up to an efficient exercise in bloodless counterrevolution.[33]

For several days Manila's newspaper readers devoured every morsel on the affair. Within a week, however, something resembling satiation materialized in the city. The story's international repercussions vanished first. Shortly after the police crackdown, an explicit denial arrived from Yokahama: "I do not belong to any secret society in the Philippine Islands," cabled General Artemio Ricarte, ". . . I wish to warn the public against those using my name."[34] Minus its Japanese ingredients, the Constabulary action lost its remaining savor. Closer inspection of much publicized Tangulan weapon caches revealed little in the way of serious war-making capacity. At the society's headquarters, for example, arresting officers had seized flags, some nondescript uniforms, several unreliable *paltiks* (homemade guns), a few clubs and daggers, and an odd assortment of "house bolos." Dionisio's automobile yielded an unlicensed revolver. That appeared to be the extent of the association's arsenal. Against such revelations, the preceding week's rumors of assaults on government buildings began to appear inane. Free on bond, Dionisio furthered public disenchantment. Queried about attacks on the Governor General's Palace, he retorted: "That is ridiculous. How are we to take Malacañang? With our mouths?"[35] Dionisio's answer permitted the *Philippines Free Press* to lampoon the whole episode. The weekly opened its report on the "uprising" with a rollicking jingle:

> Tangulans would have sacked the town
>   With eloquence and boloes,
> The wealthy they'd have harried down
>   In groups and squads and soloes,
> Until the coppers ran them down
> A hundred ragged hoboes![36]

33. The best summation of the Tangulan affair appeared in the *Manila Daily Bulletin*, Dec. 14, 1931.

34. *Philippines Free Press*, Dec. 19, 1931, 4. Ricarte's denial failed to alter Constabulary evaluations. Its report on the movement listed "General Artemio Ricarte, now in Japan, [as] the supreme head." See Hayden, *The Philippines*, 915.

35. *Philippines Free Press*, Dec. 19, 1931, 4.

36. *Ibid.*

Other prominent members of the fourth estate were not amused. A. V. H. Hartendorp saw something far more fundamental than a "cops and robbers" charade in the confusing incident. Interpreting it as another distressing sign of the times, he maintained "latent discontent among the poor . . . is developing into a . . . definite state of unrest." Calling again for sweeping social reforms and broad economic development to remedy the deteriorating situation, he asked, "Who will bring this about? Our *principales* and *ilustrados?* That is to be doubted. We need a more democratic leadership in this country, men and women of ability who, though they themselves may have risen in the world, still feel themselves identified with the people from whom they sprang."[37]

Surprisingly, the chief *ilustrado* echoed Hartendorp's theme. Manuel Quezon, disturbed by mounting discord in the Philippines and shaken by economic dislocations in the United States, refused to dismiss the Tangulan as an unimportant manifestation. Lamenting the near hysteria of early December, he said, "We are doing . . . ridiculous things and creating an impression that does not help our cause." He ascribed the movement and its counterparts to conditions emanating from the world depression, and urged ordinary Filipinos to ignore the siren songs of "agitators and reds." At the same time, he spoke directly to his prominent countrymen. Patience, Quezon reminded them, could not be expected from distraught people. Basic reforms were long overdue; the "commission of injustices to the poor, to the peasants, the small farmers [and] the laborers, should be prevented." The Senate President also endorsed the claims of workers for adequate compensation, free association, collective representation, and medical care: "rights," he pointed out, "which every progressive country has already recognized." Quezon ended his statement on a thoroughly humane note: "The best foundation of peace and order is social justice, not government force."[38]

Editorial punditry and statesmanlike pronouncements notwithstanding, the Tangulan trouble exerted little perceptible influence over the course of affairs. Like its ephemeral rural predecessors, the urban tumult soon ceased to be a subject for either debate or polite con-

37. *Philippine Magazine,* Jan. 1932, 408.
38. *Philippines Free Press,* Dec. 19, 1931, 5.

versation. By the end of the holiday season, sophisticated Manileños tended to regard the affair as "but one more typhoon in a water tumbler." Late in February insular legal machinery meshed. Charged with conspiracy to commit sedition, Dionisio and one hundred twenty-five of his followers were brought to trial. The proceedings aroused minimal public interest. On March 15, the Manila Court of First Instance handed down its decisions. All the defendants were found guilty. Depending on degrees of responsibility, they were sentenced to Bilibid Prison for terms ranging from one to six years.[39] Another popular movement, apparently, had been demolished.

Appearances, however, proved to be deceptive. Before the year ended, Dionisio's downfall took on the character of a personal blessing in disguise. The *supremo* spent precious little time behind bars. A model prisoner, he was paroled, with abundant time off for good behavior. In December 1932 the source of his premature freedom became manifest. Manuel Quezon summoned the Tangulan leader to an off-the-record discussion of labor problems.[40] After a straightforward exchange on the topic, the Senate President brought forth an astonishing proposition. If Dionisio would agree to guide restless Tagalog workers into legitimate protest channels, Quezon would guarantee him an influential government position. The Senate President also promised to consider any well-conceived reform proposal his prospective associate might suggest. Dionisio accepted the challenging arrangement. Early in 1933 he joined other newly recruited radicals on Quezon's unofficial staff. They were quickly promoted to formal posts.[41] Acting as special investigators for Labor Secretary Ramon Torres, Dionisio and his controversial colleagues compiled the 1936 exposé on rural problems in the Philippines.[42] If nothing else, the Tangulan experiment transformed Patricio Dionisio into a relatively powerful member of the Commonwealth bureaucracy.[43]

39. Stubbs, 124.
40. Dionisio interview.
41. Among those participating in the experiment was Jacinto Manahan, a radical leader of central Luzon's tenantry. Manahan was one of the founders of the Communist Party of the Philippines. In 1922 he organized the Confederación Nacional de Aparceros y Obreros Agrícolas de Filipinos. The union is discussed in *Fact Finding Report,* 87–88.
42. See *Fact Finding Report.*
43. Dionisio's later career bore out his Quezon revelations. He remained a responsible official in the Labor Department until his retirement in 1955. Im-

Quezon's calculated maneuver, however, achieved only partial success. While it diverted some peasants and proletarians from violent activities, many continued to become involved in unorthodox rectification schemes.[44] The result should have been predictable. Dionisio, after all, was one of the few Tangulans who gleaned tangible benefits from the shattered organization. In the final analysis, most of his old followers found themselves in worse straits than before the Constabulary rout. Still dedicated to radical change, they sought more dynamic leadership. Other men supplied it. By the time Dionisio affiliated himself with Quezon, the Tangulan's vital remnants had been incorporated into a more elaborate mass movement.

Inadvertently, Patricio Dionisio had helped set in motion an intricate chain of events. His tentative probing tapped deep wells of discontent in the predepression Philippines. When economic contraction began to squeeze ordinary Filipinos, many of its victims turned to the Tangulan leader for solutions. His failure to provide acceptable answers did not end the popular quest. In oversimplified terms, he unleashed powerful forces without any real idea of how to control them. Other aspiring *supremos* grasped the significance of Dionisio's achievement. If only briefly, he had combined elements from the city and the countryside behind middle-class leadership. His successors continued the effort to direct restless poor people toward revolutionary goals. The technique appeared simple. It involved ardent patriotism, social criticism, calls for militant action, and assurances of Japanese support. Properly manipulated, the volatile mixture promised impressive results. By refurbishing Artemio Ricarte's tarnished methods, Patricio Dionisio had produced an attractive strategy for Filipino extremists.

---

portant positions in the bureaucracy, needless to say, were not normally granted to former convicts. The metamorphosis can only be attributed to intervention from the highest levels. Dionisio interview.

44. Dionisio was able to retain the loyalty of between 10,000 and 15,000 Tangulans. The remainder of the society shifted their allegiance to the emerging Sakdal movement. Dionisio's associations with Quezon alienated many of his former followers so much, he said, that some of them formulated plans to assassinate him. Dionisio interview.

CHAPTER 11

Sakdalism

The decade leading up to the attack on Pearl Harbor began on notes of social discord. The Tayug and Tangulan incidents in January and December bestowed on 1931 a disturbing, if highly artificial, symmetry. Since the early years of "pacification" insular authorities had not been confronted with juxtaposed rural and urban conspiracies. Predictably, American and Filipino administrators attempted to link the outbreaks into a comprehensible whole. Their efforts produced deceptive results. Despite deep-seated official suspicions, the organizations were not related. Secretiveness and vindictiveness constituted the only connections between the dissident movements. In all other respects, the associations devised by Calosa and Dionisio were strikingly different. If anything, they represented contradictory tendencies. On the one hand, Pangasinan's "Colorums" symbolized a dying form of popular insurgency. On the other, Manila's Tangulans revealed the shape of upheavals to come.

The contrast—largely unapparent to contemporaries—sprang from divergent trends in Philippine culture. Toughness and conspiratorial competence notwithstanding, Pedro Calosa reflected the insurrectionary techniques and aspirations of the past. The local flare-up he helped ignite, moreover, followed a pattern thoroughly in keeping with village precedents. Particularistic in structure and parochial in orientation, the activities of his Philippine National Association denied its grandiose title. In oversimplified terms, Calosa's small, tightly knit society mirrored the little tradition. Dionisio's amorphous fraternity, the Tangulan, however, materialized on a different scale. Ineptness and opportunism did not prevent the inexperienced *supremo* from forging a broadly based and potentially influential organization. His ephemeral rural-urban alliance, furthermore, typified the altered circumstances of Philippine life. With all its defects, the Tangulan emerged as a logical outgrowth of the great tradition. As such, it exposed the outlines of future challenges to the status quo.

Distinctions between the movements emanated from subtle and dramatic changes in the fabric of insular society. By 1931 the paradoxical nature of American policies had resulted in a variety of unsettling consequences. For one thing, Filipinization produced a political system directed by indigenous leaders, but failed to provide practical methods for contesting or transforming the landed elite's conventional economic values. For another, mass education created literacy rates and aspiration levels well beyond the range normally associated with colonial milieus, but neglected to supply adequate routes for upward mobility. More disturbing still was the demographic outcome of efficient public-health programs. Between 1903 and 1939, the archipelago's population soared from seven to approximately sixteen million. Productivity and diversification, unfortunately, did not keep pace. Under the best of circumstances, the fourth decade of United States rule would have been a time of mounting tension. Conditions during the ten-year prelude to Pearl Harbor, however, were far from ideal. The Great Depression brought a series of disruptive new pressures to bear on Filipinos—particularly those living in Manila and its developing hinterland. Repercussions growing out of the world economic situation intensified all the sources of stress acting on Islanders and produced additional disequilibriums conducive to the generation of strident protest movements.[1] The Tangulan was simply the first of several popular efforts to challenge the prevailing order.

The second attempt revolved around another alienated intellectual from Bulacan. Like Patricio Dionisio, Benigno Ramos was a discontented beneficiary of the America era.[2] The son of a municipal bureaucrat who served both colonial administrations, Ramos was born in

1. Detrimental effects were pronounced in provinces specializing in export crops. Sharp declines in American copra consumption, for example, caused difficulties for small producers in Laguna, Tayabas, Batangas, and Cavite. American prices for copra also plummeted from $87.00 a ton in 1928 to $22.00 a ton in 1934. See Stubbs, "Philippine Radicalism," 180.

2. For biographical information on Ramos, see Hayden, *The Philippines,* 382–387; Stubbs, 130–135; and G. K. Goodman, "Japan and Philippine Radicalism: The Case of Benigno Ramos," in *Four Aspects of Philippine-Japanese Relations, 1930–1940,* Yale University Southeast Asia Studies, no. 9 (New Haven, 1967), 133–194.

Bulacan town on February 10, 1893. He attended public schools in Malolos and worked briefly after graduation as a government clerk in the historic provincial capital, where, as part of his job, he had an opportunity to become proficient in Spanish and English. In 1910 he passed the language examination for an elementary teaching certificate. Two uninspiring years as a village schoolmaster permitted him to expand his knowledge of both European tongues. In 1912, eager to test his skills on a larger stage, Ramos and his bride of one year moved to Manila.

He devoted his first half-decade in the city to literary activities. Dividing his energies between political reporting and poetry, Ramos free-lanced for several dialect newspapers, translated Spanish and English verse into graceful Tagalog, and composed patriotic poems which appeared occasionally in *Taliba* and a variety of obscure little magazines.[3] Although most of his works went unheralded, they won sufficient recognition in journalistic and political circles to gain him an appointment to the influential Spanish daily *El Ideal*. Ramos' capable performance for the paper opened important new doors. In 1917, Manuel Quezon employed him as a full-time translator for the newly formed Philippine Senate. Two years later, Ramos received a civil-service classification. In 1929, Quezon again rewarded his protégé by making him director of the Senate Clipping Division.[4]

Recognition and promotion did not satisfy Ramos. The legislative atmosphere, in fact, stirred his political ambitions. He continued to compose chauvinistic poetry in the vernacular and strove to win Quezon's endorsement as a candidate for electoral office. He even wrote a flowery tribute to the Senate President which portrayed him

3. Among other associations developed by Ramos during his early years in Manila was a close relationship with Patricio Dionisio. The men became neighbors and *compadres* and, as *coprovincianos*, relied on one another's advice until late 1934. Dionisio interview.

4. Mundane title notwithstanding, the section represented a key component of the *Nacionalista* machine. Established senators named only promising young men to the Clipping Division. Appointees held posts approximating sinecures and were encouraged to continue their professional development while serving their patrons. Isabelo de los Reyes, Jr., private secretary to Gregorio Aglipay, the Supreme Bishop of the Philippine Independent Church, was another Quezon selection. He knew Ramos well, but their association tended to be restricted to Division business. Ramos' promotion to director of the talented staff indicated his standing with Quezon and other senators. Isabelo de los Reyes interview.

as the worthy successor of José Rizal. Impressed by Ramos' undeniable way with words, Quezon began to use him as a speaker at party functions in Manila and Bulacan. Tagalog oratory proved to be Ramos' forte. Rousing platform performances in the city and countryside quickly established his reputation as a reliable Quezonista. The appearances also won for him a small but devoted personal following.

In 1930, Ramos' promising governmental career came to an abrupt end. Like many personal and political tragedies the debacle began in a thoroughly improbable manner. Ill-considered statements by an American teacher provoked unrest at the Manila High School.[5] When intramural efforts failed to resolve the dispute, an ugly situation developed. Student leaders at the elite academy—spurred on by Filipino instructors—fomented a strike to dramatize what they regarded as blatant racism. Sensing a possible *cause célèbre,* Ramos joined the pickets. In the process, he placed himself on the right side of an emotionally charged issue but on the wrong side of his powerful sponsor. Unwilling to alienate American opinion—which was then shifting rapidly in favor of Philippine independence—Manuel Quezon reluctantly supported the beleaguered teacher. Ramos was scandalized. He rejected the warnings of colleagues who advised him to dissociate himself from the embarrassing confrontation and assumed command of the demonstrating students. Temporarily, at least, Ramos lost his sense of political balance. Pulling out all the oratorical stops, he engaged in bitter public attacks on Quezon, Osmeña, and other prominent *Nacionalistas.* The Senate President finally responded in kind. On June 18, he dispatched a pointed letter to his insubordinate protégé calling for an immediate resignation. Ramos complied. But he also dedicated himself to a vendetta against his former *compadre* and political benefactor.

His unique approach soon became apparent. Combining financial contributions from friends with his own limited savings, Ramos scraped together enough money to start a newspaper.[6] Called *Sakdal,*

5. Miss Mabel Brummit, the offending instructor, purportedly referred to Filipinos as "a bunch of sweet-potato eaters" and "monkeys." Goodman, "The Case of Benigno Ramos," 136.

6. Gregorio Aglipay and prominent Aglipayan laymen contributed to the cause. The close association of Ramos and the Supreme Bishop, in fact, made Sakdalism and the Philippine Independent Church synonymous in the minds of many humble Aglipayans. Isabelo de los Reyes interview.

meaning "to accuse" or "to strike," its first number appeared on October 13, 1930.[7] From the outset, the Tagalog weekly lived up to its title. Throwing canons of taste aside, Ramos pounded out editorials like a man equipped with an ink-stained sledge hammer. In each issue, he castigated the *Nacionalista* oligarchy, accused its leaders of every political crime imaginable, and attempted to steal the independence issue from the party that had monopolized it for a generation. More importantly, he spoke out in defense of the weak, the impoverished, and the exploited elements of Philippine society. An early editorial captured *Sakdal's* caustic style; on December 15, 1930, Ramos concluded an anti-*Nacionalista* diatribe with a series of provocative associations: "In Manila we see our so-called leaders growing fat and rich on money amassed from taxing the poor. They have fine automobiles and fine homes for themselves, but for us they have only fine and empty words. They have learned to promise as much as the Americans and to deliver as little."[8]

Ramos, however, did not limit his campaign to indictments of Filipino politicos and their American mentors. He opened *Sakdal's* columns to any Manileño or *provinciano* with grievances against the regime. Early in 1931, guest editorials by Patricio Dionisio, Vicente Almazar, and other Tangulan spokesmen began to appear regularly in the tabloid. Ramos also started to accompany Dionisio on recruiting campaigns. The arrangement was mutually beneficial: it provided the Tangulan *supremo* with a convenient means of publicizing his movement; and it enabled Ramos to expand *Sakdal's* circulation in the provinces.[9] More significantly, the informal collaboration exposed Ramos to a variety of alienated rural and urban citizens, while introducing him to the manipulative techniques of the political underground. By late 1931, his personal connections in Rizal, Laguna, and Cavite were as extensive as those previously established in Manila and Bulacan.

While Ramos capitalized on his Tangulan affiliations, he was too wily to permit himself to be identified with rumors of insurrection.

7. Priced at five centavos and therefore within the reach of poor Filipinos, *Sakdal* stressed nationalistic issues. Under portraits of José Rizal and Marcelino del Pilar, Ramos ran his publication's slogan, "Independent with no master but the people." Conrado Benitez, "Sakdal," *Philippine Magazine*, XXXII (1935), 240.
8. Stubbs, 135.
9. Dionisio interview.

On December 2, 1931, a *Sakdal* editorial denied any links between Dionisio and Ramos and denounced all movements dedicated to violence. The timely disclaimer permitted him to avoid arrest or prosecution during the ensuing crackdown. His associations with Tangulan leaders, however, were too well established to escape official notice. In early January 1932, postal authorities revoked *Sakdal's* mailing privileges on the grounds that "it was libelous and inspiring of sedition."[10] At roughly the same time, the Philippine Constabulary established a separate dossier on Benigno Ramos.[11]

The controversial publisher-editor restricted his activities for a time and waited for the storm set off by the Tangulan episode to blow itself out. *Sakdal's* street-peddled issues became models of journalistic propriety, and Ramos avoided any public utterance which might be construed as seditious. His circumspection won a restoration of mailing rights on March 21, 1932. At first, Ramos was hesitant about returning to the offensive, but his animosity toward prominent *Nacionalistas* and his vituperative genius could not be restrained. By the beginning of the rainy season, he was again heaping abuse on officialdom in every issue of *Sakdal*. His cavalier attitude toward the libel laws and his affinity for radical causes won additional readers. By the middle of 1933, *Sakdal* was prospering.[12] Known as "Ben Ruben" by a growing corps of admiring villagers and slum dwellers, Benigno Ramos seemed to be taking on many of the engaging attributes of a potential David girding for combat with Quezon and his Goliath-like party.[13]

An unexpected opportunity to crystallize anti-*Nacionalista* sentiments came with the passage of independence legislation in the United States. Throughout 1932, American congressmen and senators con-

10. Stubbs, 140.
11. The Tangulan associations of Ramos constituted the first entry in his police file. A 1935 report on his activities began by declaring "The Tangulan uprising . . . was precipitated by . . . the 'Sakdal' publications." G. B. Francisco, Chief of Staff, Philippine Constabulary, "The Sakdal Party," (typescript) May 7, 1935, 1. J. R. Hayden Papers, Michigan Historical Collections, Ann Arbor, Michigan. Hereafter materials from the collection will be cited as Hayden Papers.
12. The tabloid's circulation climbed from 5,000 in early 1931 to 15,000 by mid-1933. In April 1935, it stood at 40,000. Goodman, "The Case of Benigno Ramos," 184.
13. Benitez, 240.

ducted hearings on the Hare-Hawes-Cutting Bill.[14] The measure finally passed, only to be rejected by Herbert Hoover. Early in 1933, however, angry members of the lame-duck Congress overrode the presidential veto. After a generation of normally concerted efforts, the *Nacionalista* Party had achieved its goal. Instead of celebrating, the party immediately fell into clamorous disarray. While American solons argued over the law's merits, more heated debates echoed through the chambers of the Philippine Legislature. The graceless outcome in Washington added injured feelings to the raw tempers of insular politicians. For the first time in more than a decade, deep splits appeared in the majority party. Followers of Sergio Osmeña and Manuel Roxas—who had lobbied for the enactment in Washington— and supporters of Manuel Quezon—who opposed the Bill because it did not bear his personal trademark—became involved in a political free-for-all.[15] With the oligarchs at one another's throats. Ramos decided to exploit the opening.

On October 29, 1933, rural and urban delegations led by professional men assembled at an inconspicuous convention in Manila. The dissenters completed their work quickly. By nightfall they had adopted Sakdal Party bylaws, elected Benigno Ramos *tandis* (leader), designated provincial functionaries, and endorsed a platform which drew together all the disconnected causes *Sakdal* had been advocating for three years.[16] Their campaign statement accused the *Nacionalistas* of

14. The Hare-Hawes-Cutting Bill and the Tydings-McDuffie Act, which succeeded it in 1934, both provided for a ten-year transition toward national sovereignty. Political rivalries in Washington and Manila delayed approval of the legislation. With minor modifications, however, the Tydings-McDuffie Act followed the broad outlines of its predecessor. It called for the creation of the Commonwealth of the Philippines (established in 1935) and guaranteed independence after a decade of autonomy. The best contemporary analysis of the issue, with particular emphasis on the role of American economic interests, was compiled by G. L. Kirk, *Philippine Independence* (New York, 1936).

15. For a discussion of the split, see Friend, *Between Two Empires*, 124–135.

16. The backgrounds of other officers elected that day revealed the middle-class nature of Sakdal leadership. Felino Cajucom, a seventy-nine-year-old revolutionary veteran, was given the honorary post of counselor. Elpidio Santos, a lawyer from Pasig, Rizal, and Celerino Tiongco, a large landholder from Santa Rosa, Laguna, were named cochairmen of the national committee. José E. League and Gregorio Tobias were elected treasurer and secretary, respectively. Provincial chairmen and their assigned areas were: Isidro Torres (former Tangulan), Nueva Ecija; José Timog, Tayabas; José Abanag, Cavite; Apolinario Villacarte, Bulacan; José E. Corima, Laguna; Mario Argosina, Rizal;

hypocrisy on the independence question; hurled charges of maladministration at Quezon, Osmeña, and their political confederates; attacked the unjust nature of prevailing tax policies; and stressed the coinciding interests of Sakdalism and the common man.[17]

With the Sakdal Party launched, Ramos and his aides prepared strategy for the 1934 general election. As a means of dramatizing the principal issue, Ramos announced he would sail to America to appeal for "complete, immediate, and absolute independence." His eleventh-hour intervention was arranged to coincide with the departure of a Washington-bound delegation headed by Manuel Quezon, whose special commission had been hastily organized to bring about revisions in the Hare-Hawes-Cutting Act. Predictably, readers of *Sakdal* concluded that Ramos and the *Nacionalista* leader were leaving on identical missions.

Sailing dates, however, constituted the only similarities between the political expeditions. Quezon led his influential associates directly to Washington and began negotiations which produced an acceptable independence law. Ramos proceeded at a more leisurely pace. He stopped first in Japan. There, he paid a call on Artemio Ricarte and interviewed the general for *Sakdal's* subscribers.[18] After identifying himself with the symbol of resistance to American rule, he continued his journey. Ramos next stopped in northern California. He visited Tomas Española, the proprietor of a Stockton pool hall and long-time *Sakdal* subscriber, to discuss the feasibility of establishing party chapters in the United States.[19] When Española urged him to make the effort, Ramos devoted several weeks to winning over Stockton's sizable Filipino community. Disappointed by infinitesimal results, he again embarked on his travels. His odyssey ended in Washington in late March 1934. His arrival, ironically enough, coincided with congressional clearance of the Quezon-approved Tydings-McDuffie Bill. Ramos penned a formal protest to Franklin Roosevelt and immediately booked passage for Manila.

Quintin Santos de Dios (another former Tangulan), San Juan, Manila; and Venancio Aznar, downtown Manila. Of the thirteen party officials, four were lawyers, three were former government employees, two were merchants, one a dentist, one a school teacher, and one a retired judge. Stubbs, 154–155.

17. Party goals were summarized by Francisco, "The Sakdal Party," 1. Hayden Papers.

18. Goodman, "The Case of Benigno Ramos," 139.

19. Stubbs, 159.

During Ramos' absence, his subordinates finished preparations for the June campaign. Under the guidance of Celerino Tiongco, candidates entered the race for two seats in the Senate and three in the House of Representatives.[20] A full slate of party hopefuls also filed petitions for provincial and municipal offices in Manila and eight provinces. In the meantime, *Sakdal* continued to level verbal barrages on both *Nacionlista* camps, and neighborhood activists quietly went to work in slums and villages. During April and May, when the preelection debate reached fever pitch, the logic of Tiongco's techniques became apparent. Followers of both Quezon and Osmeña raced along well-worn *Nacionalista* campaign routes, pausing only to vilify one another before disinterested voters in major plazas. Sakdalista candidates, however, appealed to urban workers at squalid Tondo intersections and visited remote barrios to harangue delighted *taos* by the light of flickering oil flares.[21]

Sakdal orators built their addresses around issues which appealed to impoverished audiences. Spokesmen promised that the party would acquire "complete and absolute independence" for the Philippines by December 31, 1935. They indicted the majority coalition for enriching itself at the expense of the populace. They also maintained that all *Nacionalistas* were satisfied with the status quo and unwilling to change it. Emphasizing the point, they vowed Sakdalistas would abolish taxes when they took control of the government. To their standard political entreaties, however, they added the vote-laden issue of caciquism. Calling for equal or common ownership of land, they proclaimed that large holdings should be confiscated and redistributed to tenant farmers. Finally, they attacked the Church for operating vast estates and accumulating wealth "through dishonest means."[22]

Sakdal speakers, furthermore, refused to limit themselves to inflam-

20. While Ramos was away, Tiongco edited *Sakdal* and assumed leadership of the party. An estate owner and old school *ilustrado,* who devoted his leisure time to constructing a genteel Tagalog translation of *Don Quixote,* he was respectfully known as "Don Celerino" by the people of Santa Rosa. His involvement in Sakdalism revealed the growing alienation of many prominent *provincianos* with *Nacionalista* leadership. Disinterested in violence but committed to political and economic reforms. Tiongco attempted to act as a moderating influence in the party's inner circle. In 1965 his son Angel Tiongco, then mayor of Santa Rosa, was kind enough to discuss his father's Sakdal activities. Information from the conversation will be cited as Tiongco interview.
21. Hayden, *The Philippines,* 384.
22. Francisco, "The Sakdal Party," 2. Hayden Papers.

matory polemics. Some of them supported charges of *Nacionalista* chicanery with fraudulent evidence. They linked lurid descriptions of Manuel Quezon's behavior with dignified depictions of Benigno Ramos' conduct, and underscored the message by distributing copies of two photographs. The first featured Quezon enjoying the company of an American movie queen. The second portrayed Ramos in earnest conversation with Franklin Roosevelt. Scandalized voters, of course, were not informed that the Quezon print was a standard Hollywood publicity shot, while the rendition of Ramos was a cleverly devised composite.[23] Contrasts between the photos clinched the argument for strait-laced hamlet dwellers. Distrust of *Nacionalista* leaders spread in the wake of Sakdalista orators, and hatred for Manuel Quezon permeated many barrios.

The activities of Sakdal rabble-rousers and the content of their speeches were ignored by everyone in authority except the Philippine Constabulary. When returns from the general election began to roll in, however, political professionals discovered that Sakdalism had become a force to be reckoned with. All three contenders for seats in the House of Representatives won impressive victories. Laguna elected Marcano Untivero and Aurelio C. Almazon; and Tayabas, Quezon's native province, sent Antonio Argosino to the insular legislature.[24] The people of Marinduque chose a Sakdal to govern their subprovince. In Laguna, Bulacan, Nueva Ecija, Rizal, and Cavite the party's candidates made remarkable showings and won scores of important municipal offices. By any standard, the results amounted to an impressive performance for a party founded by a Quezon castoff.

Basking in the glow of victory, Benigno Ramos granted an interview to Manila journalists and indicated that he was ready to appeal to a broader political spectrum. He denied claims that party successes rested on revolutionary rhetoric. "If the Sakdalistas are growing," he

23. Bernstein, *The Philippine Story,* 121.
24. Aurelio Almazon's career again exposed the bourgeois character of Sakdalista leadership. Born in Los Baños, Laguna, in 1898, he migrated to the United States in 1923. He worked three years in Seattle and then moved to Los Angeles where he attended night school. In 1932 he received a law degree. Victimized by the Depression, he worked his way home early in 1933. His unusual background, together with his intelligence and common touch, made him a natural Sakdal candidate. The retired mayor of Los Baños—he served in that capacity from 1947 to 1955—Mr. Almazon cooperatively discussed the "old days" in 1966. His revealing observations will be cited as Almazon interview.

said, "it is not because we preach revolution as some people mistakenly believe. As a matter of fact we are against revolution and against violence. If all Filipinos were Sakdalistas, the country would not need any constabulary soldiers or policemen, because Sakdalism is based on peace, on the free development and moral perfection of the individual." Ramos also rejected accusations of xenophobia. Admitting the antiforeign character of some party statements, he traced it to patriotic motives. Total independence, Ramos said, was essential because only national freedom would ensure the maximum development of insular human and natural resources. After promising to withdraw all Sakdalista officials if full sovereignty were not granted "by the end of 1935," Ramos outlined new objectives. He called for: (1) investigation of friar lands; (2) formation of a 500,000-man Philippine Army; (3) teaching of native dialects in the public schools; (4) retention of lawyers to defend poor clients; (5) reduction of official salaries; (6) pay increases for teachers, policemen, laborers, and constabularymen; and (7) adoption of voting machines to prevent election frauds. Ramos terminated his remarks on a positive note. "We fight only for things that are reasonable," he said. "Given the chance, we hope to make good."[25]

Ramos had reason to be confident. By championing the rights of the poor and downgrading *Nacionalista* performance, Sakdalism had generated impressive support. Philippine-style Populism, in fact, appeared to have unlimited possibilities. Some political observers, among them Frank Murphy, believed that it might represent the oligarchy's ultimate rival. Sent to the Islands to carry out the delicate transition from colonial to commonwealth status, the new Governor General voiced guarded optimism: "It is conceivable," he cabled the U.S. Secretary of War, "that the *Sakdal* party may become dangerous, but at present a [true] opposition . . . might be a welcome development."[26]

Events shattered both evaluations. Sakdalism's instant success led to equally sudden disaster. Confronted by the specter of a radical opposition, *Nacionalistas* set aside their differences over leadership and roads to independence and forged an efficient united front behind Manuel Quezon. Members of the reconstituted majority party, furthermore, leaped on the Tydings-McDuffie bandwagon and launched a

25. *Philippines Free Press,* July 21, 1934, 28.
26. Stubbs, 166.

well-organized campaign advocating commonwealth status as the first step toward national freedom. Their counterattack caught Ramos and his celebrating Sakdals completely by surprise.

Before he could react to the change, Ramos was confronted by a new problem. One month after the June electoral runoff, Filipino voters returned to the polls to select representatives for a Constitutional Convention. Unable to devise an acceptable alternative, Ramos ordered party loyalists to boycott the election. As a result, Quezonistas won handily. Sakdal orators characterized the whole process as a thinly disguised technique to perpetuate oligarchic controls on a foundation of American bayonets.[27] Their protests went unheeded. The delegates, whom Ramos labeled a collection of "half-breeds and betrayers," assembled on July 30, 1934.[28] Their deliberations ended on February 8, 1935. President Roosevelt signed the Philippine Constitution in early March and simultaneously issued a proclamation calling for ratification by plebiscite on May 14, 1935.

The mending of the split in *Nacionalista* ranks, together with rapid progress toward autonomy under elitist auspices, constituted a near catastrophe for the Sakdalistas. Unity among the established leaders made inconceivable a rapid rise to power by the small opposition group. It also precluded action as the fulcrum in a delicately balanced legislature. Above all, it placed Sakdal lawmakers in an untenable position. Three members of a hostile legislature could not hope to influence the operations of Quezon's potent coalition. The gloomy outlook splintered Sakdal solidarity. Some party members, particularly newly elected office holders, advocated the formulation of more realistic objectives to meet altered circumstances.[29] Others, especially a core of one-time Tangulans and their chauvinistic allies, called for less-rational tactics. Ramos and his principal aides, consequently, found themselves caught between the grindstones of their own demagoguery and the relentless *Nacionalista* drive toward commonwealth status. The squeeze left them only two alternatives: a major modification of their program, or an all-out effort to frustrate the plebescite.

27. Hayden, *The Philippines,* 388.
28. Stubbs, 173.
29. Moderates—particularly the Sakdal congressmen—urged Ramos to modify party goals, but their appeals "fell on deaf ears." Almazon interview.

CHAPTER 12

The Uprising of 1935

Ramos withstood the pressures on his party for several months. Compelling influences from a third source, however, compounded his private agonies. In late August or early September 1934, Manuel Quezon attempted a reconciliation with his former protégé. His emissary for the secret negotiations was Patricio Dionisio. Ramos pondered the advantages and disadvantages of the proposal, but finally rejected it as a solution for either his own or Sakdalism's accumulating problems.[1] Back in his original quandry, Ramos tried to resolve party difficulties by gradually aligning himself with the extremists.[2] Indirect confirmation of his ultimate decision came late in the year. On No-

---

1. Quezon offered Ramos a bargain similar to the one agreed to by the Tangulan *supremo*. Dionisio, moreover, reminded Ramos of his own difficulties with unruly followers and urged the Sakdal leader to accept the proposal. Ramos declined. "Don't worry," he told Dionisio, "I can control my people." During the same conversation, Ramos endorsed the idea of carefully organized local insurrections "because violence of a highly dramatic nature will set off a general uprising throughout the Philippines." Quezon, consequently, dropped the reconciliation effort. Dionisio further maintained that the Senate President was fully informed of Ramos' intentions. In addition to intelligence supplied by the Tangulan leader, Quezon received information from prominent Sakdalistas "who were more loyal to Quezon than Ramos," and from government agents who had infiltrated the movement. Dionisio also said Quezon ordered his "spies" to try to dissuade Sakdal leaders from violence, but if that proved impossible, to "tell them to go on with the rebellion." The remark led Dionisio to conclude that "provocateurs" helped to foment the uprising. Dionisio interview. Many Sakdalistas and, for that mattter, non-Sakdalistas held similar views on Quezon's behind-the-scene role. Several veteran *Nacionalistas* in Laguna, for example, were convinced "the clever rascal engineered the whole thing." Tiongco interview.

2. With all his talents, Ramos had always been inclined toward violent solutions for political problems. At the height of a cabinet crisis in 1923, Ramos volunteered to resolve the conflict by assassinating Governor General Leonard Wood. Quezon rejected the offer as a ridiculous proposal. Isabelo de los Reyes interview.

vember 25, 1934, Ramos set forth on his travels again, announcing
before his departure that he was returning to Washington to fight for
repeal of the Tydings-McDuffie Act. But he made no effort to carry
his followers' anti-Commowealth views to America. Instead, he
journeyed directly to Japan where he sought support for a more
spectacular enterprise.[3]

While Ramos searched for help in Tokyo, Sakdal leaders in the
Philippines grappled with a variety of external and internal complexities. Aside from the gathering *Nacionalista* drive to gain approval of
the Constitution, senior Sakdalistas were confronted by growing insubordination in the ranks. Inadvertently, Ramos and his middle-class
associates had taken the lid off a political Pandora's box. Zealous
commoners from the city and the countryside flocked to the Sakdal
movement. Some of them took control of the party's local destinies.
Once unleashed, their basic anarchism threatened all authority. By
the time Ramos left the country, Sakdalism had begun to take on new
attributes. Village true believers, in fact, were transforming a bourgeois challenge to the *Nacionalista* oligarchy into rampant patriotism
of a millennial variety. Celerino Tiongco recognized the dangers of
the situation and tried to avert them.[4] When resolution proved impossible, he urged the contending factions to concentrate their ire on
the majority coalition. Two months before the Constitutional plebiscite he managed to create a semblance of unity. Returning to the successful techniques of the general election, he soon had the party
functioning with a degree of efficiency.[5]

By early April, Sakdal activities in the provinces surrounding
Manila were causing real concern in governmental circles.[6] *Nacional-*

3. Ramos relationships with Japanese extremists and their peripheral in-
volvements in the Sakdalista uprising have been dealt with by Goodman,
"The Case of Benigno Ramos," 142–183. For the reactions of a Filipino
scholar to Ramos' Japanese affiliations see, T. A. Agoncillo, *The Fateful
Years*, II, 917.
4. Differences between Sakdal leaders accounted in part for the failure of
some party members—particularly those in Tayabas and Marinduque—to participate in the May uprising. Basilio Valdes, "Peace and Order in the Philippines," *Philippines Herald Year Book, 1935*, III (Manila, 1935), 141.
5. By late April, official estimates of Sakdal Party strength ranged as high
as 300,000. Acting Governor General J. R. Hayden, "Preliminary Report on
the Sakdalista Disturbance" (typescript), Manila, May 7, 1935, 4. Hayden
Papers.
6. A member of the cabinet informed the Acting Governor General of the

ista attempts to explain the Constitution to the *taos* of Laguna encountered hostile silence or jeers and catcalls. In Bulacan, municipal
police broke up a party rally by arresting the speaker, but had to fight
their way to jail through ranks of his angry supporters.[7] The intensifying Sakdal opposition drove Filipino officials to a series of questionable actions. On April 11, 1935, Secretary of the Interior Teofilo
Sison ordered local authorities to require permits for public meetings
and specified that permissions should not be granted until applicants
had filed an "'acceptable program.'"[8] On April 12, Secretary of Agriculture and Commerce Eulogio Rodriguez called on provincial employees to counter Sakdal propaganda by stressing the benefits deriving
from departmental services.[9] Neither repression nor education worked.
Disdaining official measures, Sakdalistas continued to hold meetings.
Sakdal, furthermore, gleefully reported on the government's "legal
transgressions" and encouraged its readers to evolve new patterns of
harassment. On April 23, accordingly, *Nacionalista* authorities took
the next logical step. The Director of Posts again revoked *Sakdal's*
mailing rights on the grounds that it was "publishing libelous matter
inciting to rebellious conspiracies, stirring up the people against law-
ful authorities, and tending to disturb the peace of the community."[10]

With *Sakdal* silenced, officialdom settled back to watch the political
thunderheads disperse. The last week in April was comparatively
calm. Committed Sakdalistas kept on meeting, but their rallies appeared to have lost momentum. The only sign of continuing pressure
was a deluge of petitions from provincial Sakdals protesting restrictions on their right to assemble.[11] During April's closing days, the
documents descended on Malacañan Palace like litter from a dying
monsoon gale. Some insular administrators concluded the turbulence
had run its course. Their optimism, however, was premature. As

situation in a confidential memorandum and suggested that "irresponsible
speakers" guilty of "defamatory and seditious denunciations" be arrested to
"stop this campaign of exaggerated misrepresentation." Eulogio Rodriguez to
Hayden, April 2, 1935. Hayden Papers.

7. *Philippines Free Press,* April 13, 1934, 25.

8. Benitez, "Sakdal," 253.

9. Department of Agriculture and Commerce, Office of the Secretary, General Circular no. 11, April 12, 1935. Hayden Papers.

10. *Philippine Magazine,* XXXII (1935), 270.

11. G. A. Malcolm, *The Commonwealth of the Philippines* (New York,
1936), 282.

events quickly demonstrated, diminishing tensions merely represented the final lull before a larger storm.

The bureaucratic constraints failed to check the flood of Sakdalista propaganda. In late April, it appeared in new forms from unforeseen sources. Large numbers of Filipinos—including some prominent politicians—received personal letters from a Japanese artillery officer stationed in Formosa.[12] The communications accused Manuel Quezon of insincerity on the independence question and labeled the Senate President a traitor to the Philippine nation. After parroting other editorial themes from *Sakdal*, the letters concluded with assurances of sympathy and support for Filipinos in their imminent hour of need.

While authorities considered the disturbing implications of that development, a second result of Ramos' activities materialized.[13] On April 29 and 30, thousands of copies of *Free Filipinos,* a "news sheet" printed in Japan and smuggled into Luzon, were secretly distributed in Manila and the countryside.[14] The four-page tabloid continued *Sakdal*'s violent verbal tradition, but added several provocative new ingredients. Its front page, for example, featured a lengthy statement in Japanese of American abuses in the Philippines. Few, if any, readers could decipher the characters. But they did not have to be linguists to conclude that Japan supported Sakdalista aspirations. Other columns in English, Spanish, and Tagalog anticipated the themes of the "Greater East Asia Co-Prosperity Sphere." Calling for a "revival of the Filipino oriental family tradition, oriental culture and civilization, and . . . the attainment of a strong and eternal union between all countries of the Far East," *Free Filipinos* emphasized the advantages of Asian solidarity as a bulwark against further Western domination.

Returning to more familiar issues, the tabloid linked demands for immediate national freedom with agrarian conditions, and reminded

12. The letters, signed by Major Hiroshi Tamaru, came to Hayden's attention directly after the uprising. Inquiries to the American Embassy in Tokyo revealed only that the officer was attached to the headquarters staff of the Imperial Army in Formosa. Hayden to Grew, May 8, 1935; and Grew to Hayden, May 9, 1935. Hayden Papers.

13. Several propaganda efforts came out of Ramos's residence in Japan. A newspaper called the *Filipino Tao* was distributed in Stockton, California, in late April 1935. For a summary of its contents, see Goodman "The Case of Benigno Ramos," 146–147.

14. The Hayden Papers contain a rare copy of *Free Filipinos.* All the quotations which follow are from that source.

rural Filipinos of their turbulent heritage. Two photographs of the Tayug incident awakened particularly bitter memories. One, taken before the disturbance, portrayed the freshly scrubbed faces of the Filipina high school students who perished defending the *convento*. The other, taken after the uprising, pictured dead "Colorums" at the feet of steel-helmeted constabularymen. The caption read:

Land-grabbing, pauperization system [*sic*] are the striking characteristics of American domination in the Philippines. The uprising in Tayug . . . was only one of the direct consequences of the people's stifled rights. Women assumed the leadership of this people's revolt, and these pictures show that they preferred death than [*sic*] to see their country still agonizing under American domination. Their bodies are no more but their defeat in unequal struggle, their bravery and courage had open [*sic*] the eyes of the people to see the naked truth that even if there are Filipinos in this government, it is not Filipino government, but American government, the enemy of Filipino welfare.

Sakdal-style abuse in the hands of Japanese typesetters produced a volatile literary mixture. Spelling and syntax suffered, but the newssheet's provocative message came through. In regard to the Tydings-McDuffie Act, *Free Filipinos* asked, "How many 'Ten Years' does the U.S. government need to kill our independence, and . . . confiscate all the lands of the Filipinos? How many 'Ten Years' does this very benevolent government need to Hawaiianize our country?" A resolutely ungrammatical editorial warned that anyone who opposed the law would be labeled "a demagogue, an agitator, an outlaw, a rabble-rouser, a self-styled leader, etc., and they the promise-breaker [*sic*], and the great forgotter [*sic*], are *saints, perfect people, great statesmen, honorable men, honest, earnest, purest.*" The paper also assembled a rogue's gallery of Hollywood-inspired monsters. It classified Governor General Frank Murphy as a "Frankenstein," and characterized Speaker of the House Quintin Paredes and Governor Juan Cailles of Laguna as "good Frankenstein Slaves." In a final assault on established leadership, *Free Filipinos* labeled Manuel Quezon and Sergio Osmeña "Super-Servants of the Americans" and printed photographs of the "Arch-collaborators" that could have been used to discipline unruly village children.

In spite of *Free Filipinos* contents, authorities failed to acquire copies of the document until after the uprising. The fact that inflammatory literature of foreign origin could be disseminated in the face of Constabulary surveillance was but one symptom of a breakdown in government security measures. On April 27, Acting Governor General Joseph R. Hayden consulted law-enforcement officials concerning possible disturbances on May Day. Secretary Sison and Brigadier General Basilio Valdes, Commander-in-Chief of the Constabulary, assured him there would be "no disorders in the immediate future."[15] Hayden, consequently, left the capital on April 30 to inspect remote sectors of Mountain Province. As predicted, May 1 passed with no untoward incidents. Manila's Labor Day parade, in fact, was a model of civic solidarity. Administrators relaxed and looked forward to a respite before the plebiscite. On the evening of May 2, even General Valdes joined the elitist exodus from the city by boarding a steamer destined for Cebu.[16]

The success of Sakdal organizers in secretly distributing *Free Filipinos* was equaled by their skill at surreptitious preparations for violence. Late on May 1, 1935, activists passed the word that the endeavor to achieve independence would begin within twenty-four hours. They shored up faltering followers by guaranteeing an easy victory. Dubious party members were told that constabularymen had affiliated themselves with the cause. When the liberation effort began, they said, sympathetic troopers would refuse to fire on their fellow patriots. In the event of American military action, they promised Japan would intervene with air and naval support. Some of them probably concluded their calls to arms with the unsubtle Sakdal slogan "Independence will appear magically like the burst of a sunrise."[17]

15. Hayden, "Preliminary Report," 1. Hayden Papers.

16. Aside from dry-season vacationers, other important figures were away from the colonial capital. Frank Murphy was convalescing from an operation at White Sulphur Springs, West Virginia; Manuel Quezon was in Washington and New York on an official trip; and Major General William Parker, the Commander of American forces in the Philippines, was on leave in China. *New York Times,* May 3, 1935. Valdes' departure, however, constituted the only mystery. On the morning of the uprising, Valdes notified the Superintendent of the Constabulary that trouble was brewing. In part, his confidential memorandum read as follows: "X reported to me this morning that the Sakdalistas last night were preparing an uprising against the government to be held tonight. . . . One thing queer on this supposed . . . movement is that no Sakdalista leaders could be located in their houses the whole day and night yesterday. X could not tell me the definite plans of attack . . . but he insisted this is a very serious situation." Valdes to Manley, May 2, 1935. Hayden Papers.

17. Luis Taruc, *Born of the People* (New York, 1953), 29.

Administrators were not the only insular residents deceived by the
conspirators. Many influential Sakdalistas found themselves in similar positions.[18] On April 30, Celerino Tiongco, Marcano Untivero,
and Aurelio Almazon received reports of an imminent uprising. After
comparing notes, they agreed to track down the rumors. Early on
May 1, they fanned out across Laguna. The party strongholds of
Santa Rosa, Calamba, Los Baños, and Santa Cruz proved all too placid.
Sakdal functionaries, in fact, could not be found anywhere in the
province. Rank-and-file Sakdalistas, moreover, were close-mouthed.
Warning their constituents to avoid violence, Almazon and Untivero
returned separately to Manila. Reunited around 11:00 A.M. on May
2, the congressmen attempted to convey their growing fears to Tiongco.
He was not available. Determined efforts to find the *Sakdal* editor also
failed; like other key party members, "Don Celerino" had disappeared.[19] Convinced they had been duped, the weary house members
registered at a Manila hotel for a few hours' sleep.[20]

While Almazon and Untivero attempted to rest, scattered pieces of
the puzzle suddenly fell into place. By 3:00 P.M. on May 2, the political atmosphere in the lowlands surrounding Manila had become as
dense as the weather. Around mid-day, municipal and provincial
authorities began to receive reports that a major outbreak was about
to occur.[21] Local officials in Bulacan and Laguna informed Constabulary commanders, who relayed their warnings to superiors in the

18. Almazon interview.
19. Tiongco interview. Celerino Tiongco did not appear for ten days. On
May 12, he surrendered himself voluntarily to the Constabulary. At that time
he claimed he had tried futilely to dissuade "a small group of irresponsible
men in our party from the use of force." Tiongco attributed the uprising to
Ramos and said his orders for violence had been disseminated by Elpidio de
los Santos. On April 30, Tiongco left Manila to seek out the Sakdal co-
chairman who reportedly was hiding in the hills with a column of men. "I
wanted to get in touch with him" he said, "to determine the veracity of the
rumors and to find out if there was time to avoid an uprising by issuing a
counterorder. I found Santos [and his men]. They would not let me leave and
made me stay with them." Tiongco's account of his activities was borne out by
a statement he issued to Sakdalista voters to boycott the procedure, warning
them to avoid "the stupidity of violence or disturbances." *Philippines Free
Press,* May 18, 1935, 34–35.
20. Almazon interview.
21. G. C. Dunham, L. J. Van Schaick, F. W. Manley, and E. G. Chapman,
"Report of the Committee Appointed by Acting Governor-General J. R.
Hayden to Investigate the Uprisings of May 2 and 3, 1935" (typescript),
Manila, May 21, 1935, 3. Hayden Papers. Cited hereafter as Sakdal Uprising
Report, appendixes to the Report will be listed by their titles.

capital. By late afternoon, government detachments throughout the region had been alerted. Up to that point, however, intelligence on specific Sakdal objectives was not available. Around 6:00 P.M., Constabulary headquarters learned that dissidents planned to dynamite the RCA transmitter at San José del Monte, Bulacan.[22] Manila notified Captain Zacarias Imperial, the provincial commander in Malolos. He promptly ordered a rifle squad to the radio installation. With minimum precautions taken, constabularymen in the city and the countryside waited for the political storm to erupt.

The period of anticipation was brief. At 8:30 P.M., Manila headquarters received word that all telephone lines north of Marilao, Bulacan, and south of Biñan, Laguna, had been cut.[23] Within an hour, urgent calls for assistance from unaffected municipalities in Bulacan, Rizal, Laguna, and Cavite jammed the switchboard at the Santa Lucia Barracks. Hoping to acquire concrete information on the provincial situation, Colonel Guillermo Francisco, the chief of staff, Lieutenant Colonel Miguel Nicdao, the sector commander, and two agents from the Intelligence Section drove south to check conditions in Mutinglupa, Rizal.[24] Aside from abnormally chaotic traffic, they encountered no hazards. Mutinglupa seemed quiet and orderly. Worried town officials, however, said large bands of armed villagers had been seen in the vicinity. They also expected an attack on the *municipio* at any moment. Before the staff officers could verify or disprove the reports, Manila notified them that a clash between Sakdalistas and constables had occurred at Santa Rosa, Laguna.[25]

By the time Francisco and Nicdao received the information, affairs in the neighboring province verged on anarchy. Indications of an impending disturbance had begun to accumulate at the Santa Cruz Constabulary *cuartel* early that afternoon. Around 4:00 P.M., the message center was inundated with pleas for help from Calamba, Cabuyao, Biñan, and Santa Rosa. At 6:30 P.M., Captain Leon Angeles—the provincial commander—ordered two officers and fourteen men to reconnoiter the danger zone. Traveling in two trucks, they reached Calamba without incident. There, the small contingent di-

22. Sakdal Uprising Report, Appendix II, "Action by the Constabulary," 2. Hayden Papers.
23. Hayden, "Preliminary Report," 1. Hayden Papers.
24. Sakdal Uprising Report, Appendix II, 2. Hayden Papers.
25. Sakdal Uprising Report, Appendix II, "Santa Rosa, Laguna—Narrative," 4–5. Hayden Papers.

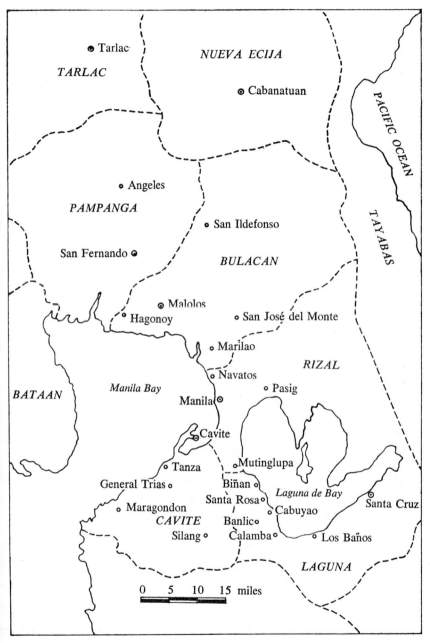

8. The Manila Hinterland, 1935

vided. First Lieutenant Jorge Velasco and seven troopers paused to investigate conditions in the community. The remainder of the unit was to proceed toward Santa Rosa. Before separating, the patrol leader advised his newly commissioned aide to exercise caution. Velasco also told him to remain on Santa Rosa's outskirts until the Calamba detachment caught up.

Propelled by the valor of inexperience, Second Lieutenant Juan Bondad hastened to his objective. North of Cabuyao town the truck-load of insular policemen was almost side-swiped by a motorist careening down the south highway. The errant driver proved to be an excited official from Santa Rosa. His municipality, he said, had been captured by hundreds of Sakdalistas. Bondad urged the man to carry his news to Velasco in Calamba and rushed northward into the night. Instead of waiting along the road, he ordered his sergeant to drive directly to the central square. Bondad's truck eased into Santa Rosa around 10:00 P.M. The town was totally blacked out. Attempting to adjust to the darkness, his driver doused the headlights and ground slowly toward the plaza. The troopers saw no one until they turned into the square. There, a bright light before the municipal building revealed a hostile crowd. Again, Bondad did not hesitate. Signaled forward, his fatalistic sergeant relentlessly parted milling Sakdals with the truck bumper and stopped at the *presidencia*'s steps. Shotguns immediately erupted on all sides. Bondad and every member of the patrol were wounded. Almost instantaneously, however, they returned the fire. Dragging injured comrades, Bondad and his bleeding constables fought their way into the municipal building. Somehow, they managed to hold on until Velasco and his men arrived from Calamba. Their ordeal lasted only fifteen minutes. But the brutal encounter claimed the lives of three constables and four rebels; it also resulted in severe wounds for Bondad, his four survivors, and six of their adversaries.

After a wild drive south from Mutinglupa, Colonel Nicdao arrived in Santa Rosa around midnight. He surveyed the scene, received Velasco's report on the engagement, and telephoned details to Manila. Colonel Francisco, who had returned to the Santa Lucia Barracks, immediately ordered a reserve Constabulary company to Santa Rosa. With reinforcements on their way, Nicdao attempted to analyze the uprising's emerging pattern. Frightened travelers soon began to congregate near the recaptured municipal building. They told Nicdao that Sakdalistas controlled barrio Banlic nine kilometers down the highway. Led by an energetic woman, the rebels were stopping all vehicles, searching passengers, and confiscating arms and ammunition.[26] Before Nicdao could devise a sensible response to the new challenge, Francisco notified him that fighting had broken out at San Ildefonso, Bulacan. Unable to keep pace with the turmoil, Nicdao relinquished sector command to Colonel Francisco and remained in Santa Rosa to oversee Constabulary operations in Laguna.

To Francisco, the situation north of Manila seemed equally bleak.[27] Since early afternoon, conditions in Bulacan had duplicated those prevailing around the great lake. By 7:00 P.M., however, the provincial commander at Malolos found himself in more precarious circumstances than his southern counterpart. Shortly after the departure of the squad sent to guard the RCA installation, appeals for help from threatened municipalities began to arrive. Captain Imperial reassured telephoning *presidentes* but kept the thinned ranks of his company intact. At 8:30 P.M., he lost direct communication with Manila. From then until well past midnight, reports on assembling Sakdalistas poured in from *municipios* across Bulacan, but there was still no indication of real violence anywhere in the province. At 2:20 A.M. on May 3, a municipal policeman from San Ildefonso arrived at the *cuartel* with word that dissidents had commandeered his town's *presidencia*. Imperial ordered Lieutenant Manuel Jimenez and sixteen men —the bulk of Bulacan's Constabulary company—to reoccupy San Ildefonso.

The detachment drove thirty-five kilometers through edgy *municipios* and hostile barrios in less than an hour. Abandoning their truck outside San Ildefonso, the constables formed a skirmish line and moved cautiously toward the rear of the municipal building. Approximately 200 yards from the structure, Jimenez halted his men. He informed the insurgents of the Constabulary's presence and demanded immediate surrender. The barricaded Sakdalistas shouted defiance and opened fire; their ricocheting buckshot killed one constabularyman and wounded two others. Jimenez gestured riflemen into position, and led a systematic assault on the *presidencia*. After thirty minutes, the out-

26. For accounts by individuals who participated in the uprising, see Appendixes C and D of this volume.
27. Sakdal Uprising Report, Appendix II, "San Ildefonso, Bulacan—Narrative," 6–7. Hayden Papers.

maneuvered Sakdalistas displayed white flags. On command, eighty-nine *taos* filed from the building with their hands held high. Waiting troopers frisked the emerging rebels and forced them to lie on the ground. Jimenez then checked casualties. Two Sakdals died and eleven were wounded during the skirmish. To the lieutenant's satisfaction, his attackers had avoided additional losses. Around 5:30 A.M., the constabularymen marched their prisoners to San Ildefonso jail.

At that hour, Jimenez and his men were the only elated constables in Manila's environs. Daylight revealed the scale of the rebellion: in addition to engagements in Laguna and Bulacan, Constabulary headquarters was confronted with mounting discord in Rizal and Cavite; timely patrols in the former province had prevented the fall of Mutinglupa and Pasig, but conditions in the latter threatened to deteriorate beyond repair; the *municipios* of Tanza, General Trias, Silang, and Maragondon had either been cut off or entered by Sakdalistas;[28] armed bands collecting behind Cavite town's Chinese cemetery endangered the provincial capital and its American naval station. To make matters worse, a garbled telephone call from somewhere in Cavite claimed rebels had captured Governor Ramon Samonte.

Colonel Francisco unquestionably faced a critical situation. Before dawn, intelligence agents from Manila's Tondo and Sampaloc districts told the chief of staff that both working quarters were on the verge of riot.[29] Francisco, with a dwindling contingent, hoarded his remaining men to meet the new menace. The end, however, was not yet. A preliminary report on the San Ildefonso action caused consternation at the Santa Lucia command center. Lieutenant Jimenez informed his superiors that captured Sakdals expected Japanese air and naval support at sunrise.[30] Francisco relayed the news to Malacañan Palace. Since repeated efforts by radio had failed to reach Acting Governor General Hayden, Richard Ely—the ranking executive official—assumed responsibility and alerted American armed forces to prepare for action.[31]

28. Sakdal Uprising Report, Appendix III, "Action of Municipal Authorities," 1–14. Hayden Papers.

29. Sakdal strategists planned supporting uprisings in Manila. At least 20,000 party loyalists were expected to swarm into the streets of Tondo and Sampaloc during the early morning hours. Communication breakdowns and the first heavy rain of the season frustrated their effort. Hayden, "Preliminary Report," 2. Hayden Papers.

30. Hayden, *The Philippines*, 391.

31. Ely to Hayden, May 4, 1935. Hayden Papers.

While rumors soared to crescendo levels in Manila, preparations for the insurrection's bloodiest encounter supplied an ominous counterpoint in Laguna.[32] Accompanied by Captain Angeles, Governor Juan Cailles—Sakdalism's local *bête noire*—arrived in Santa Rosa around 3:30 A.M. Perversely exhilarated by a harrowing three-and-a-half-hour trip from Santa Cruz, the old revolutionary confirmed the existence of a roadblock at barrio Banlic and warned Colonel Nicdao that several hundred Sakdalistas had overrun neighboring Cabuyao town. Continuing requests for reinforcement brought a trickle of constabularymen into Santa Rosa. By 7:30 A.M., Nicdao had assembled a piecemeal force of four officers and thirty-two enlisted men from four separate companies. Surrounded by grisly reminders of Bondad's fate, the troopers readied themselves for battle. Nicdao emphasized the situation's gravity by issuing each man 110 rounds of rifle ammunition before they headed south. With Governor Cailles riding in Angeles' command vehicle, their convoy covered the intervening four kilometers without incident. On Cabuyao's outskirts, drivers braked the trucks to a halt. Dismounting troopers buckled helmet straps, dispersed into combat formation, fixed bayonets, and began a cautious advance toward the *municipio*.

Cabuyao appeared to be abandoned. When the constables turned off the south highway, however, an unobstructed view of the plaza revealed a scene of hectic activity. Scores of armed Sakdalistas were evacuating Cabuyao's *presidencia,* hurrying across the littered street, and dropping behind a waist-high wall surrounding the ancient churchyard. Outwardly cool, government troopers continued their deliberate advance. When they reached a point approximately 150 yards from the stone barrier, the Sakdals fired prematurely. Realizing he was still beyond the range of their crude weapons, Captain Angeles kept his men in formation and moved forward. Sixty yards from the wall he halted his riflemen. Governor Cailles then stepped forth and called for an insurgent capitulation. The beleaguered farmers and fishermen answered with scattered shots. Splitting into three groups—two flanking parties and a covering assault line—the constables sprang into action. Cailles made a last effort to head off disaster when he leaped to a park bench only thirty yards from the wall and pleaded with the Sakdals to surrender or run away. In the midst of his appeal, the dis-

32. Sakdal Uprising Report, Appendix II, "Cabuyao, Laguna—Narrative," 8–12. Hayden Papers.

sidents unleashed another ragged volley. Three constabularymen, including a lieutenant near Cailles, fell wounded. The incensed Governor promptly gunned down the two Sakdalistas who shot at the officer and charged—side arms blazing—into the melee.[33] While Cailles ran forward, government flankers triggered a raking enfilade on the rebel position. Troopers in the street then ceased firing and rushed to the wall. Beyond the barrier they heard terrified survivors moaning *"Suko Na! Suko Na!"* (We surrender). Angeles signaled an end to the rifle fire on the flanks. When his men hurdled the wall, they discovered that seventy-nine of the original 300-man Sakdal force had stood fast. Of these, seven were physically unscathed, twenty-two had suffered multiple wounds, and fifty were dead.

Government casualties, consisting of the injured lieutenant and three wounded troopers, were sent back to Colonel Nicdao's command post in Santa Rosa. The Cabuyao contingent—soon strengthened by seventeen reserves from Manila—began preparing immediately for an attack on barrio Banlic. Informed that a thousand Sakdalistas held the highway settlement, Nicdao left nothing to chance. While his constables rested and received a new ammunition issue, the Colonel called for more reinforcements. Nicdao's anxieties were clearly revealed by a follow-up message. Around 10:00 A.M., he asked the Santa Lucia Barracks for 1,000 additional army rifles.[34] The field commander was apparently ready to arm loyalists among Laguna's civilian population. His communication appeared on the front pages of Manila's afternoon newspapers. Linked to lurid accounts of the night's hostilities, it produced near-hysteria in and around the capital. Prominent citizens from the suburbs joined fleeing *principales* from the countryside in a frantic competition for downtown hotel rooms. By the evening of May 3, the influx of well-to-do refugees had placed a severe strain on Manila's better accommodations.[35] Civil strife, quite obviously, brought agonies in one form or another to rich and poor alike.

No one realized the hailstorm of bullets at Cabuyao had shattered the rebellion—no one, that is, except the *taos* who managed to escape before havoc converged from the flanks. The odor of cordite lingered

33. In his official account of the engagement Cailles boasted that he shot seven Sakdalistas, *Ibid.*, 11.

34. *Manila Herald*, May 3, 1935.

35. *Manila Daily Bulletin*, May 4, 1935.

longer than Sakdalism that hot May morning. Fleeing survivors carried descriptions of the slaughter to comrades in neighboring barrios, and the Sakdal force in Banlic melted away before Cabuyao's constables had finished administering aid to their victims. Word of the clash spread rapidly. By noon of May 3, dissident bands along the village grapevine surrounding Manila had vanished. By evening, rebel leaders were in hiding or in flight throughout Bulacan, Rizal, Laguna, and Cavite. Like three more of Cabuyao's hapless defenders, Sakdalism was in its death agonies.

The reasons for the sudden disintegration should have been evident. For more than a generation, insular politicians had been painting halcyon portraits of the blessings that would flow from national freedom. Benigno Ramos marred the beckoning vision. He told credulous villagers that the Tydings-McDuffie Act made independence unobtainable. All that remained, he prophesied, was a prolongation of the humiliating dependence and exploitation they and their families had experienced for generations. A desperate uprising seemed to be the only hope. Local Sakdal leaders, furthermore, maintained that a show of strength would overwhelm the opposition. Many hamlet dwellers came to believe that sovereignty could be achieved with ease.

On the evening of May 2, therefore, carrying clubs, bolos, sickles, daggers, rusting pistols, and homemade shotguns, peasants had collected at prearranged assembly points. Fervent with patriotism, they had marched on the municipalities, expecting to be welcomed as liberators. When the Constabulary appeared, troopers who were supposed to join them did not throw down their weapons. Instead, they sent well-aimed rifle fire crashing through Sakdal ranks. Exaltation turned to astonishment, followed quickly by blind panic. As one disillusioned veteran of Cabuyao put it, "If every day of independence is like this, I'll go out and hide."[36]

Party leaders, of course, had proceeded on different assumptions. Sakdalista extremists recognized the limitations of the expedient. While sixty-eight thousand peasants and proletarians equipped with a motley array of weapons had no real hope of overthrowing an emerging nation of 12,000,000 people supported by the armed might of the United States, in all likelihood the men who planned the venture believed they were acting in the best interests of their country. Motivating factors aside, however, a thread of rationality ran through their ap-

36. Hayden, *The Philippines,* 397.

parent madness. A successful uprising could frustrate the plebiscite, hinder the establishment of the Philippine Commonwealth, make manifest the opposition of large numbers of Filipinos to the Tydings-McDuffie Act, and perhaps lead the United States to modify its views on independence. The position of the party on that issue, in fact, made such a course almost inevitable.

Safe in Tokyo, Benigno Ramos surveyed the shambles. During an interview on May 4, he said, "We know the American Government in the Islands is so strong that revolt against it means suicide. But what else can we do?"[37] He attempted to shrug off the outcome as a temporary setback, but the disastrous results could not be dismissed. The plebiscite took place on schedule. Insular voters overwhelmingly endorsed the Commonwealth. Shortly thereafter, they heaped additional indignity on surviving Sakdals by electing Manuel Quezon president of an autonomous Philippines.[38] Everything Ramos hoped to prevent had come into being. Everything he aspired to create had vanished. For all practical purposes, by noon of May 3, 1935, Sakdalism was as cold and dead as the corpses twisted against the Spanish wall in Cabuyao.

What began as a promising experiment ended in tragic futility. For the peasantry it was not an unprecedented experience. Unlike their *supremo,* many humble Sakdalistas had been driven by motives far more lofty than vengeance. Like their mystical predecessors they had struggled courageously, if ineffectively, to create a better world. Prisoners spoke longingly of national freedom to American interrogators, but their remarks indicated they sought something far more important. At San Ildefonso, a captured Sakdal stated his ultimate purpose with eloquent simplicity:

> I want independence. I want our country to be free. . . . I am opposed to the present leaders because they put in the Commonwealth. I don't want it. It would be sweet to my heart to have independence even if I with my children must suffer every kind of hardship. . . . We didn't settle this like they do in America . . . because in America they count the ballots fairly. Here I have no confidence in the ballots being counted. Under independence they would be . . . because everyone would purify himself inside.[39]

37. *New York Times,* May 5, 1935.
38. See O. S. Villasin, "Inauguration Day in a Sakdal Town," *Philippine Magazine,* XXXII (1935), 608.
39. Hayden, *The Philippines,* 396.

CHAPTER 13

The Aftermath

Ramos' use of the word "suicide" proved devastatingly apt. Sixty villagers died in the uprising. At least forty, and perhaps many more, suffered incapacitating injuries. The debacle also discredited both Ramos and his movement. Almost immediately, Filipino radicals joined conservatives in pillorying him. Artemio Ricarte dismissed the Sakdal *supremo* as "extremely unworthy of the cause he leads," describing him as a man whose "weakness of character" would permit "him to drown in a glass of water."[1] Some disillusioned extremists went even further. Narciso Lapus—who had gained a degree of notoriety by challenging author Nicholas Roosevelt to a duel—again achieved celebrity status by offering his services to Malacañan Palace. On May 6, the one-time Sakdal organizer volunteered to travel to Tokyo for the express purpose of capturing Benigno Ramos, vowing that he would drag the disgraced *supremo* back to Manila to be publicly hanged for "unprecedented cowardice."[2]

The decline in Ramos' reputation was not the only result of the upheaval. Sakdalism's untimely demise caused much soul-searching among Filipinos. Initially, *Nacionalista* spokesmen attempted to discredit the rebellion by tracing it to demagogues, racketeers, and religious fanatics. Their conventional view was challenged by a few prominent politicians who pointed to inequitable social and economic conditions as the real villains and called for basic reforms to ease the lot of the rural population. Journalistic reactions to the uprising passed through three distinct stages. Alarmed amazement yielded to relieved amusement, which, in turn, gradually gave way to sober assessment of the eruption's multiple sources. The resulting demands for ameliorative policies were not unanimous. But the fact that power-

1. Stubbs, "Philippine Radicalism," 157.
2. *Philippines Free Press,* May 11, 1935, 26.

ful officeholders and leading editors sought an underlying explanation created the beginnings of understanding in respect to the peasants and their plight.

During the days following the outbreak, conflicting statements by *Nacionalistas* indicated that a change in official attitudes had begun. Speaker of the House Quintin Parades offered the time-honored explanation. He found the loss of lives "deeply regrettable," and voiced hopes that "the tragic occurrences will be a blessing in breaking up these fanatical movements."[3] At first, Manuel Quezon adopted a similar stand. Interviewed at his hotel suite in New York City, the Senate President called Ramos an "irresponsible demagogue," and maintained the Sakdal Party was "operated on a purely racketeering basis."[4] Within twenty-four hours, however, Quezon adopted a new tack. Apparently able to judge infinitesimal shifts in the political winds from a distance of 11,000 miles, he traced the uprising to dislocations growing out of the Great Depression and attributed general restlessness in the provinces to the detrimental effects of American import quotas.[5]

Colonial officials disputed Quezon's evaluation.[6] Ramon Torres, the conscientious Secretary of Labor, interviewed captured Sakdalistas in Bulacan and Laguna. He uncovered no evidence of cults, cultists, or political racketeers, but at San Ildefonso he learned that *canons* on the estate exceeded the annual earnings of most tenants. "The people of the town are worried," Torres reported, "because May 31st will be the last day to pay . . . rent and if they fail . . . they will probably be ejected from their homes." In Laguna the role of impersonal *hacenderos* was less obvious. The Depression and severe typhoons, however, had caused widespread hardships. Recognizing the marginal nature of village existence, Torres concluded "hard times are at the bottom of the trouble."[7] While the reactions of the Labor Secretary were not sensational, they marked a sharp departure from traditional *Nacionalista* complacency toward rural problems.

3. *New York Times,* May 5, 1935.
4. *Manila Daily Bulletin,* May 4, 1935.
5. *New York Times,* May 5, 1935.
6. The acting governor general said: "Restrictive laws passed by Congress regarding Philippine products have as yet had no serious effect upon economic conditions." Hayden, "Preliminary Report," 5. Hayden Papers.
7. Torres to Hayden, May 7, 1935, 2–3. Hayden Papers.

Torres' interpretations were reinforced by the findings of a four-man American investigating team sent into the provinces by Acting Governor General Hayden. Their analysis ascribed the rebellion to political factors. Their conclusion, however, stressed the contributing role of social conditions.

> The government was more or less out of touch with the pulse and thought of the barrio people who are basically good citizens. The condition of the lower strata of them has not changed materially since 1898. They eat out of the same common bowl. They are protected against the worst epidemics. . . . They have some chance for a little education if they are not too poor, and they are afforded some protection in the matter of civil rights. But they do not see or feel much change except that they watch the middle and upper classes, whose standards have risen, ride in automobiles, live in better houses, and possess more than formerly. Their poverty and grievances make it possible for unscrupulous of misguided men to lead them.[8]

Press responses underwent a similar tranformation. At the height of the trouble journalists expressed fears of a general uprising and called upon all Filipinos to respect constituted authority.[9] The rapid dispersion of dissidents, however, led to efforts to lampoon Sakdalism. One of the better attempts to portray Ramos as an extortioner and his followers as pawns appeared in a new magazine:

> From the many rustic hamlets
> That have slumbered long in peace,
> Sakdalistas came with hatchets
> And with deadly guns and kris.
>
> And they danced with maddened fury,
> And they raised their weapons high,
> And their paths were red and gory,
> When they raised their frenzied cry.
>
> There was slaughter in the midnight;
> There was laughter, there was fright;
> And the darkness mocked the starlight
> As if ignorance were right.
>
> They would block the Constitution;
> There's no freedom there they say.

8. Sakdal Uprising Report, 10. Hayden Papers.
9. Under a photograph of two dead Sakdalistas appeared the warning: "The government must be respected and those who would destroy it will share the lot of these two." *Manila Herald*, May 3, 1935.

They should try to court perdition,
Toward Hell to pave the way.

In the land of Cherry Blossoms,
In the Kingdom of the Sun,
Far away from bleeding bosoms,
Their Supremo has the fun.

O the blood of Sakdalistas
It has dried upon the sod.
But the funds of Sakdalistas
Whence and whither, O my god![10]

The same periodical tried to link Sakdalism with Colorumism. In Bulacan, according to a satirical account of the uprising, "about 100 fanatics went to the hills, led by a seventeen-year-old girl mystic whose chief claim to divinity was that she could turn the bark of trees wrapped in paper into guns." But the editor abandoned humor in his final castigation of the government. Calling for an end to "complacent forbearance" toward "radicalism," he declared, "a continued namby-pamby policy in dealing with mountebanks is suicidal for the government itself, and dangerous to the ordered peace of its citizenry."[11]

Other molders of public opinion also held the insular administration responsible. Newspapers owned by *hacenderos* carried their accusations to unprecedented heights. The *Manila Herald*, for example, placed the ultimate blame on "democracy." Popular forms of government, complained an anonymous feature writer, tend "to pamper the masses." Peasants, he grumbled, "behave like spoiled children . . . demanding more and more." Echoing the age-old lament of threatened elites, he maintained that *taos* no longer knew their place: "Belief in injustice, fancied or factual, nerves the masses to heights of insolence if not revolution. The recent Sakdal uprising is an unfortunate example. Impudence, of course, usually precedes violence, be it in the individual or in the mob. As long as our masses harbor the belief that they are being persecuted they will be sullen and insolent."[12]

While the majority of Manila's press tried to discredit Sakdalism, a

10. *New Philippine Republic*, I (1935), 3–4. There was some merit to the magazine's claim. Antonio Argosino, the Sakdal congressman from Tayabas whose constituents did not participate in the uprising, maintained that Ramos carried $35,000 in party funds when he departed for Japan. *Philippines Free Press*, May 18, 1935, 34.
11. *New Philippines Republic*, I (1935), 4.
12. *Manila Herald*, June 15, 1935.

few journalists dissented. The *Philippines Free Press* and *Philippine Magazine* held the thick-skinned leaders of insular society accountable.[13] A. V. H. Hartendorp, summing up liberal viewpoints, asked: "Exploiting landlords, bloodsucking money lenders, the indifference of those in better circumstances . . . what better grounds could agitators desire?" He then compiled a wholesale indictment:

> Granted that Benigno Ramos is a "racketeer" and his lieutenants are scoundrels, the Sakdal party remains a party of protest, and that is where its strength lies. Its members are not sycophants feeding at the political trough, but belong to the common people. Granted that the principles the Sakdalistas have espoused are vague, foolish, and uncoordinated, they show, nevertheless, a groping for remedies that have not been brought them by the politicians.
>
> We cannot brush the matter aside by stating that the Sakdal movement is instigated by racketeers or that it is due to a temporary depression. Its roots go much deeper than that—go down into a substratum of class conflict that is present here as elsewhere in the world. It is a movement of the dispossessed, of the exploited, of those who are given no chance. . . .
>
> The only answer is to give these people a chance. The political party that can arrange that will be the political party of the future.[14]

Hartendorp's interpretation came to be widely accepted in the months and years following the uprising. Sakdalism, consequently, exerted a profound influence on the course of Commonwealth affairs. The attempt to avoid another Cabuyao manifested itself in several forms. *Nacionalista* leaders, hoping to frustrate future violence, forced their party to adopt social reforms. *Hacenderos,* fearing their days of affluence and influence were numbered, organized private armies and emphasized cooperative efforts to restrict the activities of belligerent peasant movements. Agrarian leaders, stunned by the bloodshed of May 2–3, 1935, re-examined their assumptions and sought more effective means to organize the rural population. In the years leading up to Pearl Harbor the contradictory tendencies created in the provinces an atmosphere heavy with tension.

The first indication of a changing climate appeared in the humane treatment accorded jailed Sakdalistas. On June 28, 1935, the *taos* who surrendered at San Ildefonso were found guilty of rebellion and

13. "Hundreds, even thousands, of poor, downtrodden peasants can be killed, but the demand for social justice, for equality before the law, for a helping hand in time of need, cannot be quelled by bullets." *Philippines Free Press,* May 11, 1935, 8.
14. "The Sakdal Protest," *Philippine Magazine,* XXXII (1935), 233.

were sentenced to prison terms ranging from two to seventeen years.[15] Within sixty days Governor General Murphy extended conditional pardons to seventy-four of them.[16] By the end of October, practically every Sakdal arrested for participating in the uprising had been convicted and consigned to Bilibid's overflowing cells. But the precedent established in the San Ildefonso case worked to their collective advantage. On November 15, 1935, as his last official act, Murphy released most of the prisoners. The retiring Governor General justified his intervention by stating that he wanted "to set an example of tolerance where differences of opinion are concerned."[17]

Murphy's astute redefinition of sedition appealed to Manuel Quezon, and in an early address before the Commonwealth National Assembly, the new chief executive picked up the cue. Quezon challenged the legislators to grapple with basic questions. "The problem involved in the relationship between tenants and landlords," he proclaimed, "whether within large or small estates, owned by individuals or corporations, public or private, transcends in importance practically all other social problems of the Philippines."[18] His declaration marked the inauguration of a presidential drive for reform legislation. Quezon even found a beguiling label for the endeavor. Dusting off the phrase he coined after the Tangulan episode, he launched a crusade for "Social Justice." Impressed by Franklin Roosevelt's landslide victory in 1936 and urged on by High Commissioner Murphy and his progressive aides, Quezon struggled to achieve the reputation of an economic liberal. During the six years prior to the Japanese invasion the Commonwealth President used every trick in his repertoire, from persuasion and patronage to charm and coercion, to push enlightened measures through the *hacendero*-dominated assembly.

A degree of success crowned his efforts. Quezon carried forward the program of estate purchases and land redistribution begun by Murphy. At the President's behest, the National Assembly established settlement projects in the Koronadel Valley of Mindanao for Luzon's depressed and crowded population. At his urging, legislators created the National Rice and Corn Corporation to provide convenient storage facilities for small farmers and to circumvent the influence of

15. *New York Times,* June 29, 1935.
16. *New York Times,* Aug. 18, 1935.
17. *Philippine Magazine,* XXXII (1935), 597.
18. Bernstein, *The Philippine Story,* 148.

usurers and sharp municipal merchants. In addition, assemblymen voted funds for public defenders to protect impoverished defendants, and gave unions the right to organize and bargain collectively. They also established a Court of Industrial Relations to mediate rural and urban labor disputes. By 1940, Quezon's legislative program and supporting executive orders amounted to a vest-pocket version of Roosevelt's New Deal.

Parliamentary victories in Manila, however, did not end misery in the municipalities. Blocking tactics by provincial governors and legislatures and foot-dragging by local politicos hindered the applications of Social Justice.[19] Persistent efforts notwithstanding, Quezon and his advisers could not implement their reforms at the barrio level. The glaring difference between legislative achievements and rural realities haunted both the Commonwealth President and his supporters. Quezon, nevertheless, took a series of dramatic steps toward a more equitable order. If nothing else, his speeches and actions on behalf of "little people" further exposed the depths of the social schism revealed by the Sakdalista uprising.

Much of Quezon's difficulty sprang from elitist determination to maintain the status quo. Large landholders resisted Social Justice at every level. With the appearance of agrarian unions, *hacendero* disapproval intensified. In 1941, a member of the National Assembly from Pampanga attributed all the woes of his province to reform programs. The growth of Marxism in central Luzon, he argued, resulted directly from the "government's policy of pampering labor." Social Justice had been carried too far. The enactment of legislaiton to protect workers from exploitation was praiseworthy, he said, but it was also essential "to protect capital and prevent it from being abused by labor."[20]

Conservatives, however, did not limit their opposition to rhetoric. They resorted to proven techniques in a determined effort to restrict village challenges.[21] During the years between Cabuyao and Pearl

---

19. Ramos had foreseen the problem. During the debate over a share-tenancy law in 1933, which placed the enforcement burden on municipal councils, he editorialized: "Depend upon the corrupt Municipal Councils to help us and we can as well expect our politicians to give us back our taxes." Stubbs, 142.

20. Fausto F. Gonzales-Sioco, "The Cause of Communism in the Philippines," *Living Age*, CCCLX (1941), 548–549.

21. Landlord associations constituted the chief weapon. One of the first was

Harbor, landlord associations appeared throughout Manila's hinterland. The governor of Cavite, for example, recruited and equipped a sizable vigilante group called the National Volunteers. When urban journalists and politicians criticized the experiment, Governor Ramon Samonte defended his retainers. "During the abortive uprising," he declared, "they more than once showed their . . . capacity to handle delicate situations."[22] Governor Sotero Baluyot of Pampanga developed the largest and most powerful provincial organization. He described the Cawal ning Capayapan, or Knights of Peace, as a "conservative labor union." At a recruiting rally in San Fernando, Baluyot proclaimed admirable objectives. The Cawal, he said, "does not believe in violence but in peace; respects the rights of the poor as well as the rich; has absolute faith in the government; and goes to the proper authorities for its grievances."[23] On the same occasion, he urged his brawny followers—who wore blue uniforms with white plow and spade insignias—to seek reconciliations between proprietors and tenants through "understanding."[24]

Politically aware Filipinos questioned Baluyot's commitment to pacifism. The *Manila Tribune* suggested the Pampanga association was "predicated on its ability and intention to use force." Prospective members, the newspaper pointed out, were offered free legal services —an unusual inducement which automatically placed the organization in the category of a "private army."[25] The Communist Party of the Philippines went further and labeled the Cawal a "strike-breaking, Fascist outfit."[26] But the Commonwealth government ignored urban protests and permitted Baluyot's organization, together with its well-armed counterparts elsewhere in Luzon, to develop into large paramilitary forces. President Quezon contributed to the growth of provincial satraps. Threatened by mushrooming anti-*Nacionalista* sentiments in the Central Plain, he stepped out of his adopted role as

---

the Batung Maputi (White Stone) which flourished in Pampanga during the late 1920's. Designed to resist "tenant encroachments," its bylaws declared "members . . . should not accept as tenants those who have deserted another member of the association without reasonable cause." Macaraig, *Social Problems*, 257.

22. *Manila Tribune*, Aug. 10, 1937.
23. *Manila Daily Bulletin*, July 20, 1939.
24. Crippen, "Philippine Agrarian Unrest," 355.
25. *Manila Tribune*, March 19, 1938.
26. *Manila Daily Bulletin*, July 31, 1939.

defender of the masses and endorsed the Cawal. "The whole country," he congratulated Baluyot, "should organize into this legion."[27]

Wealthy constituents of the Pampanga governor also took the lead in evolving new tactics to constrain the peasantry. Members of the provincial legislature passed restrictive measures of a constitutionally dubious nature, and well-to-do citizens extended largess to municipal law-enforcement agencies. In 1938, over Quezon's strenuous objections, *"Tambuli* [meeting horn] Ordinances" went into effect throughout Pampanga. The laws forbade the "gathering of two or more people after dusk."[28] In the same year, landowners and businessmen in San Fernando town purchased a truck for the local police to "facilitate the transportation of . . . patrols during an emergency."[29] As if all that were not enough, Baluyot urged the mayors of Pampanga "to stop all radical activities."[30] Inevitably, his heavy-handed approach provoked more peasants than it controlled. Baluyot's methods, moreover, were imitated by professional politicians throughout the region.[31] The ill-conceived techniques of his fellow *Nacionalistas,* in short, countered all of Quezon's endeavors to calm the village population. Pampanga and its tenant-ridden neighbors, consequently, again began to seethe with discontent.

The attention accorded barrio affairs constituted an indirect tribute to a new model *supremo.* After Ramos' failure, dissenters looked elsewhere for guidance and inspiration. Almost automatically, the mantle of peasant leadership fell on the emaciated but capable shoulders of Pedro Abad Santos. His rise to radical prominence shifted the focus of discord from the cloud-draped mountains of the southern Tagalog region to the sunny plains and sullen population of central Luzon. Pampanga, which W. Cameron Forbes once called "a most peaceful province," replaced Laguna in the Constabulary's catalogue of potential trouble spots.[32]

Abad Santos, or "Don Perico" as he was known by friends and

27. *Manila Daily Bulletin,* July 20, 1939.
28. *Manila Daily Bulletin,* Oct. 3, 1938.
29. *Manila Daily Bulletin,* April 16, 1938.
30. *Manila Daily Bulletin,* March 7, 1938.
31. Governor Molina of Bulacan, for example, advocated that local police forces in his province be increased by 600 men. Two officers in each barrio, the Governor said, would eradicate lawlessness in the form of "robberies, cattle rustling, and gangsterism." *Manila Tribune,* Jan. 22, 1938.
32. He made the observation in an entry on provincial law and order dated April 29, 1906. Forbes, "Journal," II, 2.

and admirers, reflected the expanding awareness of sensitive elitists. An established member of Pampanga's prerevolutionary *principalia,* Abad Santos had taken advantage of all the opportunities that came with social prominence. Accomplished lawyer, member of the insular House of Representatives from 1917 to 1922, Commissioner on Independence Missions to the United States, recognized scholar equally proficient in Spanish, English, French, German, Latin, and Greek, he deserved the normally misapplied superlative *"ilustrado."* Until the late 1920's his career seemed totally orthodox. Private affinities for Marxism, however, finally caught up with Don Perico. In 1929, he founded the Socialist Party of the Philippines.[33] From then on, most of Abad Santos' peers regarded him as a traitor to his class.

Ostracized by elitists he gradually won the respect and affection of commoners. Abad Santos became a student of rural rebellions. Close examination of the Sakdalista movement and its leader revealed to him strong possibilities for uniting alienated villagers behind intellectual leadership. It also disclosed the narrow confines within which successful challenges to authority might occur. In simple terms, Abad Santos attempted to emulate Ramos' accomplishments while avoiding his errors. To a remarkable degree he succeeded. Under his guidance, popular protest patterns shifted from impossible schemes for revitalization toward pragmatic efforts at rectification: union membership drives, mass demonstrations, strikes, boycotts, and open political activities, replaced intuitive revolutionary endeavors and conventional conspiracies. After 1935, Abad Santos fashioned a working coalition that included devout tenants, pious day laborers, and doctrinaire materialists. It was an unparalleled accomplishment. At long last, enlightened radicalism appeared to be winning the allegiance of a large segment of central Luzon's peasantry.

Perhaps Don Perico's greatest contribution was to deny the possibility of immediate gratification. More Fabian than Marxist, he constantly stressed the advantages of evolution over revolution. He also tried to divert the attention of his followers from political sources of discontent toward more fundamental economic issues. For a variety of reasons he opposed Quezon's Social Justice campaign. Abad Santos regarded the program as a transparent technique to mislead poor people. He looked upon capitalism as the ultimate evil and believed

33. For a reliable brief analysis of Marxism and its development see A. B. Saulo, *Communism in the Philippines* (Manila, 1969).

that sooner or later it had to be abolished. "We do not believe in social justice," he said. "We believe that if the masses are to be saved it is by their own efforts."[34] To his young protégé Luis Taruc—the future leader of the Hukbalahap—he passed on his philosophy: "The poor must learn to make what they want come true. Every strike must be a school, even if it is lost."[35] As for the government, Abad Santos hoped only for tolerance; in return, he guaranteed legal actions by his followers:

What we expect is a sincere and unprejudiced approach to the masses, a sympathetic hearing of their complaints and grievances, without bias and deceit. The laborers' actions are justifiable, their demands reasonable, and the government should take no cause for alarm over the prospect of the masses rising in armed resistance against constituted authority. We call this kind of suicide, "Pooch," and I can assure the public that so long as the Socialist Party is dominant in Pampanga there will be no Cabuyao or San Ildefonso incidents in this province.[36]

Unlike Ramos, Abad Santos shunned the limelight. Quiet, retiring, an unimpressive orator, he remained aloof and withdrawn from the party's rank and file. The Socialist leader permitted only trusted aides to enter his "big house" in San Fernando. Since he was not in good health, he sometimes conducted strategy conferences at his bedside, where, rich or poor, powerful or impotent, occasional visitors to his book-lined study and pamphlet-strewn bedroom were all treated the same. If Manuel Quezon desired a conversation with Abad Santos, he had to travel to the sprawling compound in San Fernando. Don Perico frowned on the President and all magnetic leaders. To him, Sakdalista adoration of Benigno Ramos smacked of Fascism. "Sakdalism is essentially hero worship," he said. "We don't believe in such silly stuff. We believe in mass action to secure our end—the welfare of the masses."[37]

A sophisticated man who avoided demagoguery, Abad Santos posed a difficult problem for both the insular government and regional *hacenderos*. Peasant or middle-class agitators could be silenced, but a Gandhi-like *ilustrado* could neither be manhandled nor gagged. While estate owners fumed and Quezon sought an answer, Socialism spread

34. A. H. Scaff, *The Philippine Answer to Communism* (Stanford, Calif., 1955), 17.
35. Taruc, *Born of the People*, 63.
36. *Manila Tribune*, Feb. 6, 1938.
37. *Manila Tribune*, Feb. 7, 1938.

across central Luzon. In 1939 the Socialist and Communist Parties merged into a United Front, coordinated their union activities, and launched a concerted drive to gain political influence in the provinces and Manila. The 1940 election revealed the alliance's success. Sotero Baluyot—with all the wealth and weight of the *Nacionalista* Party behind him—managed to eke out a narrow victory over Pedro Abad Santos in Pampanga's gubernatorial race. United Front candidates, however, won eight of twenty-one mayoralty run-offs in the province. Their colleagues in neighboring administrative units, moreover, captured one *presidencia* in Tarlac, and four in Bulacan.[38] Abad Santos had accomplished a unique feat. If only imperfectly, he had fused the little and great traditions into a viable form of secular radicalism.

All too few Filipinos and Americans recognized the positive nature of that achievement. Officials in Manila tended to regard the course of events in central Luzon as ominous. From their viewpoint, violence rather than progress was brewing north of the capital. Terse annual reports of American High Commissioners chronicled a menacing situation. Between the summers of 1938 and 1939, agrarian unrest began to increase. Noting the development, Paul McNutt declared that "efforts on the part of the Commonwealth government to obtain settlement of tenancy problems in Bulacan and Pampanga have been of little avail."[39] Twelve months later, Francis Sayre observed that "disagreements between landlords and tenants . . . in Central Luzon continued and became more serious during the year."[40] Sayre's final summation revealed a tortured state of affairs:

> The agrarian socialist element, particularly that led by Pedro Abad Santos in Pampanga province was exceptionally active. . . . The viewpoint of . . . dissident groups was expressed not only in speeches, parades, demonstrations, and passive resistance, but also, in several instances by violence. Several persons were killed or wounded in a number of tenant uprisings. As a result, Pampanga . . . was placed under Constabulary control. By June 1941, the Constabulary had taken over . . . all municipal police forces in the provinces of Central Luzon: Pangasinan,

38. Scaff, 21.

39. *Third Annual Report of the United States High Commissioner to the Philippine Islands to the President and Congress of the United States Covering the Calendar Year 1938 and the First Six Months of 1939* (Washington, D.C., 1943), 36.

40. *Fourth Annual Report of the United States High Commissioner to the Philippine Islands to the President and Congress of the United States Covering the Fiscal Year July 1, 1939, to June 30, 1940* (Washington, D.C., 1943), 50.

Pampanga, Tarlac, Bulacan, Nueva Ecija, Bataan, Zambales, Cavite, Rizal, Bantangas, and Laguna. Tenant troubles at Candaba, Pampanga province resulted in the murder of six persons. On June 18, the Secretary of the Interior announced that the Constabulary had been strengthened and was prepared to strike quickly against radical elements at any time.[41]

On December 8, 1941, bomb-laden Japanese aircraft roared by Tayug, Pangasinan, bound for Clark Field and Fort Stotsenburg near Angeles, Pampanga. Their flight covered the intervening hundred kilometers in less than fifteen minutes. The Philippine peasantry's meandering trek toward the same general destination via San Ildefonso and Cabuyao had required a decade. In terms of popular protests, however, several light-years separated Pedro Calosa's Tayug from Pedro Abad Santos' Pampanga. The two leaders represented poles of an agonizing transition. Directly between them stood the figure of Benigno Ramos. More than either of his appealing contemporaries, however, Ramos deserved credit for the transformation. His Sakdal Party marked the shift from blind responses against real or imagined sources of frustration toward rational movements dedicated to purposeful change. Sakdalism and Socialism together broke the traditional supernaturalistic mold of rural rebellions. In time, Philippine Communism profited from the dual achievement. Separately and inadvertently, the contradictory activities of a myopic former bureaucrat and a farsighted patrician set the stage for attempted revolution in the postwar era.

41. *Fifth Annual Report of the United States High Commissioner to the Philippine Islands to the President and Congress of the United States Covering the Fiscal Year July 1, 1940, to June 30, 1941* (Washington, D.C., 1943), 43.

Epilogue

On a Sunday morning in May 1967, leaders of the Philippine Republic faced an incongruous situation. A peasant uprising had erupted in the heart of the nation's largest urban complex. For more than a week tensions had been mounting in a strange confrontation between government representatives and spokesmen for a flamboyant religious movement called Lapiang Malaya.[1] Around 1:00 A.M. on May 21, accumulated frustrations exploded into bloody conflict. Fighting broke out along a cordoned-off section of Taft Avenue in Pasay City near the Manila corporation line. The anachronistic encounter, involving heavily armed Constabulary units and bolo-wielding sectarians, raged for more than an hour. When it was over, casualties proved to be extremely one-sided. One constable had been hacked to death, and five had been wounded. Thirty-three rebels, however, died during the course of the melee, and at least thirty-nine more suffered serious injuries. While hastily assembled medical teams sorted through the human wreckage and treated living victims, constabularymen disarmed their defeated adversaries and collected the dead. They deposited the broken bodies along a nearby sidewalk. Dawn revealed the final irony: inadvertently, the religious rebels' corpses had been laid out beneath a church steeple. The remains—

1. Before the uprising, Lapiang Malaya (usually translated as Independence Party) was also known as Bukal Na Pananampalataya (The Nature of Faith). Information on the movement came from observations and interviews conducted during 1966. Details on the uprising were drawn from accounts appearing in *The Manila Daily Bulletin, The Manila Times, The Manila Herald,* and *The Manila Chronicle* of May and June 1966. To avoid repetitious notes only feature articles will be cited. The description of the incident is drawn from D. R. Sturtevant, "Rizalistas—Contemporary Revitalization Movements in the Philippines," in *Agrarian Unrest in the Philippines* (Athens, Ohio, 1969). It is reproduced with permission of the Southeast Asia Program of the Ohio University Center for International Studies.

partially covered by newspapers—were left in that symbolic setting until Sunday noon.

On Monday morning, Manila's dailies began to perform more conventional functions. For the next few weeks reporters and feature writers regaled readers with a series of particulars on Lapiang Malaya. From an interpretative standpoint, the exposés left a great deal to be desired. From a factual viewpoint, however, the accounts revealed a number of important, if somewhat incredible, details. The militant sect—a 40,000-member organization much given to ornate uniforms, patriotic posturing, and martial Rizal Day rallies—had emerged on the Philippine scene during the late 1940's. It had been founded by a magnetic Bicolano named Valentin de los Santos who was eighty-six years old at the time of the uprising. His authority over LM members emanated from impressive worldly and otherworldly claims: on the secular side, he portrayed himself as the inventor of automobile turn signals with patents pending in Washington, D.C.; on the spiritual side, he pictured himself as a medium in regular communication with the Deity and the living personalities of dead Filipino heroes. Both of the ostensible accomplishments appealed strongly to disgruntled villagers in southern Luzon. Peasants from the Bicol region were among the first to rally to the new *supremo*. As his fame spread, he was joined by numerous converts from Quezon (Tayabas) and Laguna; he established a headquarters for the growing movement in Pasay City, and he created a central administrative staff reinforced by paramilitary echelons at the provincial, municipal, and barrio levels.

Until 1957 the organization attracted scant attention from the authorities. In that year, however, two events brought a degree of notoriety to Valentin de los Santos and his movement: (1) the *supremo* proclaimed himself a presidential candidate; and (2) the Constabulary uncovered evidence of a postelection plot in Albay province which involved LM members.[2] The two developments, moreover, seemed to be related: de los Santos suffered a resounding defeat at the polls; and when some of his disappointed disciples tried to instigate a general uprising their plans were frustrated by the police. While both efforts failed, each in turn indicated that Lapiang Malaya was profoundly antagonistic to the prevailing order. The abortive

---

2. Data on early challenges—from General Pelagio Cruz, who was Chief of the Constabulary in 1957—appeared in a feature article. See José de Vera, "The Story Behind 'Bloody Sunday' in Pasay," *Manila Times*, May 26, 1967.

efforts also revealed that leaders and followers alike were willing to resort to either legitimate or illegitimate techniques in their desire to refashion Philippine society.

Contrary to expectations, the misadventures of 1957 did not set back the movement. They acted, instead, as stimulants to further growth. De los Santos became a perennial presidential candidate. His followers, furthermore, continued to provoke minor confrontations with provincial and national authorities.[3] Each electoral challenge to the establishment, each brush with officialdom, created additional popular interest in Lapiang Malaya. To a growing number of southern Luzon's forgotten peasantry, Valentin de los Santos took on the qualities of an articulate champion and a potential deliverer. Inevitably, the venerable *supremo* attempted to live up to the impossible expectations of converts to the fold. The effort deepened profound messianic traits within his personality. He continued to denounce social ills and to call for the creation of a more equitable order. But he added millennial ingredients to his standard appeals and began to issue apocalyptic pronouncements. Among other prophecies, he proclaimed the "Second Coming." The imminent reappearance, Valentin warned, would be characterized by the arrival of a Savior with "piercing eyes," and by "slashing swords" which would "chop off the heads of the anti-Christ."[4] Only the faithful would survive that reckoning. In preparation for Judgment Day, LM members were ordered to perform a series of patriotic drills and spiritual exercises. They were advised also to accumulate prescribed paraphernalia guaranteeing invulnerability—sacred bolos, bullet-defying uniforms, *anting-anting,* and protective *oraciónes* (spoken or written formulas). By 1966, Valentin de los Santos and his retainers shared a sense of developing omnipotence.

Secretarian overconfidence and governmental complacency led to the slaughter on Taft Avenue. Lapiang Malaya's gathering militancy manifested itself in a variety of forms, but national authorities refused to take the movement seriously. During the 1966 summit conference on Viet Nam, for example, approximately 1,000 bolo-equipped LM members assembled in Manila for the express purpose of interrupting

3. Jeremias Adia, leader of the Rizalist sect *Iglesia Sagrada ng Lahi* (Sacred Church of the Race), described LM tactics to the author in April 1966.
4. Vera, "Story Behind 'Bloody Sunday.' "

the deliberations. On that occasion, policemen and constabularymen managed to disperse the religious enthusiasts without incident. Six months later, however, similar dispersal efforts failed. Early in May, Valentin de los Santos called for the resignation of President Ferdinand Marcos and the formation of a Lapiang Malaya government. When Marcos summarily rejected the *supremo*'s dramatic demands, the stage was set for violence. Before officials recognized the critical nature of the situation, more than 500 followers had rallied to de los Santos' cause. The sect's headquarters in Pasay City suddenly became the center of an armed encampment. Constabularymen sealed off the area to prevent a further influx of rebels from the provinces south of Manila. But repeated attempts either to break up the concentration of true believers or to initiate effective mediation procedures collapsed. The gulf between the contending parties was simply too broad to bridge. Valentin de los Santos and his peasant protectors regarded the encounter as the long-awaited moment of deliverance, while aspiring peacemakers from Manila's elite looked upon the dispute as an irritating interruption of the urban way of life. Inevitably, tensions increased to the point of senseless bloodletting.

Again, post-mortems on the episode followed prewar precedents. Journalists captured the pathos of "Bloody Sunday"—an appellation used by the *Manila Times*—and editorialized at length on the governmental ineptitude which had produced the incident. Politicians traded accusations and called for official investigation of Lapiang Malaya. Criticized for overreacting, the Constabulary released a series of confused intelligence reports on the sect and attempted to connect the movement with Communist machinations.[5] In a welter of conflicting diagnoses and scapegoat hunting, popular interest in the flare-up dwindled. Even the mid-June death of Valentin de los Santos passed almost unnoticed.[6] By the end of July, the dead rebels and their defunct organization had been relegated to that special place in the

5. *Manila Times*, May 28, 1968.
6. Rizalists were quite bitter about Valentin de los Santos' fate. A sophisticated sect leader, who must remain anonymous, described it in a letter to the author: "Valentin was taken . . . to the Mental Hospital and pronounced insane. He was put in a cell with a hopelessly violent case. Soon he was mauled and beaten while sleeping. He lost consciousness and was taken to an isolation ward. . . . After more than a week, he died without regaining consciousness. . . . The verdict of the attending physician was that he died of pneumonia."

public mind reserved for luckless victims of typhoons, volcanic eruptions, earthquakes, and other natural calamities.

Aside from death and injury, the most disturbing outcome of the
affair was the apparent willingness on the part of prominent Filipinos
to dismiss it as a relatively unimportant and largely inexplicable
event.[7] Philippine leaders—particularly senior law-enforcement officers—seemed oblivious to the peasantry's turbulent tradition. A
third of a century, the most disruptive in insular history, had elapsed
since Pedro Calosa's "Colorums" sacked Tayug. In the rush of
worldly upheavals after 1931, village religious rebels and their intermittent challenges to the status quo had been forgotten. The new
generation of officials, consequently, could neither comprehend nor
assimilate the motives behind their countrymen's aggressive conduct.
Sophisticated Manileños, in fact, failed to recognize Lapiang Malaya
as but another manifestation of what Felix Kessing called the "high
messianic potential of Philippine culture."[8]

Given the rural population's stormy heritage, a revival of millennialism should have been predictable. Cataclysmic events during World
War II had subjected Filipinos to awesome pressures. After 1946,
discredited oligarchs attempted to build a sovereign republic on the
Commonwealth's smoldering ashes. Few nations in history have begun
their independent existence under less auspicious circumstances. Torn
by dissension over the issue of collaboration with the Japanese and
weakened by physical devastation resulting from the American liberation campaign, a divided and exhausted people faced spirit-crushing
problems. Postwar agonies were further compounded by the disruptive activities of guerrilla squadrons in the Central Plain. All the
rebellious tendencies expressed by Luzon's peasantry prior to Pearl
Harbor converged in the Communist-led Hukbalahap. The ensuing
upheaval almost toppled a shaky government. In the final analysis,
however, elitist political flexibility triumphed. Ramon Magsaysay—a
charismatic "Filipino of heart and face"—took over the reins of
leadership, won back most alienated hamlet dwellers, and stymied his

7. Several feature writers attempted to point up the upheavel's underlying
significance. One of the most penetrating treatments was that of E. P. Patanne,
"A Round-up of Religious Rebels," *The Sunday Times Magazine* (Manila),
June 18, 1967, 20–21.

8. The provocative phrase was coined by Professor Keesing in a graduate
anthropology seminar at Stanford University.

Marxian opponents.[9] Dynamic and extensive as it might have been, the Hukbalahap went down to defeat.[10]

Secularism was the foremost casualty of the debacle. Between 1933 and 1956, rural dissenters had turned to a variety of leaders committed to basic modifications of Philippine society. Sakdalism, Socialism, and Communism, in turn, attracted the allegiance of scores of thousands of impoverished Filipinos. For the first time in history, provincial rebels received comparatively realistic guidance in their quest for a better world. But the experiments came to naught. Sakdalism collapsed after the uprising of 1935. Socialism and Communism withered to impotence after the disintegration of the Hukbalahap. The sequential failures wiped out or dishonored an entire generation of radicals. In 1956, when an airplane carrying Ramon Magsaysay crashed against a Visayan mountainside, lingering popular hopes for a more equitable order died with the commoner president. Adrift in a sea of frustration, some of the peasantry turned to mysticism for solace and solutions.

The demise of secularism led to an apparent resurgence of supernaturalism. Scores of organizations similar to Lapiang Malaya appeared in the municipalities. Half-forgotten folk cults also took a new lease on life. Priests and priestesses, faith healers and spiritualists, prophets and proselytizers crisscrossed the countryside ministering to the rural poor. The revival, however, was not limited to the provinces. Converts carried the message of salvation to relatives and former neighbors in urban working districts. Crude chapels and churches sprouted in barrios and municipalities, materialized along the cluttered streets of Tondo, and in Manila's burgeoning squatter communities. By 1960 the various movements were firmly established throughout Luzon and the Visayas and were taking root among Christian settlers in Mindanao.[11]

In many ways the reanimated revitalization efforts were similar to their mystical predecessors. Like the militant sects of the 1920's and the chiliastic cults at the turn of the century, the new movements

9. For good treatments of the Magsaysay years, see F. L. Starner, *Magsaysay and the Philippine Peasantry* (Berkeley and Los Angeles, 1961), and J. V. Abueva, *Ramon Magsaysay, A Political Biography* (Manila, 1971).
10. For a provocative interpretation, see Victor Lieberman, "Why the Hukbalahap Movement Failed," *Solidarity* I (1966), 22–30.
11. A chiliastic movement, perhaps Rizalist in origin, initiated an uprising in Bukidnon in 1966. See Patanne, "Round-up of Religious Rebels," 21.

attracted support through an ingenious merging of indigenous and Christian religious elements. Like their forerunners also, the proliferating faiths developed around prepossessing figures who claimed divine or semidivine attributes. In one important respect, however, their appeal rested on another foundation. Almost without exception they incorporated patriotic ingredients into their evolving creeds. That emphasis has created a popular religious atmosphere revolving around the worship of national heroes. While sectarian adoration has not been restricted to José Rizal—Andres Bonifacio and Apolinario Mabini, for example, have also attracted numerous disciples—the overriding reverence for the revolutionary martyr has led students of the phenomenon to label it "Rizalism."[12]

In recent years, endless variations on the theme have manifested themselves. Complementing Lapiang Malaya and its 40,000 members were: Sambahang Rizal (Rizal Church), with 7,000 devotees; Bathalismo (Godism), with approximately 10,000 followers; the Adarnistas (Mother Adarna's disciples), who boasted 20,000 worshipers; the Divine Crusaders of Christ, with a proclaimed membership of 30,000; the Iglesia Sagrada ng Lahi (Sacred Church of the Race), with an estimated 50,000 attending services; and the Iglesia Watawat ng Lahi (Pride of the Race Church), with a following of 125,000.[13] Those organizations, together with thriving offshoots and reanimated "Colorum" groups, have won the primary loyalites and absorbed the energies of numberless Filipinos.

Competition for converts, divergent goals, and personal antipathies between leaders have prevented cooperation between the groups. But the ostensible differences have not been sufficient to obscure a series of common characteristics. All of the organizations have introduced the worship of Rizal into their services: hymns and rituals, in fact, elevate him to a position beside the Father and the Son. All of them have developed similar iconography: images, paintings, and photographs of the patriot, together with his writings, occupy revered positions in every church and chapel. All of them have come to observe

12. Pioneer research on the development has been conducted by Marcelino A. Foronda of De La Salle College. For introductory information, see his *Cults Honoring Rizal.*
13. Membership estimates came from interviews with Professor Foronda and Jeremias Adia. The best study of the oldest and most influential Rizalist group is that of P. R. Covar, "The *Iglesia Watawat ng Lahi:* A Sociological Study of a Social Movement" (Master's thesis, Department of Sociology, University of the Philippines, 1961).

the same holy occasions: Rizal Day, of course, constitutes the most significant observation. All of them have recognized the same sacred sites: Calamba in Laguna, and Luneta Park in Manila have become the Bethlehem and Golgotha of Rizalism. All of them, more ominously, have evolved eschatological views of the universe. Like their violent millennial precursors, therefore, they are all potentially subject to explosive transformations comparable to the Lapiang Malaya seizure of 1967.

By 1970 the peasantry's turbulent heritage appeared to have moved full circle: from supernaturalism to secularism to supernaturalism again. The meaning of that repetitious pattern, however, constituted another matter. Historians have sometimes assigned to their subjects far more order and coherence than the events under scrutiny could legitimately bear. Recognizing that tendency, Sir George Sansom warned that the past should not be seen as a disciplined or colorful pageant studded with bright banners; instead, it should be viewed "as a motley procession with . . . many dingy emblems, marching out of step, and not very certain of its destination."[14] The chaotic caravan surveyed in the book demonstrates the validity of his observation. Certain general conclusions, nevertheless, suggest themselves.

For one thing, the millennial experiences of Filipinos are not unique. In both hemispheres and in every clime people under comparable conditions of stress have responded similarly. The nativistic prophets, social bandits, millenarian saviors, and impractical secular leaders who crowd Philippine history have materialized regularly in other cultures undergoing fundamental dislocations. From South and East Asia to Latin America, from North and Central Africa to Southeast Asia analogous protests have occurred.[15] Violent expressions of dissent, moreover, have not been restricted to the so-called "developing" world. They have become manifest in medieval and modern Europe and across North America. The response, in short, represents a frequent human reaction to difficult or intolerable circumstances.

The ubiquitous phenomena also reflect—no matter how unrealistic they might appear to pragmatic urban or Western observers—creative

14. G. B. Sansom, *Japan, A Short Cultural History* (New York, 1943), viii.
15. The accumulating bibliography on the subject is simply too voluminous to cite. For an introduction to the subject in the Philippines and neighboring areas, however, see H. J. Benda, "Peasant Movements in Southeast Asia," *Asian Studies*, III (1965), 420–434.

efforts to cope with a hostile world. What Eric Hobsbawm labeled the "extraordinary impracticality" of many abortive mass movements has camouflaged their significance.[16] In the Philippines, as elsewhere, even the most unsophisticated hamlet insurgents have realized the improbability of ultimate deliverance. The forces arrayed against them have defied the power of any village or any assemblage of villages. While recognition of that fact has not restrained determined rebels in their struggles to create a more acceptable social system, it has led them to seek external assistance to equalize an inherently uneven struggle. Charismatic leaders who guaranteed powerful intervention of either terrestrial or extraterrestrial origins have encountered few difficulties in attracting followers. "Impossibilism," then, has been a common component of small- and large-scale revitalization efforts.

That quixotic element, however, should not be dismissed as unimportant or irrelevant. Throughout history it has been the connecting link between otherworldly and worldly revolutionaries. The belief that a total transformation is feasible, that everything can be changed, "changed utterly," has the power to remake normally subservient human beings.[17] Utopian visions have repeatedly driven Filipino peasants to march on municipalities. Millennial dreams of another variety have also propelled gigantic upheavals such as those that overturned the complex societies of France, Russia, and China. Under the right circumstances, the seemingly contradictory strands can intertwine. As Eric Wolf has pointed out, in a culture experiencing basic inconsistencies and disequilibriums a peasant uprising "can, without conscious intent, bring the entire society to the state of collapse."[18]

Even when that improbability occurs, unfortunately, the village victors are destined to lose more than they gain. Caught between tradition and modernity, peasant revolutionaries are anachronisms. Their actual enemy is the depersonalized and incomprehensible world that has emerged around them. They long to destroy it. But they also yearn to build a social universe which is basically anarchistic in style and content. Such a milieu, of course, has no place in the contemporary world. "The peasant's role," as Wolf again observed, "is thus essentially tragic: his efforts to undo a grievous present only usher in

16. Hobsbawm, *Primitive Rebels*, 65.
17. *Ibid.*, 61.
18. E. R. Wolf, *Peasant Wars of the Twentieth Century* (New York, 1969), 296.

a vaster, more uncertain future."[19] That, paradoxically, is the peasantry's ultimate strength. Individually they might falter and give up; yet collectively they persist. Deathless hope fuels their never-ending quest for the millennium. Their stamina and perseverance grant them a rugged dignity which survives in the face of continuous defeats. Anyone who has examined their condition and their history must conclude that they deserve a better fate.

Only one thing is certain. At long last the destiny of Filipino villagers is no longer in the hands of aliens. Their future will be determined by their own countrymen. But that development, strangely enough, might represent the real problem. Most of the peasantry's agonies in the nineteenth and twentieth centuries have emanated either directly or indirectly from the *principalia* and their influential descendents. Scions of the old landed elite continue to dominate the island nation. If hamlet dwellers are to become full participants in insular life, farsighted, creative, and socially responsible leadership must emerge in Manila and the municipalities. Above all, those who govern the Philippines must develop an understanding of the desires and needs of rural Filipinos. If their minimal requirements are not met, many peasants will again turn to conventional redeemers.

The widespread recrudescence of mysticism in the contemporary Philippines indicates the growing desperation of impoverished *provincianos*. It also reveals the basic tension besetting insular society. Conflicts between the competing demands of the little and great traditions persist. Time and again segments of the peasantry have risen up in futile efforts to create an ethical scheme of things. Since 1896, their atavistic struggles have been couched increasingly in patriotic terms. Before 1946, they fought for "independence." After Magsaysay's death, they deified Filipino heroes and sought spiritual answers to the burdens of chronic stress. Within the narrow conceptual confines of the barrio, they regard themselves as earnest "nationalists." But most hamlet dwellers believe that "nation" and "justice" are, or should be, synonyms. Sovereignty, lamentably, has not brought about that blissful state.

Until now, nationalism in its larger ideological sense has been a near monopoly of the elite and the politically conscious middle class. All too frequently, they have manipulated the abstraction to serve

19. *Ibid.*, 301.

their own ends. This does not have to be the case. The idea of nation-hood is one of the few truly integrating factors that prevail through-out the island commonwealth. Without question, the conception, the emotion, or the shared delusion, beckons Filipinos of all strata. It could still become a convenient device for welding the rural popula-tion into a developing society. Before that can occur, however, peas-ants must begin to acquire more—tangibly and intangibly—than they surrender. Concern for the welfare of one's less fortunate countrymen has frequently been a trait of mature patriotism. If the chasms be-tween contending traditions and antagonistic social groups are to be bridged, Philippine nationalism must develop a compassionate ele-ment. Survival of the young nation might very well depend on the recognition of a simple, yet difficult, truth, familiar to many devout villagers. The time must come, according to the Gospel by Saint Matthew, when the "first shall be last; and the last *shall be* first."

A Letter to Governor General
Leonard Wood on Flor Entrencherado*

Manila
June 10, 1927

Dear General:
The following outline of the Emperor, Flor Intrencherado's plans for the establishment of a Philippine Empire may be of some interest. They are translated extracts from a printed pamphlet circulated among the adherents of the "Emperor" in Iloilo and Negros provinces.

The residence of Flor Intrencherado is in Gigante Island, Carlos, Iloilo. Only Flor Intrencherado possesses the power and ability to save the Filipino people from impending calamities. When he actively ascends the imperial throne the people not only will be freed from the payment of taxes. They will be paid salaries and bonuses.

The Emperor will create: 6 Kings, 28 Counts, 1,267 Generals, 2,534 Brigadier-Generals, 5,068 Colonels, 10,136 Majors, 20,272 Captains, 40,544 Lieutenants, 81,088 Sergeants, 162,776 Corporals, 648,704 Privates.

The aggregate of their salaries will be P270,333,000 annually.

The revenues will be derived from commerce and industry, and from a cedula tax of 20 centavos. The whole Filipino nation will be organized on a military plan as follows:

Seven Battalions of "Defenders," which will provide legal, educational, religious, and medical service *gratis*.

Twenty-eight Battalions of Engineers, in charge of mines, railroads, repair shops, bridges, etc., with an annual revenue of P504,000,000.

Fourteen Battalions of Artillery, responsible for the sale of foreign products. Total annual revenue (profit) P76,000,000.

Five Hundred Sixty Labor Battalions, in charge of the sugar, corn, tobacco, and camote industries. Revenue, P333,600,000.

Two Hundred Eighty Battalions of Marines, in charge of cigar factories, wine refineries, and fisheries. Annual revenue P118,661,200.

*From the Leonard Wood Papers, Manuscript Division, Library of Congress, Washington, D.C.

One Hundred Forty Battalions of Naval Seamen in charge of inter-island steamers, fishing boats, and ships of war. Annual revenue P2,653,200. [The Navy seems to be the Emperor's Cinderella!]

Two Hundred Ten Battalions of Constabulary, responsible for the care of cattle, other domestic animals, and *chickens*. Annual income P12,306,400.

Total annual revenue: P1,049,605,532

After payment of the salaries of the Emperor, kings, counts, generals, captains, corporals, etc., there will be a surplus of P779,272,532.

The debts due the United States will be paid off by annual installments of from twenty to forty million pesos.

Salary List

The Emperor	P510 a month and an annual bonus of P2,100.
Kings	P480 (no bonus)
Counts	P450 a month and an annual bonus of P1,100.
Generals	P420 a month and an annual bonus of P600.
Brig. Generals	P390 a month and an annual bonus of P300.
Colonels	P360 a month and an annual bonus of P100.
Majors	P180 (no bonus)
Captains	P150 (no bonus)
Lieutenants	P120 (no bonus)
Sergeants	P60 (no bonus)
Corporals	P45 (no bonus)
Soldiers	P30 (no bonus)

A government store will be established in every town, from which the people will buy all their supplies. They will no longer buy from the Chinese, who will be forced to go back to China.

If these things do not transpire before the year 1928, the Emperor will become a Hermit, live in a cave, and let everything be destroyed in the Deluge.

Very Sincerely,

R. A. DUCKWORTH-FORD
Lt. Colonel, Asst. Chief
P.C., ADC.

APPENDIX B

An Interview with
Pedro Calosa*

With Calosa and his followers behind bars, the Philippines returned to a semblance of normality. Manila's memories of the rebellion quickly faded before the rush of more cataclysmic events. Officialdom gradually released the penitent rebels. In 1939 a fit of executive leniency even led to the parole of Pedro Calosa. He returned to eastern Pangasinan.

Manila might have forgotten the terrible night in 1931, but Tayug could not. Something far more precious than innocence and graciousness had been lost. Trust between classes had also vanished. Recollections of the vest-pocket civil war were too fresh. Eardrums still recalled the muscle and bone-cleaving crunch of bolos, the terrifying concussion of heavy rifles in the darkness, and the eerie crackle of burning bamboo. Pangasinan's profound social divisions, moreover, had deepened during the intervening years. Some prominent townspeople traced the dangerous deterioration to Calosa and his uprising. Predictably, they looked upon the middle-aged rebel as a resurrected demon. Villagers, however, adopted a contrary view. Many regarded him as a potential deliverer. His reappearance in that volatile atmosphere inevitably stirred visions of a greater holocaust.

Calosa sought anonymity. He never found it. His quest for obscurity led him to move his wife and children to a remote *sitio* above the tumbling Agno River in the foothills overlooking San Nicolas, where they lived as quietly as possible. Calosa performed odd jobs and collected firewood for sale in the *municipio*. Somehow or other he made

*The interview, together with edited portions of the introduction, is taken from D. R. Sturtevant, "Epilog for an Old 'Colorum,'" *Solidarity*, III, (1968), 10–18. It is reproduced with the permission of F. Sionel José, the journal's editor-publisher.

ends meet. Occasionally, he visited friends in or around Tayug. Notoriety, however, followed him everywhere. To the Ilocano farmers of eastern Pangasinan and northern Nueva Ecija, Calosa represented something far more complex than a threadbare charcoal seller. To them, he symbolized a heritage of folk religion and social upheaval stretching back to the turn of the century and beyond.

Prominence created problems. Above all, it led to unsolicited attention from a variety of outsiders. Real and aspiring rebels sought him out for advice and assistance. Members of unorthodox religious sects came to him for spiritual sustenance. From time to time, intellectuals and reformers from Manila interviewed him concerning the roots of the 1931 rebellion. Local authorities, consequently, kept him under close watch. In time, Calosa recognized that he was a prisoner of his own past. He stopped fighting his reputation and fatalistically accepted the role society had thrust upon him. He received inquisitive visitors courteously but kept them at a respectable distance. In his declining years he moved deeper into mysticism. By 1966, he had taken on the serene qualities appropriate to an elder statesman of rustic dissent.

Among those who sought out the former rebel that year were the author and F. Sionel José, the editor of *Solidarity*. On an unspeakably hot Sunday in late March he and I waded through three inches of powdered grit along the trail to the desolate *sitio* above San Nicolas. As acquaintances of Frankie José, Calosa and his wife received us warmly. They also accepted our offer of a ride to Tayug and agreed to discuss the old days. Both of them were impressive people. Calosa, a stocky man in his late sixties or early seventies, carried himself with great dignity. His well-muscled arms bore the elaborate tatoos of an ex-convict, his rugged face showed the ravages of a turbulent career. Under a shock of thick grey hair, his eyes—spectacular brown irises edged with blue in a fiery red setting—sized up his guests from Manila. When Calosa excused himself to prepare for the trip to town, his wife discussed the sad state of Philippine affairs. Much younger than her husband and the possessor of a magnificently expressive face, she moved with the agility and self-assurance of a mountain cat. "There is no equality, under this government," she said to Frankie. "You are rich and important, a big man. We are poor and unimportant, we are little people. If someone like you harms us and there is a dispute, we will go to jail. Is that not so?" He agreed. "Then," she concluded, "there is no justice." Everyone laughed.

On that straightforward note the day of talk began. Questions concerning Guardia de Honor and Felipe Salvador at first threw Calosa off balance. No one from the outside had ever asked for his views on those topics nor was he aware that outsiders knew of these matters. Over my protestations he concluded that he was confronted with a telepathic American. But by the time we had reached the base of the foothills he was talking steadily. Abandoning English he lapsed into dialect. Frankie found it difficult to keep pace with the rush of eloquent Iloko, and it was almost impossible to jot down his verbatim interpretations. The interchange continued during the jolting ride to town, and it went on over iced San Miguel beer and a meal in a run-down restaurant facing Tayug's sweltering market. While we talked, the restaurant patrons collected around our table: men in their forties, fifties, and sixties hung on to every word; adolescents smiled at the intensity of their elders and listened in amused disbelief. By the time we left the overflowing establishment Calosa had become so involved in reliving the past he found it difficult to continue. Late that afternoon—his poise restored by the bucolic surroundings of the old house west of Tayug where he had been arrested in 1931—Calosa completed his observations on men and movements. As we prepared to depart, he added a firm postscript to the day's remarks. "Write anything you please," he said. "Feel free to use everything I have said. But don't publish it in Manila. Release the story in the United States. There, I will receive a fair hearing. I have had enough trouble. A story released in the Philippines could mean more."

We agreed to his depressing stipulation and left. The interview which follows would never have appeared in *Solidarity* if Calosa were still alive. But he can have no more trouble. Unfortunately, in 1967, an unknown assailant murdered Pedro Calosa.

THE INTERVIEW

Where and when were you born?

I was born in Bauang, La Union. I don't know what year, because I was orphaned when I was very small.

What was your father's occupation?

His name was Crispolo Calosa. He was a farmer and owned land. How much I can't say because we left Bauang when I was very young and moved to Pangasinan.

How much education did your parents have? Did you go to school?

They studied. They could read and write. I went to school one year in Tayug. Then came the cholera and my mother died. I must have been about seven years old. That was when I learned of Guardia de Honor.

Why does your mother's death remind you of Guardia de Honor?

In my mind the two things go together. A day or two after she died, a proselytizer named Francisco Salvador came to Tayug preaching the new faith. He seemed gentle and kind. So I went to him and asked where my mother was. He said I should go to Cabaruan and find Maria de la Cruz. He said she would answer my questions. I went there. She told me, "If you want to find your mother come to Cabaruan during Holy Week and look for a beggar woman. She will tell you." I went, but I could not find the woman. I did see the Guardia's rituals and I found them good.

While you were in Cabaruan did you hear of or see Baltasar, Claveria, or Felipe Salvador?

I heard of Baltasar and Claveria. I saw Felipe Salvador. But I was not interested in them. I was a small boy and I was more interested in finding my mother.

Was Cabaruan very large? Do you think there were more than 20,000 people in the town?

It was larger than Tayug is now. There were more than 20,000 people living there.

If there were so many people then why did Guardia de Honor disappear?

It did not disappear. It became part of the Aglipayan Church.

Was Felipe Salvador's Santa Iglesia the same as Guardia de Honor?

The Santa Iglesia and Guardia de Honor were the same. It was an army of liberation, a legion to free the poor people and stop their suffering. Salvador tried to destroy the sources of hate. He tried to show people the beauty of love. More than 3,000 people followed him. It is true, he was captured by the Constabulary and he was hanged. But he did not die. His personality lived on and took different forms. I knew him in Honolulu. In Hawaii he was called Felipe Santiago. When I was in prison he was a crazy man in the next cell. I talked with him and he told me many things. He *was* Felipe Salvador. You understand!

Which of the old leaders impressed you most: Maria de la Cruz or Felipe Salvador?

Salvador was great, truly great. But Maria de la Cruz was above him. She was above them all.

Let us go back to the time when you were small. What happened in those days after your mother died?

I can't remember much. After several years, I went with my brother to Manila. I can't remember when. It was in the time of Taft. From Manila we went to Hawaii. I must have been twelve or thirteen years old at the time. We worked in the fields on sugar cane and pineapples. Conditions were bad in Hawaii.

While you were in Hawaii did you become involved in any political or religious movements?

I heard of several, but I never joined any of them. I was an Aglipayan. I still am—an Aglipayan and a protestant. I don't know why anyone would be a Catholic. God is God! What's good about being a Catholic?

You said conditions were bad in Hawaii. Did those conditions spur you to action? Did you get in trouble with the authorities?

Yes, I usually get in trouble. I helped organize a society called "Beginning of Progress." We talked of a general strike. The authorities learned of my association. I was then working on a plantation near Pearl Harbor. The overseer told me to forget about those things. He told me to forget about the Philippines. He told me to settle down and be a good worker. But we went on with our plans for the strike. It didn't work. I ended up in jail. It was there I got to know Felipe Salvador, and we talked of the old days and the needs for the future. That was in 1927.

When did you become a Colorum? What does the word mean? Did you know Pedro Kabola?

As far as I know the word doesn't mean anything. It was coined by the Constabulary after Tayug. I never knew Kabola, but I heard of him. He was killed by the constables in 1925. I learned of his death through a letter from a friend. Also some of his old followers joined me when I came back to the Philippines.

When did you come home? When and why did you form your society?

I was deported from Hawaii after I got out of prison. I came home late in 1927. Conditions were still bad. The personalities of Rizal, Bonifacio, and Felipe Salvador appeared before me. They told me to form an association to end the suffering of the poor. I know Rizal's personality well. When I was in chains on Corregidor, after the uprising—it was in July of 1934—his personality told me, "I will come again." He did not say when. He helped me to escape.

Escape?

Not that way. My body stayed, but my personality escaped. I sent it to haunt three people: Manuel Quezon, Aurora Quezon, and the American Secretary of War.

Getting back to your association, what did you call it? How large did it become?

The PNA, Philippine National Association. I formed it early in 1928. It grew quickly. We soon had over 1,200 members. They came from this part of Pangasinan and from over in Nueva Ecija. The Constabulary learned of the society. In 1929, constables arrested me and several of my friends near San José in Nueva Ecija. They accused us of crimes but the court declared us innocent.

Were you set free?

Yes, but I didn't get very far. Just outside of town four constables grabbed me and tied me to a tree. They beat me with rifle butts.

Did they break any bones?

No, they were very expert at beating. They drove the butts into my belly again and again until I was hanging from the ropes, and blood oozed from my mouth. Two of the soldiers took pity on me. They told their companions to stop before they killed me. They stopped. Then one of them grabbed me by the hair and lifted my head. He told me to stop my activities. He told me, if I did not stop I would rot in jail. One said, "We might even roast you alive." I was not in very good condition, but I spat out a mouthful of blood and said, "Constables, the day will come when you will run from our women." They laughed. On the night of the uprising that is exactly what happened. Our women helped take the town, and the constables ran.

How did you organize the people? Did you have secret handshakes, code words, blood pacts, and anting-anting?

Yes, we had all those things, but we need not discuss them. You already know all about them or you wouldn't ask the question.

When did you decide to have the uprising?

I can't remember exactly when we planned the attack. The Kabola people decided that the time had come for the revolution. They said they would rise up whether I agreed or not. But they asked for my help. I told them I would consider their proposal. I went to see Maria de la Cruz in Urdaneta. I went alone, riding my horse Liwayway (Dawn of Freedom). I told the wonderful old woman of my followers' plans. She advised me to avoid trouble. "Wait," she said, "the people will suffer if they rebel now." I told my associates of her warning. But they said, "We will attack with your help or without it."

Did you plan any other attacks on other towns? What did you hope to gain?

No, only Tayug. We wanted independence. We hoped others would join us. We believed that all of the oppressed people would rise up. The men of Manila, the men of Mindanao, we hoped they all would join us when they learned of our struggle. Of course they didn't. Even the people of Tayug refused to join us. In fact, the townspeople all ran. They fled the town, left it empty, and ran into the fields.

Some of us did not believe we could gain independence, but we still believed the revolution was worthwhile. By rising up, we would show the Americans—the ones in Manila, but even more important, the Americans in America—show them that there was no town without people; no town, no matter how small, without *real* people.

Did the Tangulan promise to help you?

The Tangulan knew of our plans. We asked them for help and we discussed the possibility of a joint uprising, a general uprising. But the plans never jelled. The Tangulan were part of the same great tree. It was a tree with many roots.

Speaking of the Tangulan, what did you think of their leader Patricio Dionisio?

Don't ask me that. You have talked to Dionisio, you already know the answer.

Was there no alternative to violence? Was there no one to whom you could appeal?

There was no other choice. There was no one who understood our situation. Life was very difficult. The Constabulary and their American friends were like gods. No one dared tell them of true conditions.

On the night of the uprising what happened?

You know the story. The people gathered outside San Nicolas, thirty to forty of them in the beginning. They took over the Pantranco buses and rode into town. That was the night the constables ran from our women. But it is very difficult for me to talk of this. You already know all about it anyway. I cannot tell you of minor details because I wasn't there. I was in my house during the attack on Tayug.

If you were not in the attack, why were you sent to prison?

I was punished because I was the leader. I ordered the attack. It was my responsibility. The sentences varied. Most of them were light. Because of my record, and because they needed an example, I was sent to Bilibid for forty years.

Did you get to know any Sakdals in Bilibid? What did you think of them? What did you think of Benigno Ramos?

I was not in Bilibid very long. They transferred me to Corregidor and kept me in chains. That is when I haunted the Quezons and the Secretary of War. I was released in 1939.

Yes, I knew some of the Sakdalistas. Some of them were all right. But their leaders were not sincere. Ramos was not good. I do not know much about them, so I would rather not discuss them.

Why do you say Ramos was not good?

He was a traitor.

Did you get to know any Communists? What did you think of the Huks?

I did not agree with their principles. In 1949, a large group of them, around fifty, came to see me. They came up the trail, the same way you did this morning. They asked me to join them, to help them with their struggle. I told them I did not agree with their views. I told them I would neither help them nor hinder them. I told them to leave.

What did they do?

They left.

What about the Rizalino (Rizaliists)? Do they come to you? Do they ask for your help?

Yes, they come to my place often. There is an *obispo* [bishop] in San Fabian who thinks he is José Rizal. Another fellow believes he is Andres Bonifacio. One man is a complete fool. He thinks he is Jesus Christ. But he is very influential. Many people believe in him. He has many followers clear over in the Cagayan Valley.

There are many people around here who wish to follow me. How many would be difficult to say—somewhere between 1,000 and 3,000. They come to my chapel in the *sitio* and worship in small groups. They want me to lead them. But I am old and tired. I have had much trouble. The burden is too heavy to bear.

Do you think the present movements—the Rizalistas, the Divine Crusaders of Christ, the Watawat—are like the old ones? Are they like the Colorums of your day, the Santa Iglesia of Felipe Salvador, and the Guardia de Honor?

It's all the same banana.

Will they make trouble? Will they rise up to right wrongs?

They will talk a great deal. They love to talk. They will even sign papers. But they will not fight. They are like the people of Tayug in 1931. They will save themselves first.

Are conditions better now than they were then?

They are much worse. Then, there were some honorable men. On the whole, the Americans were good. But some of them had muddy hearts and behaved like Spaniards. The laws were good, but some of the people who enforced them were not.

What did you think of Manuel Quezon?

He did not impress me. He was not a good leader. He was a collaborator. He began life as a poor man. He collaborated with the Americans and became a rich man—rich, comfortable, and powerful. His life became good. But the people continued to suffer.

Getting back to the other question, are conditions worse now than they were in 1931?

I said they are worse. In those days the laws were all right and there was some justice. Now men speak clearly but their hearts are dirty. In those days things were better. There were no hoodlums, there were no teenagers, there were not many false gods. Now we have all these things.

It is late in the day and you have been kind enough to discuss many things, but would you answer one more question? As a protestant, how do you feel about God?

God is goodness. God is justice. God is in people. He was in Felipe Salvador. He was present in Maria de la Cruz. He is everywhere. He is in the mountains. He is in the forests. God lives in the fields and in the water. Since He lives in the people, and in the land, and in the water, there can only be love and justice when the people, the land, and the water are one.

Field Reports on Individual Participants in the Sakdalista Uprising*

No. 1. Higino Javier (Sakdal)

Barrio Gulod, Cabuyao, Laguna. Age 22. Married, one child less than a year old. Never attended school. Cannot read or write. Takes care of forty ducks. Makes less than five pesos a month. Owns small hut worth P10.00. Owes P30.00. Paid cedula [poll tax certificate] last year. Not this year. Worse off than formerly because of the *baguios* [typhoons].

His story: "The Chief told me to come into town to help capture the municipality. When he captured it we would have independence. Juan de la Cruz, our leader, said we would capture it without trouble. I don't know anything about the Constitution. I don't know what the Commonwealth is. They told me independence would be a good thing. No cedula to pay or a cedula for a peseta. I had no arms. I saw three guns in the hands of my companions. There were three hundred of us. They told us the Constabulary would not fight us. After the firing started, Juan de la Cruz put up his hands after about two shots. They did not stop shooting. I squatted down and put up my hands. A great many others put up their hands. We called out, 'We surrender; we surrender.' The Constabulary kept on firing. We fell on our faces. From the time Juan de la Cruz put

---

*The interviews come from two sources. Items #1 through #13 were included in the Sakdal Uprising Report (G. C. Dunham, L. J. Van Schaick, F. W. Manley, and E. G. Chapan, "Report of the Committee Appointed by Acting Governor-General J. R. Hayden to Investigate the Uprisings of May 2 and 3, 1935" [typescript], Manila, May 21, 1935; Hayden Papers), Appendix I, pp. 5–12. Items #14 through #19 were taken from the penciled field notes of Colonel Louis Van Schaick ("Field Notes," May 10, 1925; Hayden Papers). His verbatim renditions of interviews with captured Sakdals, together with pungent reactions scrawled across the margins, proved far more revealing than the official report. Since neither document has been reproduced, and since, to the writer's knowledge, no duplicates exist in the National Archives of the United States, this information is included to remove some of the anonymity surrounding participants in the uprising. The interviews were presented in my dissertation, "Philippine Social Structure and its Relation to Agrarian Unrest," copyrighted by David Reeves Sturtevant, Stanford, 1959.

up his hands no one inside the patio was shooting. I didn't read the 'Sakdal' because I can't read. I joined the Sakdals and paid them all together a half peso. Juan de la Cruz was the collector. He said the money was to be used to get independence and it is a good thing. Ramos is the only leader I know of. Juan de la Cruz told me of him."

No. 2. Nasario Javier (Sakdal)

Barrio Gulod, Cabuyao, Laguna. Age 40. Married, four children, nine to twenty-three years of age. Went to private barrio school two years and can read and write. Sent his girl to school one year but got sick and quit. The boys had to help. Makes *bancas* [canoes]. Makes seven to fifteen pesos a month. Made seven pesos last month. Has house on the beach worth P100.00 (no one owns the land) and a cow and a calf worth P24.00. Owes P50.00. Got into debt over the ducks he cared for belonging to another person. They died during the *baguio*. One boy catches fish. In ordinary times, with the ducks to help can get along. Paid cedula. Worse off than last year because of the loss of the ducks in the *baguio*.

His story: "We came in because we understood if we captured the town we could have independence. We expected no opposition. The Jones Law promised independence so we came in to take it. I don't want the Constitution because it is only a promise. I'm opposed to the Government of the United States. I have no objection to the way we have been treated but we want liberty. We were forbidden to hold a meeting in Marnatid. The Governor-General heard of it and said we could hold it. If we have independence we can take the land from the foreigners. Severo Generalia [*sic*] sent word to Juan de la Cruz that we should come in, take the municipality, and have independence. I saw four guns in the hands of my companions. When they fired I lay on my face because I was afraid. I couldn't run because those who stood up were falling down after being shot. All standing up near me were shot down. One in front of me, one on one side, one on the other. They had no guns. Juan de la Cruz told us not to leave. He told the ones with guns to shoot. The fight lasted fifteen minutes. One of our men had five rounds of ammunition, one three rounds of ammunition, one one round. I don't believe our men shot over four times. Many of our men put up their hands but they didn't stop shooting at us. When the Constabulary were sticking us with bayonets to make us get up, Governor Cailles stepped up and asked them to have mercy on us. Juan de la Cruz said if we defeated the Constabulary, we would govern, and that the United States would recognize our independence. I read the 'Sakdal.' Buy it once a month. I joined the Sakdals two years ago. I like their constitution and principles and joined voluntarily. I paid in small amounts two and three centavos at a time. Paid P2.00 in all. Benigno Ramos, Franco and Elpidio Santos were our leaders."

No. 3. Primitivo Algabre (Sakdal)

Barrio Banay, Cabuyao, Laguna. Age 25. Brother of Salud Algabre, woman leader who held up the trucks. Married, no children. Finished fourth grade in public school in Cabuyao. Raises 80 cavans of rice (P160.00) and P200.00 worth of sugar cane. Owns a *solar* [residential lot] worth P200.00 and a carabao worth P160.00. Owes P110.00 on mortgage on lot. Pays P1.20 property tax.

His story: "I don't know anything about the Constitution. I am opposed to the present administration because of the principles of our leaders. They are against it, so am I. I was denied the right of free speech and assembly on April 6th. Our leaders tell us foreign business kills the business of the Philippine Islands. I think it better to have our own government. When Almazon and Untivero [Sakdal representatives] had their meeting here we met in the house of Algabre. Untivero and Almazon told us not to be afraid. Ramos was in Japan making arrangements for assistance in arms and men to take over the government and get independence. They talked secretly. This was in March. On April 30th, Severo Generalia [*sic*] told me to go to their house in Banilio. Elpidio Santos was there. José Liage was there and someone was there who was introduced as a Captain of Scouts. They told us not to be afraid, but to take over the municipality on the evening of May 2nd. Ramos would come with a hundred airplanes and men and ammunition on the morning of the 3rd. They said the Scouts and Constabulary would assist in taking over the government. I am a Sakdal. I gave them about P2.00. Under independence I would pay no taxes. No cedula. Business would be in the hands of Filipinos. They know about things. I'm just a follower. They told me all municipalities were being seized and we would have independence."

No. 4. Salud Algabre (Sakdal)

Barrio Banlic, Cabuyao, Laguna. Woman leader. Age 42. Five children, one to sixteen years of age. Fifth grade in school. Sent some of her children to school in Tondo.

Her story: "We cannot send the children to school without money. Times are bad. What mother wouldn't send her children to school if she could. Two years ago we made a sugar crop for Julia Lumpaco in Calamba. We were to take what they gave us after the sugar was sold. We harvested 122 tons of cane. We have received no pay as yet. We owe Julia P137.00. The account is mixed up. Some times when we got a peso she would put down P1.15 or P1.20. When we got P5.00 she would put down P5.75. We were dissatisfied. Couldn't stand the charges so we left. She said for every ton we harvested she would collect fifty centavos on the land. We were supposed to get a fourth of the harvest. They wouldn't let us raise chickens. We needed chickens to get spending money for the children; where we are now we get P1.20 a week for the chickens, have fruit trees and get odd jobs cutting cane. We had two carabaos, but both have been sold. We borrowed P400.00 on a mortgage when my child got sick. A surveyor agreed to survey our solar and get a title for P50.00. He did it in our absence and made mistakes in the boundary. Then he sued us for P130.00. We spent the P50.00 we had to pay for the title in the lawsuit. We haven't been able to pay the land tax for four or five years. My husband was put in jail because he had no cedula. We are against the Constitution. We are against the leaders because they promise us independence and never get it. We think there is no hope for us in our hardships without independence. We were told the same thing was being done in every municipality. They thought when they got the town they would have independence. Wednesday night I was at home putting the children to sleep. A man came saying he was sent by José Abueg. He said all trucks should be held up for confiscation of arms. About three hundred people came at 3 A.M., May 3rd. Said they had not been able to capture Calamba. An auto came very fast. A man in a bus had a revolver and acted as though he were going to use it. We took it away. We stopped other trucks and took away firearms. Our leaders were Benigno Ramos, Celerino Tiongco, Elpidio Santos, and Simeon Ducena."

No. 5. Pio Tatlonghari (Sakdal)

Barrio Mamatid, Cabuyao, Laguna. Age 35. Married, three children, three to ten years old. No schooling. Cannot read or write. Has a hut on someone else's land, a small pig and some chickens. Owes P5.00 he borrowed from the landowner to get something to eat. Makes P12.00 a year. Has not paid cedula for three years.

His story: "I don't know what the Constitution is. I don't oppose any-thing. Don't know anything about it. People say independence would be a good thing. I don't know. I joined the Sakdals. They told me it was a good thing. By this means we would become independent. They told us it was a good thing to have liberty. How could I make a speech. I told you I am ignorant. When I saw the Constabulary, I turned and ran. Ran my head against the stone wall and fell down. Stayed there. Then the shooting started. I did not see any guns among my companions. The constabulary did most of the shooting. I put up my hands. There was some shooting after I put my hands up but not much. We were not abused."

No. 6. Marcelo Alintinahan (Sakdal)

Barrio Banlic, Cabuyao, Laguna. Age ?. Can read and write. Has five children from 8 to 22 years of age. Laborer-carpenter. Makes 60 centavos a day when he works. Works two or three days and then not again for a month. Wife goes out harvesting. Owns house worth P80.00. Pays P3.00

tax. Has a pig and five chickens. Owes P10.00. Has no money. Has not bought a cedula for four years.

His story: "I'm poorer now than before. No chance to make money. I am opposed to the Constitution. Ramos says it is no good because under it we are not given independence. Every election they renew the independence promise but we never get it. I was at Cabuyao and had a club about twenty inches long. Severo Generalia [sic] was in charge. We asked the Presidente to turn over the municipality so that we could show the American people we really want independence. We entered the municipal building peaceably. No one opposed us. We sat around in front of the Presidencia. Along toward morning I went home. Our chief told us we had independence. Didn't even eat breakfast. I woke up and heard the Constabulary had fought the Sakdals. I don't want to do it any more. Our Chiefs told us we would take over the country peacefully. I gave a cent or two to the Sakdals. Probably five centavos in all. We read our names in the paper.

No. 7. Jacinto Aliliran (Sakdal)

Barrio Gulod, Cabuyao, Laguna. Age 38. Married, three children, three to sixteen years old. No education. All children finished first grade. Took care of ducks. When they died he became a *cochero* [carriage driver]. Makes 60 centavos to a peso a day. Owns house and lot worth P300.00 Pays P1.20 taxes. Has a carabao worth forty-five pesos and a cow and a calf. No debts. No money. Used to buy cedula. Now no more. Waiting until he sells cow.

His story: "Our leader, Juan de la Cruz, told us not to approve the Constitution because it delays freedom. Our leaders put off independence ten years. The Jones Law promises it immediately. Salud Algabre said that if we have independence living will be easy to get. There will be many ways like mining to earn a living if we are independent. I was at Cabuyao. Had a shotgun. It wasn't to fight with. They told us we wouldn't have any trouble. I wasn't ready to fight. I would get killed which would be a pity. I had four rounds of ammunition. When I saw the Constabulary I ran. They told us any time we took over the government our Chief would arrive and arrange everything. I had reached the railroad tracks when the firing started. I am a Sakdal. I gave probably a peso in all. We read about our contribution in the newspaper. I don't know about the rest but I am not going to fight any more. If I had stayed around I would have been killed."

No. 8. Domingo Paulmino (Sakdal)

Barrio Banlic, Calamba, Laguna. Age 25. Single. Finished fourth grade. Farmer. Makes P400.00 a year. Owes P20.00 he borrowed to buy food. No money. Paid P2.00 for cedula.

His story: "Last year we could not pay our land tax. I am accused of holding up the trucks. I don't know what the Constitution means or says. We don't like the government because it is severe. Difficult to bear. If you cannot pay your cedula, next year you pay double. Filipinos are losing the means to make a living. Many are out of work. If the Filipinos keep quiet the Jones Law will be put aside and the Commonwealth put in. Under independence, I believe we would have better business and better harvests because it would be our own. They told us that in every province the Sakdals were taking over the government. I saw Salud Algabre and others stopping the trucks. When I saw what they were doing I went home. I joined the Sakdals about two years ago and contributed in all about fifty centavos. They called me group secretary, but I never did anything really. I do not know what secretary means. I hope I won't be severely sentenced because I did not intend to do anything wrong. Almazon told us not to break the law because we were under the American government."

No. 9. Pacencia Alvaree (Sakdal)

Barrio Gulod, Cabuyao, Laguna. (Wife of Juan de la Cruz, the leader who was killed at Cabuyao.) Age 32. Two children, one-and-a-half to eleven years old. She had no schooling as her parents were too poor but she learned to read and write a little in Tagalog. Husband was a fisherman. Made sixty centavos to a peso a day. Owns a sixty peso house, a cow, a calf and some chickens. Owes P27.00, borrowed this when they could not catch fish. No money. "How can we get money when we don't have enough to eat?" Paid land tax but no cedula.

Her story: "I was opposed to what the Sakdals were doing. I tried to stop my husband. He used to read the 'Sakdal,' I told him to pay attention to earning a living. We never had any trouble until he joined the Sakdals. I told him to let it alone. He wouldn't take my advice so we frequently quarreled."

No. 10. Dencio Lapiderio (Sakdal)

Barrio Gulod, Cabuyao, Laguna. Age 40. Single. No education. Fisherman. Fishes three times a week. Makes 25 to 50 centavos a day. Owns fishing gear worth P30.00. Owes about P30.00. Does not pay cedula now because living is not easy.

His story: "I oppose the Constitution because we want independence. It is a good thing because living will be easy under independence. Thursday night we were invited into town by our leaders who told us we had independence. They told us there would be no headbreaking. The Constabulary say the Sakdals shot first. I don't know. I had my head on the ground. . . . I saw many of my companions raise their hands to surrender. The Constabulary stopped shooting when they raised their hands. I joined the Sakdals to work for independence. I contributed fifteen centavos in all."

No. 11. Epifanio Lupena (Sakdal)

Barrio Mamatid, Cabuyao, Laguna. Age 46. Married, seven children, from three to sixteen years old. No education. Fisherman. Makes 60 to 80 centavos or P1.20 a day when he fishes. Has house worth P50.00 and a lot worth P95.00. Pays P1.60 land tax. Owes for ducks which all died in the *baguio*. No money.

His story: "We were told if we had independence it would be easy to make a living. We were ordered to the churchyard. The Constabulary arrived and began firing. The only Sakdal I saw with a gun was Juan de la Cruz. He fired his gun. I put up my hands when the Constabulary ordered it. I was wounded lying on my back. The Constabulary fired after the Sakdals were through. I don't know if the Sakdal shot back. I was down and out. If we succeeded we were just going to have independence, but I don't know what that is. I joined the Sakdals. The most I gave at any time was ten centavos."

No. 12. José Lactan (Sakdal)

Barrio Tranka, Talisay, Laguna. Age 23. Married last January. Studies a little in Tagalog. Can read a letter and write his name. Farmer. Makes about P50.00 a year from harvesting rice as a tenant. No money. Paid cedula tax for past years, had not paid this year. "I have but little knowledge and I am willing to follow the kind of government I was born under."

His story: "I was in Gulod. Went to get watermelon. José Balutic told me to come with them or be killed. I went along. We stopped near the station in Cabuyao. I heard there might be a fight and I ran away. They sent out and arrested me."

No. 13. Marcario Aunsunurin (Sakdal)

Barrio Mamatid, Cabuyao, Laguna. Age 37. Married, two children, thirteen and seventeen. Has house worth 15 pesos and one old hen. Has second-grade education. Fisherman. Makes 20 to 30 centavos a day. Borrowed P300.00 to buy ducks. They all died in the *baguios*. Has 50 centavos in money.

His story: "I heard the Sakdals had taken the Presidencia. I came out of curiosity to see what was going on. I was near the beach when I heard the shooting. I saw three guns among the Sakdals. The Chief of Police sent for me because someone told him I was in the fight. The Constabulary Lieutenant looked at the dobie itch on my back and said it was a wound."

No. 14. Eriberto Jaurigue (Sakdal)

[Location of home not indicated.] Age 19. Single. Finished third grade in school. Farmer. Makes P80.00 a year. Owns house and lot and one old carabao. Has no debts. Had cedula last year. Couldn't borrow the money to buy one this year. Has no money.

His story: "I am opposed to the Constitution because they say we won't get our independence under it. I'm opposed to the leaders who promised independence for 27 years and didn't get it. I didn't vote against the Constitution instead of fight against it because I'm not an elector yet. Under independence all means of life will be controlled by the Filipinos. There is no way of making a living now. At the fight they told us that if the Constabulary fired into the air, we were not to fire either. The Constabulary did begin shooting high. I saw one gun in the hands of my companions. I had a bamboo club."

No. 15. Gregorio Declaro

[Location of home not indicated.] Age 27. Married, one three-year-old child. Can read a little but can't write. Farmer. Makes P55.00 a year. Has a house worth P30.00 and a carabao. Owes ten pesos he borrowed when a child died. No money. Had a cedula two years ago. None since.

His story. "I'm not a Sakdal. I was coming to market. They brought me in by force. I saw seven long guns. I was shot by the Sakdals with bird-shot when I tried to run away."

No. 16. Antonio Alcasabas

[Location of home not indicated.] Age 60. Married, four children. Cannot read and write anymore. Could once when young. Farmer. Owns a house worth P10.00 and lot worth P35.00. Has pigs and chickens. Makes his living and P10.00 a year. Pays cedula and 80 centavos land tax.

His story: "I don't know what the Constitution is. I don't know anything about the government. I pay attention to my work and care for my family. I don't know what the Commonwealth is. I'm telling you the truth when I tell you whoever is in power, I'm going to obey them. I didn't participate. Wasn't there. They sent out and arrested me. I was caring for my sick wife."

No. 17. Bartoleme Batario (Sakdal)

[Location of home not indicated.] Age 38. Married, seven children from five to eighteen years old. Got to third grade in school. Fisherman. Makes 30 to 50 centavos a day. Owns house worth P150.00. Raises P10.00 worth of rice. Owes P80.00 spent for ducks lost in the *baguio*. Hasn't paid land or cedula tax for two years. "I didn't have enough to support us."

His story: "If the Constitution doesn't bring independence I am against it. If the Commonwealth doesn't bring independence I'm against it. I don't know what benefit I would get from independence, but I'm told it would be a good thing. Juan de la Cruz told me we would get independence. We came with him into town. I had a club. When someone said the Constabulary are here, I left and went home to my family. I saw four Sakdals with guns."

No. 18. Pasqualla Lapinid (Sakdal)

[Location of home not indicated.] Age 70. Mother of three children, one a Sakdal prisoner. Can't read or write.

Her story: "My boy Jacinto (38 years old) joined Juan de la Cruz. I joined too. They told us we would get our independence. That it was a good thing, and that we would have no disturbance. I'm an old woman and ignorant. I was in the barrio sick when they said they were going to take the town. We've given probably five pesos to the Sakdals. They told us Ramos was going to the States and needed money. My boy took care of the ducks. I buy and sell bread. Make 50 cents a day. We own a house and a lot, a carabao and a cow. I owe P50.00 on account of the ducks. I can't pay it now, I have no savings. That's why I'm selling things. My son has three small children. I pay 98 centavos land tax. I don't know what the Constitution is. They told us there wouldn't be any more taxes if we got our freedom. I have two hens and thirty ducks. What will become of my grandchildren?

No. 19. Sebastian Parducho (Sakdal)

[Location of home not indicated.] Age 25. Single. No schooling. Can read and write Tagalog. Farmer. Makes P200.00 a year. With his brother owns six hectares land and house worth P100.00. Has a hundred-peso carabao. Mother pays the land tax. No cedula for three years. "We are poorer than four years ago, don't get enough to eat now."

His story: "I give the jueting collector 5 or 10 centavos a day. Never won anything. I don't know what the Constitution is. I don't know anything about the leaders. I don't know what the Commonwealth is. I was not at Cabuyao. They said I was a Sakdal. I joined but I don't know what it is. I gave P10.00 in all."

An Interview with
Salud Algabre*

Participants who lived through the fusilade at Cabuyao, Laguna, constitute a breed apart among Sakdalism's silent survivors. One of them is Salud Algabre. By a quirk of fate she evaded the hellish crossfire and lived on to tell her story. Until now, it has been shared only with relatives and comrades-in-arms. Occasionally, a few Sakdal veterans assemble to honor the night of defiance which gave special meaning to their lives. In small groups they listen attentively to one another's memories. But the gentle hum of separate conversations ends, and they gather respectfully to hear the recollections of Salud Algabre. They call her "Generala." The title is deserved.

A beautiful, restless woman, she was thirty-six when she became a disciple of Benigno Ramos. Like many others she followed Sakdalism out of frustration. Her involvement grew from a deep-seated desire to build a better world for her children. Severo Generalla, her husband, shared Salud's discontents and aspirations. Both of them possessed more formal education than most village residents. *Sakdal*'s system-shattering eloquence captured the couple's imagination and loyalty. They were among the first to subscribe to the volatile weekly. They were also instrumental in forming the original party units in Cabuyao town.

While each of them became profoundly involved in Sakdalism, Salud's fierce attachment exceeded that of Severo. Relatives and friends testify to the minor breach between husband and wife. Severo

*Most of this material appeared first in David R. Sturtevant, "No Uprising Fails—Each One Is a Step in the Right Direction," *Solidarity*, I (1966), 11–21. It is reproduced with the permission of F. Sionel José, the journal's editor-publisher.

was a good Sakdal, but he retained a large measure of skepticism concerning the party's ultimate possibilities. As an old labor leader, wise in the snares and pitfalls that await popular movements, he counseled moderation. Salud rejected his arguments. Like most converts she was captivated by the promise of salvation. She became a true believer. As such, she devoted herself completely to the transforming cause.

The degree of Salud's commitment became apparent that wild May night a generation ago. She was forty-one at the time of the uprising. Impulsively decisive and gracefully quick of movement under normal circumstances, she became an inspiring figure of resolute command when the men of Banlic barrio began their march on the municipality. During fifteen hours of turbulence, she oversaw the placing of ties across the main rail line south from Manila, supervised the cutting of telephone and telegraph wires, ordered and assisted the bolo wielders who felled trees across the pavement of the south highway, assumed command of the resulting roadblock, stopped and searched all vehicles bound for Manila, and confiscated one scout car after disarming its occupants—four United States Marines. It was an excellent night's work for a ninety-pound mother of five.

While the interview which follows is primarily a personal account of those events, it incorporates far more than vivid reminiscences of the uprising. Her responses to questions expose a taproot of rebellion deeper than the surface runners emanating from Sakdalism. They also reveal motives far more complex than the political, economic, and social drives commonly attributed to dissident Filipino farmers by students of agrarian unrest. She fought for land. She fought to throw off foreign domination. She fought to rectify an inequitable social system. She fought for all those things, but she sought something more. Her basic motives sprang from a popular tradition of resistance and a village view of history which bore little or no resemblance to the scholarly versions current in the lecture halls of the University of the Philippines and Ateneo de Manila. She was driven by faint memories of a golden age—a distant time of freedom and ethical relationships. Whether or not such a society ever existed is utterly beside the point. To Salud and her fellow rebels it was real. Consciously or unconsciously they struggled to create a *moral* world. Like most idealists, their only transgression in an age of realists was the sin of simplicity.

But the Generala can speak for herself. The answers which follow are her own. They have been edited slightly for purposes of brevity. Questions were posed by the author and four Filipinos. Gratitude is hereby extended to Mrs. Lettie Ramos Uyboco, Attorney Juan Sulijon, Mr. Jeremias Adia, and Salud's son, the Reverend Conrado Generalla. Without their understanding assistance the dialogue would have missed much in its impact. Without their limitless hospitality, furthermore, an outlander would have experienced a far less rewarding year in the Philippines. The only pity is that the wonderfully soft tones of Salud Algabre's genteel Tagalog cannot be transferred to the printed page.

I. Her Early Life

Where and when were you born?
In Cabuyao, October 10, 1894.
What were your parents' names?
Father, Maximo Algabre; Justina Tirones, mother.
Did they have Chinese or Spanish blood?
I do not think so. As far as I know I am pure Tagalog.
You are very fair, perhaps . . . ?
My skin is light; mother said this is because after she conceived, she saw a beautiful Spanish lady.
What were your parents' occupations?
My mother was a seamstress. Father was a landowner. He managed extensive lands.
How extensive?
There were five warehouses—three large old buildings, and two smaller ones. The granary was big.
How many hectares in your estimate?
Perhaps a thousand hectares.
How long had the land been owned by the family?
I do not know for certain. Grandmother told me that grandfather was a *capitán* [*gobernadorcillo*]. Only men with land became *capitánes*. The land must have belonged to them for a long time.
Did your parents have any formal education?
Yes. They studied Spanish in Manila. For about six years, I think. I do not know how long.
Did your father fight against the Spaniards?
Yes. In 1896–1897, in the War of the Katipunan. Father and grandfather were both soldiers. They fought between Calamba and Santa Cruz, Laguna, for about six months.
Who was their commander?
General Juan Cailles. One of my uncles also fought under Cailles. He is still alive, aged 102. He was a lieutenant.

Was that the same Juan Cailles who was Governor of Laguna in 1935?
The same Cailles.
Did your father and grandfather fight the Americans?
They did not fight in 1898–1899.
Getting back to you again, how many brothers and sisters did you have?
We were ten, but many are no more. Only six are alive.
Did you go to school?
In Manila. From 1903 to 1909, about five years. I finished grade four.
I was going to continue, but I did not. I stopped.
If you wished to continue, why did you stop?
Because of Mrs. Brown. She was my music teacher. A nice lady, I
liked her very much. My mother asked me to stop school. She was afraid
Mrs. Brown would take me home with her to America.
Then you had only four years of schooling?
No, I had more. I wanted to continue, so my parents sent me to a
Filipino teacher. I studied with him through first year of high school.
*Did your education have anything to do with your revolutionary activities
in later life?*
Nothing.
*They say that you were a very beautiful girl. Please pardon a personal
question, but were you ever a beauty queen?*
Yes, in 1913.
Where?
In Josefina, there in Cabuyao.
On Rizal Day?
Yes, on December 30, 1913. In those days we were much better off.
Each barrio was represented in the fiesta. Everyone contributed to the
occasion. There were the farmers, then the boatmen, then the porters—
some of them wore *salakots* [broad-brimmed, conical-crowned hats].
Others prepared sweets. There were representatives of all the groups on
the horse-drawn carriage. It was a wonderful day.
You must have had many suitors?
A few.
When did you marry?
1915.
Was your marriage to Severo Generalla arranged by your parents?
Mother and father were gone. Severo's father desired the match; it was
his wish.
But didn't Severo court you?
Of course. I was courted for a long time. Is there anyone who marries
without being wooed?
What was Severo's occupation then?
He was a master baker. They had a bakery in Pandacan.
What was your occupation at the time of the wedding?
Seamstress.

How much education did your husband have? Also, did he follow any occupations other than his work at the family bakery?
He was born November 8, 1892. He studied nine years in Manila. He also studied two more years in the night school of the Liceo de Manila. He received an Associate of Arts degree from the Liceo.
He worked at several jobs, first as a baker in Pandacan, then as a cigar maker for Tabacalera. Severo was a strong union man. He was president in Pandacan of Unión Obreros de Tabaco de Filipinas. This led to some trouble and he moved to the province. He ran a *sari-sari* store in the public market of Calamba. He also farmed.

II. Her Grievances

When did you begin to consider the government as unjust to the people?
1930.
Why?
Because of the abuses against the people. The needs of the laborers were ignored. The leaders paid no attention to the people.
Before you became a Sakdal, were you a member of any other political group or party?
I was a *Nacionalista*. When I became disgusted with them, I joined the *Democratas* under old Sumulong.
Why were you disgusted? You said your family was well-to-do. Was there no property left?
None. It was all gone, even before I came of age. Father managed the lands. I did not bother about them. I was in Manila when it happened. The properties must have been sold. I do not know.
You said Severo was a part-time farmer. Did you become tenants?
Yes.
As tenants were you abused?
When we worked the land, we were cheated. The terms on the estate were 50-50. If the tenants harvested 1,000 tons, 500 were to go to the *proprietario* and 500 to the farmers. But we never got the agreed 50 per cent. We would get a mere 25 per cent, sometimes even less.
Did you share the 25 per cent?
We divided it among ourselves. But even then it amounted to less. They got all the disbursements back. All the expenses in planting were borne by us, even the land tax. We were very poor.
Then the basic problem was one of poverty or having enough to live?
Having enough, but without abuses.
Did you not protest?
Of course. But nothing happened. We even sent our case to Mr. Quezon and to Malacañang.
What happened?
Nothing.
It was poverty, then, and abuses which caused your discontent?
No, it was more. There was a root cause behind everything. Nothing could solve our problem except independence, as the United States had

promised. Freedom was the solution. From the time we were *Nacionalistas*, until we became *Democratas*, that was our goal. There was no other answer to the abuses and the poverty. With independence the leaders would cease to be powerful. Instead, it would be the people who were powerful. The people would have their freedom. We would have our own lands; they would no longer be the monopoly of the *proprietarios* and of the government officials. As it was, we had nothing.

The problem, in short, was poverty and power?

You might say that; that was our belief. Under independence, no one would be powerful, because the people would exercise power.

Did you have any other reasons to be discontented?

Yes.

What were they?

The religious situation in our town was very bad.

In what way?

The parish priest in Cabuyao was an evil man.

The Catholic priest?

Yes. His name was Padre Lucas. He was a Filipino, but he did not live by his vows. He committed many sins. Among other things, he fathered several children in Cabuyao. The people did not trust him. They called him Padre "Ucan" [stud] and refused to go to church.[1] Some of them requested that he be removed, but his superiors denied their request. He stayed on and the people began to leave the church. They had their children baptized and married by Aglipayan priests.

Were you and Severo among the people who abandoned Catholicism?

No. We were never Catholics. We were brought up as Aglipayans. As members of the Independent Church, we tried to get Protestant ministers into Cabuyao to provide religious services for the people. In 1929, Severo and I helped two American missionaries (they were Seventh-Day Adventists) to go about their work in Laguna. We introduced them to many people.

How did Father Lucas react to that?

He was extremely angry.

Did you do anything else to challenge him?

Yes. We turned our house into a chapel. On many Sundays, the Aglipayan priest from Santa Rosa came to our place and conducted mass for people in the neighborhood. When he couldn't come because of other duties, another friend of ours offered services. He was a Bantangueño named Ciriaco Llages. He had left the Independent Church and established his own sect. It was called Iglesia Filipino Kristiano. He often came over from Bantangas and delivered sermons at our house.

What did Father Lucas do?

He complained to the authorities about our activities. But there was

1. Liberties were taken in translating the term. "Stud" is the only English word to approximate its general meaning. *Ucan*, a Tagalog insult of the off-color variety, was delicately defined by a Filipina friend as "a man who uses his reproductive functions to the fullest possible extent."

nothing they could do. We stood on our right of freedom of religion and went on holding services. Padre Lucas lost most of his congregation. But the old man got even with his ex-parishioners during the uprising.
How?

I will discuss that when we talk about the revolution.
There were many reasons, then, for you to be discontented?

Very many.
Is that why you became a Sakdal?

Yes. It was the only thing left to do.
Did you know Benigno Ramos?

Yes. I met him in 1930 when he was establishing the movement. He was a good man. We agreed completely with his purposes. We helped organize the party in Cabuyao.
How did you go about it?

We talked to our friends. We read copies of *Sakdal* to them and discussed common problems. We also spoke out against injustice.
Is that all?

No. We held regular meetings in our house. More and more people began to come to our place, particularly on Sundays. We expanded the chapel to take care of the crowd.
How many came?

By late 1931, as many as four or five hundred every Sunday.
It must have been a large house?

Not very. The chapel was on the ground floor. We made it larger by building bamboo frames out from the sides and covering them with palm leaves. The arrangement provided shelter for lots of people.
Did any important people come to the meetings?

Oh yes. Celerino Tiongco often came to the meetings, as did Benigno Ramos. Early in 1932, Ramos, Tiongco, Bishop Aglipay, and lots of other big politicos from Manila and the provinces came to our house to dedicate the chapel. Gregorio Aglipay blessed our house that day. He was like a father to me. He baptized all my children. He conducted mass that Sunday. There must have been at least 500 people at the service. It was like a fiesta.
Were the people from Banlic and other barrios of Cabuyao town?

Some. But most of them came from other places. Sakdal delegations came from Tayabas, Batangas, Cavite, Rizal, and Bulacan. Sometimes they even came from more distant provinces. It was very pleasant. Every Sunday the people came, four or five hundred. Bishop Aglipay was often there. Benigno Ramos frequently came and spoke to the people. Everyone brought their own food. The cooking fires burned all day and well into the night. It was exciting. Religion in the morning and politics all day.
How long did this go on?

Every Sunday from late 1931 right up to the time of the uprising in 1935.

Were there no efforts by the authorities to prevent Sakdal activities?
Many. The police visited our house often when people were there.
They would rush in and say, "What are you discussing?" We told them
of the abuses, but nothing happened. The abuses kept right on.
Is that all that they did?
Oh no, they did many things to block the growth of the party. They
restricted freedom of speech. They denied us the right to assemble. They
imprisoned Sakdalistas on unfounded charges. They even arrested our
leaders in Cabuyao for refusing to pay the *cedula.* Many people did not
pay, but only Sakdal leaders were jailed. My husband was one of them.
He and the others were forced to haul sand from the river beds. They
were also made to wear uniforms with stripes like those of the tiger.
I took a picture of Severo in that tiger shirt and mailed it to the
United States. I wanted the Americans to know what their compatriots
here in the Philippines were doing to the people. What kind of government did we have if men who refused to pay the *cedula* were forced to
wear tiger suits. Nothing happened. I don't know whether they received
it or whether it was intercepted.
Which authorities gave you the most trouble?
The provincial and municipal officials all worked for Governor Cailles.
He was against the Sakdalistas. The municipal police were always
around. They gave us the most trouble. They came to the night meetings
and broke them up. "You cannot do that," they would shout. "That is
prohibited!" Once I said, "Why are you so tough? You are supposed to
keep the law. Why do you break it? Why do you ignore our sufferings?
After all, you get your salary from us." It did no good.
What about the Constabulary?
They didn't bother us very much. Now and then, several constables
would visit our place. The same ones every time. They were all right.
They liked *cerveza negra.* We always kept some for them. They drank
their beer and we talked. They would hear us out and agree with us.
When they finished the beer, they would leave.
Did they ever try and improve conditions for you?
They told their superiors and the *proprietarios* of our grievances, but
nothing happened. When they were with us, they agreed with us. When
they were with the *proprietarios,* they agreed with the *proprietarios.*
After realizing your complaints were in vain, what did you do?
We decided to rebel, to rise up and strike down the sources of power.

III. Her Role in the Uprising

How and where was the uprising planned?
There was a meeting in our house on April 7, 1935. Only the local
leaders were there. We talked of the rebellion and what each of us was
to do.
What were your orders?
Just before the revolution I was to spread the word. On April 30, I
went to San Pedro, then to Calamba and Los Baños, and from there to

Calauan. I told leaders in each town along the way of our plans. I returned to our house in Banlic late on May 1.

Were all the Sakdals in Laguna informed of the uprising?

No. Only key leaders in each town. They were to rally their followers when the time came to strike. Some important party members, such as Almazon and Untivero were purposely kept in the dark. If they had known of the plot it might have caused them trouble. Neither of the Sakdal congressmen favored violence. They were good men but somewhat passive.

What was the plan?

The people were to march to their municipal buildings, capture them, raise the Sakdal flag, and proclaim independence.

What kind of weapons did the Sakdals have?

Bolos, clubs, sickles, some shotguns, and a few revolvers.

In your plans, did it not occur to you that you would be fighting trained Constabulary soldiers equipped with rifles and, if necessary, with machine guns and cannons?

In my experience, the abused fellow does not care if there are cannons.

That might be, but behind the constables there was the power of America. Did you really think you could achieve independence?

We had reason to believe the Constabulary and Philippine Scouts would join the uprising. We also believed other abused people would rebel when they learned of our action. If everyone joined the revolution we would have independence.

Exactly what happened on May 2? Please explain in detail.

As planned, we began to assemble near the railroad station late in the afternoon. Our group marched up the tracks to Cabuyao. That was when we blocked the rails with ties and cut the telegraph wires. In the plaza we met other Sakdals coming from other barrios. All the groups assembled in front of the municipal building.

Was there any fighting at the municipal building?

No. We entered the building—it was not locked—and ordered that the Sakdal flag be raised.

Who raised the flag?

The Sakdalistas, we!

Were there no officials or policemen at the municipal building?

The *presidente* was there and three policemen. The *presidente* asked if it would not be possible to stop the whole affair. We said no, it could not be stopped. "Very well," he said, "touch nothing, not even pencils and papers, and take nothing from the building." That is all there was to it.

What about the police?

They did nothing. One was even my uncle.

Did you take away their guns?

No, we didn't do that to them.

What happened then?

Severo and some other leaders took charge of the group at the municipal building, and I led another group to the highway. We felled several trees across the road. It must have been about six o'clock in the evening when we began to stop the traffic.

What about the incident with the Marines?

The Marines came up the highway from Los Baños at seven o'clock. I walked up to the scout car. The sergeant asked "What is going on? Who are you? What do you want?"

I said, "We are Sakdals! We want immediate, complete, and absolute independence."

The sergeant said, "We don't know anything about any of this. I suggest you write to Congress. They have the answer for everything. Tell them what you want."

I asked them for their side arms and the keys to the car. They gave me four .45's and the keys. I wrote them a receipt.

What happened then?

They stayed with us there until about one o'clock in the morning. We gave them some food and something to drink. But they seemed uneasy about the long bolos of all the men, so we released them.

Did you go back to the municipal building?

Around dawn, I returned to the plaza of Cabuyao. The Sakdals were in a good mood. The women began to prepare food. It took several hours to feed all the men. They ate standing or sitting on the ground. I even got some.

Where were you when the Constabulary came?

As I said, the men ate a lot. Around eight o'clock in the morning I went back to our house in Banlic to get more rice. While I was there, the constables and Governor Cailles came.

Was your husband in the plaza?

No, he was also away when they arrived. He was going from house to house asking for guns. He received one from an old Algabre. That was where he was when the fighting broke out.

Did any of the men who were in the churchyard tell you how the firing began?

Governor Cailles and the constables spread out and advanced slowly down the street. The Governor called on the men to surrender. They refused. Governor Cailles gave the command, *"Fuego!* Attack!" That's what he said.

Some fought back. Others ran away because they had no arms to fight with.

You said earlier that Father Lucas got even with the Sakdals. Did he gain vengeance during the fight?

Yes. When the Sakdalistas took the municipal building, the priest locked the doors to the church and *convento* and remained inside all night. When the Constabulary came the next morning he joined the attack on the people in the churchyard.

What did he do?

According to men who were there, "Ucan" had a rifle. He took it to the upper floor of the *convento*. When Governor Cailles and the constables opened fire on the men behind the wall, the priest shot at them also from a window of the *convento*. Several men who were there say Father Lucas hit some of the Sakdals. A few say he killed as many as twelve.

What happened to Father Lucas?

Nothing. His activities were not mentioned in the Manila newspapers. Only the people in the churchyard knew what he did, and most of them died. Not long after the uprising he was transferred to another parish. He was an old man. He died quietly in bed just before the war.

Where did you go after the uprising failed?

No uprising fails. Each one is a step in the right direction.

But you did not achieve your goal. Is it not the same as unsuccessful since your plan to take control of the Philippines did not succeed?

True. We succeeded in Cabuyao, but other Sakdals did not take control of their municipalities. That was their responsibility.

Why did some of them not act? Why didn't the Sakdals in Tayabas and Marinduque rebel?

I do not know. I suppose they were not informed. They are rather far away. They wanted to fight later, but it was too late.

Getting back to you, what did you do after the fight in the plaza?

News of the battle spread very quickly. I went as fast as I could to the house of a friend where the children were staying. When I heard the Constabulary was coming, I ran from the back of the house to the irrigation canal. Some constables arrived around ten o'clock in the morning. They fired in the air, and searched the houses.

I stayed in the canal for about four hours, letting myself up and down in the water. It must have been about one or one-thirty in the afternoon when the soldiers left. I returned to the house of our friends. They gave me dry clothes and two eggs, and I fled.

There were soldiers everywhere. But I got away through the paddies. In some places the mud came up to my knees. Several patrols were after me.

One thing I remember very well. It was raining very hard, and I was hurrying along a dike. Suddenly I heard a sound. I looked up and there was a soldier. "Hiss! Hiss!" he said, and gestured for me to come close to him. I drew myself straight and tall and walked up to him. He had on a Constabulary hat, but was wearing only an undershirt and trousers. He also had a rifle with a fixed bayonet in his hands. We just stared at each other over the bayonet. After a long time, he lowered the rifle, turned and left. I continued on across the paddies.

I believe he knew who I was. Perhaps he had heard that I had a powerful *anting-anting*. People said I did. But my only *anting-anting* was help from God.

After the incident with the soldier, where did you go?

I continued hiking, crossing rivers, paddies, and mountains, on my way to Silang in Cavite. Two parties of constables were searching for me. I saw them but they did not see me. There was even an airplane.

Where did you hide?

I hid behind banana trunks and bamboos.

Where were you captured?

I was not captured. I was taken to the authorities by my uncle.

By your uncle?

Yes. It was like this: I got to Silang early in the morning of May 5. When I passed by Santo Domingo, which is part of Silang, the lieutenant of that place was brushing his teeth. He did not hear or see me. The constables were looking for me even there, so I hid in the forest. They did not see me.

Although they knew I was around, they finally returned to the barrio. It rained some more. The ants kept biting me. My uncle, Miguel de la Cueva, started his own searching. He also went to the same places searched by the constables. I was not seen, not until the *cogons* were parted. He looked down at me sitting there in the bamboo grove. "Uncle Miguel!" I said. "Shhh . . . my daughter," he said, "I am already tired looking for you. I could not find you." "Well," I said, "here I am, visibly white."

Then I took eggs in their house. I was already hungry. It was still raining. I covered myself with the shirt of my uncle, covered my head using the sleeves as a hat. I also wore his underwear.

It was your uncle then who took you to the authorities?

Yes, to justice.

From Silang, where were you taken?

To Calamba, and then back to Cabuyao.

Were you bailed out?

Not right away. I was in jail from May 5 until October. In October, I was bailed out for the amount of P2,400.

Was that not an unusually long time?

Rather long.

While you were in jail, were you questioned by any representative of Acting Governor General Hayden?

Yes, five Americans questioned me.

Were they in uniform? How did they treat you?

They wore civilian clothes. A man named Manley asked the questions. They treated me decently. They said that they wanted to know why we had risen up against the government; that I could feel free to talk, because they would not use what I said as evidence.

What did you tell them?

When he asked me what we wanted, I said "Immediate, complete, and absolute independence!"

What did they say?

They agreed with me.

Where were you tried? What was your sentence?

There was a mass trial of Laguna Sakdals in Santa Cruz. The decision was appealed to the Supreme Court, but my appeal was denied. I was sentenced to the Women's Correctional in Mandaluyong, Rizal, for a

term of six to ten years and fined P5,000. I was the only woman Sakdal to be imprisoned. I served one year, seven months, and three days. I was pardoned by President Quezon at the intercession of Vicente Soto.
Was your husband also sent to prison?

Not then; he escaped to the mountains. He hid on Mount Makiling for seven months after the uprising, then made his way secretly back to Manila. Friends hid him in their homes in Sampaloc and Tondo. The police did not capture him for four years. In August 1939 he received the same sentence as I did. He was pardoned just before the war broke out.

This is a difficult question to answer, but how did you avoid becoming bitter? How did you remain a lady through that time in prison?

I was not bitter. I did what I thought was right. We lost and I was punished. The principles we fought for, and my faith in God, strengthened me.

I also kept very busy. I learned everything I could about chickens.

IV. Her Heritage as a Rebel

You have thought your way through your positions very well. How did you learn to reason so closely? Did you learn it from Sakdal?

From *Sakdal*, from all the publications, from conversations, from political meetings.

But did not Benigno Ramos admonish all Sakdalistas to become more knowing in the pages of the newspaper? Did he not induce them to hate the government?

We had our own convictions.

You had your own convictions?

Yes, we knew what the people in the government were doing. Actually we did what we ourselves had decided upon—as free people, and power resides in the people.

Some people say the Sakdals expected help from Japan?

Foolishness! Foolishness! We did not expect help from Japan or from anywhere else. It would be utter foolishness to lead the nation to war, particularly a war between America and Japan.

What we did was our heritage, from our fathers and our fathers' fathers. My family has always resisted. Some were put into exile merely for refusing to kiss the hands of the priests. Some were exiled to Jolo, that's where some died. During the early revolutions, to rise up was voluntary, of one's own will. Someone in the family was always involved. For these activities they were dispersed—to Laoag, to Nueva Ecija, some to Pampanga, some to Rizal. In my visits to those places, I found out they were all Sakdalistas, and that they were all our relatives.

Why did they rebel so often?

Because they were rebels, they rose up in arms!

Rebels?

Ah, rebels! And aside from that they refused to kiss the priests' hands.

Nationalism and rebellion then go hand-in-hand in your family?

From the beginning. That is why I can really be proud of Cabuyao. Cabuyao would never allow tyranny to go unchallenged. Even when I am gone—when we are all gone—someone in Cabuyao will stand up and protest.

Why? Because the king of all Laguna ruled from Cabuyao. When the Spaniards came, there was no Santa Rosa, no Biñan, no Calamba, no San Pedro. The emblem of our municipal building is Tabok, King Tabok. There, according to my father and to my father's father, the King of Tondo would discuss with the King of Laguna the problems of the country. There, near the shore of Laguna, they would discuss the problems of the people and find solutions.

It is an old town—a very old town. In fact, there is a golden bell. I shall point out the place to you. During summer, when the water was clear, you could see down through the depths, down to where it stood. The reason they disposed of it was because mothers—early in their pregnancy—would give birth prematurely upon hearing it toll.

One of the reasons my ancestors rebelled was to protest against the church that held the bell. When the Spaniards came they forced the people to build the church. Many were killed by the Spaniards—flogged to death, there on the shore where the church was built.

How did you learn these things?

From my father and my father's father.

By word of mouth, could you call it hearsay?

It is not hearsay, it is true! The professor here would call it history.

You have answered many questions and we know you are tired, but would you be good enough to answer one or two more about Sakdalism?

We have talked for a long time, but I am not tired. Whenever there is talk about the Sakdalistas, I become younger and stronger. I feel like it is 1935 again. That was the moment. Everything led up to the uprising. That was the high point of all our lives. Afterward things were never the same. Later people and principles became confused. Few people think well of Sakdalism these days. They should remember what happened in May 1935. They should also remember why.

Are conditions better or worse now than they were then?

They are worse—*far worse.* All we are free to do now is talk.

After all you have been through and knowing the course of events, if you had it all to do again, would you do the same?

I am reluctant to say I will do something I cannot do. I am old. But I would do it again.

Bibliography

One of the chief problems confronting students of Philippine history is the diverse nature of source materials. Investigators discover that they must devote inordinate amounts of time and energy to an intercontinental search for reliable raw data. Documentation of the primary variety exists, but it is scattered across Spain, the United States, and the Philippines. Since the bulk of this study pertains to relatively recent developments, it is based essentially on Filipino and American sources. Spanish materials undergirding portions of the analysis were acquired from special collections in the United States and Manila.

Listing such a range of sources also presents difficulties. To avoid repetitious entries, certain basic items—available in major American and Philippine libraries—can best be referred to by their general titles. Among these are the Annual Reports of (1) the Philippine Commission (Washington, D.C.), (2) the Governors General (Washington, D.C., and Manila), (3) the High Commissioners (Washington, D.C.), and (4) the Philippine Constabulary (Manila). The findings of the Philippine Census Bureau for 1903, 1918, and 1939, fall under the same general category. These published materials for the years 1898 to 1946 are of such fundamental importance that no valid inquiry into the American colonial period can be made without constant reference to them. Of almost equal value for the Spanish era are the documents compiled and translated by Emma H. Blair and James A. Robertson, eds., *The Philippine Islands, 1493–1898*, 55 vols. (Cleveland, O., 1903–1909). Since sources from this collection were used somewhat sparingly, they will be listed under a separate category.

Of even greater significance to the historian, of course, are manuscripts which have never been used in conventional accounts of the past. Many were relied on in compiling this study. For convenience they will be listed under subheadings by order of their appearance in the text. The locations of all manuscripts will be indicated. Information drawn from the unpublished records of the Bureau of Insular Affairs, now in the National Archives of the United States, will also be entered independently with record group and card index numbers enumerated.

MANUSCRIPTS

A. Spanish Documents

Sancho, Manuel. "Relaciónes expresivas de los principales acontecimientos de la titulada Cofradía del Señor San José." August 16, 1843. Newberry Library, Chicago.

Pampliega, Cipriano. "Documento curioso sobre los guardias de honor de Pangasinan y otras cosas curiosas de los katipuneros." No date. Dominican Archives, Manila.

Maurin, José Maria. "Recuerdos de una expedición a la Pampanga . . . Antecedentes acerca del célebre tulisan conocido con el nombre de Tancad." Manila, August, 1877. Newberry Library, Chicago.

B. Bureau of Insular Affairs Records

Governor General James Smith on Dionisio Sigobela. N.A., B.I.A., F.E. 19077.

Governor General Leonard Wood on the Colorums of Surigao. N.A., B.I.A., F.E. 4865-A-57.

Florencio Entrencherado to Calvin Coolidge, N.A., B.I.A., Personal Name Information File.

Newspaper Clippings on Florencio Entrencherado. N.A., B.I.A., Personal Name Information File.

Constabulary Reports on the Theft of Plans for Corregidor by Ricartista Agents. N.A., B.I.A., F.E. 4865-77.

Constabulary Surveillance of Ricartista Agents. N.A., B.I.A., F.E. 4865-106C.

Governor General Francis Harrison on Artemio Ricarte. N.A., B.I.A., F.E. 4865-106C

Newspaper Clippings and Correspondence on Artemio Ricarte. N.A., B.I.A., Personal Name Information File.

C. Library of Congress, Manuscript Division

Forbes, W. Cameron. "Journal" (typescript).

Duckworth-Ford, R. A., to Leonard Wood, Manila, June 10, 1927.

D. Miller Papers, New Concord, Ohio

"The Colorum Uprising in Surigao as Told by a Surviving P. C. Hero, Sergeant Leonard Tecson, to José Navallo Eñano." Gigaguit, Surigao del Norte, 1966. 3 pp.

"History of the Death of Captain Valentine Juan in the Prewar P.C." Colonel Rizalina M. García, Commander, Surigao del Norte Province, 1966. 3 pp.

"An Interview with Mr. Pablo Cosigna." Surigao, January 24, 1966. 5 pp.

"Records of Miguel G. Calderon," Municipal Secretary (Retired), Surigao, Surigao del Norte, January 1966, 3 pp.

E. Hall Papers, New Concord, Ohio

"An Interview with Dr. José Fernández." Manila, March 23, 1966. 10 pp.

Hall, Anne T. "The Entrencherado Revolt." Unpublished seminar paper, Institute of Asian Studies, University of the Philippines, April 19, 1966.

"Some Observations on the 'Personal History' of Florencio Natividad by Dr. José Fernández" (Handwritten). Manila, May 25, 1927. 20 pp.

F. Hayden Papers, Michigan Historical Collections, Bentley Historical Library, Ann Arbor, Michigan

1. Confidential Memoranda

Cailles, Juan, Governor of Laguna, to Secretary of Interior Teofilo Sison. "Regard to Activities on May 2–3, 1935." May 10, 1935.

Dominquez, Juan, Chief of Police, City of Manila, to Superintendent, Intelligence Division, Philippine Constabulary. "Regard to Possible Sakdal-Communist or Sakdal-Socialist Alliance." May 24, 1935.

Ely, Richard, to Acting Governor-General Joseph R. Hayden. "Regard to Activities during the Night of May 2–3, 1935." May 4, 1935.

Guido, Captain José P., to Superintendent of Constabulary Colonel F. W. Manley. "Regard to Sakdalistas and Japanese." May 9, 1935.

Rodriquez, Eulogio, Secretary of Agriculture and Commerce, to Acting Governor-General Joseph R. Hayden. "Regard to Sakdal Propaganda." April 2, 1935.

———. "Regard to Campaign of Suppression against Sakdals." May 8, 1935.

Torres, Ramon, Secretary of Labor, to Acting Governor-General Joseph R. Hayden. "Regard to Peaceful Celebration of Labor Day." May 2, 1935.

———. "Regard to Future Investigation of Social and Labor Conditions by the Department of Labor." May 7, 1935.

Valdes, Brigadier General Basilio J., to Superintendent of Constabulary, Colonel F. W. Manley. "Regard to Planned Uprising by Sakdals." May 2, 1935.

Van Schaick, Colonel Louis J., to Acting Governor-General Joseph R. Hayden. "Regard to Sacdal [sic] Uprising." May 4, 1935.

———. "Field Notes." May 10, 1925.

2. Radiograms and Telegrams

Cailles to Chief of Constabulary, Cabuyao, Laguna, May 3, 1935.

Hayden to Grew, Manila, May 8, 1935.
Grew to Hayden, Tokyo, May 9, 1935.

3. Government Circulars
Department of Agriculture and Commerce, Office of the Secretary, General Circular No. 11, Subject, "Sakdalista Propaganda." Manila, April 12, 1935.

4. Sakdal Literature
"An Open Letter to All Sakdalistas." No date.
Free Filipinos. Manila, April 1, 1935.

5. Reports
Dunham, Major George C., Colonel Louis J. Van Schaick, Lt. Colonel F. W. Manley, Captain E. G. Chapman. "Report of the Committee Appointed by Acting Governor-General J. R. Hayden to Investigate the Uprisings of May 2 and 3, 1935."
——. "Minority Report on Action by the Constabulary in Suppressing the Uprising at Cabuyao, Laguna." No date.
Francisco, Lt. Colonel G. B., Chief of Staff, Philippine Constabulary. "The Sakdal Party." May 7, 1935.
Hayden, Acting Governor-General J. R. "Preliminary Report on the Sakdalista Disturbances." May 7, 1935.
Van Schaick, Colonel Louis J. "Minority Report on the Action at Cabuyao." May 23, 1935.
——. "Partial Reports on the Sakdal Investigation." May 7, 9, 11, 12, 1935.

G. *Fact Finding Report*

Philippine Commonwealth, Department of Labor. *Report of the Fact Finding Survey of Rural Problems in the Philippines Submitted to the Secretary of Labor and to the President of the Philippines.* Manila, 1937.

MATERIALS FROM BLAIR AND ROBERTSON

de la Matta, Juan Manuel. "Communication from the Intendant of the Army and Treasury of the Philippine Islands, to the Captain General Don Marcelino de Oraa, in Regard to the Moral Condition of the Country after the Insurrection of a Portion of the Troops of the Twenty-First Regiment of the Line," LII, 91–111.
de Plasencia, Juan. "Customs of the Tagalog." VII, 173–196.
"Extracts from Diaz' *Conquistas*," XXXVIII, 85–138.
"Extracts from Murillo Velarde's *Historia de Philipinas*," XXXVIII, 139–215.

Nuñoz, José. "Present Beliefs and Superstitions in Luzon," XLIII, 310–319.

Ortiz, Tomas. "Superstitions and Beliefs of the Filipinos," XLIII, 103–110.

INTERVIEWS

Salud Algabre, Manila, March and April, 1966
Aurelio Almazon, Los Baños, Laguna, February, 1966.
Pedro Calosa, San Nicolas and Tayug Pangasinan, March, 1966.
Patricio Dionisio, Manila, February and March, 1966.
Guillermo B. Francisco, Manila, March, 1966.
Isabello de los Reyes, Jr., Manila, March and April, 1966.
Angel Tiongco, Santa Rosa, Laguna, November, 1965.

UNPUBLISHED STUDIES

Coats, George Y. "The Philippine Constabulary, 1901–1917." Doctoral dissertation, Ohio State University, 1968.

Covar, P. R. "The *Iglesia Watawat ng Lahi:* A Sociological Study of a Social Movement." Master's thesis, University of the Philippines, 1961.

Larkin, John A. "The Evolution of Pampangan Society: A Case Study of Social and Economic Change in the Rural Philippines." Doctoral dissertation, New York University, 1966.

Legardo, Benito Jr. "Foreign Trade, Economic Change, and Entrepreneurship in the Nineteenth-Century Philippines." Doctoral dissertation, Harvard University, 1955.

Santos, Dom R. "The Guards of Honor, 1872–1910." Unpublished seminar paper, Ateneo de Manila University, 1966.

Stubbs, R. M. "Philippine Radicalism: The Central Luzon Uprisings, 1925–1935." Doctoral dissertation, University of California, Berkeley, 1951.

Tauli, Alejandro R. "The 'Colorums' of Tayug," Unpublished seminar paper, Institute of Asian Studies, University of the Philippines, 1966.

NEWSPAPERS

Christian Science Monitor, 1920–1940.
The Manila Chronicle, 1960–1970.
The Manila Daily Bulletin, 1920–1940.
The Manila Herald, 1934–1940.
The Manila Times, 1960–1970.
The Manila Tribune, 1920–1940.
The New York Times, 1920–1940.

PERIODICALS

Khaki and Red (Manila), 1930–1935.
The Philippines Free Press, 1920–1972.
Philippine Magazine, 1920–1940.

ARTICLES

Allen, James S. "Agrarian Tendencies in the Philippines," *Pacific Affairs,* XI (1938), 52–65.

Arens, Richard. "Witches and Witchcraft in Leyte and Samar Islands, Philippines," *Philippine Journal of Science,* LXXXV (1956), 451–465.

——. "The Early Pulahan Movement in Samar and Leyte," *Journal of History,* VII (1959), 303–371.

Benda, Harry J. "Peasant Movements in Southeast Asia," *Asian Studies,* III (1965), 420–434.

Benitez, Conrado. "Sakdal," *Philippine Magazine,* XXXII (1935), 240, 252–253.

Chapman, Abraham. "American Policy in the Philippines," *Far Eastern Survey,* XV (1946), 164–169.

Clark, Victor S. "Labor Conditions in the Philippines," *Bulletin of the Department of Labor,* X (1905), 721–905.

Crippen, Harlan R. "Philippine Agrarian Unrest: Historical Backgrounds," *Science and Society,* X (1946), 337–360.

Dalisay, Amando M. "Types of Tenancy Contracts on the Rice Farms of Nueva Ecija," *Philippine Agriculturist,* XXVI (1937), 159–191.

Dawson, Owen L. "Philippine Agriculture: A Problem of Adjustment," *Foreign Agriculture,* IV (1940), 383–456.

Eggan, Fred. "The Philippines and the Bell Report," *Human Organization,* X (1951), 16–21.

—— and Pacyaya, Alfredo. "The Sapilada Religion: Reformation and Accommodation among the Igorots of Northern Luzon," *Southwestern Journal of Anthropology,* XVIII (1962), 95–113.

Fernández, J. A. "Florencio Natividad, Alias Flor Intrencherado," *Journal of the Philippine Islands Medical Association,* XII (1932), 627–634.

Fey, H. E. "Farmers' Revolt in the Philippines," *Christian Century,* XLVIII (1931), 1004.

Foronda, Marcelino. "The Canonization of Rizal," *Journal of History,* VIII (1960), 1–48.

Gonzales-Sioco, Fausto F. "The Cause of Communism in the Philippines," *Living Age,* CCCLX (1941), 547–549.

Goodman, Grant K. "General Artemio Ricarte and Japan," *Journal of Southeast Asian History,* VII (1960), 48–60.

Guerrero, M. C. "The Colorum Uprisings, 1924–1931," *Asian Studies,* V (1967), 67–78.

Hart, Donn V. "The Filipino Villager and His Spirits," *Solidarity,* I (1966), 65–71.

Hartendorp, A. V. H. "The Tayug 'Colorums,' " *Philippine Magazine,* XXVII (1931), 563–567.

——. "The Sakdal Protest," *Philippine Magazine,* XXXII (1935), 233.

Hester, Evett D. and Mabbun, Pablo N. "Some Economic and Social Aspects of Philippine Rice Tenancies," *Philippine Agriculturist,* XII (1924), 367–444.

Leiban, Richard W. "Sorcery, Illness, and Social Control in a Philippine Municipality," *Southwestern Journal of Anthropology,* XVI (1960), 127–143.

Lieberman, Victor. "Why the Hukbalahap Movement Failed," *Solidarity,* I (1966), 22–30.

Linton, Ralph. "Nativistic Movements," *American Anthropologist,* XLV (1943), 230–240.

Manawis, Mariano D. "The Life of a Nueva Ecija Peasant," *Philippine Magazine,* XXXI (1934), 12; 42.

Plehn, Carl C. "Taxation in the Philippines," *Political Science Quarterly,* XVIII (1902), 684–689.

Redfield, Robert. "The Natural History of the Folk Society," *Social Forces,* XXI (1953), 224–228.

Robb, Walter, "What Ho, the Guard," *American Chamber of Commerce Journal,* XL (1931), 18.

Roosevelt, Theodore. "Land Problems in Puerto Rico and the Philippines," *Geographic Review,* XXIV (1934), 182–204.

Serrano, Leopoldo, "Vibora, the Misunderstood Patriot," *Philippine Herald Magazine,* July 26, 1958, 3–6.

Stephens, Robert P. "The Prospects for Social Progress in the Phillippines," *Pacific Affairs,* XXII (1950), 139–152.

Stoodley, Bartlett H. "Some Aspects of Tagalog Family Structure," *American Anthropologist,* LIX (1957), 236–249.

Sturtevant, David R. "Sakdalism and Philippine Radicalism," *Journal of Asian Studies,* XXI (1962), 199–215.

——. *"Guardia de Honor:* Revitalization Within the Revolution," *Asian Studies,* IV (1966), 342–352.

——. "No Uprising Fails—Each One Is a Step in the Right Direction," *Solidarity,* I (1966), 11–21.

——. "Epilog for an Old 'Colorum,' " *Solidarity,* III (1968), 10–18.

Valdes, Basilio. "Peace and Order in the Philippines," *Philippines Herald Year Book, 1935,* III (Manila, 1935), 140–141.

Velmonte, Jose E. "Farm Security for the Tenant," *Philippine Agriculturist,* XXVI (1937), 395–398.

Villasin, O. S. "Inauguration Day in a Sakdal Town," *Philippine Magazine,* XXXII (1935), 608.

Wallace, Anthony F. C. "Revitalization Movements," *American Anthropologist,* LVIII (1956), 264–281.

Wells, Henry. "Communism in the Philippines," *American Perspective,* IV (1950), 82.

Wickberg, Edgar. "The Chinese Mestizo in Philippine History," *Journal of Southeast Asian History,* V (1964), 62–110.

Woods, Robert G. "Origin of the Colorum," *Philippine Magazine,* XXVI (1929), 428–429.

——. "The Strange Story of the Colorum Sect," *Asia,* XXXII (1932), 450–454, 459–460

GENERAL WORKS

Abaya, Hernando J. *Betrayal in the Philippines.* New York, 1946.

Abelard, Pedro E. *American Tariff Policy toward the Philippines, 1898–1946.* New York, 1947.

Abueva, Jose V. *Ramon Magsaysay, A Political Biography.* Manila, 1971.

Agoncillo, Teodoro A. *The Revolt of the Masses: The Story of Bonifacio and the Katipunan.* Quezon City, 1956.

——. *The Fateful Years.* 2 vols. Quezon City, 1965.

——. *Malolos: The Crisis of the Republic.* Quezon City, 1960.

Agoncillo, Teodoro A., and Oscar M. Alfonso. *A Short History of the Filipino People.* Quezon City, 1960.

Aguinaldo, Emilio, and V. A. Pacis. *A Second Look at America.* New York, 1957.

Bastin, John, and Harry J. Benda. *A History of Modern Southeast Asia.* Englewood Cliffs, N.J., 1968.

Beqiraj, Mehmet. *Peasantry in Revolution.* Ithaca, N.Y., 1966.

Bernstein, David. *The Philippine Story.* New York, 1947.

Blunt, J. Y. Mason. *An Army Officer's Philippine Studies.* Manila, 1912.

Castillo, Andres V. *Philippine Economics.* Manila, 1949.

Chamberlain, Elinor. *The Far Command.* New York, 1952.

Cohn, Norman. *The Pursuit of the Millennium: Revolutionary Messianism in Medieval and Reformation Europe and Its Bearing on Modern Totalitarian Movements.* London, 1962.

Corpuz, Onofre D. *The Philippines.* Englewood Cliffs, N.J., 1965.

Coulborn, Rushton, Ed. *Feudalism in History.* Princeton, N.J., 1956.

Cressey, George B. *Asia's Lands and Peoples.* New York, 1944.

Cushner, Nicholas P. *Spain in the Philippines.* Manila, 1971.

de la Costa, Horacio. *The Jesuits in the Philippines, 1531–1793.* Cambridge, Mass., 1961.

——. *The Background of Nationalism and Other Essays.* Manila, 1965.

de la Gironier, Paul P. *Twenty Years in the Philippines.* New York, 1854.

Devins, John B. *An Observer in the Philippines.* New York, 1905.

Duran, Joaquin. *Episodias de la revolución filipina.* Manila, 1900.

Elarth, H. H. *The Story of the Philippine Constabulary.* Los Angeles, 1949.

Felix, Alfonso, Jr., Ed. *The Chinese in the Philippines, 1570–1770.* Manila, 1966.

Forbes, W. Cameron. *The Philippine Islands.* 2 vols. New York, 1928.

Foreman, John. *The Philippine Islands.* London, 1899.

Foronda, Marcelino. *Cults Honoring Rizal.* Manila, 1961.

Friend, Theodore. *Between Two Empires.* New Haven, Conn., 1965.

Gates, John. *Schoolbooks and Krags: The U.S. Army in the Philippines, 1898–1902.* Westport, Conn., 1973.

George, Henry. *Progress and Poverty.* New York, 1883.

Golay, Frank H. *The Philippines: Public Policies and National Economic Development.* Ithaca, N.Y., 1961.

Goodman, Grant K. *Four Aspects of Philippine-Japanese Relations, 1930–1940.* Yale University Southeast Asia Studies, No. 9. New Haven, 1967.

——. *Davao: A Case Study in Japanese-Philippine Relations.* New York, 1967.

Grunder, Garel A. and Livezey, William E. *The Philippines and the United States.* Norman, Okla., 1951.

Harrison, Francis B. *The Corner-Stone of Philippine Independence.* New York, 1922.

Hayden, Joseph R. *The Philippines: A Study in National Development.* New York, 1942.

Heiser, Victor. *An American Doctor's Odyssey.* New York, 1936.

Herrero y Sampedro, Upanio. *Nuestra Prisión.* Manila, 1900.

Hobsbawm, Eric J. *Primitive Rebels: Studies in Archaic Forms of Social Movement in the 19th and 20th Centuries.* New York, 1963.

Hurley, Victor. *Jungle Patrol: The Story of the Philippine Constabulary.* New York, 1938.

Jacoby, Erich H. *Agrarian Unrest in Southeast Asia.* New York, 1949.

Jenkins, Shirley. *American Economic Policy toward the Philippines.* Stanford, Calif., 1954.

Joaquin, Nick. *Prose and Poems.* Manila, 1963.

Kalaw, Maximo M. *The Development of Philippine Politics, 1887–1920.* Manila, 1929.

Keesing, Felix, *Taming Philippine Headhunters.* Stanford, Calif., 1934.

——. *The Philippines: A Nation in the Making.* Shanghai, 1937.

Kirk, Grayson L. *Philippine Independence.* New York, 1936.

Kurihara, Kenneth K. *Labor in the Philippine Economy.* Stanford, Calif., 1945.

Lanternari, Vittorio. *The Religions of the Oppressed: A Study of Modern Messianic Cults.* Trans. by Liza Sergio. New York, 1963.

Larkin, John A. *The Pampangans.* Berkeley, Calif., 1972.

Laskar, Bruno. *Human Bondage in Southeast Asia.* Chapel Hill, N.C., 1950.

Lava, Horacio C. *Levels of Living in the Ilocos Region.* Institute of Pacific Relations, Philippine Council. Manila, 1938.

LeRoy, James A. *Philippine Life in Town and Country.* New York, 1905.

——. *The Americans in the Philippines,* 2 vols. New York, 1914.

Liang, Dapen. *The Development of Philippine Political Parties.* Hong Kong, 1939.

Macaraig, Serafin E. *Social problems.* Manila, 1929.

Majul, Cesar A. *The Political and Constitutional Ideas of the Philippine Revolution.* Quezon City, 1957.

——. *Mabini and the Philippine Revolution.* Quezon City, 1960.

Malcolm, George A. *The Commonwealth of the Philippines.* New York, 1936.

Mas y Sanz, Sinibaldo de. *Secret Report on the Condition of the Philippines in 1842.* Manila, 1963.

Mayo, Katherine. *The Isles of Fear: Truth about the Philippines.* New York, 1925.

Miller, Hugo H. *Economic Conditions in the Philippines.* Boston, 1920.

——. *Principles of Economics Applied to the Philippines.* Boston, 1932.

Montero y Vidal, José. *Historia general de Filipinas,* 3 vols. Madrid, 1895.

Pelzer, Karl J. *Population and Land Utilization.* Shanghai, 1941.

——. *Pioneer Settlement in the Asiatic Tropics.* New York, 1945.

Phelan, John L. *The Hispanization of the Philippines.* Madison, Wis., 1959.

Philippine Commonwealth, Department of Agriculture and Commerce. *Atlas of Philippine Statistics.* Manila, 1939.

Philippine Islands, Bureau of Forestry. *Spanish Public Land Laws in the Philippine Islands.* Washington, D.C., 1901.

Philippine Islands, Department of the Interior. *Slavery and Peonage in the Philippine Islands.* Manila, 1913.

Philippine Islands, Office of the Governor General. *The Friar Land Inquiry.* Manila, 1910.

Philippines, Republic of, Bureau of the Census. *Yearbook of Philippine Statistics, 1946.* Manila, 1947.

Polotan, Kerima. *The Hand of the Enemy*. Manila, 1963.

Quezon, Manuel. *The Good Fight*. New York, 1946.

Recto, Claro M. *Three Years of Enemy Occupation*. Manila, 1946.

Redfield, Robert. *The Primitive World and Its Transformation*. Ithaca, New York, 1953.

———. *The Little Community*. Chicago, 1964

———. *Peasant Society and Culture*. Chicago, 1965.

Reel, Frank A. *The Case of General Yamashita*. Chicago, 1949.

Ricarte, Artemio. *Memoirs of General Artemio Ricarte*. Manila, 1963.

Romani, John H., and Thomas, M. Ladd. *A Survey of Local Government in the Philippines*. Manila, 1954.

Runes, I. T. *General Standards of Living and Wages of Workers in the Philippine Sugar Industry*. Institute of Pacific Relations, Philippine Council. Manila, 1938.

Sansom, George B. *Japan: A Short Cultural History*. New York, 1943.

Saulo, A. B. *Communism in the Philippines*. Manila, 1969.

Sawyer, Frederick H. *The Inhabitants of the Philippines*. London, 1900.

Scaff, Alvin H. *The Philippine Answer to Communism*. Stanford, Calif., 1955.

Schott, John L. *The Ordeal of Samar*. Indianapolis, Ind., 1964.

Schurz, William L. *The Manila Galleon*. New York, 1939.

Starner, Francis L. *Magsaysay and the Philippine Peasantry*. Berkeley and Los Angeles, Calif., 1961.

Steinberg, David J. *Philippine Collaboration in World War II*. Ann Arbor, Mich., 1967.

Sturtevant, David R. *Agrarian Unrest in the Philippines*. Ohio University Center for International Studies, Southeast Asia Series No. 8. Athens, Ohio, 1969.

Taruc, Luis. *Born of the People*. New York, 1953.

Taylor, George E. *The Philippines and the United States: Problems of Partnership*. New York, 1964.

Taylor, John R. M., comp. "The Philippine Insurrection against the United States." Galley proofs, 5 vols. Washington, D.C., 1906. [Available in microfilmed copies from the Bureau of Insular Affairs Records, United States National Archives].

Thrupp, Sylvia L., ed. *Millennial Dreams in Action: Essays in Comparative Study*. The Hague, 1962.

United States, War Department, Bureau of Insular Affairs. *Compilation of Philippine Insurgent Records: Telegraphic Correspondence of Emilio Aguinaldo, July 15, 1898, to February 28, 1899, Annotated*. Washington, D.C., 1902.

United States, War Department. *Report, 1900*, Washington, D.C., 1901.

United States, War Department. *Report, 1901*, Washington, D.C., 1902.

United States, War Department. *Report, 1902,* Washington, D.C., 1903.
United States, War Department. *Report of Major General E. S. Otis: September, 1899 to May 5, 1900.* Washington, D.C., 1900.
Villamor, Ignacio. *Criminality in the Philippine Islands.* Manila, 1909.
White, John R. *Bullets and Bolos.* New York, 1928.
Wickberg, Edgar. *The Chinese in Philippine Life, 1850–1898.* New Haven, Conn., 1965.
Wolf, Eric R. *Peasant Wars of the Twentieth Century.* New York, 1969.
Wolff, Leon. *Little Brown Brothers.* New York, 1961.
Worcester, Dean C., and Hayden, Joseph R. *The Philippines Past and Present.* New York, 1930.
Zaide, Gregorio F. *The Philippines since Pre-Spanish Times.* Manila, 1949.
———. *Philippine History.* Manila, 1961.

Index

Abad Santos, Pedro, 251-255
Abé, Cesario, 185, 188, 189
Absentee landownership, 40, 57, 63, 70
Adarnistas, 262
Adia, Jeremias, 288
Aglipay, Gregorio, 105, 198, 292
Aglipayans, *see* Philippine Independent Church
Agraviados, 102-105, 110, 112
Aguinaldo, Emilio, 14; and Guardia de Honor, 102-107; capture by Americans, 118; and secret societies in Negros, 159, 195; and Artemio Ricarte, 197; and Patricio Dionisio, 207
Agusan, 143, 152-153
Alcasabas, Antonio, 284
Algabre, Primitivo, 279
Algabre, Salud, 279-280; interview with, 286-299
Aliliran, Jacinto, 281
Alintinahan, Marcelo, 280-281
Alitao, 89-94
Almazar, Vicente, 219
Almazon, Aurelio, 224, 233, 279, 294
Alvaree, Pacencia, 282
American colonial policies, 42-60; public health, 43-44; education, 44-45; transportation and communication, 45; political program, 46-49; economic policies, 50-51; land policy, 51-56; social change, 56-60
Angeles, Leon, 234, 239-240
Anting-anting, 25, 117, 120, 129, 145, 258, 274, 296
Argosino, Antonio, 224
Aunsunurin, Marcario, 283

Babailanes, 79, 119, 121-125, 131, 138, 158, 172
Bahao, Juan, 144, 154
Bais, Estate, 159
Baltazar, Julian, 98-102, 111, 272
Baluyot, Sotero, 250-251, 254
Banditry, 115-138
Banlic, Laguna, and Sakdal uprising, 237, 240-241, 287, 292, 294, 295
Barangay, 21-25, 31
Batario, Bartoleme, 284-285
Bathalismo, 262
Bernales, Felix, 144-154, 175
Bohol, 79-80, 129, 143, 172
Bondad, Juan, 236, 239
Bonifacio, Andres, 145, 206, 262, 273, 275
Bopp, Edwin C., 202
Bowers, C. H., 152-155
Bucas Grande, 142-153
Burgos, José, 94, 160, 164

Cabaruan, 101-102, 107-113, 132, 172
Cabezas de barangays, 28
Cabuyao, Laguna, and Sakdal uprising, 239-241, 247, 253, 255, 277-285, 286-299
Caciquism, 57-58, 67, 69, 190-191, 223
Cailles, Juan, 231, 239-240, 288-289, 293, 295
Calosa, Pedro, 17, 183-192, 209, 215, 255, 260; interview with, 269-276
Canon, 63
Capistrano, Maximina, 68
Catalonans, 79
Cawal ning Capayapan, 250-251
Cazadores, 119
Cebu, 80, 143, 172

*Popular Uprisings in
the Philippines, 1840–1940*

Designed by R. E. Rosenbaum.
Composed by York Composition Company, Inc.,
in 10 point linotype Times Roman, 2 points leaded,
with display lines in monotype Bulmer.
Printed letterpress from type by York Composition Company
on Warren's Number 66 text, 50 pound basis.
Bound by John H. Dekker & Sons, Inc.
in Columbia book cloth
and stamped in All Purpose foil.